Nineteenth-Century
American Activist Rhetorics

Nineteenth-Century American Activist Rhetorics

Edited by

Patricia Bizzell and
Lisa Zimmerelli

Modern Language Association of America
New York   2021

MLA and the MODERN LANGUAGE ASSOCIATION are trademarks owned by the
Modern Language Association of America. For information about obtaining permission to reprint material from MLA book publications, send your request by mail
(see address below) or e-mail (permissions@mla.org).

Library of Congress Cataloging-in-Publication Data

Names: Bizzell, Patricia, editor. | Zimmerelli, Lisa, editor.
Title: Nineteenth-century American activist rhetorics / edited by Patricia Bizzell
    and Lisa Zimmerelli.
Description: New York : Modern Language Association, 2021. | Includes biblio-
    graphical references. | Summary: "Essays cover nineteenth-century American
    activists' rhetorics and their echoes in contemporary American activism using
    a variety of theoretical lenses, such as classical rhetorical tropes, feminism,
    gender, and race. In addition to texts such as letters, sermons, and speeches, a
    variety of rhetorical contexts such as monuments, strikes, protests, and theater
    are considered"—Provided by publisher.
Identifiers: LCCN 2020029643 (print) | LCCN 2020029644 (ebook) | ISBN
    9781603295208 (hardcover) | ISBN 9781603295215 (paperback) | ISBN
    9781603295222 (EPUB) | ISBN 9781603295239 (Kindle)
Subjects: LCSH: English language—Rhetoric. | Rhetoric—Political aspects—
    United States—History—19th century. | Politics and literature—United
    States—History—19th century. | Speeches, addresses, etc., American—History
    and criticism.
Classification: LCC PE1405.U6 N56 2021 (print) | LCC PE1405.U6 (ebook) | DDC
    810.9/003—dc23
LC record available at https://lccn.loc.gov/2020029643
LC ebook record available at https://lccn.loc.gov/2020029644

Published by The Modern Language Association of America
85 Broad Street, Suite 500, New York, New York 10004-2434
www.mla.org

For it is not light that is needed, but fire; it is not the gentle shower, but thunder. We need the storm, the whirlwind, and the earthquake. The feeling of the nation must be quickened; the conscience of the nation must be roused; the propriety of the nation must be startled; the hypocrisy of the nation must be exposed; and its crimes against God and man must be proclaimed and denounced.

—Frederick Douglass,
"What to the Slave Is the Fourth of July?"

Contents

Part Three: Listening for Contemporary Echoes

Introduction

Patricia Bizzell and Lisa Zimmerelli

We first conceived of *Nineteenth-Century American Activist Rhetorics* as a pedagogical collection, one that might fit in the Approaches to Teaching series of this press. Both of us have been immersed in nineteenth-century scholarship for many years, and we imagined the benefit of a book that presented some ideas for how best to take advantage of the rich texts of this era in the classroom. But as we talked and planned, we realized that the collection that may better serve the academy in this cultural moment was in fact a more theoretical and rhetorical collection, centered around the foundational issues and moments of the nineteenth century and how they still manifest today.

We realize that applying *activist* to nineteenth-century rhetoric is anachronistic, but we do not think it is inaccurate. The period abounded with diverse intellectual, social, and civic issues with which people across race, creed, class, and gender were passionately engaged, and contributors to this volume have found many echoes with activist issues in the United States today. The term *activist* thus highlights the kinds of textual and contextual elements that comprise the rhetorical perspective our contributors take on this plethora of civic activity. The essays contained in this collection, in offering a distinctly rhetorical point of view and theorized position, contribute both to our historical understanding of the nineteenth century and to our contemporary engagement in sociocultural disputes.

Rhetorical Analyses

This collection fits within the discipline of English studies, a field rich with a complex history and varied foci, and a field that deserves a bit of explication. In her 2019 Modern Language Association Presidential Address, the rhetorician Anne Ruggles Gere describes different emphases within English studies: a primary emphasis on reading for literary critics and on writing for people in writing studies, also known as composition and rhetoric, or comp/rhet ("Re-visioning").

We agree. Although the distinctions between literary critics and composition and rhetoric scholars are increasingly blurred and sometimes overlap in productive ways, we find naming some differences helpful. We see literary critics focusing primarily on texts deemed to have aesthetic value and aiming to teach readers to elucidate their fine qualities. We see scholars in writing studies focusing primarily on texts deemed to be doing work in the world; these scholars may aim to teach writers to do this work more effectively (often, a focus of work in composition studies) or to understand how people have used or are using texts to accomplish this work (often, a focus of scholarship in rhetorical studies). This latter focus comprises the contributions to this volume.

Of course, literary studies and rhetorical studies have diverged and converged in Western intellectual history many times since Aristotle left separate treatises on rhetoric and poetics. While the New Criticism moved literary study far away from rhetoric, rapprochement began later in the twentieth century, through such important works as Wayne Booth's *The Rhetoric of Fiction* (1961), which rehabilitated attention to a text's effects on its consumers, and Judith Fetterley's *The Resisting Reader* (1978), which broke ground for feminist approaches to literature. While these works focus on readers, later developments in literary studies have come even closer to rhetoric studies in increasing attention to the many contextual elements that draw rhetoricians' analytic eye: political agendas, cultural allusions, delivery media, diverse audiences' responses, and more. Nevertheless, in studying how rhetors deal with the many factors influencing their performances, rhetoricians may value ingenious and effective rhetorical solutions that produce texts of little inherent literary merit. Examples in the present volume include Sarah Hallenbeck's analysis of the lists of women inventors compiled by Charlotte Odlum Smith and Brian Fehler's treatment of newsboys' protest signs.

In *A Grammar of Motives* (1945) and *A Rhetoric of Motives* (1950), Kenneth Burke, one of the most important rhetoric theorists of modern times, outlines a theory of rhetorical analysis that helps to explain rhetoricians' interests. He describes what he calls a "pentad" of elements comprising any communicative event: act (the event itself), scene (political, social, and historical contexts), agent (creator or initiator), agency (means or media), and purpose (what the communication is intended to accomplish). This pentad extends textual analysis to any communicative event, whether textual, visual, or material in medium, whether aesthetically valuable or commonplace.

Burke's pentad forms an important theoretical horizon within which the contributors to the present volume are working, as they study what activist interventions rhetors attempted in the nineteenth century, what media they used, what kinds of education equipped them, what theories describe their practices, and what historical contexts shaped their aims and accomplishments (see capsule summaries in our account of the table of contents, below, for more examples of the sorts of rhetorical analyses we characterize here). This theoretical horizon also prompts many of our contributors to detect echoes with twenty-first-century social issues.

Taking the scope of Burkean rhetorical analysis as a paradigm helps to explain why, even though literary theory moved closer to rhetorical theory in the mid–twentieth century, the two subfields of English studies remain somewhat distant, as Gere recognizes in her description of contrasting foci of study in these subfields ("Re-visioning"). Gere's own position as president of the MLA evidences current movement toward rapprochement; but at the same time, the consequences of a one-hundred-year-old rift are still felt, primarily as a result of the structural reorganization of post-secondary language studies that took place at the end of the nineteenth century. Rhetoric in the classical tradition had formed a principal part of the liberal arts curriculum in nineteenth-century colleges (see Clark and Halloran). But by the turn of the twentieth century, literary history and criticism dominated English departments, and rhetorical studies were demoted. In place of rhetoric as an advanced discipline in verbal persuasion, first-year courses in expository writing functioned as gate-keepers, teaching basic skills (see Carr; Miller). Some rhetoricians remained in English departments and were largely relegated to teaching these first-year courses. Others dispersed to departments of classics or philosophy or to newly formed departments of speech-communication. By the mid–twentieth century, rhetoricians gathered themselves into their own professional organization, the Rhetoric Society of America (see Halloran). Here, interdisciplinary connections helped to develop the diverse agenda of interests that characterizes rhetorical analysis.

Rhetoricians in the present volume contribute to scholarship in the many forms outlined above. However, their work here zeros in on rhetorical activity that is overtly political and social-reform-minded. In this, their scholarship is cutting-edge. Surprisingly, given nineteenth-century America's plethora of passionate reform causes, little work on the era's activist rhetorics was done before the end of the twentieth century. Indeed, in the 1990 edition of a standard bibliography, *The Present State of Scholarship in the History of Rhetoric*, Donald Stewart remarks on the dearth of studies in this period (172). One reason for the dearth of studies may be that, at that time, available rhetorical theory tended to work better to analyze classical sources or mainstream political rhetoric, rather than the necessarily nonnormative and marginalized work of those who were trying to effect radical social change. Yet, innovation in the field was coming: witness the 2010 edition of *The Present State of Scholarship*, in which coeditor Lynée Lewis Gaillet stresses how "the tide has turned . . . in favor of a broadened and inclusive canon" that moves beyond the "preceptive" (largely pedagogical) focus of the texts Stewart listed to encompass activist rhetorics (153). What happened?

Feminist Theory and Activist Rhetoric

A key breakthrough occurred in 1990, when the speech-communication scholar Karlyn Kohrs Campbell delivered the keynote at the Rhetoric Society of America conference "Genre and Culture: The Test Case of Women's Rhetoric" (Halloran 237). Her landmark two-volume study had just appeared: *Man Cannot Speak for Her, Volume I: A Critical Study of Early Feminist Rhetoric* and *Volume II: Key Texts of the Early Feminists* (1989). Campbell's groundbreaking work instantiated two principal activities for rhetoricians beginning to explore nineteenth-century activist rhetoric: to do the archival work necessary to discover and recover relevant texts, and to submit these texts to rhetorical analysis.

Women (cisgender, gay and straight, white and Black) took the lead in this research. The women researchers' engagement with the twentieth-century civil rights and women's movements enhanced their affinity with the passionate causes to which nineteenth-century rhetors were devoted. The nature of the rhetorical canon played a part, too, as Jessica Enoch has explained:

> For more than two thousand years, conventional rhetorical history has recorded the work of elite male rhetors and rhetoricians as well as masculine forms of rhetorical practice, inscribing it as agonistic, competitive, public, and linear. In so doing, rhetorical history has ignored not only women's rhetorical production but also alternative ways of theorizing and practicing rhetoric. Given the rhetorical history feminist scholars have received, altering the rhetorical tradition becomes the most obvious and important mode of scholarly production. (58)

One important means of "altering the rhetorical tradition" would comprise recovering and analyzing texts by activist women rhetors. Scholars quickly realized that archival work must head in new directions, because often the activists' work may not have been thought worth preserving or may not even have existed in traditional rhetorical formats. Moreover, as new activist texts were discovered, scholars often could not understand the works best by parsing them into the sections of a classical oration. Cultural contexts began to play a much larger role in rhetorical analysis as a means to appreciate the rhetors' strategies for claiming a public voice and resisting restrictive ideologies of gender, race, and class.

These scholarly challenges gave rise to new feminist rhetorical theory, and feminist studies of activist rhetoric burgeoned at the end of the twentieth century. The 1990s was a remarkable decade in which work by and about women flourished. With the floodgates opened, more innovative work, by and about women and men, emerged in the twenty-first century.

The 1990s and After:
Twenty-First-Century Studies of Activist Rhetoric

Campbell's groundbreaking study included important Black rhetors Maria W. Stewart and Sojourner Truth, although Campbell herself does not identify as a person of color. It is imperative for us to acknowledge, then, that from the beginning of the modern upsurge of activist rhetoric scholarship, there exists as well the potential of cultural appropriation. Although several scholars of color make important contributions to the present volume, we are mindful of this ongoing concern, and we don't have any easy answers for addressing it. At the same time, we want to highlight that when early scholarship in the 1990s sought to recover texts by women activists and provide historical and biographical information to contextualize their works, Black rhetoricians produced key texts. Frances Smith Foster collected the speeches, essays, and poems by freeborn Black activist Frances Ellen Watkins Harper and added a lengthy analytic introduction (1990); Foster's work is still the authoritative source on Harper. Shirley Wilson Logan's anthology of Black women's texts (1995; *With Pen and Voice*), followed by her analysis of their rhetoric (1999; *"We Are Coming"*), introduced many scholars to the variety of accomplished Black women rhetors, beyond the well-known names of Stewart and Truth. Carla Peterson provided special emphasis on the political activism of Black women speakers and writers "in the North" (1998). Moreover, we are very fortunate to have a magisterial essay by Jacqueline Jones Royster, author of *Traces of a Stream* (2000), to pronounce the final word in the present volume.

As the remarkable 1990s unfolded, a sign of the times emerged as nineteenth-century activist topics began to appear in the *Rhetoric Society Quarterly*, most dramatically in 1995 when the major figure treated in a special issue was not a well-known male from antiquity, as in previous years, but a white Quaker woman, Lucretia Coffin Mott, an early activist for women's rights and abolition. Moreover, rhetoricians investigated, neglected, or ignored movements where rhetorical activity flourished: Gere explored rhetorical production in the women's club movement (1997; *Intimate Practices*); Carol Mattingly analyzed Frances Willard's dynamic effects on rhetoric in the Woman's Christian Temperance Union, which empowered many women activists to address a variety of reform causes (1998).

This early work tended to treat the subject of woman as an unproblematic category and women's rights as an unmitigated social good. Scholarship in the twenty-first century began to complicate this picture, however. Some work looked at rhetorical situations that were not comfortably feminist by today's standards. Nan Johnson detailed the kinds of rhetoric women developed while bending to the gender ideology that confined them to the domestic sphere

(2002). Lindal Buchanan used the classical canon of delivery to show how women found purely decorous ways to challenge the era's restrictions on women's public speaking (2005). Moreover, new work began to acknowledge that some activism, even if well-intentioned, still promoted attitudes and actions that did harm to individuals and groups. Mattingly's work on the Woman's Christian Temperance Union had acknowledged the organization's racist tendencies; later, Wendy Hayden traced the problematic compromises with eugenics made by both male and female nineteenth-century feminists who devised interrelated arguments about "sex, science, and free love" (2013). Even more problematic—indeed, completely reprehensible—was the pro-slavery rhetoric produced by a "tragedy of consensus" that Patricia Roberts-Miller analyzed (2009).

Today's expansive reach of rhetorical theory derived from late-twentieth-century feminist work is both symbolized and acknowledged by the recent decision of the Coalition of Women Scholars in the History of Rhetoric and Composition (founded in 1989) to change the organization's name. Now, the Coalition of Feminist Scholars in the History of Rhetoric and Composition invites all with a feminist theoretical orientation, not only (implicitly cisgender) women (see Bizzell and Rawson). Now, rhetoric scholarship informed by feminist theory is mainstream, and Cheryl Glenn has recently shown how its reach extends across historical periods and public venues. As Andrea Lunsford prophesied in 1995, feminist rhetoric has "[opened] up possibilities for multiple rhetorics . . . [and incorporated] other, often dangerous moves: breaking the silence; naming in personal terms; employing dialogics; recognizing and using the power of conversation; moving centripetally towards connections; and valuing—indeed insisting upon—collaboration" (6). Given this origin story for the modern upsurge of scholarship on nineteenth-century activist rhetoric, it is not surprising that our contributors found so many echoes here with issues of social justice that still agitate the public sphere.

Nineteenth-Century Reform Issues and the Structure of This Volume

We have devised a three-part structure for the volume: "Reframing Activist Issues," "Locating Rhetorical Activities," and "Listening for Contemporary Echoes." The essays in part 1, "Reframing Activist Issues," fall under four themes: engaging with new theoretical lenses, challenging received wisdom, highlighting obscured figures, and looking at understudied activist movements. For new theoretical lenses, Meaghan Brewer uses the classical concept of kairos to illuminate both Frederick Douglass's familiar "What to the Slave" oration (quoted in this volume's epigraph) and today's Black Lives Matter protest by Colin Kaepernick. Julie Prebel uses Black theorist Christina Sharpe's concept of "wake work" to bring together the embodied activism of Harper and Ida B. Wells. Martin Camper repurposes classical stasis theory to analyze arguments about Methodist women's preaching in both Black and white congregations.

In the essays with the theme of challenging received wisdom, iconic figures are revisited. Nancy Myers analyzes the "rhetorical missteps" of Elizabeth Cady Stanton that allied her with white supremacist elements in her era's political landscape. Mollie Barnes examines not only Margaret Fuller's well-known reluctance to espouse abolitionism but also her little-known tendency to change her mind about the movement near the end of her life. Paul Stob rehabilitates Booker T. Washington's reputation as an advocate for Black rights.

Three essays in part 1 are focused on highlighting obscured figures. Wendy Hayden discusses the feminist anger of Lillie D. White, who called out male progressives for their less-than-progressive attitudes toward women activists. Patty Wilde explains the Black rights advocacy of Susie King Taylor's little-known wartime memoir. Sarah Hallenbeck shows how the working-class activist Charlotte Odlum Smith sought recognition for women inventors.

The last four essays in part 1 look at protest movements by Indigenous peoples and by labor activists. Elizabeth Lowry shows how a Yurok ritual embodied resistance to colonialist incursions in California. Megan Vallowe explains why three Indigenous men were willing to risk the charge of "race traitor" in advocating for their people. Activism for workers' rights forms the focus of essays by Brian Fehler and Brenda Glascott; Fehler shows how newsboys organized as workers, and Glascott details the "affectional bonds" that united women labor activists who preferred not to be identified as lesbians.

Part 2, "Locating Rhetorical Activities," comprises essays that focus on different material and print venues for rhetorical activism: on the stage, in memorials and monuments, and in the periodical press. The first two essays look at the stage: Angela G. Ray recounts the career of impersonator Helen Potter, who dispelled the era's harridan caricatures by depicting feminist activists positively on the stage, and Lisa Suter chronicles young women's initiatives to write and perform plays that dramatized women's rights issues but also problematically perpetuated racialized stereotypes.

The next three essays look at memorials and monuments. Jessica Enoch discusses how conservative, white supremacist women memorialized their version of American history in the activities of the Daughters of the American Revolution. Shevaun Watson shows how monuments dedicated to Confederate heroes have been attacked by Black people almost from the moment the monuments were erected in the postbellum period and up to today's protests against the Mother Emanuel Church shootings. Jessica A. Rose and Lynée Lewis Gaillet recount a cautionary tale about preserving women's history by exploring how even widespread and well-funded memorial programs, such as the Woman's Christian Temperance Union's projects to build water fountains and establish archives in a monumental building, can eventually disappear from public view.

The final two essays in part 2 focus on the periodical press. Kristie Fleckenstein documents how the periodical press provided a venue for competing images of the New Negro Woman as a talented but vulnerable young girl, or as an accomplished and powerful activist matron. Coauthors Suzanne Bordelon and Elizabethada Wright turn the classical enthymeme to use for recovering the subtle feminist themes in journalism by Louise Clappe and Fanny Fern.

While many of the contributors in parts 1 and 2 notice parallels between nineteenth-century rhetoric and today's controversies, the four contributors in part 3, "Listening for Contemporary Echoes," more deeply explore these resonances. Patricia Roberts-Miller uses her work on pro-slavery rhetoric as a lens through which to detect and condemn the rhetorical moves of today's white supremacists. Morris Young finds that themes either attacking or defending Chinese immigration at the end of the nineteenth century carry forward into today's immigration debates. Michael-John DePalma develops a plan for contemporary interfaith social justice collaboration from the work of Andover Settlement House's nineteenth-century founders. Jacqueline Jones Royster looks at key nineteenth-century developments—the rise of literacy and the periodical press, the battles over imperialism, colonialism, and slavery—and links them with ongoing twenty-first-century concerns over access to multimodal knowledge and the unjust effects of sociopolitical hierarchies.

We are aware that the nineteenth-century sources our contributors analyze did not typically critique the category *woman*; people who looked like women were simply regarded as heterosexual and female. Same-sex relationships were not labeled as gay or lesbian, and people in such relationships sometimes actively resisted such labeling (see Glascott, this volume). Transgender people were not recognized as such. Racial mixing was condemned, when it was acknowledged at all. Our contributors are cautious not to impose twenty-first-century political agendas on their research subjects, but at the same time they cannot set aside their twenty-first-century commitments to social justice across diverse racial, sexual, gender, and social-class identifications.

As editors, we have attempted to assemble a selection of essays that gives due attention to individual activists while reflecting the field's increasing emphasis on movements rather than individuals. We hope that our readers, like our contributors and ourselves, appreciate the contemporary resonances in the struggles examined here and find inspiration for understanding our era's social issues and crafting rhetorical agendas to engage them.

Works Cited

Bizzell, Patricia, and K. J. Rawson. "Coalition of Who? Regendering Scholarly Community in the History of Rhetoric." *Peitho*, vol. 18, no. 1, Fall-Winter 2015, pp. 110–12, peitho.cwshrc.org/issue/18-1.

Booth, Wayne. *The Rhetoric of Fiction*. U of Chicago P, 1961.

Buchanan, Lindal. *Regendering Delivery: The Fifth Canon and Antebellum Women Rhetors*. Southern Illinois UP, 2005.

Burke, Kenneth. *A Grammar of Motives*. 1945. U of California P, 1969.

———. *A Rhetoric of Motives*. 1950. U of California P, 1969.

Campbell, Karlyn Kohrs. *A Critical Study of Early Feminist Rhetoric*. Praeger/Greenwood, 1989. Volume 1 of *Man Cannot Speak for Her*.

———. *Key Texts of the Early Feminists*. Praeger/Greenwood, 1989. Vol. 2 of *Man Cannot Speak for Her*.

Carr, Jean Ferguson. "Composition, English, and the University." *PMLA*, vol. 129, no. 3, 2014, pp. 435–41.

Clark, Gregory, and S. Michael Halloran. "Introduction: Transformations of Public Discourse in Nineteenth-Century America." *Oratorical Culture in Nineteenth-Century America*, edited by Clark and Halloran. Southern Illinois UP, 1993, pp. 1–26.

Enoch, Jessica. "Releasing Hold: Feminist Historiography without the Tradition." *Theorizing Histories of Rhetoric*, edited by Michelle Ballif. Southern Illinois UP, 2013, pp. 58–73.

Fetterley, Judith. *The Resisting Reader: A Feminist Approach to American Fiction*. Indiana UP, 1978.

Foster, Frances Smith, editor. *A Brighter Coming Day: A Frances Ellen Watkins Reader*. Feminist P, 1990.

Gaillet, Lynée Lewis. "The Nineteenth Century." *The Present State of Scholarship in the History of Rhetoric: A Twenty-First Century Guide*, edited by Gaillet with Winifred Bryan Horner. 3rd ed., U of Missouri P, 2010, pp. 152–84.

Gere, Anne Ruggles. *Intimate Practices: Literacy and Cultural Work in U.S. Women's Clubs, 1880–1920*. U of Illinois P, 1997.

———. "Re-visioning, Language, Texts, and Theories." *PMLA*, vol. 134, no. 3, May 2019, pp. 450–58.

Glenn, Cheryl. *Rhetorical Feminism and This Thing Called Hope*. Southern Illinois UP, 2018.

Halloran, S. Michael. "The Growth of the Rhetoric Society of America: An Anecdotal History." *Rhetoric Society Quarterly*, vol. 48, no. 3, 2018, pp. 234–41.

Hayden, Wendy. *Evolutionary Rhetoric: Sex, Science, and Free Love in Nineteenth-Century Feminism*. Southern Illinois UP, 2013.

Johnson, Nan. *Gender and Rhetorical Space in American Life, 1866–1910*. Southern Illinois UP, 2002.

Logan, Shirley Wilson. *"We Are Coming": The Persuasive Discourse of Nineteenth-Century Black Women*. Southern Illinois UP, 1999.

———. *With Pen and Voice: A Critical Anthology of Nineteenth-Century African-American Women*. Southern Illinois UP, 1995.

Lunsford, Andrea A. "On Reclaiming Rhetorica." *Reclaiming Rhetorica: Women in the Rhetorical Tradition*, edited by Lunsford. U of Pittsburgh P, 1995, pp. 3–8.

Mattingly, Carol. *Well-Tempered Women: Nineteenth-Century Temperance Rhetoric*. Southern Illinois UP, 1998.

Miller, Susan. "The Feminization of Composition." *The Politics of Writing Instruction: Postsecondary*, edited by Richard Bullock and John Trimbur. Heinemann/Boynton/Cook, 1991, pp. 39–54.

Peterson, Carla. *"Doers of the Word": African American Women Speakers and Writers in the North, 1830–1860*. Rutgers UP, 1998.

Roberts-Miller, Patricia. *Fanatical Schemes: Pro-slavery Rhetoric and the Tragedy of Consensus*. U of Alabama P, 2009.

Royster, Jacqueline Jones. *Traces of a Stream: Literacy and Social Change among African American Women*. U of Pittsburgh P, 2000.

Stewart, Donald. "The Nineteenth Century." *The Present State of Scholarship in the Historical and Contemporary Rhetoric: Revised Edition*, edited by Winifred Bryan Horner. U of Missouri P, 1990, pp. 151–85.

Part One

Reframing Activist Issues

Kairos Matters: Reading Colin Kaepernick's Protest through the Lens of Frederick Douglass's "What to the Slave Is the Fourth of July?"

Meaghan Brewer

During a preseason football game in 2016, Colin Kaepernick, then a quarterback for the San Francisco 49ers, linked himself to a long history of Black civil protest when he sat during the singing of the national anthem. He later clarified why he chose to sit, saying, "I am not going to stand up to show pride in a flag for a country that oppresses Black people and people of color. . . . To me, this is bigger than football and it would be selfish on my part to look the other way" (qtd. in Wyche). While Kaepernick's actions drew praise in some quarters (including solidarity from other players within the NFL and other sports venues, like women's professional soccer), many were critical, believing his actions to be unpatriotic or disrespectful to the military. This criticism came most vocally from Donald Trump and other conservatives during the fall of 2017, but even some more liberal-minded individuals (like Ruth Bader Ginsburg) initially criticized Kaepernick's protest (Graham; de Vogue).

In this essay, I argue that detractors of Kaepernick and the Black Lives Matter movement could better understand the kairos of these protests if the protests are contextualized within rhetorical history and the long tradition of peaceful protest for civil rights. Specifically, I contend that Frederick Douglass's July 1852 speech "What to the Slave Is the Fourth of July?" created an important precedent for Black expressions of dissent within the context of a patriotic event. The key to understanding the rhetoric of these protests is the Greek rhetorical concept of kairos, which I define provisionally as right or opportune timing and right measure or appropriateness. With this rhetorical lens, and when considered in conversation with Douglass's speech, Kaepernick's protest appears not as unpatriotic or disrespectful but rather as the ultimate display of patriotism: the use of his available means to correct injustice. As rhetoricians, both Douglass and Kaepernick identify kairotic opportunities—the occasion of Douglass's speech and the televised football game—to persuade their largely white audiences of the existence of inequality. They both call attention to American hypocrisy by contrasting the messages of the texts assumed to be part of the context for their protests (the Declaration of Independence and "The Star-Spangled Banner") with the realities for slaves and people of color. Yet they both also had to justify the kairos (the appropriateness or right measure) of their protests, demonstrating how kairos is unequally available to people of color.

I begin by exploring kairos in three different but interrelated senses that I argue are essential to understanding both historical and contemporary Black protest. I then move to Douglass's speech, examining how its antebellum context, and specifically the realities of slavery and the Fugitive Slave Law, created tensions in terms of his access to kairos. However, I also demonstrate how Douglass exploited these tensions to create kairos, a move that would later be used by Black rhetors in the twentieth and twenty-first centuries as well. Specifically, although Douglass's juxtaposition of protest with patriotism appears to foreclose kairotic opportunity by (potentially) drawing criticism for its inappropriateness, the juxtaposition also creates kairos because of this very tension. I then explore how Douglass's speech resonates today in the protests of Kaepernick and Black Lives Matter. I end by considering more broadly what nineteenth-century American activist rhetorics, and particularly Black rhetors, can teach us about Black protest in the twenty-first century.

Kairos as Opportunity, Right Measure, and Call to Action

Like many terms coming from another language, *kairos* is difficult to translate. James S. Baumlin contends that kairos denotes a range of meanings, including "due measure," "harmony," "fitness," "appropriateness," "proportionality," and "timeliness" (157). And when we translate the term into English we tend to account for these meanings only fractionally, when in reality "any given usage is likely to suggest several senses simultaneously" (Baumlin 157). With these difficulties in mind, I explore kairos here in three senses. For the first two senses, I draw on James Kinneavy's interpretation of the two basic (and often interrelated) elements of kairos as they appear in the work of Hesiod through Cicero: finding the right or opportune time and finding the right measure (60). I then add, based on more recent work, a third definition of kairos as a call to action, and specifically as a sense of being compelled to act, often because of circumstances that force one's hand.

Understanding kairos as right timing requires contrasting the term with the Greek concept of *chronos*, defined as traditional or linear time. Frank Kermode contrasts the two terms by depicting chronos as orderliness and linking kairos to chaos; kairos is "a point in time filled with significance, charged with a meaning derived from its relation to the end" (47). The precision involved in identifying kairos is sometimes illustrated with spatial metaphors, as the small gap that one must thread through in weaving, or the axe heads Odysseus shoots his arrow through to defeat Penelope's suitors. Both metaphors demonstrate how elusive kairos can be in that the speaker or rhetor must pinpoint exactly when to speak for the speech to be most effective. Kairos is thus, according to Sharon Crowley, a "more subjective dimension of time" that becomes available to the savvy rhetor who knows how to identify it (83). In addition to kairos as the right or good time to do something (*eukairos*), the Greeks also had terms for the wrong time (*kakakairos*) and even times with no opportunity (*akairos*; Sipiora 2; see also Crowley 83).

These definitions show how fleeting kairos can be and how one's access to the opportunity to speak can be unequally available, especially in a country that has historically tried to suppress Black citizens' rights to speak. In this sense, kairos can be linked to Aristotle's definition of rhetoric itself as the "faculty of observing in any given case the available means of persuasion" (7).

Kairos in the second sense, as right measure or appropriateness, can be elucidated by the proverb from Hesiod which charges one to "Observe good measure, and proportion *[kairos]* . . . in all things" (qtd. in Kinneavy 60). This definition demonstrates how right timing is tied to decorum and context. For example, expressing anger in one context might be deemed righteous or understandable while in another it might be judged inappropriate or out of proportion to the situation it responds to.

These first two senses of kairos are often linked. For example, the judgment of the appropriateness of Douglass's "What to the Slave" speech and of Kaepernick's protest is tied directly to both protests' timing during displays of patriotism. Black displays of dissent during the Fourth of July holiday were common during the antebellum era, but only for Black audiences (Bizzell). In delivering his address to a predominantly white audience on the fifth of July, the day after the holiday, Douglass took a risk that his audience members might judge his speech to be *kakakairotic*, even if they agreed with many of its messages.

Instead, as I will discuss, Douglass's audience judged his timing to be appropriate, and his speech created an important historical precedent for later Black protests during patriotic events, including the refusal of members of an African American Methodist church to sing the national anthem after the 1892 lynching of three men in Memphis, Tennessee, and the 1968 Olympics Black Power salute by the Black athletes Tommie Smith and John Carlos during their medal ceremony. Indeed, perhaps the defining aspect of African American rhetoric throughout its history has been, as Keith Gilyard and Adam Banks argue, its goal of persuading "American society to live up to its expressed ideals about equality and rights," a goal that necessitates aligning protest with displays of patriotism (3; see also Bacon).

Kairos as call to action is the third sense. Arguing that rhetorical scholarship has yet to draw concrete connections between kairos and action, Michael Harker contends that "it is almost impossible to consider kairos outside of . . . the realm of action, the realm of ethics" (82). As this statement suggests, ethics and action are both intimately tied together and essential to understanding kairos. In Pythagorean rhetoric, for example, kairos is almost always tied to *dikaion*, or justice (Kinneavy 61; Sipiora 4).

Harker points to Kenneth Burke's interpretation of kairos as occurring in moments of historical crisis in which "one must make a choice, even when no apparently good choices are available" (qtd. in Harker 83). As Harker argues, connecting kairos and action "charges kairos with a sense of inevitability," a recognition that "whether a writer or speaker likes it or not . . . we must often choose— as the decision to not act is a decision itself" (84). As I discuss later, Douglass created precedent for this sense of kairos in Black rhetoric by using the subgenre of the apologia to depict himself as simultaneously reluctant and compelled to speak to correct injustice.

Embedded in all these senses of kairos is the contextual nature of rhetoric itself. While different rhetorical traditions have recognized the contingency of rhetoric to varying degrees, even Platonic and Aristotelian rhetoric are sensitive to the dynamic, contingent nature of the rhetorical situation. And while kairos is often concerned with fleeting moments, the connection between kairos and ethics also shows how these moments are connected historically. As Kinneavy asserts, "[K]airos brings timeless ideas down into the human situations of historical time. It thus imposes value on ideas and forces humans to make free decisions about those values" (62). In the next section, I make the case for considering the historical moment of Douglass's "What to the Slave" speech as a precedent for Black political protest today.

From Apologia to Anger: The Creation of Kairos in Douglass's Independence Day Oration

In some ways, Douglass faced a more receptive audience for his "What to the Slave" oration than many Black rhetors would in the twenty-first century. Unlike Kaepernick, for example, Douglass was invited to give his speech by the Rochester Ladies' Anti-slavery Society and thus had allies for creating his kairos (as opportunity) at the speech's outset. He faced a crowd of mostly abolitionists, and the immediate outcome of his speech was supportive in that the audience responded by voting to endorse his speech.

Still, Douglass's speech makes clear that he could not assume his audience's support for what was still a radical statement: that he refused to celebrate the Fourth of July until slavery ended. As Patricia Bizzell points out, "[T]he event was open to the public and Douglass had to assume that there were also audience members who were undecided about abolition, or even hostile to it" (48). And although it comprised abolitionists, Douglass's audience was mostly white, a difference, as I noted earlier, in audience from similarly themed July Fourth addresses delivered to audiences of mostly African Americans (Bizzell 47–48; Forbes). Black abolitionist speakers of the time, including Douglass and Sojourner Truth, frequently faced confrontation by angry, violent pro-slavery mobs who threw eggs and rocks and even attacked members of their audiences. While on an abolitionist tour in 1843, Douglass was beaten unconscious after protecting a white abolitionist from an angry pro-slavery mob, an incident which left him with a broken hand that never completely healed (Colaiaco 20).

Douglass thus had to anticipate that white members of his audience might feel uncomfortable with a speech that points to the hypocrisy of July Fourth celebrations of liberty while so many African Americans remained in chains. Douglass also knew that his speech would be regarded (and reproduced) as a speech to the nation as a whole, meaning he had to think beyond his immediate audience. He thus goes to great lengths to establish his expertise on American history and its documents, spending twenty-six paragraphs recounting the history of the American fight for independence, citing specifics to support his account. In this section, Douglass establishes the Declaration of Independence as his primary document of reference, calling it "the RING-BOLT to the chain of your nation's destiny" (363).[1] The use of the Declaration to point to the hypocrisy of slavery was not unique to Douglass. As the early-nineteenth-century Black activist David Walker exclaims, "See your Declaration Americans!!! Do you understand your own language?" (qtd. in Bacon 55).

Douglass depicts the kairos of his speech, in the sense of the creation of his opportunity to speak, as originating much earlier and only after he had overcome a number of almost insurmountable obstacles. He demonstrates how unlikely it is that he, a former slave, would be able to speak on such a day and in such a venue, stating:

> [T]he distance between this platform and the slave plantation, from which I escaped, is considerable—and the difficulties to be overcome in getting from the latter to the former, are by no means slight. That I am here to-day is, to me, a matter of astonishment as well as of gratitude. (360)

Douglass shows how kairos (as opportunity) is unequally available and, indeed, that it is almost nonexistent for slaves or even former slaves. Douglass and his fellow Black American rhetors were risking much more when they spoke than their white abolitionist counterparts, especially after the passage of the 1850 Fugitive Slave Law, which allowed slaveholders to pursue and capture Black Americans even in states that had abolished slavery.

Although the law technically only applied to escaped slaves, Douglass and other Black abolitionists argued that it put all Black Americans in peril, and he refers to this directly in his speech, contending:

> [T]he power to hold, hunt, and sell men, women, and children as slaves remains no longer a mere state institution, but is now an institution of the whole United States. The power is co-extensive with the star-spangled banner and American Christianity. Where these go, may also go the merciless slave-hunter. . . . Your broad republican domain is hunting ground for men.   (375)

In this and the passage I cite above, Douglass reveals himself not as the polished rhetor but as one of the Black bodies in peril, and the "distance," as he calls it, between the platform of the rhetor and the plantation is one he wants his audience to bear in mind, since it is crucial to the message of his speech. Indeed, throughout his speech, Douglass creates a charged distance between himself and his audience by using the second person ("*your* National independence," "*your* fathers," "*your* Nation's history" [360, 363; emphasis mine]). Douglass creates kairos by, ironically, pointing to the unavailability of kairos for him and to the fact that the opportunity he now has to speak against slavery has come only because he fought to achieve his own liberty.

Douglass's reluctance comes in the form of an apologia. Although a common subgenre in nineteenth-century speeches, his apologia is striking in its initial hesitance, given the experience (as a former slave) and expertise (as a frequent speaker on slavery) informing his position. He states, "I do not remember ever to have appeared as a speaker before any assembly more shrinkingly, nor with greater distrust of my ability, than I do this day. . . . Should I seem at ease, my appearance would much misrepresent me" (359–60). This apologia helps set up his speech by suggesting a reluctance that would starkly contrast with the anger and even fire of his later message. He thus depicts himself as someone in a situation in which he must speak, regardless of potential, personal, negative consequences, suggesting the third sense of kairos as call to action.

The turning point of his speech, and the part he anticipates his audience might object to on grounds of appropriateness, comes when Douglass turns to the present situation of the nation. "Fellow-citizens, pardon me," he states, "allow me to ask, why am I called upon to speak here to-day? What have I, or those I represent, to do with your national independence? Are the great principles of political freedom and natural justice, embodied in the Declaration of Independence, extended to us?" Douglass then questions whether his audience means to "mock" him by asking him to speak on a day that throws into such stark contrast the celebration of liberty by American citizens with the brutality and suffering experienced by slaves (367).

Douglass thus moves from a speech largely driven by logos to one driven as well by anger, and it is an anger that could well be deemed inappropriate by his audience. Douglass gives voice to these challenges to his kairos, stating that some in his audience might say that "it is just in this circumstance that you and your brother abolitionists fail to make a favorable impression on the public mind. Would you argue more, and denounce less, would you persuade more, and rebuke less, your cause would be much more likely to succeed" (369). These charges are strikingly similar to ones Martin Luther King, Jr., Kaepernick, and others connected to Black Lives Matter would have to answer to in the twentieth and twenty-first centuries: that they have the right to protest but that they're going about it all wrong; that their anger, the fire in their messages are inappropriate, especially given, in Douglass's case, the context of a celebration. But Douglass persists, arguing that he can't merely stand up and argue for slavery's abolition or slaves' humanity because those are points that are already well established. "At a time like this," Douglass states, directly referring to the kairos his speech responds to,

> scorching irony, not convincing argument, is needed. O! had I the ability, and could I reach the nation's ear, I would to-day pour out a fiery stream of biting ridicule, blasting reproach, withering sarcasm, and stern rebuke. For it is not light that is needed, but fire. . . . The feeling of the nation must be quickened; the conscience of the nation must be roused; the propriety of the nation must be startled; the hypocrisy of the nation must be exposed; and its crimes against God and man must be proclaimed and denounced.   (371)

Douglass, like many of his contemporaries and like the many Black rhetors who would follow him, exposes and condemns the hypocrisy of white American claims of justice and liberty by identifying and maximizing the fleeting moments of kairos he worked hard to grasp hold of. Refusing to be quieted by claims that his speeches lack appropriate measure, he ultimately portrays himself as compelled for the sake of justice to make his argument for the rights of Black Americans and point out the hypocrisy of the American public.

Kaepernick and Black Lives Matter

Douglass's skillful use of kairos to connect and exploit tensions between Black protest and patriotic displays created a significant historical precedent for other Black activist rhetors. Like Douglass, Kaepernick and other Black activists today have to identify right timing along multiple dimensions. In the sense of kairos as opportunity, the available time Kaepernick and other athletes have that will maximize attention from their audience, the (perhaps largely white) American public, is during the national anthem, a nationally televised portion of a football game when millions of viewers are tuned in. The singing of the national anthem becomes their available means or opportunity to make a statement about American hypocrisy by connecting events in which agents of the state have shot, incarcerated, or inflicted violence and brutality on Black bodies to a song celebrating the land of the free.

Yet Kaepernick, like Douglass and many other Black rhetors, has been criticized for his choice of timing. For example, Steven Mnuchin, secretary of the United States Treasury, in response to a question about whether the NFL players who kneel during the anthem were exercising their First Amendment rights, stated, "It's not about free speech. They can do free speech *on their own time*" (qtd. in "September 25"; emphasis mine). Mnuchin's statement implies that a rhetor's kairos must in some way be owned by the rhetor ("their own time")—and, moreover, that there are some events, like nationally televised American football games, that are, by definition, *akairotic*.

In a segment on *The Daily Show*, host Trevor Noah mocked Mnuchin's statement that NFL players could simply protest "off the field," saying, "He's not against the players protesting. He just doesn't like it when they do it on the field—you know, when everyone's watching" ("September 25"). Noah further demonstrated how NFL players' access to kairos is perhaps only on the field (the time and place when their protest can be seen by millions of viewers) by asking whether Rosa Parks would have been as effective if she had protested from her house instead of on a bus, demonstrating how these fleeting moments of kairos are historically connected.

Kaepernick's protest, and its evolution, also suggests a broader sense of right timing in its connection to the larger cultural visibility of the Black Lives Matter movement, a movement Kaepernick has specifically linked his protests to. Even after Kaepernick was no longer employed by the NFL (and thus no longer had access to televised games), his protest gained renewed attention when several NFL teams either knelt together or linked arms in the weeks following Trump's now infamous speech in Alabama, where he asked his audience whether they wouldn't love to hear league owners say, "Get that son of a bitch off the field right now" in response to players' kneeling (qtd. in Graham). As with Douglass's speech, Kaepernick's protest suggests, then, that the most kairotic moments can be the ones that others judge to be *akairotic* or even bad timing (*kakakairos*). And that kairos can, in fact, be heightened after one's kairos, in the sense of right or opportunity to speak, is called into question. For example, Chris Conley, a wide receiver for the Kansas City Chiefs, in response to Trump's statements, asked, "When will people learn that fear won't make someone sit down? It quite possibly will make more stand up for what they believe in" (qtd. in Graham). To put it another way, when different constituents of an audience disagree on a rhetor's kairos, the disagreement can create further kairotic opportunities, revealing the link among kairos, tension, and action.

Recognizing the parallels between Kaepernick's protest and the actions of his Black activist predecessors, artist Mark Ulriksen designed a cover for *The New Yorker* depicting Martin Luther King, Jr., kneeling between Kaepernick and another NFL athlete, Michael Bennett, their arms linked and with King's head bent in prayer. Ulriksen's cover demonstrates that while King (like Douglass) is now widely accepted as one of the most important civil rights leaders in American history, he too had to justify the appropriateness of his protests. King frames his "Letter from Birmingham Jail" as an answer to challenges to his kairos, since the letter responds to clergymen who called his protests "unwise and untimely" (472). King argues that the purpose of nonviolent protest is to create discomfort, implying that there will always be those who challenge a protest's appropriateness. Yet nonviolent protest also creates kairos; King states, "[T]he purpose of direct action is to create a situation so crisis-packed that it will inevitably open the door to negotiation" (475). This sense of skillfully using tension to create openings (kairos) is, as I argued earlier, present in Douglass's speech as well.

Even with these historical precedents, Kaepernick adjusted his protest in response to others' judgment of its appropriateness. Days after his first statement about his protest, Kaepernick sat down with Nate Boyer, a former Green Beret who played in the NFL for the Seattle Seahawks; Boyer convinced Kaepernick that kneeling, rather than sitting, would be more respectful. The progression of Kaepernick's protest shows the modifications that savvy rhetors make in response to their audience and how these adjustments respond, ultimately, to kairos. At the same time, in consideration of the continued criticism Kaepernick and others received, his protest and its precedents also demonstrate the potentially unachievable nature of kairos. If kairos is both right timing and a sensitivity to what auditors of any given situation are going to deem appropriate, kairos is unstable, always shifting, and perhaps never ideal.

The sense of kairos as inevitable action fits Kaepernick's statements about his initial choice to sit after months of deliberation. Standing during an anthem and saluting the flag was a moment Kaepernick found himself in but which had become no longer tenable after the shootings of Black Americans like Tamir Rice, Philando Castile, and Terence Crutcher, all cases where officers were either not criminally charged or were acquitted after their trials. Kaepernick's protest, then, is also kairotic because it marks a moment in which he felt compelled to act, regardless of the repercussions. He states, "I have to stand up for people that are oppressed. . . . If they take football away, my endorsements from me, I know that I stood up for what is right" (qtd. in Wyche). Kaepernick's initial protest thus responded to a crisis moment (or moments) after which inaction had become impossible, linking kairos to ethical imperative.

One notable difference between Douglass and Kaepernick is that whereas Douglass delivered hundreds of antislavery speeches, Kaepernick has been relatively silent in his protests. While he is active on *Twitter*, many of Kaepernick's tweets are retweets and quotes from others in support of his protests, and he has been reticent about giving interviews. However, as Cheryl Glenn argues, silence can be a powerful rhetorical strategy, and Kaepernick's supporters have noted how his at times "deafening" silence is a savvy rhetorical strategy (Hoffman and Minsberg). According to the editors of the *GQ* issue where Kaepernick appeared on the cover as citizen of the year:

> [Kaepernick] has grown wise to the power of his silence. It has helped his story go around the world. It has even provoked the ire and ill temper of Donald Trump. Why talk now, when your detractors will only twist your words and use them against you? Why speak now, when silence has done so much?
>
> ("Colin Kaepernick")

Kaepernick's silence can thus be seen as itself a form of kairos, his judgment about the prudence of not speaking, of letting his message be carried in images and the words and deeds of others. Indeed, it is perhaps not a coincidence that he has allowed his silence to stand in stark contrast to a president who seemingly cannot stop talking, even when it incriminates him. Although some have questioned Kaepernick's decision to remain silent (see Thomas), silence has been his way of shifting the ground underneath us, of opening up the conversation, and of letting declarations of injustice fill the void that silence leaves.

Their differences notwithstanding, Douglass and Kaepernick both depict themselves as unlikely rhetors and both draw attention to their initial reluctance to speak, given the juxtaposition of their opportunities to speak with displays of patriotism. However, they both also describe themselves as being compelled to speak (the third sense of kairos) because of messages contained within the patriotic texts their protests reference. Douglass and Kaepernick are, then, linked in a longer cultural narrative about white American hypocrisy; they are both able to channel and create tensions between their messages and the displays of patriotism they found themselves reluctantly participating in to maximize their access to kairos.

Kairos and the Role of Anger in Black Activist Rhetorics

White Americans have always been uncomfortable with Black Americans' displays of anger, and some of this discomfort (and even anger) undoubtedly springs from white supremacist racism and the at times calculated erasure of Black historical activism. Ella Forbes argues that white, dominant cultural narratives deliberately refer to images of Black victimhood and subjugation. White Americans are more comfortable with such images, Forbes contends, than they are with "illustrations of Black agency and self-empowerment," which, in Forbes's view, "force Whites to confront the reason for Black activism and militancy: White racism" (155).

Yet, as Forbes argues, "the most prevalent stance for the African American community has been one of resistance," and this resistance also includes "redemptive violence," which she characterizes as "both retributive and retaliatory because it was to be committed in self-defense and for the purpose of liberation" (155–56). While Douglass does not directly call for violence in his "What to the Slave" speech, in a speech just a month later he states that "[t]he only way to make the Fugitive Slave Law a dead letter is to make a dozen or so more dead kidnappers" ("Let All Soil" 390). In the view of Douglass and other Black abolitionists like Charles Henry Langston, Henry Highland Garnet, and Samuel Ringgold Ward, redemptive violence and resistance were necessary when even free African Americans could be apprehended in any state, and these abolitionists connected the use of violent resistance with patriotism. Reverend Andrew Jackson, for example, telling how he used a hickory stick to escape five slave catchers who tried to recapture him, asserted, "[I]f it was right for the revolutionary patriots to fight for liberty, it was right for me, and it is right for any other slave to do the same" (qtd. in Forbes 157).

What does it mean, then, for our current moment, that even much more subdued displays of Black resistance are deemed inappropriate (*kakakairos*), disrespectful, and as evidence that Black protestors hate America? How do we reconcile Douglass's now centuries-old call for "a fiery stream of biting ridicule, blasting reproach, withering sarcasm, and stern rebuke" ("What to the Slave" 371) with the lack of affordance given to Black activists today, even as Black Americans are killed, beaten, and incarcerated by agents of the state? Criticism (and even hatred) of Black rhetors who stand up for the Black Lives Matter movement stems, in part, from white America's confusion between patriotism and nationalism, as well as its denial of the racist and white supremacist origins of many of its patriotic displays, including "The Star-Spangled Banner" (see Dyson).

My answer is that we need to study the nineteenth century and the long tradition of Black activism to contextualize and understand how the white American public restricts Black rhetors' access to kairos. We need to understand that Black activism today always occurs in the context of the Black activism that has preceded it, the long tradition, beginning with antebellum Black American activist rhetoric, that brought into being the "timeless ideas" that, in Kinneavy's view, create kairos.

Note

1. Douglass's metaphor purposefully invokes the imagery of the chains used on enslaved Africans, making this another moment where he juxtaposes the ideals expressed in the Declaration of Independence with the reality of people in bondage.

Works Cited

Aristotle. *Rhetoric*. Translated by W. Rhys Roberts, Mockingbird Classics, 2015.

Bacon, Jacqueline "'Do You Understand Your Own Language?' Revolutionary Topoi in the Rhetoric of African-American Abolitionists." *Rhetoric Society Quarterly*, vol. 28, no. 2, 1998, pp. 55–75, doi:10.1080/02773949809391119.

Baumlin, James S. "Ciceronian Decorum and the Temporalities of Renaissance Rhetoric." Sipiora and Baumlin, pp. 138–64.

Bizzell, Patricia. "The 4th of July and the 22nd of December: The Function of Cultural Archives in Persuasion, as Shown by Frederick Douglass and William Apess." *College Composition and Communication*, vol. 48, no. 1, 1997, pp. 44–60.

Blassingame, John W., ed. *The Frederick Douglass Papers*, series 1, vol. 2. Yale UP, 1982.

Colaiaco, James A. *Frederick Douglass and the Fourth of July*. St. Martin's Griffin, 2006.

"Colin Kaepernick Will Not Be Silenced." *GQ*, 13 Nov. 2017, www.gq.com/story/colin -kaepernick-will-not-be-silenced.

Crowley, Sharon. "*Rhetoric and Kairos: Essays in History, Theory and Praxis* by Phillip Sipiora, James S. Baumlin." Review. *Rhetoric Review*, vol. 22, no. 1, 2003, pp. 82– 85. *JSTOR*, www.jstor.org/stable/3093056.

de Vogue, Ariane. "Ruth Bader Ginsburg on Kaepernick Protests: 'I Think It's Dumb and Disrespectful.'" *CNN*, 12 Oct. 2016, www.cnn.com/2016/10/10/politics/ruth -bader-ginsburg-colin-kaepernick/index.html.

Douglass, Frederick. "Let All Soil Be Free Soil: An Address Delivered in Pittsburgh, Pennsylvania, on 11 August 1852." Blassingame, pp. 388–93.

———. "What to the Slave Is the Fourth of July?: An Address Delivered in Rochester, New York, on 5 July 1852." Blassingame, pp. 359–88.

Dyson, Michael Eric. *Tears We Cannot Stop: A Sermon to White America.* St. Martin's, 2017.

Forbes, Ella. "Every Man Fights for His Freedom: The Rhetoric of African American Resistance in the Mid–Nineteenth Century." *Understanding African American Rhetoric: Classical Origins to Contemporary Innovations*, edited by Ronald L. Jackson II and Elaine B. Richardson. Routledge, 2003, pp. 155–70.

Gilyard, Keith, and Adam J. Banks. *On African-American Rhetoric.* Routledge, 2018.

Glenn, Cheryl. *Unspoken: A Rhetoric of Silence.* Southern Illinois UP, 2004.

Graham, Bryan Armen. "Donald Trump Blasts NFL Anthem Protesters: 'Get That Son of a Bitch off the Field.'" *The Guardian*, 23 Sept. 2017, www.theguardian.com/sport/2017/sep/22/donald-trump-nfl-national-anthem-protests.

Harker, Michael. "The Ethics of Argument: Rereading *Kairos* and Making Sense in a Timely Fashion." *College Composition and Communication*, vol. 59, no. 1, Sept. 2007, pp. 77–97.

Hoffman, Benjamin, and Talya Minsberg. "The Deafening Silence of Colin Kaepernick." *The New York Times*, 4 Sept. 2018, www.nytimes.com/2018/09/04/sports/colin-kaepernick-nfl-anthem-kneeling.html.

Kermode, Frank. *The Sense of an Ending: Studies in the Theory of Fiction.* 1967. Oxford UP, 2000.

King, Martin Luther, Jr. "Letter from Birmingham Jail." *Cultural Conversations: The Presence of the Past*, edited by Stephen Dilks, et al., Bedford/St. Martin's, 2001, pp. 472–87.

Kinneavy, James L. "*Kairos* in Classical and Modern Rhetorical Theory." Sipiora and Baumlin, pp. 58–76.

"September 25, 2017." *The Daily Show with Trevor Noah*, performance by Trevor Noah, season 22, episode 160, Comedy Central, 2017.

Sipiora, Phillip. "Introduction: The Ancient Concept of *Kairos*." Sipiora and Baumlin, pp. 1–22.

Sipiora, Phillip, and James S. Baumlin, editors. *Rhetoric and Kairos: Essays in History, Theory, and Praxis.* State U of New York P, 2002.

Thomas, Etan. "'It's Time to Speak Up': An Open Letter to Colin Kaepernick." *The Guardian*, 20 Aug. 2019, www.theguardian.com/commentisfree/2019/aug/20/colin-kaepernick-open-letter-jay-z-silence.

Ulriksen, Mark. "In Creative Battle." *The New Yorker*, 15 Jan. 2018, front cover, www.newyorker.com/culture/cover-story/cover-story-2018-01-15.

Wyche, Steve. "Colin Kaepernick Explains Why He Sat during National Anthem." *NFL News*, 27 Aug. 2016, www.nfl.com/news/story/0ap3000000691077/article/colin-kaepernick-explains-why-he-sat-during-national-anthem.

"Wake Work": Frances E. W. Harper, Ida B. Wells, and Embodied Black Feminist Rhetoric in Slavery and Its Aftermaths

Julie Prebel

Frances Ellen Watkins Harper, born into a free Black family in Baltimore in 1825, and Ida B. Wells-Barnett, born to slaves in Mississippi in 1862, were arguably two of the most prominent African American activists, reformers, speakers, and writers of the nineteenth century. A well-known public figure for over half a century, Harper earned a national reputation for her lectures, speeches, and poetry by the time she was thirty years old, publishing pieces in local periodicals on topics such as women's rights and social reform and compiling her first volume of poetry by the mid-1850s. Despite experiencing both the "subtle and . . . blatant racism of her fellow feminists," who did not have to contend with the impact of white supremacist actions—such as the Fugitive Slave Act, which prevented Harper from returning to her Baltimore home—Harper established herself as a social activist dedicated to women's suffrage (Foster 21). More prominently, Harper's early work emphasizes her commitment to the antislavery struggle and Black rights as she built a radical social agenda exposing slavery as a flawed institution and validating African American embodied experiences of oppression—an agenda that spanned the antebellum and postbellum eras. Like Harper, although Wells wrote and spoke about women's rights issues, she, too, established her social justice platform in the latter decades of the century by focusing on Black politics, racial segregation, and white supremacist violence against African Americans. By the end of the 1880s, Wells had built a strong reputation as a writer, which enabled her to become an editor and publisher of the *Memphis Free Speech and Headlight*, the city's Black newspaper. Wells garnered both national and international attention for her work in the 1890s when she concentrated her writing and speeches on the rising incidence of lynching throughout the South, compiling her anti-lynching lectures and articles in the pamphlets *Southern Horrors: Lynch Law in All Its Phases* (1892) and *The Red Record* (1895).

While scholarship on Harper and Wells tends to divide their work into distinct halves of the nineteenth century, these Black feminist rhetors were joined in their shared concerns with the discrimination, disenfranchisement, and racial violence that African Americans were subject to during slavery and in the era of post-emancipation reconstruction. They often shared the lecture stage to convey their common message on the importance of enacting social justice for African Americans, traveling together and staying in one another's homes; and, despite a seeming generational divide, they shared common experiences with racial and gender discrimination that provided a basis for their mutual outrage at the violence and brutality enacted upon the bodies of Black people. In their work, Harper and Wells both focus on Black suffering, documenting the pain and brutality experienced by African Americans in slavery and its aftermaths. They both engage in crusades to tell the truth about white supremacy by calling on the embodied experiences of racism—their own and those of other Black Americans—as they trace a history of Black suffering across the antebellum and postbellum eras. In so doing, Harper and Wells can be seen to engage in what Black diaspora studies scholar Christina Sharpe defines as "wake work": the "gathering . . . collecting and reading toward a new analytic," a new way to represent, interpret, and "imagine ways of knowing" the experiences of the "denial of Black humanity" both "within and after the legacy" of slavery (13–14). As Sharpe explains, Black people "live in the wake . . . of terror, from slavery to the present," and wake work involves examining "terror's embodiment" (15) while acknowledging Black humanity—which is precisely what Harper and Wells do. While I focus on Harper's and Wells's rhetoric in the postbellum era, I also draw on selections of Harper's antebellum writing, with Sharpe's understanding of the atemporality of wake work in mind to illustrate how "the past that is not past reappears" (9), as Harper and Wells situate Black trauma, death, and subjugation as ongoing throughout the nineteenth century.

In bringing together these two prominent rhetors, in this essay I show how Harper and Wells employ a rhetorical use of the body in their wake work, as they shift the discourse and representation of violence and trauma enacted upon the bodies of African American people from a spectacle for white consumption to a critique of white supremacy. Harper and Wells use strategies and features of embodied rhetoric in their work through images of the body and narratives of bodily experiences, and in doing so challenge common white perceptions about African Americans and what it means to inhabit a racialized body. White discourse about the bodies of Black people in the nineteenth century, even white abolitionist and reformist rhetoric, often took a disembodied view of Black oppression through rhetoric that ignored or diminished bodily experiences. In contrast, Harper and Wells wrote against the white supremacist endoxa of their time, especially the widely perpetuated belief that African Americans were immune to pain and unaffected by acts of bodily brutality. As Susan Kates argues in her analysis of embodied rhetoric in the work of Hallie Quinn Brown, a late-nineteenth-century African American elocutionist, the use of embodied rhetoric by Black rhetors enables a resignification of the racist representations of Black people's bodies, foregrounding instead the stories and histories of Black experiences (64–65). I thus ground my reading of Harper and Wells in theories and definitions of embodied rhetoric, which emphasize the link between language and bodies, to examine how their embodied rhetorical practices emerge in response to experiences of violent oppression and marginalization.

Embodied Rhetorical Knowledge: Resignification and Counter-Discourse

In her work on how the Black body is used as a political and rhetorical device, Debra Walker King argues that the "persistent metaphorical use of the black body in pain" (7) often results in the abstraction of Black embodied experience, especially in racist representations where "black people disappear while their bodies are constantly renewed as memorials" or symbols "benefiting systems of American acculturation" (9). King focuses on how Black experience in the United States is frequently defined through depictions of Black bodies "stripped of subjectivity," and she suggests an "oppositional approach" to reinterpret and reinscribe meaning to representations of Black embodied experiences (21). King's emphasis on the symbolic use of Black bodies provides a starting point for an analysis of how rhetorical practices of embodiment, such as those used by Harper and Wells, enact an oppositional approach to the resignification of the meaning of Black experience in the nineteenth century.

Embodied rhetoric underscores connections between the body and discourse and highlights what Jack Selzer calls the "rhetorical nature of material realities" (9), which emphasizes how the material experiences and practices of bodies are literate acts that can be read and deployed as knowledge. For this essay, A. Abby Knoblauch's work on the rhetorical turn to embodiment in composition and rhetoric studies proves particularly useful for reading the ways in which Harper and Wells situate African American experiences in specific forms of embodied rhetoric. Knoblauch identifies three overlapping categories of rhetorical embodiment—embodied language, embodied knowledge, and embodied rhetoric (51)—which she argues all function to highlight "practices and discourses . . . that consciously position knowledge as of the body" (62). Knoblauch defines embodied language as "the use of terms, metaphors, and analogies" that refer to the body, embodied knowledge as connected bodily sensation and feeling, and embodied rhetoric as the "purposeful decision" to represent embodiment in a text (52). Knoblauch reminds us that bodies are more than metaphors "imagined only as texts" to be read (60), which Harper and Wells make clear as they speak about their own bodily experiences and the embodied experiences of African Americans more broadly—thus producing counter-discourse about the material realities of Black people living in the wake.[1]

All three categories of embodied rhetoric outlined by Knoblauch are evident in the work of Harper and Wells as they employ images of the body, depict bodily experiences, and locate or situate the body as a central point of knowledge in their writing. In particular, Harper and Wells assert their views on racist exclusionary and segregationist practices and their own marginalization as Black women through the use of embodied rhetoric. Harper, for example, in her speech to the Eleventh National Women's Rights Convention (1866), titled "We Are All Bound Up Together" (Foster 217–19), joined contemporary white feminist activists such as Elizabeth Cady Stanton and Lucretia Mott in expressing her outrage at the gendered injustices that denied women equal representation with men. However, Harper's use of embodied rhetoric highlights the particular injustices experienced by Black Americans and the racist practices that prohibited them from achieving liberty in a racially segregated nation. She criticizes white women for being complicit in the system of white supremacy by not fighting for the rights of Black Americans, "the weakest and feeblest members" of the country (Foster 217). At a time when white feminists were advocating single-mindedly for women's suffrage, Harper uses embodied language and allusions to bodily experiences to emphasize that the ballot is no "cure" for African Americans who continue to have their "hands . . . fettered" by a system in which they have been "pressed down for two centuries" (Foster 217–18). Moreover, focusing on the intersections of race and gender oppression, Harper also connects social and personal instances of racism by highlighting her embodied experiences with segregation on streetcars and trains—disputing a white woman's shouted objection that "they will not do that here"—as she narrates being removed from the women's car to the smoking section on a train from Washington, DC, to Baltimore and being forced to ride on the "platform with the driver" rather than inside with white passengers on Philadelphia streetcars (Foster 218). In this speech, Harper speaks directly of her embodied experiences as a Black woman in nineteenth-century America, calling on the experiences of her body—what spaces she is permitted to occupy as a Black woman, the physical impact of these experiences on her body, and how she is treated as a nonbeing body by white Americans—to highlight the continued subjugation of Black Americans in slavery's wake. Harper refuses to align herself with the agenda of her white female contemporaries, reminding them that such deprivations of human liberty based on the "color of . . . skin or the curl of . . . hair" are unjust and deny all Black people the privileges of "humanity" (Foster 218). Citing experiences and images of embodiment, Harper affirms Black subjectivity by asserting her own Black feminist activist position and underscoring the effects of white supremacy on African Americans more broadly.

Like Harper, throughout her work Wells uses embodied rhetoric to speak out against racial oppression and the daily indignities experienced by Black Americans under Jim Crow laws. Similar to Harper's documenting of the segregationist practices she experienced as a Black woman, Wells chronicles her experience of being thrown out of the ladies' railcar while traveling through Tennessee—and like Harper, she uses embodied rhetoric to illustrate her response to this specific incident and her broader views on such white supremacist practices. Wells's description of her experience is replete with language that refers to the body, as she describes how the conductor "tried to drag [her] out of the seat" when she refused to move and her bodily resistance to his attempts: "the moment he caught hold of my arm I fastened my teeth in the back of his hand" (*Crusade* 18). Using vivid embodied language and imagery, Wells describes bracing her body against the seat in resistance and eventually being forcibly pried from her seat by the conductor with the help of other white men. Although she reports being physically overpowered and "roughly handled" by these white men, Wells nonetheless refuses their order to change cars and elects to get off the train in an act of purposeful resistance, while the other passengers—led by the "white ladies"— cheer what they perceive as the conductor's success (*Crusade* 18, 19). Wells uses this experience as a catalyst for a lawsuit against the railroad, winning an initial settlement by a circuit court before losing to the railroad's appeal at the state supreme court.

Both this incident of physical resistance and Wells's description of the incident demonstrate many forms of rhetorical embodiment purposefully deployed to be illustrative and instructive, since she uses her body as a means to challenge social and ideological perspectives about African Americans and their rights. While white perspectives on incidents such as the one Wells describes cast her as a criminal and justify the physical treatment of her as a necessary response to maintain the white supremacist social order, as the cheering crowd of white people on the train suggests, Wells ensures through her use of embodied rhetoric that such stories from Black perspectives will not be undermined or erased. Like Harper, Wells makes use of bodily experiences to generate new forms of knowledge about Black people's bodies as more than metaphors by emphasizing, in Knoblauch's terms, "real lived experiences of [the] flesh, of *people*" (60)—in this case, people living in the wake.

Embodied Rhetorical Practices:
Black Bodies in the Wake

In addition to chronicling their own experiences with racist segregation practices, Harper and Wells use embodied rhetoric to provide knowledge of Black experiences in white supremacy by focusing on the brutality inflicted upon Black bodies. In particular, their use of embodied rhetoric to recognize the pain Black people experienced and to articulate a response to a history of Black suffering illustrates Saidiya Hartman's concept of "re-membering" the captive, enslaved, and violated Black body. As Hartman explains, the enslaved Black body was "dis-membered" through the "segmentation and organization of the captive body for the purposes of work, reproduction, and punishment," which enabled the "denial of black sentience" and the discrediting of corporeal experiences based on the myth that Black bodies were "indifferent to pain" (51). In Hartman's conceptualization, "re-membering" the body provides an alternative to white supremacist logic through the "redemption of the body as human flesh, not beast of burden" (77). The process of re-membering enacts a "redressive action" that bears witness to the "violated condition" (77) of bodily and social devastation experienced by Black people in the wake of slavery—a process that can be seen in the use of embodied rhetoric by Harper and Wells.

Harper, for example, enacts the concept of re-membering throughout her poetry in the depiction of racial and social violence inflicted on Black Americans both during and after slavery. Two poems, "The Slave Auction" and "The Slave Mother," written between 1853 and 1864 and collected in *Poems on Miscellaneous Subjects*, depict common abolitionist topics, but Harper's antislavery poems respond to racial violence through her emphasis on Black embodied experience. In "The Slave Auction," Harper re-members Black suffering by recasting depictions of the slave auction from a white supremacist spectacle that confirmed the slaveholder's dominion over the captive Black body to an experience that recognizes Black pain and suffering—and thus affirms Black humanity. Whereas Black pain was "largely unspoken and unrecognized" in the everyday practices of slavery, including the slave auction (Hartman 51), Harper opens her poem with the use of embodied language to articulate slavery's inhumane conditions:

> The sale began—young girls were there,
> Defenceless in their wretchedness,
> Whose stifled sobs of deep despair,
> Revealed their anguish and distress.   (Foster 64)

This imagery of bodies in pain permeates the poem, as "mothers stood with streaming eyes" while their "frail and shrinking children" were sold, culminating in Harper's final stanza where she concludes that African Americans experience this scene of torture as "a dull and heavy weight" which "[w]ill press the life-drops from the heart" (Foster 64–65). Through her use of embodied rhetoric, Harper's poem serves as a critical counter-narrative to white supremacist depictions of Black bodies as merely commodities lacking "feelings, ideas, desires, and values" (Hartman 21).

Harper's descriptions of Black suffering during slavery recur throughout her poems, especially in "The Slave Mother," based on a real-life incident of a woman attempting to escape slavery with her children by fleeing from Kentucky to the free state of Ohio—the same story Toni Morrison fictionalized in her 1987 novel, *Beloved*. Told from the perspective of the Black mother running with her children while "The pursuer is on thy track / And the hunter at thy door," Harper's poem depicts the physical and psychological effects of the brutality of slavery through embodied imagery that positions the mother as trying to accomplish a "deed for freedom" by "find[ing] each child a grave" rather than subjecting the children to the "cruel" and "icy hands of slavery" that will ultimately destroy them (Foster 85–86). As suggested in this poem, forced infanticide is preferable to the systematic torture that renders Black Americans victims to bodily and social violence.

Harper's poems in the last decade of the nineteenth century, focused on white supremacist acts of physical brutality and lynchings, reaffirm Sharpe's idea that wake work documents the ongoing trauma of Black experience in the United States. In their subject matter, often inspired by real-life incidents, Harper's postbellum poems also demonstrate direct connections to Wells and her activist work, as I will show below, and function as a rhetorical re-membering of Black bodily suffering. Harper's poem "The Martyr of Alabama" (1895) takes as its subject an incident of racial violence in December 1894, when a young African American boy was beaten to death for refusing to dance for the amusement of white men. Like Harper's earlier poems situating scenes of racial violence from the perspective of Black Americans, this poem opens from the imagined point of view of the Black child about to be beaten as "He lifted up his pleading eyes, / And scanned each cruel face" of the white men surrounding him (Foster 359). Although physically weak and overpowered, the boy in Harper's retelling of this incident resists "their mandates" by refusing to allow the white men to use his body for their enjoyment and instead sacrifices his body as they "trampled on his prostrate form" and "danced with careless, brutal feet" / Upon the murdered boy" (Foster 360). Through her use of embodied rhetoric in this poem, Harper humanizes the boy by showing both his abasement and his resistance to the white exercise of power as she attempts to incite indignation in her readers, calling upon them to "Avert the doom that crime must bring / Upon a guilty land" by disempowering the "reckless hands" of white supremacy (Foster 361).

One of the final poems of Harper's prolific career as a rhetor and activist, "The Lake City Tragedy," depicts another real-life incident in 1898, the white supremacist killing of Frazier Baker and members of his family. This incident in South Carolina, where a mob of two to three hundred men surrounded the Baker home, setting it afire to draw out Baker and lynch him, received considerable coverage in the press for its extreme brutality—and became a focal point in Wells's anti-lynching campaign. Baker and his two-year-old daughter were shot as the family attempted to flee and were later found burned at the site. Harper's retelling of this horrific crime situates readers in its brutality by using embodied language and body images, describing "babes upon . . . breasts," weeping "eyes" with "hot tears," the "cruel hands" of the lynch mob, "blood drops" spraying through the gunshot air, and "affrighted girls in terror" (Foster 383–84). Just as she recounts a very different experience of the slave auction than is frequently depicted in white-authored accounts of Black people as property, in this poem with its real-life reference point Harper re-members Black suffering through the depiction of bodies that bear witness to the violence of white supremacy. By calling for action on the part of "Carolina" to "disavow / This blot upon thy name; / And brand this brutal cowardice, / With everlasting shame" (Foster 385), Harper's poem thus functions as both an important means to validate Black embodied experience and as a rhetorical strategy of political resistance.

The Baker murders also captured Wells's attention and further ignited her decades-long investigation into the practice of lynching and her campaign to outlaw these acts of brutality against Black people and bring white supremacists to justice. In her appeal to President William McKinley, where she argues for legislation and reparations for the Baker family, Wells uses embodied rhetoric to describe the brutality of lynching when "bands of 50 to 5,000 [men] hunt down, shoot, hang or burn to death a single [Black] individual, unarmed and absolutely powerless" (Giddings 387). While by the end of the 1890s Wells was a frequent visitor to the nation's capital as a regular part of her activist work, her focus on lynching began in 1892 in Memphis, when one of her closest friends, Thomas Moss, was arrested and, along with two other men, was taken out of his jail cell and lynched. The lynching at the Curve, which referred to the neighborhood where the incident occurred, was the first known lynching in Memphis and Wells's first personal experience with this form of white violence. In her editorial in the *Memphis Free Speech*, published in May 1892, a few months after the Curve lynching, Wells argues that for Black people in Memphis this lynching "was our first object lesson in the doctrine of white supremacy," a realization that within the systematic "power of the State" Black Americans had no protection against such exertions of white violence (*Light of Truth* 102). When chronicling this incident and the impact of her editorial in the speech "Lynch Law in All Its Phases" (1893), Wells's use of embodied rhetoric is clear as she describes the bodily threats she received: "I was to be dumped into the river and beaten, if not killed . . . I was to be hanged in front of the court-house and my face bled . . . [shot] down on sight . . . and lynched" (*Light of Truth* 106).

Wells's response to the Curve lynching highlights important features of embodied rhetoric: the ways embodied knowledge can transform thought and inspire social action and how the use of body images can expose facts—in this case, the facts of lynching. More specifically, Wells's embodied rhetoric functions as critical counter-discourse to the prevailing verbal and visual representations of lynching in the postbellum era, as narratives and images of lynching, as Amy Louise Wood argues, tended to "affirm and authenticate white supremacy" by making lynching a "thrilling spectacle" of white dominance and Black submission (Wood 10). Wells employs a rhetoric of embodiment to acknowledge the humanity of lynching victims and to resignify the meaning of lynching from what Courtney Baker describes as a "spectacle of black criminality and racial shame" to a "hideous act" that underscores the "unjust and untimely destruction of black human beings" (51). Wells's embodied rhetorical strategies are seen throughout her work, as shown poignantly in her description of the destruction of the Black family after the murder of Tom Moss, when his "baby daughter . . . too young to express how she misses her father toddles to the wardrobe, seizes the leg of his trousers . . . and stretches up her little hands to be taken into the arms which will nevermore clasp his daughter's form" (*Light of Truth* 101). This passage shows Wells's purposeful resignification of Moss from lynched criminal to a human being and of lynching from sensationalized spectacle to devastating violence.

In her anti-lynching lectures and articles, collected in the pamphlets *Southern Horrors: Lynch Law in All Its Phases* (1892) and *The Red Record* (1895), Wells chronicles lynching as a form of racial terrorism, notably through the use of embodied rhetoric depicting in graphic detail the brutality enacted upon the bodies of Black people. Wells demonstrates her keen awareness of slavery's wake in this work, as she connects the conditions of Black Americans before and after emancipation through their embodied experiences: "In slave times the Negro was kept subservient and submissive by the frequency and severity of the scourging . . . with freedom, a new system of intimidation came into vogue; the Negro was not only whipped and scourged; he was killed" (*Red Record* 10). Connecting bodies to facts, in *Southern Horrors* she demonstrates through case after case the falseness of white claims of Black depravity and shows in contrast through vivid body readings the murder of Black men without any pretense, such as "Ebenezer Fowler [who] was shot down . . . by an armed body of white men who filled his body with bullets" simply because Fowler showed kindness to a white woman (*Light of Truth* 67). Wells also points to the white supremacist hypocrisy of the rape narrative when she notes that while claims of rape by white women are often fabricated, proven rape of Black women and girls by white men goes un-punished, as shown in her use of embodied rhetoric in reporting the assault by a white man of a "little Afro-American girl" who was "ruined for life," so devastat-ing were the "physical injuries she received" (*Light of Truth* 67–68).

Wells's investigative method and sociological approach to analyzing lynch-ing and American race relations depend in part on her use of harrowing and gruesome details to describe Black people's bodies in pain and death, a rhetori-cal method she employs throughout *The Red Record*. For example, she describes the killing of Henry Smith in Paris, Texas, using body language and imagery to show how his "agony was awful" as he "writhed in bodily and mental pain" while he "lay fastened to a torture platform" with "hot irons thrust into his quivering flesh," his "eyes . . . burned out and [hot] irons thrust down his throat" (32–33). Examples such as this recur throughout Wells's detailed taxonomy of lynchings by year and state, and along with graphic details about the deaths of Black peo-ple she also describes the white mobs and spectators, who "looked on [scenes of lynching] with complaisance, if not with real pleasure" and often "laughed as the flesh cracked and blistered" (*Light of Truth* 139–41). In her anti-lynching work, rather than gratuitous in her focus on the Black body in pain or a reuse of the body as a site of spectacle, Wells's descriptions of the bodies of Black peo-ple instead function to incite critique of white supremacy and its lawlessness. While her use of graphic body details may horrify her readers, Wells constructs her anti-lynching narrative to ask her audience to "look" differently, with what Baker calls "humane insight," as a way to "see and recognize the body as human in order to condemn its violation" (39). According to Paula Giddings, Wells's anti-lynching campaign "gave her the means to reorder the world and her and the race's place within it" (229), a reordering that unfolds through a focus on Black embodiment.

As shown above, Harper's and Wells's work amplifies this idea that rheto-ric functions as a means to reorder self and social perspectives. Through their use of multiple and intersecting forms of rhetorical embodiment, both rhetors highlight the unjust authority of white supremacist ideology while documenting and validating Black experience and humanity. In their use of embodied rheto-ric to articulate Black body knowledge, Harper and Wells seize the authority to reinscribe Black agency and give meaning to Black experience as they facilitate social change.

Rhetorical Embodiment and Black Feminist Social Activism

Among many social platforms they shared, Harper and Wells were joined in their protest of the exclusion of African Americans from the World's Columbian

Exposition in Chicago in 1893—a World's Fair designed to showcase the United States' progress and achievement in commemoration of Columbus's arrival four hundred years before. Harper delivered one of her most renowned speeches, "Woman's Political Future," to the World's Congress of Representative Women; she was one of only six Black women given a speaking platform at the fair. Employing embodied rhetoric to highlight the continued subjugation of African Americans in the postbellum United States, Harper charges white women with the task to "demand justice [and] brand with infamy" the "brutal and cowardly men, who torture, burn, and lynch their fellow-men" (Logan 44). Harper's argument that Black people are brutalized by "red-handed men in our republic, who walk unwhipped of justice" underscores an embodied history that belies the performances of the United States' progress on display at the exposition (Logan 44).

While not invited to speak, Wells joined Frederick Douglass in publishing and distributing the pamphlet *The Reason Why the Colored American Is Not in the World's Columbian Exposition*, contesting the lack of Black representation at the fair by exposing white supremacist practices of degradation and brutality.[2] Similar to Wells's *Southern Horrors* and *The Red Record*, the Columbian Exposition pamphlet provides a detailed taxonomy of lynchings by year, state, and accused charges, drawing on such data as a form of embodied rhetoric to tabulate and make matter these deaths of Black people. Some of Wells's most graphic embodied details are included in this pamphlet, in descriptions of bodies hung and swung from telegraph poles, "blood streaming down from . . . knife wounds," "convulsive movements of the limbs," and the "human body burned to ashes" (*Light of Truth* 139–41). Thus, in what was considered a display of American exceptionalism on the world's stage, Harper and Wells disrupt a nationalism "that erases the historical experience of particular members of a diverse citizenry" (Kates 66–67) through strategic rhetorical choices of embodied knowledge.

As Chanta M. Haywood reminds us, the late nineteenth century is recognized as a "critical moment in the development of black feminist thought," a time of such prevalence in "black women's public and social presence" that, in her speech at the World's Congress of Representative Women, Harper declared the 1890s to be the "women's era." Taking to the platform throughout the nineteenth century to describe the conditions for Black people of captivity and racial brutality, Harper and Wells were critical in shaping the social consciousness and activism of Black feminist speakers and writers. Knoblauch emphasizes that "writers utilizing an embodied rhetoric work against what might be seen as the . . . hegemony of . . . discourse" by foregrounding the ways bodies matter, "locating a text in the body" and "locating the body in the text" (59)—rhetorical moves that Black women writing and speaking in the nineteenth century make throughout their work. As I have shown, in reconstituting the representation of

Black experiences of suffering and pain through their wake work, Harper and Wells emphasize Black subjectivity and offer new narratives that dislodge or disrupt dominant rhetoric perpetuating racism and oppression. Their representations of the suffering and pain of Black people are radical acts of Black feminist activism, since they challenge social and rhetorical depictions of the effects of racial violence and demand rights for those living in the wake.

Notes

1. Scholarship on embodied rhetoric underscores the connections between body and discourse evident from antiquity to the present. Debra Hawhee, for instance, reminds us that rhetors from Isocrates to Gorgias, from Aristotle to Plato, and from the Sophists to Cicero emphasize the link between the body and language. Kate Ronald and Hephzibah Roskelly revisit Peter Elbow's iconic work in a contemporary example of embodied rhetoric, pointing to Elbow's connections between speech and the body.

2. Douglass was one of many speakers, writers, and activists with whom Wells interacted throughout the anti-lynching movement. Despite Wells's pivotal role in "making lynching a national issue," the prolific literature on lynching either fails to mention her at all or mentions her only briefly, as Giddings notes (6). As Giddings also points out, two of the "widely cited references texts" on lynching do not mention Wells: Walter Francis White's *Rope and Faggot* and Arthur Raper's *The Tragedy of Lynching* (6). Moreover, the NAACP's historical documentation of anti-lynching activism "gave her . . . role short shrift" when Wells is mentioned at all (Giddings 6). As noted in this essay, the response of the Black press in the late nineteenth century to lynching and the subsequent consciousness raised against lynching is in large part because of Wells's work.

Works Cited

Baker, Courtney. *Humane Insight: Looking at Images of African American Suffering and Death.* U of Illinois P, 2015.

Foster, Frances Smith, editor. *A Brighter Coming Day: A Frances Ellen Watkins Harper Reader.* The Feminist Press, 1990.

Giddings, Paula J. *Ida: A Sword among Lions.* Harper Collins, 2008.

Hartman, Saidiya V. *Scenes of Subjection: Terror, Slavery, and Self-Making in Nineteenth-Century America.* Oxford UP, 1997.

Hawhee, Debra. "Rhetorics, Bodies, and Everyday Life." *Rhetoric Society Quarterly*, vol. 36, no. 2, Spring 2006, pp. 155–64.

Haywood, Chanta M. *Prophesying Daughters: Black Women Preachers and the Word, 1823–1913.* U of Missouri P, 2003.

Kates, Susan. "The Embodied Rhetoric of Hallie Quinn Brown." *College English*, vol. 59, no. 1, Jan. 1997, pp. 59–71.

King, Debra Walker. *African Americans and the Culture of Pain*. U of Virginia P, 2008.

Knoblauch, A. Abby. "Bodies of Knowledge: Definitions, Delineations, and Implications of Embodied Writing in the Academy." *Composition Studies*, vol. 40, no. 2, 2012, pp. 50–65.

Logan, Shirley Wilson. "Frances E. W. Harper, 'Woman's Political Future.'" *Voices of Democracy*, vol. 1, 2006, pp. 43–57.

Ronald, Kat, and Hephzibah Roskelly. "Embodied Voice: Peter Elbow's Physical Rhetoric." *Writing with Elbow*, edited by Pat Belanoff et al., UP of Colorado / Utah State UP, 2002, pp. 210–22.

Selzer, Jack. "Habeas Corpus: An Introduction." *Rhetorical Bodies*, edited by Selzer and Sharon Crowley, U of Wisconsin P, 1999, pp. 3–15.

Sharpe, Christina. *In the Wake: On Blackness and Being*. Duke UP, 2016.

Wells, Ida B. *Crusade for Justice*. Edited by Alfreda M. Duster, U of Chicago P, 1970.

Wells-Barnett, Ida B. *The Light of Truth: Writings of an Anti-Lynching Crusader*. Edited by Mia Bay and Henry Louis Gates Jr., Penguin, 2014.

———. *The Red Record: Tabulated Statistics and Alleged Crimes of Lynching in the United States*. 1895. Cavalier Classics, 2015.

Wood, Amy Louise. *Lynching and Spectacle: Witnessing Racial Violence in America, 1890–1940*. U of North Carolina P, 2009.

Analyzing the Methodist Debate over Women's Preaching with the Classical Interpretive Stases

Martin Camper

Around 1809, Jarena Lee was startled by a voice from God calling her to preach. Desiring to preach among the Methodists, she approached Richard Allen, pastor of Bethel Church in Philadelphia, who would soon help found the African Methodist Episcopal Church. He responded that while women could exhort and hold prayer meetings, the *Doctrines and Discipline* did not authorize women to preach (Andrews 35–36). Years later, Allen, now the African Methodist Episcopal Church's first bishop, affirmed Lee's call to preach, but Lee was never officially licensed (6, 44–45). Women's preaching rights fared no better among white Methodists. In the 1820s, Sally Thompson traveled as a popular itinerant preacher in the northeastern United States. However, in 1830, a group of ministers in upstate New York approved a resolution barring any clergy in their district from supporting her. Undeterred, Thompson continued to preach, triggering an ecclesiastical trial. She was found not guilty, but one of the New York ministers appealed the case to the circuit conference and won, resulting in Thompson's excommunication (Richey et al. 148–49). Neither the African Methodist Episcopal Church nor the Methodist Episcopal Church would permanently grant women preaching rights until the twentieth century.

The stories of Lee and Thompson represent broader trends in the American Methodist movement concerning women's preaching in the first half of the nineteenth century. From the movement's start in the mid–eighteenth century, women played an important, even public, role spreading the gospel and discipling converts. In the beginning of the nineteenth century, when Methodism was surging to become one of the country's largest religious sects, there were several female preachers, some quite popular. But beginning in the 1830s, as part of a strategy to establish their legitimacy, multiple Methodist denominations officially banned women from the pulpit (Richey et al. 147–48). The suppression of women's preaching across Methodism sparked multi-denominational activism and debate that continued for more than a century.

Today, all of the major Methodist denominations in the United States officially allow women to preach. How was this remarkable reversal achieved? Critical to this about-face were the arguments that proponents of women's preaching made, beginning in the second quarter of the nineteenth century. The nineteenth-century controversy over women's preaching among American Protestants in general, and sometimes Methodists in particular, has been studied predominantly by historians, who have done important work recovering this debate and tracing its contours. However, historians have primarily attended to the social, cultural, economic, and institutional factors that shaped the dispute (Brekus; Chaves; Dodson; Keller; Richey et al. 147–52). While these factors were important, this perspective ignores the primary instrument activists employed to change minds and denominational policies: argument.

Only a few scholars have focused on this key aspect of the debate (Donaworth 73–104; Zikmund; Zimmerelli). These scholars have identified common arguments that Protestant women employed in support of their right to preach, including arguments about the Bible's meaning. Focusing on biblical arguments within American Methodism by activist women and men on both sides, I extend this scholarship by analyzing these arguments not according to their content but according to their motivating issue and type. I do not consider, here, the social justice issues involved in women's right to preach; rather, I provide close analysis of the biblical arguments made concerning this right. To conduct this analysis, I turn to the main line of classical rhetorical thought on disagreement: stasis theory.

Stasis Theory: The Interpretive Stases

Disagreement was a central concern for classical rhetoricians, many of whom wrote courtroom speeches or taught others how to do the same. The exigence of efficiently composing effective legal orations inspired these rhetoricians to devise a method for systematically discovering the possible issues that could emerge in such a setting. The result was stasis theory, which identifies general, recurring points of contention, or stases, that can arise in a debate. Classical rhetoricians quickly discovered that this system described the basic logic of virtually all human disagreement, and stasis theory became a central component of rhetorical education in Europe for almost two millennia.

For contemporary scholars, stasis theory provides a useful heuristic for analyzing controversies. In the first place, it helps analysts identify the fundamental issue that must be addressed for a disagreement to be resolved. Focusing on the root issue can be clarifying because, even as the arguments in a debate change, an analyst can see if the underlying point of contention has shifted or if rhetors have simply changed their argumentative strategy. Stasis theory also postulates that rhetors move through these issues in a predictable, presuppositional sequence. A debate can only move forward successfully through the stases if issues in prior, presupposed stases have been addressed to all parties' satisfaction. Thus, stasis theory can explain why certain debates get stuck, usually because there is a disagreement in a more fundamental stasis. The theory further views all arguments within a dialogic frame: every stasis point has at least two sides. Additionally, classical rhetoricians cataloged lines of reasoning, or topoi, particular to each stasis, which can help analysts understand the argumentative mechanics of a disagreement and its resolution.

Contemporary rhetoricians are likely most familiar with the situational stases recognized by several classical rhetoricians: conjecture, definition, and quality (Cicero 1.8.10; [Cicero] 1.11.18; Quintilian 3.6.66). These stases respectively concern whether something exists or has occurred, belongs in a particular category, or should be assigned a certain value. Classical rhetoricians also recognized another set of stases, largely ignored by contemporary scholars, which pinpoint the types of issues that can arise when a text's meaning is the subject of a dispute: the interpretive stases (Cicero 1.12.17–13.18; [Cicero] 1.11.19; Quintilian 3.6.66). Based on classical rhetorical theory, six interpretive stases can be identified, which cover hermeneutical issues concerning ambiguous words and phrases in a text, definitions of terms in a text, clashes between a text's letter and spirit, conflicting passages in the same text, the adaptation or assimilation of a text to address a new context, and the preliminary conditions necessary for a legitimate reading of a text. Together, the interpretive stases constitute a critical tool for analyzing how people use argument to construct and dispute the meaning of any type of text (see Camper). The next section of this essay applies the interpretive stases to the American Methodist debate over women's preaching during its first phase from 1833 to 1873, shedding light on the root interpretive issue and attending to a key argumentative strategy.

The Stasis of the Women's Preaching Debate: Conflicting Passages

The first order of business is to identify the main interpretive issue at the center of the Methodist debate over women's preaching. By locating the stasis of the disagreement, we discern the disputational frame that shaped arguments on both sides. Notably, this frame was not endemic to American Methodism but appears to have been established by early-nineteenth-century British Methodist Bible commentators who were highly influential in the United States, most prominently, Thomas Coke, Adam Clarke, and Joseph Benson. Each of these commentators, who were cited by American Methodists debating women's preaching, advocated a different position on this question. Coke contended that women should never be allowed to speak authoritatively in church for an audience containing men. Oppositely, Clarke argued that women should be allowed to preach in church regardless of the audience's makeup. Benson took a more moderate position, asserting that in general women should not authoritatively speak in church before a mix-gendered audience, but there should be exceptions for women uniquely inspired by God.

When one reads these multivolume commentaries, it becomes clear that the main interpretive problem that divides them is an issue in the stasis of conflicting passages. In this stasis, rhetors recognize that two passages in the same text appear to contradict one another, and they advance arguments to resolve the apparent contradiction to support their agendas. As Quintilian observes, "[O]ne law can never be contrary to another in juristic principles, because if there were distinct principles one law would be cancelled out by the other" (7.7.2). For these commentators, the debate hinged on an apparent contradiction in the Pauline epistles. The first two problem passages are 1 Corinthians 14.34–35: "Let your women keep silence in the churches: for it is not permitted unto them to speak; but they are commanded to be under obedience as also saith the law. And if they will learn any thing, let them ask their husbands at home: for it is a shame for women to speak in the church"; and 1 Timothy 2.11–12: "Let the woman learn in silence with all subjection. But I suffer not a woman to teach, nor to usurp authority over the man, but to be in silence." Both passages seem to forbid women's ecclesiastic speaking. However, in 1 Corinthians 11.4–5, Paul writes, "Every man praying or prophesying, having his head covered, dishonoureth his head. But every woman that prayeth or prophesieth with her head uncovered dishonoureth her head: for that is even all one as if she were shaven" (*Holy Bible*). This third passage appears to permit women's public speaking in church, since it is generally assumed that a regulation of an action implies that the action is allowed.

All three commentaries acknowledge that Paul appears to contradict himself in these texts. Coke, the more conservative of the three, writes, "Here [1 Cor. 11.5] then the Apostle gives directions about the woman's praying and prophesying in an *assembly*, or where *others* were present, and yet, in the above quoted places [1 Cor. 14.34–35], he expressly enjoins silence, and forbids her *speaking*, and consequently *prophesying*, in the *churches*. —How shall we bring these things to a consistency?" (*New Testament* 160; see also Benson, *New Testament* 197; Clarke 290). For Methodists on both sides of the Atlantic at this time, the Bible as divine revelation could not contain any contradictions; thus, this apparent discrepancy was a serious problem. American Methodist activists in the mid–nineteenth century accepted this problem, as outlined by these commentators, as the fundamental interpretive issue in this debate and worked to argumentatively resolve this problem in favor of their positions on women's preaching.

One problem with resolving this apparent biblical inconsistency in either direction is the lack of verses that speak directly to the issue of women's preaching. Rhetors on both sides therefore had to infer support for their positions from passages that did not explicitly address this issue. This topos shares its name with one of the other interpretive stases: assimilation. An assimilation argument employs inferential reasoning to elicit a nonexplicit meaning from a text, and one way to reconcile discordant passages, as Cicero explains, is to "develop from the written word something that is not expressed" (2.50.148, 1.48.142).[1] Assimilation played an important role in this period of the debate, and the following section explores how activists employed this argument type to interpret the Bible to support their positions.

Assimilation in the Methodist Debate over Women's Preaching

In the first place, activists on both sides employed assimilation to align Paul's words with their beliefs about women's preaching. Specifically, in the words of Quintilian, activists "deduce[d] something which is uncertain from the Letter of the [text]" based on various assumptions (7.8.3). Several writers defending women's preaching argued that Paul's regulation of women's ecclesiastic speech in 1 Corinthians 11.5 indicates that he must have approved of it. In her spiritual autobiography, Ellen Stewart, associated at different times with the Methodist Episcopal Church and the Methodist Reform Church, deduces that "where [Paul] speaks of women prophesying with their heads covered or uncovered: [this statement] plainly shows that he allowed women to prophesy" (168; see also Lee 94; Palmer 6–7; Boardman 27–28, 42). In her book-length defense of women's preaching, Mary Boardman, who converted to Methodism upon reading testimonies in a book, makes a similar deduction with regard to 1 Timothy 2.8–10,[2] which she argues is another example of Paul regulating women's clothing when they are publicly speaking in church—in this case praying—and therefore further evidence of his general endorsement of women's ecclesiastic speech (27–28, 54–55). Those who opposed women's preaching viewed the Pauline prohibitions as universal injunctions and argued that Paul's regulation of women's clothing while praying or prophesying therefore must refer to worship settings where only women were present—another assimilation by deduction (Coke, *New Testament* 160).[3] Each side thus assimilated 1 Corinthians 11.5, along with similar passages, to either universalize or limit this verse in support of its position on women's preaching.

Another assimilation strategy, in this case just among defenders of women's preaching, involved taking the premises of an opposing interpretation to what the fourth-century Roman rhetorician Fortunatianus calls their "logical consequences" (67; sec. 1.25). For instance, Luther Lee, an abolitionist and Wesleyan Methodist leader, notes that people on all sides believe that the "law" Paul cites in 1 Corinthians 14.34 is Genesis 3.16,[4] in which Eve is punished for her sin: "[A]nd thy desire shall be to thy husband, and he shall rule over thee" (96). Since this verse concerns wife-husband relations, Lee concludes that Paul's injunction in 1 Corinthians "is binding only upon married women," having no bearing on "unmarried females and widows," and that it "imposes silence on married women, only in obedience to the will of their husbands," meaning that wives may speak in church if their husbands allow (97; see also Palmer 47). With this assimilation, Lee also makes sense of Paul's directive to women in 1 Corinthians 14.35 to "ask their husbands at home" if they have questions and of "the man," whom Paul says women are not to "usurp authority over" in 1 Timothy 2.12 (97–98). Lee's assimilation thus narrows the women Paul prohibits from speaking in church, provides even these women the possibility of speaking, and makes these verses more congruent with 1 Corinthians 11.5.

While Lee's argument clarifies the Pauline prohibitions according to premises agreed to by the opposing side, another form of assimilative reasoning, the reductio ad absurdum, was used to ridicule more conservative interpretations. With this argumentative strategy, a rhetor, according to Aristotle, shows that "an impossible conclusion follows from the assumption of the contradictory [i.e., opponent's] proposition," thus refuting the opposing argument "by reducing it to a fallacy" (41a.26–27, 62b.30–31). Phoebe Palmer, mother of the Methodist-rooted holiness movement, observes that Episcopalians violate Paul's injunctions, which they claim to strictly follow, whenever their women participate in liturgical responses, say the Lord's Prayer, or sing a hymn (5–6). Stewart likewise strings out an absurd conclusion based on a strict reading of 1 Corinthians 14.35: "and what if the husband be more ignorant than the wife? then of course she must not add to *his* stock of knowledge. . . . They [wives] must not go to meeting or any public place, lest they may chance to hear preaching or lecturing, and God has given them a memory as retentive as that of men" (135). Through reductio ad absurdum, rhetors like Palmer and Stewart argue that those who oppose women's preaching are hypocrites because they do not strictly adhere to a literal reading of Paul. Further, by showing that a strict reading of these passages can lead to bizarre results, this argumentative strategy advances the idea that understanding the Pauline prohibitions as narrow restrictions rather than universal mandates is the best way to resolve their apparent clash with other words by Paul and other biblical authors.

One of the challenges of supporting women's preaching in the nineteenth century was that many Christians believed that there were no female preachers in the Bible. A common assimilation by opponents to women's preaching thus consisted of an argument from silence: since no female preachers are mentioned in the Bible, female preaching is not sanctioned by God. As the author of the *Rhetorica ad Herennium* explains, rhetors can argue that "the absence of a text concerning the matter here involved was intentional, because the framer was unwilling to make any provision" ([Cicero] 2.12.18). William Johnston, writing in dialogue with Stewart in the *Church Advocate*, asserts, "Nor does it appear from the Scriptures that God chose his *preachers* from the *sexes indiscriminately*; for *all* the preachers we have any account of were men" (Stewart 172). And the author of an 1852 editorial in the African Methodist Episcopal Church's *Christian Recorder* observes that "God appropriated the labors and toils of his Church in all past time" to men, not women, citing the biblical examples of Noah, Abraham, Moses, the Levite priests, the apostles, and even Jesus himself (Payne 301). Supporters of women's preaching, like Stewart, answered these assertions with the classic rebuttal of an argument from silence, that absence of evidence is not evidence of absence: "the females' names not being mentioned, is no proof that there were none, any more than their not being mentioned at any public assembly, is proof that there were none present" (Stewart 174).

But advocates of women's preaching did not simply settle for this defense, and they responded to these arguments from silence with their own assimilations. Arguing that prophecy was a form of preaching, a definitional argument, supporters of women's preaching rights claimed that the Bible in fact records a long history of female preachers (Brekus 217; Donawerth 74, 77, 88, 91, 92; Zikmund 199; Zimmerelli 190). Once this definition was in place, these rhetors could make additional assimilations through deduction to support their case. Nancy Towle, an itinerant preacher who traveled among various Protestant groups, including the Methodists, deduces that female prophets were more likely than their male counterparts to be true prophets. Comparing the ratio of true to false female prophets and true to false male prophets in the Bible, she concludes that "one, to the number four [of the female prophets], was proved false: but of the opposite gender . . . in the days of the Prophet Elijah, were found four hundred and fifty that were false, to the little number 'one' that was true" (28; referring to 1 Kings 18.22). Palmer quotes J. J. Gurney, a Quaker advocate for women's preaching, who points out that, in Ezekiel 13.17, God tells the eponymous prophet to preach against false female prophets; Gurney thus deduces that such "a circumstance . . . clearly indicates that there were *true* prophetesses" (67). Other advocates named false female prophets in the Bible, including Naodiah (Neh. 6.14) and Jezebel (Rev. 2.20), sometimes without comment, but to the same end (Foster 311; Lee 87; Stewart 128; Towle 28).

Another set of assimilation arguments concerned the equality of the sexes: are men and women equal or are women inferior to and therefore supposed to be subordinate to men? A key biblical passage in this debate was the story of humanity's creation in Genesis 1–2. The story itself does not explicitly state that women were created inferior to men. Indeed, the more conservative British Methodist Bible commentators Coke and Benson, in their commentaries on Genesis, interpret this story as narrating how God created the sexes equal, with inequality being introduced after the fall as part of Eve's curse (Coke, *Holy Bible* 17–18; Benson, *Holy Bible* 27). But in later volumes of their commentaries, these commentators revise this reading and argue that women were created inferior and subordinate to men, aligning the Genesis story with their interpretation of Paul's words in 1 Timothy 2.13 and 1 Corinthians 11.7–9.[5] This revision stuck and American Methodists opposed to women's preaching in the mid–nineteenth century continued to assimilate the Genesis creation story to support this position.

For example, Albert Barnes, a Presbyterian, deduces the following in one of his Bible commentaries, with which multiple Methodists in this debate engaged: "Man was made as the Lord of this lower creation . . . and then the woman was made of a rib taken from his side, and given to him, not as a Lord, but as a companion. All the circumstances combine to show the subordinate nature of her rank, and to prove that she was not designed to exert authority over the man" (155). Similarly, using the analogy of multiple editions of a book, J. F. W. (John Frederick Weishampel), in dialogue with Stewart, deduces that "[w]oman is the 'second and revised edition' of man." And while he notes that women's "feminine passions" are "improvements in her nature, over the harsher and more unfeeling nature of man," J. F. W. asserts that these improvements "do not elevate her above man, nor do they raise her up to be equal with man" (Stewart 184). By employing such assimilations of the Genesis narrative, these and other rhetors grounded Paul's injunctions against women's preaching in God's original design of men and women. Thus, such rhetors supported their contention that these prohibitions are universal. Activists in support of women's preaching, however, objected that these assimilations were illogical. Stewart, for example, counters J. F. W.'s interpretation by asking two rhetorical questions: "[D]oes not this idea depreciate the Divine wisdom beneath that of human writers? For what writer or editor ever issued a second edition of any work, but with the intention that it should occupy at least as high a position as the first?" (185). In a similar vein,

Palmer writes, "That which was twice modelled and fashioned by the Creator, and of course doubly refined, cannot be inferior" (96).

But occasionally proponents of women's preaching conceded some degree of biblically affirmed gender inequality or subordination, whether within the context of the family, marriage, or the church, or in terms of physical strength or vocation outside the home (Andrews 61–62; Boardman 52, 131; Foster xxvii; Palmer 96; Stewart 174). Nevertheless, these advocates often turned such Bible-based beliefs around in their favor through various assimilative arguments. Towle, quoting from Isaiah 41.14–15, metaphorically compares the status of women to that of an insect, writing, "The Lord grant that 'Worms may thresh mountains, and beat them small, and make the hills as chaff!'" (93). Boardman likewise cites God's use of a nonhuman species, specifically a donkey, as an instrument of God's will in Numbers 22.21–39 to argue that if God uses "a dumb brute," why not a woman (84)? Methodist itinerant preacher Zilpha Elaw, who notes her low status as a Black female, validates her call by quoting 1 Corinthians 1.27: "But God hath chosen the foolish things of the world to confound the wise; and God hath chosen the weak things of the world to confound the things which are mighty" (Andrews 51, 75; see also Palmer 74; Stewart 132). Similarly, quoting from Luke 1.37, Jarena Lee contends that "as unseemly as it may appear now-a-days for a woman to preach, it should be remembered that nothing is impossible with God" (Andrews 36). Based on the uncontested, biblically derived premise that God regularly chooses the lowly to accomplish God's will, these advocates deduce that if women are lower than men, then God may actually be more likely to call them to preach.

The Analytical Power of the Classical Interpretive Stases

Previous scholarship has noted that activists in this debate both observed and tried to reconcile the discrepancy within Paul's statements on women's ecclesiastic speaking in 1 Corinthians 11.4–5 and 14.34–35, and 1 Timothy 2.11–12 (Brekus 219; Donawerth 88, 91, 92; Zimmerelli 192). However, a classical stasis analysis reveals that this discrepancy was the principal interpretive issue during this period of the debate. Consequently, in this controversy, these Pauline verses functioned as linchpin passages: their interpretation was central to the biblical debate over women's preaching.[6] Moreover, most other interpretive arguments identified by scholars—including contextualizing Paul's prohibitions, constructing lists of biblical women who preached, and appealing to the original language of verses concerning women's ecclesiastic authority and speaking (Brekus 216–21; Donawerth 77; Zikmund 197–202; Zimmerelli 190–93)—were ultimately employed to resolve this central issue. Additionally, the topoi that classical rhetoricians associated with the stasis of conflicting passages help bring a heretofore unnoticed but key argumentative strategy in this debate to the surface: assimilation.

Stasis analysis, which is necessarily dialogic, further illuminates similarities and differences between the two sides' rhetorical challenges and strategies. One might assume that assimilation arguments would have been primarily employed by those in favor of women's preaching since they were fighting a supposedly clear biblical prohibition against the practice. However, this analysis shows that both sides faced the same problem of finding sufficient explicit biblical evidence for their positions, especially in light of Paul's apparent self-contradiction, and therefore both sides had to infer such support from the text. Yet this overlap in challenge and strategy does not mean that the two sides were on equal rhetorical footing. Without further context, the two Pauline prohibitions do appear to explicitly forbid women's ecclesiastic speaking, while the Pauline passage that appears to permit women's authoritative speaking in church seems less explicit. As Cicero explains, "[W]hat is plainly stated seems to be stronger and more binding" (2.49.147). Thus, women's preaching activists faced a more difficult rhetorical obstacle in rebutting arguments that Paul disapproved of women's preaching.

Many social and political disputes in nineteenth-century America, inside or outside the church, rested on particular interpretations of the Bible. The classical interpretive stases and their topoi are well suited for systematically analyzing the biblically grounded arguments in these controversies to elucidate the complex relations between issues, arguments, and opposing positions. And the American Methodist debate over women's preaching provides a rich case study for demonstrating the analytical power of the classical interpretive stases. But the interpretive stases are useful not only for analyzing biblical arguments. Nineteenth-century America was rife with arguments based on other texts, especially the Declaration of Independence and the Constitution, and the interpretive stases here too would be a great aid to the rhetorical critic. While modern methods of rhetorical analysis have enriched our understanding of rhetorical practices, the contemporary rhetorician would be wise not to forget the methods of classical rhetoric, which have successfully served rhetors and rhetoricians for thousands of years.

Notes

1. This line comes from Cicero's discussion of the stasis of letter versus spirit; however, since he considers the stasis of conflicting passages to consist of a double letter-versus-spirit dispute, this topos applies in both stases (2.49.147).

2. "I will therefore that men pray every where, lifting up holy hands, without wrath and doubting. In like manner also, that women adorn themselves in modest apparel, with shamefacedness and sobriety; not with braided hair, or gold, or pearls, or costly array; But (which becometh women professing godliness) with good works" (*Holy Bible*).

3. See also "Should Females Pray," where the refutation of this line of argument suggests that it was common among American Methodists.

4. Benson (*New Testament* 197–98), Clarke (290), and Coke (*New Testament* 267) all agree on this point.

5. "For Adam was first formed, then Eve"; "For a man indeed ought not to cover his head, forasmuch as he is the image and glory of God: but the woman is the glory of the man. For the man is not of the woman: but the woman of the man. Neither was the man created for the woman; but the woman for the man" (*Holy Bible*).

6. The concept "linchpin passages" is an extension of the concept "linchpin terms," individual words or phrases whose interpreted meaning governs how the rest of a passage or text is read (see Camper 59–62).

Works Cited

Andrews, William L., editor. *Sisters of the Spirit: Three Black Women's Autobiographies of the Nineteenth Century*. Indiana UP, 1986.

Aristotle. *Prior Analytics*. Translated by Hugh Tredennick, Harvard UP, 1938.

Barnes, Albert. *Notes, Explanatory and Practical, on the Epistles of Paul to the Thessalonians, to Timothy, to Titus, and to Philemon*. New York, 1845.

Benson, Joseph. *The Holy Bible, Containing the Old and New Testaments*. Vol. 1, New York, 1846.

———. *The New Testament of Our Lord and Savior Jesus Christ*. Vol. 2, New York, 1847.

Boardman, Mrs. W. E. [Mary]. *Who Shall Publish the Glad Tidings?* Boston, 1873.

Brekus, Catherine A. *Strangers and Pilgrims: Female Preaching in America, 1740–1845*. U of North Carolina P, 1998.

Camper, Martin. *Arguing over Texts: The Rhetoric of Interpretation*. Oxford UP, 2018.

Chaves, Mark. *Ordaining Women: Culture and Conflict in Religious Organizations*. Harvard UP, 1999.

Cicero. *De Inventione*. Translated by H. M. Hubbell, Harvard UP, 1976.

[Cicero]. *Rhetorica ad Herennium*. Translated by Harry Caplan, Harvard UP, 1981.

Clarke, Adam. *The New Testament of Our Lord and Savior Jesus Christ*. Vol. 2, New York, 1831.

Coke, Thomas. *A Commentary on the Holy Bible*. Vol. 1, London, 1801.

———. *A Commentary on the New Testament*. Vol. 2, London, 1803.

Dodson, Jualynne E. *Engendering Church: Women, Power, and the AME Church.* Rowman and Littlefield, 2002.

Donawerth, Jane. *Conversational Rhetoric: The Rise and Fall of a Women's Tradition, 1600–1900.* Southern Illinois UP, 2012.

Fortunatianus. *The Art of Rhetoric.* Edited and translated by Mary Elene Brightbill, 1930. Cornell U, PhD dissertation.

Foster, John Onesimus. *Life and Labors of Mrs. Maggie Newton Van Cott: The First Lady Licensed to Preach in the Methodist Episcopal Church in the United States.* Cincinnati, 1872.

Holy Bible. King James Version. *Bible Gateway,* 1987 printing, www.biblegateway.com/versions/King-James-Version-KJV-Bible. Accessed 17 Apr. 2018.

Keller, Rosemary Skinner. "Conversions and Their Consequences: Women's Ministry and Leadership in the United Methodist Tradition." *Religious Institutions and Women's Leadership: New Roles inside the Mainstream,* edited by Catherine Wessinger, U of South Carolina P, 1996, pp. 101–23.

Lee, Luther. *Five Sermons and a Tract by Luther Lee.* Edited by Donald W. Dayton, Holrad House, 1975.

Palmer, Phoebe. *Promise of the Father; Or, a Neglected Specialty of the Last Days.* Boston, 1859.

Payne, Daniel A. *History of the African Methodist Episcopal Church.* Arno / The New York Times, 1969.

Quintilian. *Institutio Oratoria: The Orator's Education.* Edited and translated by Donald A. Russell, vol. 3, Harvard UP, 2001.

Richey, Russell E., et al. *The Methodist Experience in America, Volume I: A History.* Abingdon, 2010.

"Should Females Pray in Our Public Prayer-Meetings?" *Christian Advocate and Journal,* June 1847, p. 98.

Stewart, Ellen. *Life of Mrs. Ellen Stewart, Together with Biographical Sketches of Other Individuals.* Akron, 1858.

Towle, Nancy. *Vicissitudes Illustrated, in the Experience of Nancy Towle, in Europe and America.* 2nd ed., Portsmouth, 1833.

Zikmund, Barbara Brown. "The Struggle for the Right to Preach." *Women and Religion in America, Volume 1: The Nineteenth Century,* edited by Rosemary Radford Ruether and Rosemary Skinner Keller, Harper and Row, 1981, pp. 193–241.

Zimmerelli, Lisa. "'Heaven-Touched Lips and Pent-Up Voices': The Rhetoric of American Female Preaching Apologia, 1820–1930." *Mapping Christian Rhetorics: Connecting Conversations, Charting New Territories,* edited by Michael-John DePalma and Jeffrey M. Ringer, Routledge, 2015, pp. 180–202.

Elizabeth Cady Stanton's Rhetorical Missteps: Metonymy and Synecdoche in the Women's Suffrage Arguments

Nancy Myers

> I am a white woman who has been angry in my life and my work, occasionally on my own behalf but more often about politics, about inequity, and the grotesque *unfairness* of the world, this country, how it was built and who it still excludes and systematically diminishes.
>
> —Rebecca Traister, *Good and Mad*

Examining the "nexus of women's anger and American *politics*," Rebecca Traister situates her own ongoing and simmering anger within the context of the 2016 presidential election and American women's responses to its outcome (xviii). Almost 150 years before this election, Elizabeth Cady Stanton was expressing the same angry sentiments in her arguments about a white woman's right to vote, because in 1869 the United States Congress passed the Fifteenth Amendment (ratified in 1870)—which protected all male citizens from being discriminated against in voting because of race—an amendment excluding women. Stanton's anger was justified. She had fought for women's suffrage since the Woman's Rights Convention in Seneca Falls, New York, in 1848. Similar to Traister, Stanton wanted more than just voting rights; she wanted equity and fair treatment for women, and women's ability to vote would enable those desired societal, cultural, and legal shifts toward gender equality. Unfortunately, Stanton's advocacy from 1866 to 1870 for universal suffrage, as preferable to solely male suffrage, undercut both her ethos as a champion for women's rights and the ethos of the women's movement across the nation. With the movement in disarray and national interest waning, Stanton, working to regain momentum for women's rights, compounded her first rhetorical misstep with her second when she—along with Susan B. Anthony—associated herself with Victoria Claflin Woodhull and rhetorically supported Woodhull's unorthodox positions on marriage and divorce in 1871 and 1872. Stanton's first rhetorical strategy caused the women's movement to be equated with racism and elitism, and her second rhetorical strategy resulted in suspicion and ridicule of suffragists' moral beliefs and practices. Her fearless public arguments ultimately delayed progress toward women's suffrage and women's equality for twenty years (Kerr 76). Jane S. Sutton argues that women's authority is continually undermined by patriarchal rhetoric in public and political spaces, even when a woman embraces her agency in the name of equality and change for all. From 1866 to 1872, Stanton experienced this public deprecation as the rhetorical and political contexts worked together to discredit Stanton and her women's rights agenda.

During these six years, Stanton's two rhetorical missteps transformed her longstanding metonymic arguments—as the contiguity of two distinct social agendas working for change—into synecdochic ones—as ones in which a quality or essence of one movement becomes what that movement stands for. The tropes of metonymy and synecdoche are easily misunderstood because they are often working together in the same sentence or discourse and because the differences in their abilities to change meaning through substitution are subtle. However, their distinction is crucial in Stanton's arguments because the two rhetorical strategies, according to Frank J. D'Angelo, "are not just incidental ornaments, but systems of human conceptualization operating deep in human thought" (211). Tropes as ideological frames reflected in words, sentences, and discourses "describe logical relationships among phenomena in the world of experience" (206).

For Quintilian, metonymy "consists in the substitution of one name for another" (8.6.23). This form of substitution is what Krista Ratcliffe refers to as "juxtaposition" because "it assumes that two objects do not share a common substance but are rather merely associated" (98). As such, these two distinct entities create meaning through their adjacency, simultaneously separate and related, "thus foregrounding both commonalities *and* differences" (68). Stanton's metonymic argument for universal suffrage undercuts her social and political women's rights agenda because her rhetoric highlights differences in this juxtaposition, and those differences become synecdochic word tropes that label and libel her cause.

Stanton's twenty years of metonymic arguments for comprehensive social change become reduced through synecdoche to two either-or arguments: educated white women's suffrage versus Black men's suffrage, and women's self-protection versus the sanctity of marriage. Synecdoche, as a substitution in which a part represents the whole, allows an understanding of "many things from one, the whole from a part" (Quintilian 8.6.19). With this trope the two elements in Stanton's arguments operate symbiotically, with the substitution representing the essence or quality of the other. With phrases such as "educated white women first" and "free love," Stanton's metonymic arguments on universal suffrage and on the legal aspects of marriage and divorce transform into synecdochic ones that threatened not only her hard-fought agenda of women's equity with men but also the women's suffrage movement. From 1866 to 1872, Stanton's advocacy demonstrates how, in the urgency of the moment, a social movement leader can destabilize her own long-held arguments through tropes. As Lee Ann Banaszak contends, "Understanding the success and failure of social movements requires a careful examination of both their political context and their values and beliefs" (222). Metonymy's capaciousness and synecdoche's reductionism help explain how a women's social movement can be easily derailed and vilified.

Stanton's Metonymic Rhetoric, 1840–66

Before the Civil War, Stanton's ideologies metonymically associated women's legal and social plight with the oppression of slaves in the United States, not as a metaphor or as a part of a whole ideology of social oppression but as a correspondence with two sets of oppressions being related but unique in their focus and approach. At an 1840 antislavery convention, Stanton realized the correlation between a woman's and a slave's legal situations. As she writes in her autobiography, "[A]ccording to common law, both classes occupied a similar legal status" (*Eighty Years* 79). Her arguments on women's suffrage and on marriage and divorce, as just two issues in her more expansive view of women's rights, demonstrate metonymy as heuristics reflecting D'Angelo's "modes of thinking" on two ideological levels (211). First, women's activism operates alongside antislavery advocacy and Black rights, and second, women's suffrage functions in conjunction with men's suffrage. Women's restrictions in marriage and divorce run through both metonymies in that, if women can vote, all legal and social injustices for themselves and others can be remedied. Stanton recognized these inequities and worked to highlight the oppressive social attitudes about the sanctity of marriage and the laws limiting avenues to divorce for women.

Newly married in 1840, Stanton attended the World's Anti-Slavery Convention in London with her abolitionist and lawyer husband. During the two-week convention and across the month of touring and pleasure in London, she befriended Lucretia Mott and other American women and men who were both abolitionists and advocates of women's rights (*Eighty Years* 73–91). These encounters of side-by-side discussions on emancipating slaves and women, with the first women and men she "had ever met who believed in the equality of the sexes," established for Stanton a two-pronged agenda of rights for all women and rights for Black people (83). While across the next years she attended and spoke at antislavery meetings and conventions, her women's rights activism began at the Seneca Falls Convention. With the "Declaration of Sentiments and Resolutions," a result of that convention, Stanton, Mott, and others established the women's movement platform as one of women's equality under the law: "in view of this entire disenfranchisement of one-half the people of this country [women], . . . we insist that they have immediate admission to all the rights and privileges which belong to them as citizens of these United States" (Gordon, *Selected Papers* 1: 80). This capacious understanding of "all the rights and privileges" for women, including those connected to social and legal concerns, continued to inform Stanton's agenda throughout her life.

In personal and public statements, Stanton established women's rights and antislavery issues metonymically, reflecting both their independent distinctions and their correlations. In a 26 November 1841 letter to Elizabeth J. Neall, Stanton writes about her inclusion of women's rights in her first public speech on temperance to a large audience of women, because, as she says, she intends to keep women's rights "before the people" (Gordon, *Selected Papers* 1: 25). In that same letter and contiguous with her rights explication, she addresses the male abolitionists and their potential voting power: "now our abolitionists are the best men in our country, & I should be unwilling that as a body they should exert no political influence. Slavery is a political question created & sustained by law, & must be put down by law" (1: 25). Almost twenty years later, in her 8 May 1860 address to the American Anti-Slavery Society, Stanton, while acknowledging the differences in the slave's and white woman's plights, argues their parallel principles: "The health of the body politic depends on the sound condition of every member" (1: 410). Showing the correspondence between women's rights and antislavery advocacy and Black rights, she argues that "the mission of this Radical Anti-Slavery Movement is not to the African slave alone, but to the slaves of custom, creed and sex, as well; and most faithfully has it done its work" (1: 412). This last clause, and with her use of "most faithfully," moves the sentence from the movement's principles to Stanton's belief and judgment as a white woman. In referring to the slave trade and the separation of Black family members and Black women's misery, Stanton offers a third correlation between white women's standing and the slaves' condition: the "privileged class can never conceive the feelings of those who are born to contempt, to inferiority, to degradation. Herein is woman more fully identified with the slave than man can possibly be, for she can take the subjective view" (1: 414). Since women's plight was socially and legally paired with the slaves' condition, a woman could better identify with slaves' sentiments. In this speech, Stanton's use of metonymy demonstrates the ideological correspondences through principles, beliefs, and affect.

Stanton established the right of women's enfranchisement alongside the already privileged position of white male suffrage. According to Ann D. Gordon, after Seneca Falls, Stanton gave a women's rights address several times across the state of New York (*Selected Papers* 1: 94). In the address, she systematically demonstrates the imbalance by pairing a white woman's restrictions with a man's privileges within a question of constitutional rights and argues for suffrage as the linchpin to balancing the inequities in this metonymy: "Had we [women] a vote to give might not the office holders and seekers propose some change in woman's condition?" (1: 106). This rhetorical demonstration of injustices toward women and advocacy of women's suffrage establishes her expansive women's rights agenda. By 1851, after meeting Anthony at an antislavery meeting, Stanton joined forces with this abolitionist and temperance advocate for over fifty years in an ongoing campaign for women's rights. Immediately, they were writing "addresses for temperance, anti-slavery, educational and woman's rights conventions" (Stanton, *Eighty Years* 164). Stanton and Anthony quickly took their arguments beyond the borders of New York. Sutton contends that Stanton, Anthony, and other women at this time united to create a rhetorical shift "marked by a move from women using speech to speak about slaves' rights to using it to address women's rights" (82).

At the end of the Civil War, and in a July 1865 *National Anti-Slavery Standard* article on universal suffrage, Stanton made the claim that all men should have suffrage. Indirectly referencing the current legislators, she asks, "Where does the aristocrat get his authority to forbid poor men, ignorant men, and black men, the exercise of their rights?" (Gordon, *Selected Papers* 1: 551). This advocacy for universal suffrage of all men reflects her metonymic correspondence between women's and African Americans' rights. However, by 26 December 1865, in a second *National Anti-Slavery Standard* article and only a week after the ratification of the Thirteenth Amendment, Stanton had expanded that term to include an argument about Black women in her metonymic parallel between women's and men's suffrage: "If the two millions of Southern black women are not to be secured in their rights of person, property, wages, and children, their emancipation is but another form of slavery" (1: 564). In addition, she warns that white women who have worked "for the last thirty years to secure freedom for the negro" will not stand aside but wish "to walk by his side" in claiming enfranchisement (1: 564). With this image, Stanton's ideological metonymy is now embodied with the Black man and white woman side by side.

Stanton continued with her expansive metonymic agenda for women's rights as she and Anthony established *The Revolution*, a weekly newspaper that ran from January 1868 through 1872. Stanton was the lead editor and Anthony the publisher from the newspaper's inception until its sale in May 1870. From the beginning, *The Revolution* claims that women's rights encompass more than attaining voting rights. The articles regularly addressed arguments for women's suffrage and activist activities, but they also focused on all social problems and possible reforms related to women, including working women's labor and treatment by their employers. As Bonnie J. Dow contends, *The Revolution* "defined woman suffrage as a movement with an independent and multifaceted existence"

(79). In addition, Dow argues that for every woman's social struggle that Stanton addressed "she asserted that the enfranchisement of women would lead to the solution of the ills she exposed" (77–78). *The Revolution's* masthead, "Principle, Not Policy, Not Favors—Men, Their Rights and Nothing More; Women, Their Rights and Nothing Less," indicates both the major focus of the newspaper as women's suffrage and suggests the foundation for that suffrage lies on principle and rights. Both words reverberate with meaning, for *principle* is associated with cause, as in Aristotle's first principles, and law, as in the standard for a society, while *rights* is associated with justice, entitlements, and redress, as in *to make right*. The words joined in this masthead indicate that women and men are entitled to the same principles of justice and that the law must be corrected to ensure equity across gender, race, and class lines.

From Metonymy to Synecdoche, 1866–70

Stanton's words on suffrage in *The Revolution* and her remarks at conventions between 1866 and 1870 transformed her metonymic arguments of twenty years into synecdochic ones. While her political redirection from appealing to Republican congressmen to Democratic ones had begun earlier, it is with her association to the racist Democrat George Francis Train and the publishing of *The Revolution*, partly funded by Train, that Stanton's universal suffrage argument (voting as the right of all citizens) becomes a hierarchical argument (voting as the right of all educated white women first). Stanton and Anthony saw the insertion of the word *male* before *citizen* in the Fourteenth Amendment, passed in 1866 and ratified in 1868, as a blow to their women's suffrage cause. The exclusion of women in regards to citizenship was compounded when, in 1869, the Fifteenth Amendment on voting rights was being debated in Congress. Until this amendment, voting rights were completely controlled by the states and territories, and Stanton and Anthony had worked with women on voting rights state by state. This constitutional amendment would make voting rights a federal concern (Tetrault 31–32). After twenty years of crusading for suffrage, Stanton and Anthony believed that the probable passage of this amendment was the kairotic moment for achieving women's enfranchisement. Across 1869, they campaigned throughout the northern and midwestern states, fighting fiercely to put women's voting rights in the Fifteenth Amendment, then against the amendment's ratification when it passed, its text addressing race but not sex.

What resulted was Stanton's first, and most damaging, rhetorical misstep in which her rebuttal to the position of narrowing voting rights to only men worked on two levels to undermine the women's movement. First, Stanton's association with and defense of the Copperhead Train required that she systematically set women's rights against Black men's rights, and second, even though her advocacy was for universal suffrage, Stanton regularly privileged and prioritized white educated women through her rhetorical appeals to race, class, gender, and education, further compounding this differentiation. Racism and attitudes that non-white people were inferior were pervasive across the states and territories and within the women's movement, and Stanton's attitudes were no exception (see Tetrault). Rather than unifying white men and women in supporting women's voting rights, Stanton's metonymic appeals, as parts of her larger argument for universal suffrage and women's equality, operate divisively, for through their repetition and angry wording they become synecdochic appeals, as qualities of Stanton's character and women's suffrage.

Even though *The Revolution*'s masthead and Stanton's years of appeals for emancipation and Black rights are evidence of her stance on universal suffrage, her rhetoric in defense of Train and against the wording of the Fourteenth and Fifteenth Amendments caused a loss of national credibility for women's suffrage and the political rupture in the women's movement. Within the first month of *The Revolution*'s publication, in the 29 January 1868 issue, Stanton describes her disappointment with the Republicans' inclusion of the word *male* in the Fourteenth Amendment and their recent debate to exclude women in the wording of the Fifteenth Amendment: "The Democratic party, on the contrary, has done all it could to keep our question alive in the State and National councils, by pressing Republicans, in their debates on negro suffrage, to logical conclusions" (1: 49). All of these conclusions work against Black men's suffrage, of course. In that same article, Stanton declares the importance of recognizing that by separating Black men's suffrage from women's suffrage, lawmakers have compromised the chance for universal suffrage: "Every far-seeing woman who has a proper self-respect or an intelligent love of country will protest against the enfranchisement of another man, either black or white, until the women of this nation are crowned with all the rights of citizenship" (1: 50). With the expression "far-seeing woman," Stanton is appealing to the white women from the middle and upper classes who have both the time and the money to actively promote reform; and if suffrage is the goal, then these women need to support it universally and work against a bifurcated approach politically and rhetorically. However, this appeal to education and privilege trumping sex also implicates negatively on Black freedmen and Irish male immigrants, among others. Again, a metonymic appeal asking educated women to take action by demanding universal suffrage now becomes synecdochic, meaning educated women's suffrage should take priority over Black men's or universal suffrage.

Stanton's anger and desperation accelerate her rebuttals to this ongoing political debate to exclude women from the Fourteenth and Fifteenth Amendments;

these motions continue in the issues of *The Revolution* across 1868. Somewhat trapped in an either-or rhetorical strategy, she undercuts her ongoing argument for universal suffrage. Even when she reaffirms her commitment to it, the differentiation between supposed illiterate free men and educated white women arises. For example, in the 9 April 1868 issue, she addresses the precedence issue of the debate but undermines her universal argument with her final claim: "It is not a question of necessary precedence for one or the other. . . . Our demand has long been suffrage for all, white and black, male and female, of legal age and sound mind. . . . So we say to-day, educated women first, ignorant men afterward" (1: 212–13). Instead of arguing against precedence, she decides that if she has to choose, it is educated women first, reinforcing the earlier synecdochic reading of the essence of women's suffrage as based not only in privilege but also in race and sex. This right of privilege tied to race and sex as the essence of women's suffrage again appears in Stanton's declaration on 1 October 1868: "in the name of the educated women of this country, we protest against the enfranchisement of another man of any race or clime until the daughters of Jefferson, Hancock, and Adams are crowned with all their rights" (*Revolution* 2: 200). The right and privilege of educated women to voting rights now becomes tied to the white founding fathers as a clear bloodline that other races and ethnicities in America cannot claim. In the 24 December 1868 issue, Stanton's appeals privileging educated white women over disenfranchised men become more angry and blatantly racist: "Think of Patrick and Sambo and Hans and Yung Tung who do not know the difference between a Monarchy and a Republic, who never read the Declaration of Independence or Webster's Spelling book, making laws for Lydia Maria Child, Lucretia Mott, or Fanny Kemble. Think of jurors drawn from these ranks to try young girls for the crime of infanticide" (2: 392).

Completely undermining Stanton's universal suffrage stance, these gendered appeals to difference emphasize a human binary with one side encompassing socially respected and privileged white women, English speakers, and writers with a strong knowledge of governmental and cultural history who work to support and develop the community. On the other side are a group of ill-defined and objectionable men who are illiterate, uneducated, and intellectually irrational. Including three famous women abolitionists' names as counterpoints to the racial and ethnic monikers only heightens these distinctions. The unasked question is this: Who would you rather had voting rights? These extreme stereotypes based on differentiation through gender, race, class, and education instantiate the synecdochic readings of Stanton's previous words, which destabilize not only her ethical appeal but also the ethos of the women's suffrage movement for many suffrage advocates.

At the May 1869 American Equal Rights Association Convention, long after Stanton and Anthony had disassociated themselves from Train, Stephen Foster, for the benefit of the press, verbally attacked Stanton for her association with Train and her arguments against the recent constitutional amendments (Kerr 68–70; Tetrault 27–30). Foster's statements, along with others', and Stanton's rebuttal confirmed for the audience that Stanton shared Train's beliefs. As Foster's denunciation indicates, Stanton's use of racial inferiority as a rhetorical appeal became synecdochic, as the essence of her argument for women's suffrage. With the legislators moving toward race only, again excluding women in the Fifteenth Amendment, Stanton was not just angry but desperate to promote universal suffrage over Black men's suffrage, at this time referred to as manhood suffrage. Confronted by the either-or arguments, she resorted to the race inferiority arguments that were her own but also reflected the views of many women and men across the nation.

From Metonymy to Synecdoche, 1871–72

Up to this moment, the women's suffrage associations across the nation had formed locally and independently with no connection to a regional or national organization. Stanton, Anthony, and Lucy Stone, among others, functioned as suffrage advocates, spokeswomen, and celebrities by being invited or inviting themselves to speak at small gatherings and larger conventions across the nation. Stanton's activist and aggressive rhetorical tactics tied to suffrage caused a fissure among the East Coast leaders of the women's movement, thus creating Stanton and Anthony's National Woman Suffrage Association and Stone's American Woman Suffrage Association six months apart in 1869. Stone's more conservative association politically supported the ratification of the Fifteenth Amendment and a proposed sixteenth amendment for women's suffrage and rhetorically narrowed the scope of the women's suffrage issue to voting rights and away from suffrage as a solution to women's social struggles (Dow 78–79). Stanton's first rhetorical misstep divided the movement and caused both national organizations to struggle for membership and support.

Across 1871 and 1872, this divide deepened when Stanton's advocacy of women's right to divorce combined with her support of Victoria Woodhull. While women's suffrage was still central to Stanton's advocacy of women's rights, she returned to her long-held views on women's plight in marriage and in the legal restrictions on divorce. Anthony had been working with Woodhull on women's suffrage since December 1870, but Stanton, on an extended speaking tour, learned about her through news reports and letters and in 1871 began to praise her arguments on the Fourteenth and Fifteenth Amendments, that they should allow for women's suffrage rather than exclude it (Gabriel 91–92). Writing to Mott on 1 April 1871, Stanton declares, "Victoria Woodhull stands before us to day one of the ablest speakers & writers of the century sound & radical, alike in political, religious, & social principles" (Gordon, *Selected Papers* 2: 427–28). In a 29 December 1871 letter following Woodhull's November "free love" speech, Stanton's excitement for Woodhull's views, notoriety, and audience appeal and for their similar views on marriage and divorce led her to write Woodhull about the upcoming Washington convention: "Let us have a real old fashioned protracted meeting full of enthusiasm. I would rather make a few blunders from a superabundance of life, than to have all the proprieties of a well embalmed mummy" (Gordon, *Selected Papers* 2: 463). Women's suffrage for Stanton would provide the desired changes to the social and legal structures that limited women's agency and self-determination, and Woodhull now seemed instrumental in gaining those institutional shifts.

While Stanton's advocacy for marriage as a legal contract and for more flexible divorce laws for women are in keeping with Woodhull's promotion of sexual independence for women, their views fundamentally differ. According to Wendy Hayden, advocates of free love "denounce marriage, urge its abolition, encourage sex education, and promote an agenda that included women's sexual self-ownership" (2). These are not the arguments Stanton makes. In the summer months preceding Woodhull's free love speech, Stanton regularly gave a lengthy speech on marriage and divorce during a western-states speaking tour. In her argument "[t]hat marriage is not an indissoluble tie" and "not a sacrament of the church, but a civil contract," she again restates her ideological metonymy between men's and women's rights as a legal and social issue ("On Marriage"). As early as 1850, Stanton had argued for changes in state divorce laws. That April, *The Lily*, a Seneca Falls monthly publication supporting temperance and women's rights, published Stanton's report on a divorce bill being debated in the New York Legislature. In her advocacy for its passage, she argues for the right of women to remove themselves, their children, and their property from reprobate husbands (Gordon, *Selected Papers* 1: 162). In an 1860 speech on marriage and divorce at the Tenth National Woman's Rights Convention, Stanton advocates for a redefining of marriage as a civil, legal contract so that it can be regulated as such: "A contract, to be valid in law, must be formed between parties of mature age, with an honest intention in said parties to do what they agree. The least concealment, fraud, or intention to deceive, if proved, annuls the contract" (1: 421). Marriage as a contract works within Stanton's more expansive women's rights metonymy in that she is arguing for a legal approach to marriage and divorce that balances a woman's rights with a man's rights.

Unfortunately, Woodhull's free love agenda quickly became synecdochically attached to women's suffrage and the women who advocated for it. Woodhull contends that without the social, moral, and legal pressures for women to marry, they would make reasonable and effective decisions about the relationships they engage in. This argument directly confronted the social conservatives who believed in the sanctity of marriage and the purity of respectable women. Instead of Woodhull bringing the women's movement together, her views on and espousal of free love and her notorious reputation tied to financial concerns and her personal life drove the divisions in the women's movement deeper. While Stanton's first misstep was in her appeals to the differences in her metonymic argument of universal suffrage, her second was in supporting the metonymic connections between her view of marriage as a civil contract and Woodhull's advocacy for free love.

The shifts in tropes on Stanton's angry advocacy of universal suffrage and women's marriage rights offer insight into women's social movements and the histories about them in three ways. First, strong and consistent social ties across a movement's leaders and affiliates need to be constantly and consistently maintained, with compromise being the outcome—for with that interaction a common set of values is generated. As Banaszak maintains in her study of women's movements, when successful, "values then served to filter and interpret the available information" (218). In the urgency of the moments of the Fourteenth and Fifteenth Amendments being ratified, and in her anger over their wording and her desperation to achieve women's suffrage, Stanton reduced her more capacious metonymic universal suffrage arguments to either-or synecdoches, advocating educated white women's suffrage before manhood suffrage. Second, with her defense of Woodhull in the name of women's equality in all social and cultural practices, Stanton's larger metonymic social agenda for women's self-reliance and social equity diminished to the synecdochic stigma of free love. Given both rhetorical missteps, Stanton lost male and female supporters for women's suffrage and ultimately proved that "[w]ithout a movement 'community' and intense social interaction among activists, a social movement will remain divided" (Banaszak 223). Third, over the last twenty years, scholarship on Stanton's suffrage arguments and activism has centered on issues of class and race (see Ginzberg; Kerr; Tetrault). Lori D. Ginzberg's 2009 critical biography maintains that Stanton was racist and elitist and that her arguments for universal suffrage at this time were "ugly, conscious, and unforgivable" (192, 121). Conversely, in addressing the complexity of Stanton's prolific writings and thinking, Gordon in 2007 explains that Stanton argued for universal suffrage throughout her life and claims that "[q]uoting selectively from Elizabeth Cady Stanton is risky business" ("Stanton" 124, 117). In keeping with Gordon, this essay suggests that further investigations on Stanton's rhetoric across time continue to complicate this debate and prompt feminist historiography to reconsider previous recovery work toward more nuanced conclusions. Stanton's ideological metonymies provide just one example of how rhetorical failure is an important site of inquiry for women's social movements, past and present.

Works Cited

Banaszak, Lee Ann. *Why Movements Succeed or Fail: Opportunity, Culture, and the Struggle for Woman Suffrage*. Princeton UP, 1996.

D'Angelo, Frank J. "Tropics of Invention." *Rhetoric Review*, vol. 36, no. 3, 2017, pp. 200–13.

Dow, Bonnie J. "*The Revolution*, 1868–1870: Expanding the Woman Suffrage Agenda." *A Voice of Their Own: The Woman Suffrage Press, 1840–1910*, edited by Martha M. Solomon, U of Alabama P, 1991, pp. 71–86.

Gabriel, Mary. *Notorious Victoria: The Uncensored Life of Victoria Woodhill—Visionary, Suffragist, and First Woman to Run for President*. Algonquin Books, 1998.

Ginzberg, Lori D. *Elizabeth Cady Stanton: An American Life*. Hill and Wang, 2009.

Gordon, Ann D., editor. *The Selected Papers of Elizabeth Cady Stanton and Susan B. Anthony*. Rutgers UP, 1997–2013. 6 vols.

———. "Stanton and the Right to Vote: On Account of Race or Sex." *Elizabeth Cady Stanton, Feminist as Thinker*, edited by Ellen Carol DuBois and Richard Cándida Smith, New York UP, 2007, pp. 111–27.

Hayden, Wendy. *Evolutionary Rhetoric: Sex, Science, and Free Love in Nineteenth-Century Feminism*. Southern Illinois UP, 2013.

Kerr, Andrea Moore. "White Women's Rights, Black Men's Wrongs, Free Love, Blackmail, and the Formation of the American Woman Suffrage Association." *One Woman, One Vote: Rediscovering the Woman Suffrage Movement*, edited by Marjorie Spruill Wheeler, NewSage P, 1995, pp. 61–79.

Quintilian. *Institutio Oratoria*. Translated by H. E. Butler, vol. 3, Harvard UP, 1921.

Ratcliffe, Krista. *Rhetorical Listening: Identification, Gender, Whiteness*. Southern Illinois UP, 2005.

Stanton, Elizabeth Cady. *Eighty Years and More: Reminiscences, 1815–1897*, edited by Denise M. Marshall, unabridged version, Humanity Books, 2002.

———. "On Marriage and Divorce—Aug. 18, 1871." *Iowa State University Archives of Women's Political Communication*, awpc.cattcenter.iastate.edu/2017/03/21/on-marriage-and-divorce-aug-18-1871/.

———. *The Revolution* [New York]. 1868–1872. 8 vols. *Hein Online Women and the Law (Peggy)*, home.heinonline.org/content/Women-and-the-Law-Peggy/.

Sutton, Jane S. *The House of My Sojourn: Rhetoric, Women, and the Question of Authority.* U of Alabama P, 2010.

Tetrault, Lisa. *The Myth of Seneca Falls: Memory and the Women's Suffrage Movement, 1848–1898.* U of North Carolina P, 2014.

Traister, Rebecca. *Good and Mad: The Revolutionary Power of Women's Anger.* Simon and Schuster, 2018.

The Late Abolitionist Rhetoric of Margaret Fuller: How She Changed Her Mind

Mollie Barnes

How do we read the history of a woman who changed her mind—especially a woman who changed her mind on a subject as vital as the abolition of slavery? How do we remember her antislavery writing in our own third- or fourth-wave feminist moment, when we're still struggling to realize intersectional activism? Margaret Fuller's abolitionist rhetoric is important to research now not because it's consistent or because it's always flattering to her and our desires to recognize her as a feminist social reformer but because her eventual outrage seems delayed to many people. Here, I study oft-cited antislavery passages in Fuller's late writing. I examine her strategic revisions in *Woman in the Nineteenth Century* (1845) to contextualize analyses of her *New-York Daily Tribune* dispatches (1847–50). Fuller's critics have long canonized these late moments as transformative: critics contrast writing from the 1830s and 1840s, when Fuller critiqued overt abolitionist outcries. In longitudinal studies, Francis Kearns, Margaret Allen, and Albert von Frank dilate over early texts, recounting moments when Fuller abstained from speaking on behalf of the cause and when she balked at those who did, and then ending with her turning points—the passages that are my subject here. While previous studies examine Fuller's texts over time, I linger over this late period. By unpacking the transatlantic contexts that provoked her to write—publicly, and more and more vehemently—against slavery, I reveal how Fuller's foreign correspondence shaped her feminist and abolitionist rhetoric.

Fuller's problem with abolition was rhetorical: her critiques weren't of abolitionism itself but of abolitionist rhetoric. Beyond acknowledging that Fuller was never an antislavery leader, as current scholarship reminds us, I analyze her late writing precisely because it resists expectations to connect intersectional dots. Along these lines, I place my focused reading in conversation with two patterns that Kearns, Allen, von Frank, and Michael Bennett identify: first, these authors study her early resistance by historicizing tensions that emerged at mid-century among abolitionist and feminist movements; second, they demonstrate that she criticized abolitionists' rhetorical strategies by prioritizing her own expectations for women. As von Frank observes, "Up to and including the period when *Woman in the Nineteenth Century* was written, Fuller sympathized with the burgeoning antislavery movement. . . . [S]he approved of its principles, but hesitated, as others did, before the spectacle of the associated measures and more especially before the combative language of the movement" (145). By privileging her concerns about abolitionists' words over their ideas or actions, Fuller embodies the stereotypes about intellectual elitism that biographers have sought to temper since her death. The story of how she changed her mind and, in turn, her language is complex. The story of our own critical metanarrative is, too, starting with second-wave critics' strategies for canonizing, and sometimes challenging, their first-wave subjects. These layered histories affect our reading practices. When we surface them together, the self-conscious ideological and rhetorical provocations within Fuller's late prose stand out in sharper relief.

Fuller and Her Historic Afterlives

Fuller claims abolitionist sympathies at the very moment when her understanding of the nineteenth-century nation-state was transformed. Critics have long noted the significance of Fuller's moves from Massachusetts to New York and Italy, yet long-arc discussions don't wonder over exactly what these moves have to do with her increasingly passionate appeals or exactly how her appeals changed in light of her work as a foreign correspondent—the first woman foreign correspondent, we often emphasize—for a major newspaper.[1] When we see Fuller as a journalist, our political gaze is redirected to the Texas annexation (in 1845) and the Mexican-American War (between 1846 and 1848) while Fuller was writing from Italy during the period now known as the Spring of Nations (in 1848). Fuller's experiences abroad shaped appeals she made to an American readership recovering from these events, which spurred the terms of the Compromise of 1850. In fact, Fuller's recursive allusions to Texas and Mexico—in articles documenting the Italian Risorgimento—reveal how her preoccupations with shifting borderlines and nation-states, as much as her feminism, transformed her abolitionist rhetoric. Fuller's antislavery appeals are, then, necessarily transatlantic.

Perhaps because studies work through the 1830s and 1840s to Fuller's first and most sustained rallying cries in 1845, it's become critical commonplace to wonder what would have happened had she lived past 1850. The consensus is that she would have been radicalized upon her return to the United States. This critical penchant is not something I mean to reinforce by beginning my analysis in July 1850, the moment when a series of obituaries for Fuller replaced her long-running column in the *New-York Daily Tribune*. Instead, I cite the date of her untimely death because it's useful to study how her own newspaper looked the week it reported that she drowned in a shipwreck within sight of Fire Island. Between 23 and 30 July 1850, the *Tribune* published updates on the wreck of the *Elizabeth* alongside reports of congressional debates that resulted in the Compromise of 1850, including the 1850 Fugitive Slave Law. Fuller haunted Horace Greeley's newspaper in the days immediately preceding historic votes on the compromise: the first failed on 31 July, but the second was signed into law on 20 September. The issues that provoked Fuller's antislavery writing in this newspaper appear side by side with columns that worry over her still-missing body. This historical coincidence draws our attention to the transatlantic circulation of Fuller's own contentious rallying cries. The coincidence also draws our attention to the specific geopolitical contexts that provoked her sharpest pivots toward antislavery writing: partial paragraphs about Texas and Mexico that punctuate her most famous pieces.

Fuller's afterlife in the *Tribune* that summer is a powerful archive, for it urges us to study her unfolding abolitionist rhetoric with the immediacy distinguishing her journalism. To date, almost nobody has addressed this confluence of events. One exception is von Frank: "the progress of her thought might be seen as coincident with or even slightly in advance of changes in popular feeling among educated New Englanders," he writes (128). Notice his parenthetical in the following:

> Especially is this so if one were to grant that it was only with [the Texas annexation or the Mexican War] . . . or still more decisively with the passage of the Compromise of 1850 and the Fugitive Slave Act (virtually at the moment of Fuller's death) that abolitionism ceased being a predominantly moral and religious crusade and finally emerged as a revolutionary moment.   (128–29)

When we remember the immediate contexts of Fuller's return to the United States, I argue, we also remember how the abolitionist movement itself was transformed—and so, in turn, were the reputations of its reformers—during that summer of 1850 (Delbanco 8–11).

Fuller's "Constant Revisions"

To trace the seeds of these connections, I'll backtrack from the 1850 *Tribune* to passages where many brilliant pieces on Fuller's abolition linger and end: in *Woman in the Nineteenth Century*. In the final pages of *Woman*, Fuller discloses her hope that the book will satisfy critiques leveled at "the earlier tract" that she didn't "make her meaning sufficiently clear" (99; "the earlier tract" refers to "The Great Lawsuit," the essay she published in *The Dial* in July 1843 and later expanded into

Woman). In the paragraphs immediately preceding this disclosure, Fuller turns, sharply and rather self-consciously, from her argument about marriage to current "events" that, she worries, preclude men and women from realizing transcendent partnership. "I now touch on my own place and day," Fuller writes; and she pivots from "Miss Martineau," "Miss Barrett," and her desire for women to experience "the glories of the universe" to three news stories that unnerve the transcendent possibilities she envisions (97). She devotes just one sentence to each of the three news stories: the first about William Miller's 1844 Great Disappointment; the second, Daniel O'Connell's 1844 imprisonment for demanding that the union between Great Britain and Ireland be repealed; and the third, the 1845 Texas annexation, which was signed into law after Fuller finished *Woman*. Fuller's turn from marriage to any of these news stories would be remarkable.

But Texas stands out. For Fuller, the annexation of the Republic of Texas to the Union literalizes the crisis of domestic independence that prompts *Woman* in the first place. She clarifies what Miller and O'Connell have to do with Martineau and Barrett or marriage. "But," Fuller continues, "last week brought news which threatens that a cause identical with the enfranchisement of Jews, Irish, women, ay [sic], and of Americans in general, too, is in danger, for the choice of the people threatens to rivet the chains of slavery and the leprosy of sin permanently on this nation, through the annexation of Texas" (97). Recent work emphasizes that Fuller's references to slavery and antislavery sentiment, especially in the context of the woman question, are often rhetorical.[2] Yet we should resist the temptation to dismiss this particular association, however rhetorical it may be, as passing comparison, half-hearted non sequitur, or editorial messiness or sloppiness. These are kairotic appeals.

In fact, the logic of the sequence is in the past-tense network that Fuller constructs through her seemingly linear timeline. While the preface to *Woman* is signed November 1844, the book was published in February 1845, when Texas's annexation was incomplete. The circuitous process captured the nation's attention for months preceding this moment. It was a decisive issue in the 1844 presidential election: John Tyler secured a treaty in April 1844, before the pro-annexation James Polk won the presidency over the anti-annexation Henry Clay, author of the Compromise of 1850. Polk signed the state into the Union in December 1845; Texas yielded in February 1846, after *Woman* had been in print for one year. Fuller's immediacy in this paragraph about slavery and the annexation of Texas is, then, far more complicated than it appears. She's anticipating events that weren't formalized until her book was circulating. Fuller's layered immediacies and temporalities are all the more remarkable when we remember that she edited this passage before publishing *Woman*, and that the book is a revision of her previous essay "The Great Lawsuit." While her writing in both media is predicated on her readers' familiarity with mid-century events, Fuller's sense of timing in these revisions is strategic. I emphasize this particular revision not only because of its immediate historical contexts but also because Fuller nods to "constant revision" in the first sentence of "The Great Lawsuit." Indeed, this essay actually takes constant revision as its rhetorical provocation. In Fuller's soon-to-be first-wave tome, constant revision is both her subject and her rhetorical process. When we pause over the revision history of this passage about the annexation of Texas, as Bennett urges us to do, and read it in light of her historical timeline, Fuller's reference to Texas seems all the more powerful (87).

Fuller rallies readers' sympathies about annexation just before she makes one of her most impassioned antislavery appeals: "This cause is your own, for as I have before said, there is a reason why the foes of African slavery seek more freedom for women; but put it not upon that ground, but on the ground of right" (*Woman* 98). Fuller casts her representation of "the foes of African slavery" in ways that presage institutional schisms in first-wave feminism—most famously, between the American Woman Suffrage Association and the National Woman Suffrage Association over the Fifteenth Amendment. Fuller argues that antislavery reformers advocate for women for "a reason" that she doesn't spell out and doesn't need to spell out: securing "more freedom for women" is, a priori in her mind, the antecedent to freedom for enslaved people (98). Nevertheless, Fuller's second-person petition is her first time connecting what we'd now call abolitionism and feminism in substantive ways—and asking her readers to do the same "before it is too late" (99). She draws our attention to the necessity of revision because of geopolitical exigencies in 1844 and 1845.

At this moment, Fuller reveals the radical potential—and risk—of a woman changing her mind in public letters on public debates that asseverated sectional conflict in the wake of a presidential election. Fuller pivots in 1845. What propels her constant revision after "Lawsuit" and *Woman* isn't easy reconciliation between abolitionist and feminist sympathies. Instead, the antislavery passages in this text reveal that crises of domestic independence are bound to crises of statehood. This Fuller—the person attuned to geopolitical fracture—became a foreign correspondent for the *New-York Daily Tribune*, writing about the making and unmaking of a nation-state to an audience who read her reports weeks or months later, when everything had changed again. Fuller's *Tribune* pieces return our attention to Texas and Mexico. Indeed, her time in Italy widened her perspective on statehood crises. While it's become a critical commonplace to mention that Fuller's writing changed when she lived in New York and Rome, and that she became increasingly vocal in her critiques of slavery, nobody discusses why it's so powerful for her to connect abolitionist rhetoric to Italy.[3]

Connecting the Italian Risorgimento and the Mexican-American War

Fuller's most vehement journalistic appeals are in dispatch 18, where she reflects on the differences between Old and New Worlds and urges readers to imagine the Atlantic Ocean as a watery boundary. "A new world," she imagines, "a new chance, with oceans to wall in the new thought against interference from the old!" (*"These Sad but Glorious Days"* 164). At the end of a dispatch otherwise famous for its meditation on the "three species" of American travelers abroad and the urgencies of Old and New World democracies, she catalogs a list of evils she must "confess" (165). "Then there is this horrible cancer of Slavery, and this wicked War, that has grown out of it," Fuller writes. "How dare I speak of these things here? I listen to the same arguments against the emancipation of Italy, that are used against the emancipation of our blacks; the same arguments in favor of the spoliation of Poland as for the conquest of Mexico" (166). It's critical that Fuller writes this statement in Italy—at the moment when Italy's provisional republic and liberation from Austria, France, and the Catholic Church seemed uncertain. Yet that moment alone is not enough to explain her seeming analogy between the "emancipation" of enslaved people and the "spoliation of Poland" or the "conquest of Mexico." In other words, the transatlantic context for this turn is more complicated than the fact that she was writing her dispatch from the Italian Peninsula.

Fuller's language transcends neat parallels, as we've seen elsewhere. She's paying attention to unions and disunions in these places: remembering Poland and Mexico in Italy prompts her to wonder over what a nation-state is—and how it coheres or falls apart—at precisely the moment when debates about statehood and personhood became inextricable. "I find the cause of tyranny and wrong everywhere the same," Fuller continues in her dispatch, "—and lo! my Country the darkest offender, because with the least excuse, forsworn to the high calling with which she was called,—no champion of the rights of men, but a robber and a jailer; the scourge hid behind her banner; her eyes fixed, not on the stars, but on the possessions of other men" (*"These Sad but Glorious Days"* 165). Notice the "banner" and its "stars," a trope that recurs across this column. On one hand, Fuller is calling on us to reorient our moral compass and look heavenward. On the other, her language conjures the image of a flag, revised again and again over the nineteenth century, whose symbolic "stars" remind us of states added to a Union that is, in her estimation, "a robber and a jailer" of "possessions," not just "of other men" but of enslaved human lives that were in fact reduced to "possessions."

Fuller is self-conscious—again—of her language and her earlier critiques of abolitionist language in the final lines of this dispatch. "How it pleases me here to think of the Abolitionists!" she cries. "I could never endure to be with them at home, they were so tedious, often so narrow, always so rabid and exaggerated in their tone" (*"These Sad but Glorious Days"* 166). Most critics discuss the first sentence, the exclamation, but not the second, where she returns to modes of expression. Fuller's conclusion is all the more striking since she suggests that she, too, loses control of her own language: "I do not know what I have written. I have merely yielded to my feelings in thinking of America; but something of true love must be in these lines—receive them kindly, my friends; it is, by itself, some merit for printed words to be sincere" (166). But how sincere is she when she claims to have lost control of her own words, when in actuality she's drawing readers' attention to her rhetorical disruption and political disorientation within vulnerable republics, Italy and America?

Our scholarship hasn't addressed the fact that Fuller is so self-conscious about her language in the dispatch now known for its radicalism, despite her perennial concerns for abolitionists. At the end of the letter, she doesn't recognize her own writing. Sara Ahmed might call dispatch 18 Fuller's feminist "snap": the moment when she was outraged enough to claim antislavery rhetoric as her own, even if that isolates her, and even if that makes her feel unlike herself temporarily (188, 200–12). Ahmed describes what she means by "snapping," and, riffing on Marilyn Frye and Sianne Ngai, explains that the "temporality of snapping is . . . crucial" (188). "A snap might seem sudden but the suddenness is only apparent," Ahmed writes; "a snap is one moment of a longer history of being affected by what you come up against" (190). Ahmed's formulation illuminates the transformation, even disidentification, that we witness in Fuller's pause: whatever reasoning may have stopped Fuller's tongue before is overwhelmed by deep feeling. While the idea of a snap is predicated on a kind of intersectional feminism that Fuller never realized, it's clear that she had had enough by January 1848, as the Mexican-American War was ending. By evoking crises in statehood, she aligns herself with turns in mid-century abolitionist rhetoric: the post-1850 outrage that we find in the wake of the Fugitive Slave Law. In ways that she couldn't have anticipated, Fuller's snap documents "a longer history" for this watershed moment in the United States.

Historian, Ambassador, Activist Journalist

In the last two dispatches I'll discuss, Fuller criticizes President Taylor, whose funeral procession appears alongside her obituaries just a year and a half later. As she writes, she anticipates Taylor winning the presidency on the promise of annexation. Fuller criticizes the president because he was elected for being a hero of the Mexican-American War. "I do not deeply distrust my country. She is not dead, but in my time she sleepeth, and the spirit of our fathers flames no more, but lies hid beneath the ashes," Fuller writes. "But it is not the making a President out of the Mexican War that would make me wish to come back. Here things are before my eyes worth recording, and, if I cannot help this work, I would gladly be its historian" (*These Sad but Glorious Days* 230; see note by the collection's editors, Larry Reynolds and Susan Belasco). At one point, Fuller expresses her disappointment in the Pope's uncertain support for the Roman Republic by invoking her own fractured country. "And my country," Fuller writes, "what does she? You have chosen a new President from a Slave State, representative of the Mexican War. But he seems to be honest, a man that can be esteemed, and is one really known to the people; which is a step upward after having sunk last time to choosing a mere tool of party" (245). I want to draw attention to Fuller's tenses—which are always provocative in the deliberate authorial and editorial timelines she crafts within her reports. Even at the moment when she claims an identity as "historian," her tenses shift forward in time, reflecting immediately unstable borderlines and nation-states. Fuller's point about the president from a slave state and the Mexican-American War goes beyond loose allusion, association, or metaphor. Fuller rallies her readership in the United States after the rise and fall of a republic in Italy, when disunion was immediately and violently real.

Fuller concludes one of these antislavery dispatches by envisioning herself as America's "historian" (*These Sad but Glorious Days* 230) and the other as America's "ambassador" (245). Fuller imagines her own diplomatic potential as an ambassador, however coy, as a corrective to Taylor's politics as a general and as the president-elect:

> Pray send here a good Ambassador—one that has experience of foreign life, that he may act with good judgment; and, if possible, a man that has knowledge and views which extend beyond the cause of party politics in the United States; a man of unity in principles, but capable of understanding variety in forms. And send a man capable to prize the luxury of living in, or knowing Rome: it is one that should not be thrown away on a person who cannot prize or use it. Another century, and I might ask to be made Ambassador myself ('tis true, like other Ambassadors, I would employ clerks to do the most of the duty,) but woman's day has not come yet. (245)

Notice the subjects and the cases of verbs in this passage. Fuller's shifts—from the assumed "a man," "a man," "a man" to the singular first-person, and from imperatives to conditionals ("I might" and "I would")—are polite semantic conventions that should reflect her uncertainties about "woman" serving. In fact, the passage suggests just the opposite. For when she shifts tenses, and provisional historical periods, from her immediate moment to "[a]nother century" in that last sentence, she imagines an era when the expectation is not for man but for woman to assume diplomatic leadership. We might read this line in light of *Woman*: Fuller is challenging herself (most immediately) and womankind (more abstractly, as she imagines it in her earlier writing) to assume moral authority. Like the Texas annexation in that 1844 to 1845 revision, the Mexican-American War and the Italian Risorgimento in this 1848 to 1849 dispatch prompt Fuller to imagine a world shaped by woman's moral compass.

Once more, antislavery rhetoric inspires broader musing about woman's capacities to transcend worldly corruption. Fuller implies—through her structure in which a paragraph about the president-elect and his role in the Mexican-American War precedes a paragraph about a not-yet-real ambassador and her role in a not-yet-realized Roman revolution—that this ideal diplomat could connect the dots among mid-century events. What's more, she expects her readers to do the same. In fact, she calls for "a man"—or a woman—"of unity in principles, but capable of understanding variety in forms" (*"These Sad but Glorious Days"* 245). To understand this passage, we have to follow the logic of Fuller's imperialist critique—the thing linking the Mexican-American War to the Roman revolution. What we might read as disruption, at least at first, is transatlantic perspective on Old and New Worlds whose boundaries were increasingly unsettled.

However deferential her indefinite subjects and uncertain tenses may be, it's delightful to take Fuller seriously when she imagines that she might, or she would, represent the United States abroad. As the first woman foreign correspondent, she in fact "has experience of foreign life," having captured the spring and fall of 1848 in print (*"These Sad but Glorious Days"* 245). Fuller's turn from "man" to "woman's day" dramatizes an even greater turn she makes across this paragraph sequence. Her tempered hope that Taylor would improve on Polk is precisely what makes Fuller's "might" and "would" seem so urgent. Fuller's "Ambassador" musing is even more intriguing when we read it alongside her late antislavery writing where she is, as she long was, reluctant to share abolitionists' boldness. By January 1849, Fuller hadn't followed abolitionist pathways she'd long resisted, but she had developed her own ways to write against slavery. She found her voice in foreign correspondence—where she traces precarious borderlines linking democratic crises in Texas, Mexico, and Rome to one another. The constant revision we trace in her expatriate journalism was—and is still— remarkable because it reflects her desire to mediate the most urgent political discussions of her time.

We should study these moments, then, not to celebrate Fuller as the radical abolitionist-feminist we might wish her to be—and that she was not—but to challenge the very ways we read borderlines and nation-states in mid-century texts. In fact, abolitionist reformers did change debates across the ocean just a year and a half later with the Compromise of 1850. The point in reading Fuller's references to the Mexican-American War and North-South divides isn't to compare the Roman revolution to an American civil war still a decade away (or even to suggest that her language precipitated rising sectionalism, as Reynolds argues). Instead, transatlantic reading has the potential to illuminate what we might otherwise dismiss as half-hearted allusions to free-soil politics overseas. Italy transformed how Fuller mapped domestic reform. To do justice to such imperfect reform requires our feminist critical practices to be, at once, intersectional and transnational. That's important now not because Fuller does articulate such a perspective (to call her a first-wave feminist is anachronistic, and to call her intersectional, necessarily linking feminism and abolitionism, just isn't true) but because she doesn't yet have words to name what we now trace across her late writing as a powerful change of mind.

Historicizing and Revising the Future, Inspired by Fuller

Studying Fuller's journalism and not-quite-realized abolitionist rhetoric is more urgent now than ever before. I'll close by outlining what Fuller's antislavery writing provokes readers to do in our own time. Reframing our critical approaches to her late prose has consequences, not just for scholarship related to Fuller's writing but also for our conversations about nineteenth-century activism, feminism, and journalism. Two constellations of issues arise. First, Fuller's journalism provoked her abolitionist turn. And Fuller's self-consciousness about activist language should remind us just how powerful the act of writing for the public was and still is for changing people's minds, including her own. But beyond this, her late archive urges us to consider not just what she reported but also how she reported, and why journalistic contexts matter to understanding issues over time. At a moment when we must be vigilant about the veracity, integrity, and civility of our own news media reading practices, it's useful to remember that the *New-York Daily Tribune* was a Whig paper. I want to circle back to that *Tribune* archive from July 1850, for the reports of congressional debates remind me just how difficult it is to read news from the nineteenth century as news and with sensitivity for its contexts and its authors' and editors' implicit biases, including Fuller's. The passages that are hardest for us to understand should challenge us to read her words and historical contexts with greater precision, even when that reading illuminates what seems unflattering or delayed. Part of what makes Fuller's treatment of slavery so complicated is the fact that she was writing when its abolition was still unrealized, as Martha Schoolman reminds us in her discussion of what we ought to read from this period and how (8). Ultimately, this kind of work also has serious implications for our reading practices as critics and

consumers of the news in our own times. The importance of the news—and of
activist voices in the news—shouldn't be limited to those whose views are confirmed by the verdict of history.

Second, Fuller's abolitionist rhetoric—and her long-held resistance to this
rhetoric—dramatizes philosophical differences that split white feminism and
abolitionism across the long nineteenth century. Fuller's late work can help us
to historicize, and to inspire, critiques of white feminism now. *Woman* may be a
first-wave classic, but, as von Frank notes, Fuller's difficult allegiances to abolition mean that she is missing altogether from some feminist histories (136–37);
and, as Phyllis Cole argues, this may be why both the American Woman Suffrage
Association and the National Woman Suffrage Association claim Fuller's allegiance (14). All of this must be part of Fuller's story—and part of the reception
history that we continue to write for her—if we are to do the kind of educational
justice that Fuller imagines in so much of her work. We shouldn't whitewash
what Fuller did or didn't say on abolition. We also shouldn't minimize how significant it is for a woman to revise her position and her manner of expression
in public. The timeliness of a close reading of the moment when a mother of
white, first-wave feminism was pushed to her limit isn't lost on me. Neither is
the question of whether her particular incrementalism merits academic sussing
out, beyond making white feminism's long silence on the most pressing social
justice crises even more visible. Yet Fuller's late confrontations with abolitionist
rhetoric can redirect the ways we approach our own gaps in feminist scholarship and, more important, feminist pedagogy and activism. When we surface
these tensions—which feel hauntingly relevant in this cultural moment—we
must also reckon with what made Fuller revise herself: a crisis in the idea of the
nation-state that is, at once, local and global, with difficult implications for what
citizenship has the potential to mean. In doing so, I hope, we might be able to
revise ourselves, in all the ways we need to be good and do good for one another
in our own world now.

Notes

1. For perspectives on Fuller and periodical print culture, see Bean and Myerson, Introduction; Di Loreto.

2. Critics are right to distinguish between these rhetorical analogies and the
full-throated rallying cries in Fuller's contemporaries' prose. Bennett's analysis reveals how figures of speech appropriate abolitionist language against patriarchal
oppression (71–72).

3. Many cite New York and Rome as turning points: Kearns 122; Allen 564–69,
Reynolds 41; Steele 161, 174; von Frank 145–46; Bean and Myerson. Fuller's pieces

"New Year's Day" (Bean and Myerson, *Margaret Fuller* 14–19), "Fourth of July" (149–51), "First of August 1845" (183–88), and "1st January, 1846" (323–32) contain the most important antislavery appeals in her New York journalism.

Works Cited

Ahmed, Sara. *Living a Feminist Life*. Duke UP, 2017.

Allen, Margaret. "The Political and Social Criticism of Margaret Fuller." *South Atlantic Quarterly*, vol. 72, 1973, pp. 560–73.

Bailey, Brigitte, et al., editors. *Margaret Fuller and Her Circles*. U of New Hampshire P, 2012.

Bean, Judith Mattson, and Joel Myerson. Introduction. Bean and Myerson, pp. xv–xl.

———, editors. *Margaret Fuller, Critic: Writings from the New-York Tribune, 1844–1846*. Columbia UP, 2000.

Bennett, Michael. *Democratic Discourses: The Radical Abolition Movement and Antebellum American Literature*. Rutgers UP, 2005.

Cole, Phyllis. "The Nineteenth-Century Women's Rights Movement and the Canonization of Margaret Fuller." *ESQ*, vol. 44, no. 1–2, 1998, pp. 1–33.

Delbanco, Andrew. "The Abolitionist Imagination." *The Abolitionist Imagination*, by Delbanco, Harvard UP, 2012, pp. 1–55.

Di Loreto, Sonia. "Margaret Fuller's Transatlantic Vistas: Newspapers and Nation Building." *Transatlantic Conversations: Nineteenth-Century American Women's Encounters with Italy and the Atlantic World*, edited by Beth Lynne Lueck et al., U of New Hampshire P, 2017, pp. 23–37.

Fuller, Margaret. "The Great Lawsuit: Man *versus* Men. Woman *versus* Women." *Norton Anthology of American Literature, 1820–1865*, edited by Nina Baym and Robert S. Levine, 8th ed., W. W. Norton, 2012, pp. 743–79.

———. *"These Sad but Glorious Days": Dispatches from Europe, 1846–1850*. Edited by Larry J. Reynolds and Susan Belasco Smith, Yale UP, 1991.

———. *Woman in the Nineteenth Century*. Edited by Larry J. Reynolds, W. W. Norton, 1997.

Kearns, Francis E. "Margaret Fuller and the Abolition Movement." *Journal of the History of Ideas*, vol. 25, no. 1, Jan.–Mar. 1964, pp. 120–27.

Reynolds, Larry J. *Righteous Violence: Revolution, Slavery, and the American Renaissance*. U of Georgia P, 2011.

Schoolman, Martha. *Abolitionist Geographies*. U of Minnesota P, 2014.

Steele, Jeffrey. "Sympathy and Prophecy: The Two Faces of Social Justice in Fuller's New York Writing." Bailey et al., pp. 161–78.

von Frank, Albert J. "Margaret Fuller and Antislavery: 'A Cause Identical.'" Bailey et al., pp. 128–47.

The Rhetoric of Work and the Work of Rhetoric: Booker T. Washington's Campaign for Tuskegee and the Black South

Paul Stob

Booker T. Washington's legacy is marred by everything from skepticism to condemnation. Around the turn of the twentieth century, many people viewed him as a Moses-like leader for African Americans (Hamilton 38–68). Yet a few critics, most notably W. E. B. Du Bois, rebuked Washington's leadership for supposedly accommodating the segregationist South (50). Building on Du Bois's criticism, scholars of the 1960s, '70s, and '80s effectively dismantled whatever positive assessments may have remained about Washington's work (Dagbovie 246). While a small number of commentators have begun to reevaluate Washington's career (e.g., Jackson; Norrell), his contributions remain contested (e.g., Kirkland; Walters).

Scholars of rhetoric have criticized Washington harshly as well, providing their own evidence that Washington accommodated segregation and proffered a foolhardy compromise with the white South (e.g., Heath; Howard-Pitney; Vivian). This is unfortunate because it is incomplete, if not incorrect, to view Washington as an accommodationist. Elsewhere I have argued that Washington's rhetoric, particularly his infamous Atlanta Exposition address, was not the compromise with segregation that scholars allege (Stob). In this essay, I extend the point by turning to a larger collection of Washington's speeches—specifically those delivered on behalf of the Tuskegee Institute. In a career that bridged the late nineteenth and early twentieth centuries—decades known as the nadir period of civil rights because of how difficult activism was (Bay 188)—Washington deployed a nuanced, sophisticated rhetoric that both sought to reassure white Americans that the status quo would continue and also worked to empower and strengthen Black Americans in their efforts to combat the white establishment. The central idea in this rhetoric was work. Washington spoke endlessly about work, and it allowed him to reach out differently to white and Black listeners. To whites, Washington's rhetoric of work suggested that African Americans would labor on behalf of the American economy and uphold the values of white society.

To African Americans, his rhetoric signaled the chance to seize the South, to build strong Black communities, and to transfer wealth to African Americans across generations.

Ultimately, the point of this analysis is to show how Washington's rhetoric presented different realities to different audiences as Washington charted a careful path through the violence of American society. In charting this path, Washington's rhetoric aimed to empower Black communities across the South and, indeed, the nation. Many of these communities never emerged; the southern Black utopia of which Washington preached never arrived. But that had little to do with Washington's leadership and much to do with the structures of American society, which functioned at every turn to impede empowered Black communities. Thus my goal in this essay is not to trace the effects of Washington's rhetoric. Rather, it is to show how his rhetoric of work, and the work of his rhetoric, carefully and strategically navigated a dire situation without succumbing to the accommodationism that scholars often attribute to him.

To explicate Washington's rhetoric of work, I will first explain his work on behalf of the Tuskegee Institute, as he traveled the country and spread his vision of racial progress to a diverse array of audiences. I will then explore the way his appeals carefully navigated the complex racial politics of the late nineteenth and early twentieth centuries. In the end, I underscore the need to reevaluate Washington's rhetoric and leadership.

Work of Oratory

Founded by a former slave, Lewis Adams, and a former slave owner, Wilbur Foster, the Tuskegee Normal School for Colored Teachers, later renamed the Tuskegee Institute, was just a dream on paper before Booker T. Washington became the Alabama school's first president in 1881 (Norrell 50). Washington, himself a former slave, had been educated at the Hampton Institute in Virginia after emancipation, and he used his experience at Hampton to guide education at Tuskegee. Students at Tuskegee made up what they could not afford in tuition (which was usually all of it) by working on and around campus. They worked in fields to raise the crops that fed the school; in the wood shop to prepare the lumber that framed the school's buildings; in the brickworks to bake the bricks for the buildings' exteriors; in the machine shop to construct and maintain the equipment needed to keep the school running; in the tailor shop to fashion the clothes, linens, and curtains used around campus; and more (Washington, *Working with the Hands* 43–81). Washington built the school on the idea that working with one's hands, in addition to working with one's head and heart, was necessary for learning "the dignity of labor" ("To the Editor" 140).

To keep the "Tuskegee Machine" running, faculty worked just as hard as students (Harlan 254). Faculty worked in classrooms and labored alongside students in fields, mills, and foundries. Washington sometimes joined them as well. But he spent most of his time on the road, working to raise the resources needed for Tuskegee's future; in a typical year, Washington spent around half his time raising money for Tuskegee (Norrell 153). His fundraising tours included plenty of private conversations with wealthy donors, but just as often he delivered speeches and lectures to massive crowds—of African Americans, white Americans, northerners, and southerners—on the important work happening at Tuskegee. The success of these campaigns depended on a network of associates on campus and on the road. On campus, this network included Emmett Scott, his personal secretary; John Washington, his brother and head of industrial operations; and Margaret Murray Washington, his third wife and "Lady Principal" of Tuskegee (Norrell 197). On the road, the network included Charles Fearing, another of Washington's secretaries; Warren Logan, treasurer of the Tuskegee Institute; John H. Palmer, the school's registrar; and Richard Leroy Stokes, yet another secretary. Especially crucial to fundraising was Nathan Hunt, traveling secretary and stenographer. Hunt's tasks involved, among other duties, recording Washington's speeches for posterity (Jackson 80). Though Hunt seldom transcribed every word, he carefully tracked the way Washington made the case for empowering African Americans in the rural South.

Washington's traveling coterie packed his schedule for maximal effect. Consider just a few examples. In a spring 1912 lecture tour, Washington spoke in nine towns in New York, six towns in Pennsylvania, and six towns in Ohio (Wood, Letter [Fearing]). But the number of towns only tells part of the story; he often spoke several times per day in the same locale. In a fall 1912 lecture tour, Washington swung through Michigan on a ten-day campaign, speaking in fifteen different cities. Along the way, he spoke twice in Ypsilanti, twice in Kalamazoo, twice in Grand Rapids, and four times in Detroit (Wood, Letter [Washington]).

Publicity was crucial for these lecture tours. Washington's name usually appeared in large, bold type in newspapers and broadsides, signaling the impending arrival of a historic figure. In Milwaukee, for instance, the Women's Improvement Club printed a large photo of Washington and invited men and women to witness the "elaborate" program planned for this distinguished guest. In Norfolk, Virginia, the Jamestown Exposition's Negro Day promised a keynote address by Washington, along with performances by the Hampton Institute Brass Band and the Fisk Jubilee Singers, and a closing reception featuring a fireworks display. In Atlanta, a flyer announced the "Greatest Meeting of the Races ever held in the South," all planned around a speech by Washington—"The Most Distinguish Man of his Race" and "The Most Popular Orator in America." Joining him on stage would be the mayor of Atlanta, the governor of Georgia, and members of the state legislature, along with musicians, professors, and ministers (Broadsides).

These events were orchestrated to increase the Tuskegee Institute's visibility and to reap sizable donations. Lecture programs usually began with music, followed by introductory remarks from some notable citizen. Then Washington mounted the rostrum and delivered his speech, which he often did from memory or with the help of a brief notecard carried in his coat pocket (Norrell 137). As the speech built toward its conclusion, Washington made the case for the audience to donate to the Tuskegee Institute. To facilitate the donation, Tuskegee staff distributed circulars that contained general information about the school—location, demographics, academics, finances, and ongoing needs—along with several photographs. On the back of the circular was a list of the school's trustees, followed by the most important part: the "form of bequest." The form allowed attendees to donate money on the spot or to pledge themselves to supporting the institution at a later date. "I give and devise to the Trustees of the Tuskegee Normal and Industrial Institute, Tuskegee, Alabama," read the typical bequest form, "the sum of . . . . dollars, payable, etc., Booker T. Washington" (Circulars).

The Tuskegee Machine, as Louis Harlan calls it, needed money, and Washington worked hard to provide it. Relentless scheduling, constant traveling, meeting and greeting notable citizens, pleading for funds, distributing forms of bequest—these campaigns kept Washington at the forefront of public culture and advanced Tuskegee along the way. Looking back, the relentless fundraising can make his efforts seem crass. But it is important to keep the campaigns in perspective. Washington was a college president, and college presidents routinely spend their time raising money. Not many presidents then (or today) traveled on dedicated public-speaking tours to raise funds for their institutions. But Washington was a college president as well as an orator, advocate, and race leader, so his speaking tours allowed him to perform several roles at once. More important, Washington's fundraising efforts aimed ultimately at disrupting and contesting the racial politics of the day. In traveling from Tuskegee to cities and towns across the country, Washington amassed a war chest through the donations of wealthy philanthropists and middle-class citizens. He then brought the money back to the rural South—to the site of enslavement. There, he used the money to build an impressive institution that educated former slaves and their descendants, subsequently sending them out to strengthen themselves, their families, their communities, and their race. In effect, the fundraising campaigns were exercises in wealth redistribution. Tuskegee encouraged its graduates to remain in the South so they could live apart from the white-controlled economic structures of the North and claim the land and resources needed for success across generations. At the same time, the school encouraged graduates to read, think, speak up, and organize for communal and social change. Thus Tuskegee took the wealth of white America and put it to work for African Americans in the South, empowering them as laborers, landowners, and leaders. And it did so without raising the ire of the violent white establishment that surrounded the school in Alabama (Smock 136–47).

Indeed, white audiences in the North and South came away from Washington's speeches convinced of the good work he was doing—or so various newspapers reported. In 1899, the *Detroit Free Press* maintained that "Booker Washington is doing a greater work for the advancement and elevation of his people than was ever done by Fred Douglass. The work of Booker T. Washington is eminently practical and its results are being felt all over the south" ("Working for His People"). In 1904, the *Atlanta Constitution* called a recent Washington speech eloquent and full of "arguments that were endorsed and approved by the large number of White people who hear him. He made the point that the negro should be given protection for life and property, and made a plea for mutual understanding and tolerance between the races" ("Press Thanked by Washington"). In 1906, the *Topeka Plaindealer* concluded that the "solution Washington urges with such adroitness, with such dramatic fervor and yet with such simple and convincing earnestness" makes it "almost impossible for one who hears him to doubt that Dr. Washington's method will succeed" ("Booker Washington").

Instead of seeing Washington's oratorical labor as accommodation, we ought to see it as the pursuit of covert disruption, wealth redistribution, and Black empowerment. He appealed to the American people in a way that got them excited and got them to contribute, then he used their money for education at the Tuskegee Institute and the subsequent creation of Black-owned businesses, banks, neighborhoods, schools, and industries (Denton 106–53). As I explain below, the core of his appeals was the rhetoric of work.

Work in Oratory

Washington's work on the road was matched by a rhetoric of work in his speeches. This rhetoric took several forms. Washington routinely (and unsurprisingly) spoke of the work being done at the Tuskegee Institute, describing the kind of academic and industrial labor undertaken by the student body. At the same time, he deployed a cluster of terms that directly and indirectly involved work, including *labor, toil, effort,* and *jobs,* as well as *hands, arms, brains, bodies,* and *souls.* Further still, he argued that work itself could be rhetorical, as the labor of Black Americans could change the perceptions of white Americans just as well as, and often better than, any kind of logical argument. These appeals combined in his speeches in a way that spoke in different registers to white and Black listeners.

Consider how Washington depicted work in and around Tuskegee. Because his institution was not simply about job training but about academic flourishing as well, he regularly placed labor next to learning, thereby linking work with inquiry and positioning Tuskegee as a new kind of institution. "At Tuskegee," he explained to an audience in Alabama in 1899, "it has been our aim to give the students intelligence, Christian character, to teach them how to make a living by becoming skilled in some industry—to do a common thing in an uncommon way—and to teach them the beauty, dignity, and civilizing power that there is in intelligent labor" (Untitled). "Intelligence" and "intelligent labor" rebuffed the idea, prominent with Du Bois and others, that Washington promoted menial labor at the expense of higher learning. To Washington, however, intelligent labor put Tuskegee on a new course, producing "results" for a world "interested in results"; he continued, during a 1908 address in Atlanta: "Sometimes at the Tuskegee Institute in achieving these results we use the class room; sometimes a farm twenty miles from the class room; sometimes a county fair in a distant county; sometimes we use a text book on arithmetic, sometimes a trowel; sometimes a text book in grammar, or an acre of land planted in turnips" ("Extracts" [Spelman]). Tacking back and forth between academics and labor, Washington highlighted Tuskegee's balanced pedagogy, even working to erase the supposed line between the two. Tuskegee taught people a trade, a skill, how to make a living, and it taught them the same academic subjects they could learn at any college. Tuskegee elevated work into a form of inquiry that developed people's bodies, brains, and futures.

This formulation of work at Tuskegee beckoned to white Americans and Black Americans in different ways. White listeners could hear in Washington's promotion of intelligent labor the ideals they believed necessary for African Americans: industriousness, self-help, hard work, character, intelligence, results. These were supposedly the ideals that the great industrialists of the North, the robber barons of the Gilded Age, had enacted to advance capitalist society. Now, white Americans might believe, African Americans in the South would labor in accord with the dominant culture. But Black listeners could hear something different in Washington's promotion of intelligent labor. Washington affirmed work, but the work was purportedly transformative, facilitating not just prosperity but collective resistance. In the places where the products of their labor had been taken from them during slavery, African Americans could now retain what they produced, secure new wealth, and empower generations. Washington explained the point in a 1902 speech:

Since 1881 the Tuskegee Normal and Industrial Institute has been one of the forces where we have been trying in an humble way to bring about the readjustment of conditions in the South. We are trying to use our organization at Tuskegee of 1400 students, nearly 100 teachers and the instruction given in industrial and academic and religious branches as a means towards fitting thoughts of young men and women to earn their own living through the industries that are open to them in every part of the South, and to make of themselves such useful members of the community where they live that the white people will feel that the education of man or women is of real and potent value in helping forward the interests of the community.   ("Extracts" [New Old South Church])

Educating individuals, sending them into American communities, rebuilding those communities, readjusting the South—these were central to Tuskegee's work, at least in Washington's telling.

Also central to Tuskegee's work was the location of intelligent labor. That is to say, Washington's rhetoric proceeded from and returned to the rural South, and this geographic dimension of his oratory was key to the resistive potential of his efforts. As he explained to an audience in Washington, DC, in 1905, he did not need to concern himself with "the exceptional man," for the exceptional man could make his own way in the world. Instead, he concerned himself "about the masses" (First Joint Commencement)—whom he elsewhere called "the masses of the people in the Black Belt of the South" ("Extracts" [Arlington St. Church]). These individuals, he insisted in an 1893 address to the New York Congregational Club, were the same people who suffered under slavery and now faced "industrial, mental, and moral slavery" ("Speech"). Hoping to lead them out of the new slavery, this Moses of the Progressive Era explained that the "masses of people" thrive in "an out-of-door life, an agricultural life," the kind of life he was trying to cultivate in the rural South ("Commencement Address"). That was why the masses needed to join him at Tuskegee—an institution, he declared in Atlanta in 1908, that has "kept in mind the actual needs and condition of the masses of the Negro people. We have tried as best we could to study their condition and their needs and then adapt our educational system and efforts to meeting and improving these conditions" ("Extracts" [Spelman]).

The Black Belt of the South was appealing to Washington because it afforded African Americans the space—literally—to create what they needed to thrive. In his advocacy, the South offered the masses the chance to reclaim their status as the real producers of the nation's wealth; only this time, unlike with slavery, the masses could retain the fruits of their labor. It was an important point of contrast with the North, especially the urban North, which attracted many African Americans in the late nineteenth and early twentieth centuries. In the urban

North, African Americans had to rent homes in poor, segregated neighborhoods, borrow money from white-owned banks, and send their kids to white-controlled schools. There were certainly fewer lynchings in the North, and fear of violence was not as constant as it may have been in the South. But lynchings and violence were still a reality in the North. Violence was endemic to the capitalist system, as working-class immigrants and industrial laborers were finding out in spades. Washington looked north and saw crime, vice, squalid conditions, and violent labor strikes. African Americans, he believed, should stay in the South and build their own schools, businesses, and communities.

To make the South as appealing as possible to the resistive force he was trying to create, Washington deployed images of cultivation, farming, agriculture, and the pastoral life. African Americans must "become landowners," he insisted ("Extracts" [Men's League of Chicago]). They must work in "the cultivation of the soil, the saving of money, commercial growth, and the skillful and conscientious performances of every duty with which we are entrusted" ("Extracts" [Olivet Baptist Church]). As he announced elsewhere, there is as much dignity in "tilling a field, in working in the shop or in the kitchen as in teaching school, preaching the gospel or writing poetry" ("Extracts" [Steubenville]). That is why, he explained, "We want a little more of the pioneer spirit, that dogged determination that will make us sacrifice, endure hardships, which will make the poor boy willing to go bareheaded, barefooted and without a coat if necessary, and stand there doggedly until he has wrung success out of the soil" ("Dr. Booker T. Washington's Lecture"). As intelligent farmers, hard workers, and determined pioneers, southern African Americans could carry on the American mythos of the past, yet they could use those values to restructure the economics of the South.

The rhetoric of work took still another form in Washington's advocacy. While Washington spoke about labor and work directly, he also insisted that work itself could be a kind of rhetorical practice. When people worked hard, owned their business, owned their home, and laid a material foundation for their advancement, Washington said at a celebration of Abraham Lincoln's birthday in 1896, "these are the kind of arguments that kill prejudice by the acre" ("Address" [Union League]). In 1899, he explained that "[o]bject lessons that shall bring the Southern white man into daily, visible, tangible contacts with the benefits of Negro education will go further in the solution of present problems than all the mere abstract argument and theories that can be evolved from the human brain" ("Extracts" [Springfield]). In 1905, he called on Black listeners to "present year by year to the world, tangible and indisputable evidences of our progress as a people" ("Extracts" [Augusta]). In 1914, he elaborated on the point: "Instead of giving people opportunity to explain why we failed to build a house"—a comment about the problem of explanatory words—"let us build so many houses that the world will forget about the house that we failed to build. One big, definite fact in the direction of achievement and construction will go farther in securing rights and removing prejudice than many printed pages of defense and explanation" ("Address" [Muskogee]). Labor could thus perform the suasory work that words and pages tried to perform, and it could supposedly succeed beyond any oration (a somewhat ironic point, given that his point emerged in an oration).

For Washington, work spoke through laboring Black bodies and the futures they created, through the hands and arms that pushed back against prejudice. But, he reminded listeners time and again, these were the bodies, hands, and arms of former slaves and their descendants. By reclaiming the importance of work in the South, Washington called on African Americans to join in a movement for transforming the structures that oppressed them. The result, he prophesied, would be a new day for the race. "Work more and more in these directions," he told a Black audience in Knoxville, "and neither we nor our children will be dependent upon the uncertainties of seeking for ourselves positions which no man can give nor take from us" ("Delivered at the Conservation Congress"). Far from accommodating segregationism, this work was a call for strengthening Black communities against the oppressive systems of the South.

The upheaval of oppressive systems that Washington depicted in his rhetoric of work never came to pass. Racial violence was widespread, blunting attempts to build strong Black coalitions (Wilson 215). Neither Washington nor any race leader at the time, in the South or the North, was able to upend the systematic racism and injustice of American society. But that does not mean Washington's efforts were wasted, or that he simply acquiesced to southern whites. While many race leaders at the time fled the violent realities of the South and shifted their work to the North, relocating to New York, Chicago, and other northern metropolises (Richardson 14), Washington remained in the South to stay connected to the people, issues, and locales he knew best.

To navigate the racial politics of the time, Washington crafted a language that shaped perceptions of white people and Black people in different, strategic ways. For white people, Washington's rhetoric gave the impression that Black people would perform the menial labor they had long performed in the region and develop the self-reliance, Christian character, and work ethic closely associated with the dominant society. That was why white-run newspapers such as the *Atlanta Constitution* could declare in 1900: "Undoubtedly the Tuskegee Normal and Industrial institute, under the efficient charge of Professor Washington, is doing an excellent work and one which is bound to make itself felt, not only upon the improved status of the negro, but upon the material upbuilding of the south" ("Booker T. Washington's School"). But Washington's rhetoric of work signaled something different to many African Americans: empowerment, progress, and a future in which strong Black communities did not have to bow to white America but could control their own affairs. That was why Black-run newspapers such as the *Colored American* could print in a December 1902 edition a large lithograph that showed Washington above other Black leaders and included the poem: "With the Apostle of common sense, Education as the keystone, the combined forces of Capital, Business, Labor, and Law will form an indestructible archway over the ruins of Negro serfdom. The race in solid array" ("Hang Together").

To be sure, not all Black-run papers applauded Washington, and not all white-run papers celebrated his efforts. In fact, some white southerners saw the supposedly subserve upshot of Washington's advocacy, and they got nervous. The author Thomas Dixon, Jr., wrote an op-ed for the *Saturday Evening Post* in 1905—the same year he published the novel *The Clansman*—exposing Washington's real plans at the Tuskegee Institute:

> Mr. Washington is not training negroes to take their place in any industrial system of the south in which the white man can direct or control him. He is not training his students to be servants and come at the beck and call of any man. He is training them all to be masters of men, to be independent, to own and operate their own industries, plant their own fields, buy and sell their own goods, and in every shape and form destroy the last vestige of dependence on the white man for anything.

Ironically, this bigoted perspective captured exactly what Washington was trying to do. In rallying the masses of the Black Belt of the South, he called on African Americans to secure themselves and their communities through work. The work of African Americans was not to be menial; it was to be empowering, enabling them to seize control of the land and wealth denied them for centuries.

While tracing the actual effects of Washington's rhetoric is impossible, it should be noted that the Tuskegee Institute did indeed send students into communities across the country, North and South, where they were able to prosper. In fact, the Tuskegee University Archives contain hundreds of unpublished profiles of students who attended the school during Washington's tenure and went on to work hard, start their own businesses, buy their own property, and secure the wealth that could help them, their families, and their neighborhoods ("Tuskegee Alumni"). Complete with photographs of alumni smiling brightly in tailored suits and neat dresses outside of their homes, these profiles capture at least part of how the rhetoric of work prepared individuals to seize control of their lives. Trained in the resistive rhetoric of work, the alumni supposedly prospered in big cities and small towns in Illinois, Indiana, and Kentucky as well as

North Carolina, Georgia, and Alabama, among many other states. They worked as nurses, doctors, dentists, lawyers, miners, brick masons, builders, shop owners, and teachers. According to the profiles at least, the Tuskegee alumni seized their place in a violent world. Of course, alumni profiles from every college and university depict a rosy life for graduates. But that ought not to diminish the significance of Tuskegee and Washington's leadership in helping former slaves and their descendants flourish in communities across the country.

Indeed, understanding the resistive potential of Washington's rhetoric brings his leadership into clearer focus. We ought not to mistake his careful rhetorical strategy for some kind of accommodationism or compromise with Jim Crow. Washington well understood that he could raise money from white America and use it for Black America, but only if he spoke in a way that set white America at ease. Excluding his effect on Dixon, Washington was able to do just that with a careful, sophisticated rhetoric of work that propelled him into the position of one of the greatest orators and race leaders in American history.

Works Cited

Bay, Mia. *The White Image in the Black Mind: African-American Ideas about White People, 1830–1925*. Oxford UP, 2000.

"Booker T. Washington's School." *The Atlanta Constitution*, 11 June 1900, p. 4.

"Booker Washington at Cawker City." *Topeka Plaindealer*, 3 Aug. 1906, p. 1.

Broadsides. Booker T. Washington Papers, Manuscript Division, Library of Congress, MSS44669, supplemental file, box 565.

Carroll, Rebecca, editor. *Uncle Tom or New Negro? African Americans Reflect on Booker T. Washington and Up from Slavery 100 Years Later*. Harlem Moon, 2006.

Circulars. Booker T. Washington Papers, Manuscript Division, Library of Congress, MSS44669, supplemental file, box 566.

Dagbovie, Pero Gaglo. "Exploring a Century of Historical Scholarship on Booker T. Washington." *Journal of African American History*, vol. 92, no. 2, 2007, pp. 239–64.

Denton, Virginia Lantz. *Booker T. Washington and the Adult Education Movement*. UP of Florida, 1993.

Dixon, Thomas, Jr. "Booker T. Washington and the Negro." *Saturday Evening Post*, 19 Aug. 1905, p. 2.

Du Bois, W. E. B. *The Souls of Black Folk: Essays and Sketches*. 5th ed., A. C. McClurg, 1904.

Hamilton, Kenneth M. *Booker T. Washington in American Memory*. U of Illinois P, 2017.

"Hang Together or Hang Separately." *The Colored American* [Washington, DC], 6 Dec. 1902, p. 3.

Harlan, Louis R. *Booker T. Washington: The Making of a Black Leader, 1856–1901*. Oxford UP, 1972.

Heath, Robert L. "A Time for Silence: Booker T. Washington in Atlanta." *Quarterly Journal of Speech*, vol. 64, no. 4, 1978, pp. 385–99.

Howard-Pitney, David. "The Jeremiads of Frederick Douglass, Booker T. Washington, and W. E. B. Du Bois and Changing Patterns of Black Messianic Rhetoric, 1841–1920." *Journal of American Ethnic History*, vol. 6, no. 1, 1986, pp. 47–61.

Jackson, David H., Jr. *Booker T. Washington and the Struggle against White Supremacy: The Southern Educational Tours, 1908–1912*. Palgrave Macmillan, 2008.

Kirkland, Avon. "Chapter VII." Carroll, pp. 57–67.

Norrell, Robert J. *Up from History: The Life of Booker T. Washington*. Belknap P / Harvard UP, 2009.

"Press Thanked by Washington." *Atlanta Constitution*, 16 Oct. 1904, p. A3.

Richardson, Riché. *Black Masculinity and the U.S. South: From Uncle Tom to Gangsta*. U of Georgia P, 2007.

Smock, Raymond W. *Booker T. Washington: Black Leadership in the Age of Jim Crow*. Ivan R. Dee, 2009.

Stob, Paul. "Black Hands Push Back: Reconsidering the Rhetoric of Booker T. Washington." *Quarterly Journal of Speech*, vol. 104, no. 2, 2018, pp. 145–65.

"Tuskegee Alumni." Tuskegee U Archives, 2A1.012 copy 1–3.

Vivian, Bradford J. "Up from Memory: Epideictic Forgetting in Booker T. Washington's Cotton States Exposition Address." *Philosophy and Rhetoric*, vol. 45, no. 2, 2012, pp. 189–212.

Walters, Ronald. "Chapter III." Carroll, pp. 25–31.

Washington, Booker T. "Address of Booker T. Washington, President National Negro Business League, Convention Hall, Muskogee, Oklahoma, August 19, 1914." Papers of Booker T. Washington, Tuskegee U Archives, box 118A, folder 16.

———. "Address of Booker T. Washington, Prin., Tuskegee Normal and Industrial Institute, Tuskegee, Ala., before the Union League Club, Brooklyn, Feb. 12, 1896." Papers of Booker T. Washington, Tuskegee U Archives, box 113, folder 6.

———. "A Commencement Address in Washington, DC." 16 June 1905. *The Booker T. Washington Papers*, edited by Louis R. Harlan and Raymond W. Smock, vol. 8, U of Illinois P, 1979, pp. 304–17.

———. "Delivered at the Conservation Congress, Knoxville, Tennessee, Oct. 14, 1913." Papers of Booker T. Washington, Tuskegee U Archives, box 118A, folder 7.

———. "Dr. Booker T. Washington's Lecture at Metropolitan A.M.E. Church (Rev. O.J.W. Scott, D.D., Pastor), on Friday Evening, March 18, 1904." Papers of Booker T. Washington, Tuskegee U Archives, box 115, folder 7.

———. "Extracts from Address Delivered at Steubenville, Ohio, Tuesday Afternoon, Sept. 5, 1911." Papers of Booker T. Washington, Tuskegee U Archives, box 118A, folder 6.

———. "Extracts from Address Delivered by Booker T. Washington at a Banquet Given in His Honor by the Business Men's League of Chicago, Ill., on the Evening of April 5th, 1904." Papers of Booker T. Washington, Tuskegee U Archives, bound speeches volume.

———. "Extracts from Address of Booker T. Washington, Arlington St. Church, December 7." Papers of Booker T. Washington, Tuskegee U Archives, box 115, folder 3.

———. "Extracts from Address of Booker T. Washington at Olivet Baptist Church, 27th & Dearborn St., Chicago, April 5, 1907." Papers of Booker T. Washington, Tuskegee U Archives, bound speeches volume.

———. "Extracts from Address of Booker T. Washington at the New Old South Church, Sunday Evening, December 14, 1902." Papers of Booker T. Washington, Tuskegee U Archives, bound speeches volume.

———. "Extracts from Address of Booker T. Washington before the High School, Springfield, Mass., Mar. 17, 1899." Papers of Booker T. Washington, Tuskegee U Archives, box 114, folder 15.

———. "Extracts from Address of Booker T. Washington before the Society for the Promotion of Industrial Education, Spelman Seminary, Atlanta, Ga., November 20, 1908." Papers of Booker T. Washington, Tuskegee U Archives, bound speeches volume.

———. "Extracts from Address of Booker T. Washington, Delivered in Augusta, Ga., January 2, 1905." Papers of Booker T. Washington, Tuskegee U Archives, box 116, folder 3.

———. First Joint Commencement. Armstrong Manual Training School. 1905. Booker T. Washington Papers, Manuscript Division, Library of Congress, MSS44669, box 542.

———. "A Speech before the New York Congregational Club." *The Booker T. Washington Papers*, edited by Louis R. Harlan, vol. 3, U of Illinois P, 1974, pp. 279–88.

———. "To the Editor of the *Southern Workman*." *The Booker T. Washington Papers*, edited by Louis R. Harlan, vol. 2, U of Illinois P, 1972, pp. 140–41.

———. Untitled speech. Alabama. 1899. Papers of Booker T. Washington, Tuskegee U Archives, box 114, folder 2.

———. *Working with the Hands*. Doubleday, Page, 1904.

Wilson, Kirt. "The Racial Contexts of Public Address: Interpreting Violence during the Reconstruction Era." *The Handbook of Rhetoric and Public Address*, edited by Shawn J. Parry-Giles and J. Michael Hogan, Wiley-Blackwell, 2010, pp. 203–28.

Wood, Charles W. Letter to Booker T. Washington. 12 Oct. 1912. Booker T. Washington Papers, Manuscript Division, Library of Congress, MSS44669, departmental file, box 674.

———. Letter to Charles Fearing. 22 Feb. 1912. Booker T. Washington Papers, Manuscript Division, Library of Congress, MSS44669, departmental file, box 674.

"Working for His People." *Detroit Free Press*, 29 Jan. 1899, p. C8.

"Nasty" Women, Progressive Causes, and the Rhetorical Refusals of Lillie D. White

Wendy Hayden

> In the good time coming, what a cause of wonder it will be to recall the fact that the champions of freedom, the most progressive men of the nineteenth century, denied women the right of free speech in an anti-slavery convention. . . . I am at the boiling point! If I should not find some day the use of my tongue on this question, I shall die of intellectual repression, a woman's rights convulsion.
>
> —Elizabeth Cady Stanton

> Among the greatest challenges faced by the women's movement in all its iterations has been the structural difficulty of persuading women to express sustained, public anger toward their most direct oppressors: men.
>
> —Rebecca Traister, *Good and Mad*

The 2016 presidential election narrative touts the story of the angry white man: the Donald Trump voter who deserves empathy, the Bernie Sanders supporter who feels wronged. The angry white man in this narrative could be as angry as he wanted. Hillary Clinton, however, was not allowed to express the same anger: not at the media who dismissed her hordes of supporters by reporting a lack of enthusiasm for her candidacy, not for being the most qualified candidate facing a vastly unqualified opponent, not at the centuries it took for a woman candidate to appear on the ballot, not at the lack of attention to her policy proposals, and not at the man invading her personal space as she tried to elucidate those proposals at a town hall–style debate. In her memoir *What Happened*, Clinton muses: "Maybe I have overlearned the lesson of staying calm—biting my tongue, digging my fingernails into a clenched fist, smiling all the while, determined to present a composed face to the world" (136–37). Men, conservative and progressive, are allowed to be angry and shout without being labeled shrill, or a "nasty woman," or accused of "playing the [gender] card." Clinton had to suppress her anger—even toward progressive men—until, she says, "I felt like I was in a straitjacket" (230).

The nineteenth-century feminist Lillie D. White would not be surprised at the criticisms feminist women receive today, particularly those criticisms leveled by progressive men that argue that focusing on gender perpetrates, in their derisive spin on the term, "identity politics." White described such male progressives in a speech titled "Woman's Dangerous Friends." A supporter of anarchism and free thought, White attempted to highlight the role of gender in economics, labor reform, and marriage, among other issues. Her 1893 speech "The Coming Woman" exemplifies the rhetorical challenges of feminist arguments during moments of tension and backlash among progressive men and women, both then and now—over gender roles, economics, sex, parenthood, women's places, and women's voices. The speech's central argument is a repudiation of an ideology of separate spheres. The speech attacks progressive social movements that ignore the lived realities of women, criticizes how even radical and progressive movements still expect women to fit into certain roles, urges women to resist any ideologies that reduce them to their roles as mothers, and calls for progressive men to become better allies to women.

Radical, iconoclastic, and confrontational, White does not fit in any of the molds ascribed to nineteenth-century women, even among the more revolutionary feminists of the time. White contested these molds, recognizing that none opened the door for her vision of "the coming woman," and thus crafted her speech as a series of what John Schilb calls "rhetorical refusals": when a rhetor "pointedly refuses to do what the audience considers rhetorically normal" (3). Analyzing "The Coming Woman" with this concept reveals White's defiant rhetorical moves. White resists femininity, calling gender differences "humbug" (*Coming Woman*) and rejecting the appeals we call a feminine style of rhetoric. She resists consistency, recognizing that ideas need to grow and change according to the circumstances. She resists likability, using her sarcasm and anger to chastise progressive men. She resists the expectations of the speech with its title, offering redefinitions of manhood rather than womanhood. The criticisms White received correlate to criticisms of Clinton, from her likeability to her growth on certain issues, which comes across as a lack of consistency. White reclaims these criticisms as positive in her rhetorical refusal, adopting what some would believe to be an unlikeable persona and a lack of consistency.

Never a force in the organized movements for suffrage and mainstream women's rights organizations, White's speech may seem unimportant in accounts of activist rhetoric of the late nineteenth century. However, her speech provides insight into the rhetorical outliers of this era, particularly anarchist feminists. She rejects the common feminist topoi of the era: the argument from justice and the argument from expediency, or arguments based on natural rights versus arguments based in women's supposed higher virtues. Both lines of argument did not serve White's agenda. White's rhetoric is more in line with the moves identified in Emma Goldman's work by scholars Kate Zittlow Rogness and Christina R. Foust. These scholars show how Goldman's rhetoric of free love, in rejecting the arguments from both justice and expediency, hints at later feminist theories of intersectionality (160). Similarly, White's speech demands that gender be accounted for in discussions of economics, social class, and politics, just as economics and social class must be accounted for in discussions of gender.

Playing the Woman Card

White came from a progressive family which included her mother, Hannah Hunt, a radical feminist who joined the Berlin Heights free love community (Passet 154); her brother, C. F. Hunt, who also wrote about radical causes; and her sister, Lizzie Holmes, who joined White in her activism and is more well known because of her association with the 1886 Haymarket Square protests in Chicago. White and her siblings were all frequent contributors to anarchist and free love periodicals. Though much of her life remains elusive, I was able to piece together some details through her articles and snippets in secondary sources (see Passet; McElroy). White was married at least once and had at least one son ("Light Bearer Library"). She resided in Halstead, Kansas, as well as in Chicago ("Letters from Friends"; "Various Voices"); served as secretary of the Kansas Freethinkers' Association (Rowbotham 118); and worked with Matilda Joslyn Gage to form the Liberal Suffrage Association in 1890 ("Notes and News"). This organization probably became Gage's Woman's National Liberal Union, which aimed to attract women interested in working for women's rights beyond suffrage (Grube). White and Lizzie Holmes were active in labor reform groups and brought women's issues to the forefront when, in the early 1880s, they worked in a factory where they organized "the first strike of women workers in Chicago history" (McKinley 400). The strike lasted only a few hours, after which all but White and Holmes returned to work (McKinley 400).

White became editor of the free love periodical *Lucifer, the Light Bearer* from 1892 to 1893 while its incumbent editor, Moses Harman, was imprisoned for obscenity. White used her time as editor to shed light on what she saw as the idealism of many free love advocates. Her contributions to *Lucifer* and to other periodicals illuminate the rhetorical moment "The Coming Woman" responds to. Though she supported free love as a protest to the ways women are oppressed through marriage, "The Coming Woman" responds to the progressives whose calls for women's "sexual self-ownership" increasingly focused on women's roles as mothers. White thus used the occasion of this speech to point out the hypocrisy of these freethinkers.

White emphasized economic inequality in her free love rhetoric. To her, free love is not the answer to women's inequality unless it also recognized "the financial independence of woman; not until she is a self-reliant, self-supporting, independent human being can she really be man's equal, and be to him a true companion" ("Love and Finance"). White even attacks idealistic notions of love that were popular with free love proponents: "I do not believe it possible for a deep and enduring love or even friendship to exist between any two people, when one is in comfortable circumstances and the other making a desperate daily struggle for existence, [and] 'working for a pittance'" ("Love and Finance"). She asks women to demand more than professions of love: "Love that is only expressed in sweet words, pet names, caresses, etc., and which flies away when anything practical is to be done, can not be very deep or sincere. Kisses are all very well but bread and cheese are not to be despised" ("Love and Finance"). Her writing on progressive causes may be accused of playing the woman card, like Clinton was, by pointing out the sexism of many who claim to support women's rights and by insisting that gender issues be intertwined with other progressive causes.

"Nasty" Woman

"The Coming Woman" was delivered several times during the 1890s, initially in October 1893 to the International Congress of Freethinkers in Chicago and later to the International Liberal Congress of 1898 ("Light Bearer Library"). The audience for this speech comprised progressives who frequently denounced the bondage marriage creates for women. But the speech's structure and tone reveal that all was not what it seemed among progressives.

She begins the speech with, "It is almost impossible to consider woman apart from her wrongs. To select woman as a topic for a discourse generally means to recount the story of her degradation and slavery" (*Coming Woman* 3). One might expect White to then enumerate these wrongs. Instead, she seems to refute the charge that women are the victims of men, and clarifies that there are "[i]ntelligent, broad-minded men of progressive thought . . . working earnestly for the emancipation and equality of woman" (3–4). Her opening statements acknowledge that her hearers are the progressive-minded men she speaks of; she says that the wrongs some men have done to women "can not be reproved in an audience of advanced minds like this" (3). It would seem White is attempting to evoke a shared value between herself and her audience. Carolyn Skinner explains how "the rhetor can construct her audience as sharing [her] values. . . . In the body of the speech, she can describe her audience as people who . . . implicitly share her sense of the most important virtues" (242). Schilb notes how rhetorical refusals often ask the audience to accept the values the rhetor prioritizes (3). The rhetor, in Schilb's estimation, evokes two different audiences through a rhetorical refusal: a group that expects the status quo and a second that does not: "The refuser begins by assuming that his or her actual audience is the first group. The refuser then tries to show that this group's reasoning is limited. More generally, the refuser works at converting the actual audience into the second group" (39). In "The Coming Woman," White uses sarcasm to depict how the second group is actually the first group.

Though White is speaking to progressives, an audience who seemingly shares her values, she also sarcastically attributes values to them that they do not in fact have. For example, White praises the values of the "true liberal" man, who, she says,

> does not mark out lines and spheres nor define womanly virtues nor avocations. He recognizes woman's right to grow freely, to engage in whatever occupation she chooses, to cultivate and develop every faculty and talent she possesses and he does not denounce her if she fails to grow into his ideal of womanliness. He never presumes on his power over her as granted by church and state. . . . He admits her perfect right to control her . . . person in all ways, and so it is, of course, impossible to find tyrannical monsters or poor abused . . . [women] among freethinkers. (*Coming Woman* 4–5)

The sarcasm in her speech is not always obvious, but, within the context of the particular rhetorical situation she responds to, we can see she is exactly charging these men with the very views she says they could not possibly hold, a reading confirmed by the articles she wrote in *Lucifer*, where she charged male free love advocates with replacing one restricting ideal of womanhood with another equally restricting ideal.

After criticizing the church's subjugation of women, White moves into enumerating the stereotypes of separate spheres for men and women. The qualities of each sphere, she argues, tend to subjugate women, and she rejects any characterizations of women that position them as "angels of the household" or "man's guide and sustainer" and cautions progressives against accepting ideologies "masked by pretty coverings and nice-sounding terms" (7). She engages in a rhetorical refusal by implying that her own rhetoric will not be masked by such "pretty coverings" and thus implicitly announces her intention to use more angry rhetoric, including sarcasm, denouncing the social systems that value women for their higher virtues in the process.

In attacking an ideology of separate spheres, White attacks the logic used to keep women from the workplace, a place where, she argues, women could thrive and become financially independent and thus equal with men. Yet, White is not heralding the workplace as women's salvation. For example, she elaborates on what she calls the "wage slavery" women encounter in the workplace:

When we consider the obstacles and disadvantages woman must meet in the industrial world, the question presents itself, if she is the gainer by exchanging the obscurity and safety of the fireside, with possibly a kind master, for the evils of wage slavery. Her advent into the competitive field of industry has apparently caused much mischief, not only with the ideal of domestic womanliness, but with her brother's position. She has taken his place, lowered his wages, crowded him into the ranks of the unemployed; for as a 'foreign element' she must offer to work cheaper and consent to live on less.

(*Coming Woman* 8–9)

When her fellow progressives criticized the economic conditions of women, they often focused on economic conditions within marriage, equating women's need to marry for economic protection to prostitution. White brings attention to working women and tries to shift the dialogue on women and economics within progressive, anarchist, and free love discourse. She analyzes the logic used to devalue the work women do, logic still used today against what are considered feminine jobs. She points out how progressives need to look more closely at gender, just as today progressives focus on economic inequality often without accounting for gender or race.

The rest of White's "Coming Woman" speech details the harms done by voluntary-motherhood arguments espoused by progressive men and women to support eugenics. Eugenic rhetoric had been part of the philosophy of free love since the free love communes of the mid–nineteenth century, and the 1870s and '80s saw women using new sciences to support these arguments (see Hayden). White resisted eugenic arguments because they reinforced the conservative belief that women's highest function is motherhood. Thus, White says, these arguments replace a focus on women bearing children for "god" or "the husband" to bearing children for the good of the "community" or "race": "I deny that gods, husbands, communities, or the race, have any claim whatever on woman's maternal functions or that she owes them any duty in that line" (*Coming Woman* 25). She in turn rejects values many progressives supported in basing their arguments for women's sexual rights on the superiority of the children these women would bear. The last ten pages of the forty-one-page published text of the speech consist of arguments breaking down gender dichotomies and rejecting stereotypes to prove that "[t]he coming woman repudiates spheres, departments, and lines" (19).

White's speech violates several expectations in supporting her attacks on social institutions. For example, her argument does not employ a justification for women taking traditionally masculine roles in industry; she instead blurs the boundaries between masculine and feminine. She notes how men can "cook, bake, wash, iron, sew . . . keep house and take care of babies," and shows how women have already taken what many consider masculine roles (*Coming Woman* 11–12). She redefines manhood rather than womanhood to reveal the artificiality of gender.

White's speech also violates expectations in its tone and style. She lacks a personal tone or evidence from personal experience, qualities usually associated with the feminine style that historians of women's rhetoric find popular with other women rhetors of the time. White, a labor reformer who worked in factories, uses no examples from her own personal life or experiences with labor organizing, and she rarely employs the first person in the speech. White's call for the professionalization of women explains her choice of ethical appeals. She presents herself as the independent, self-reliant woman she describes. Her speech is also self-reliant, and "the coming woman" thus does not need to justify her speech or give her credentials. If there is a personal aspect to this speech, it is her sarcastic tone.

White's use of sarcasm to actually indict the audience she praises is not always clear within the context of the speech. However, looking at the speech as a response to shifts in progressive rhetoric during this time explains her choices. A year before she first delivered "The Coming Woman," she gave a speech to the Kansas Freethinkers' Association that named both the church and "progressive men" as "woman's dangerous friends," the title of the speech. She says of these men:

> The true reformer of to-day, woman's true friend, will labor to remove the chains of bondage fastened upon her by the ignorance and tyranny of the past; but they will not make new moulds, they will not build ideas of womanly perfection and then bewail the loss of her feminine virtues if she does not conform to or fulfill them. Her true friends will work to make her *free* let the result be what it will. They will not mourn if she smashes every cherished ideal of womanly perfection. ("Woman's Dangerous Friends")

Some progressives, however, likely misinterpreted her tone and goals. In a letter written in 1901, White responds to fellow progressive Elmina Slenker's praise of "The Coming Woman": "Elmina believes that evolution will prove the superiority of the female, and says so in a letter in which she writes quite approvingly of . . . 'The Coming Woman.' The one point in my paper, if it has a point, is the injustice and wrong of considering woman superior to man, as it is to assume man's superiority to woman. . . . She can hardly endorse 'The Coming Woman' if she believes that woman is man's superior" (White, "Men, Women and Emotions").

White frequently debated free lovers who extolled the virtues of love instead of acknowledging women's actual experiences. She believed some progressives to be more focused on celebrating women rather than enacting actual reforms:

"Woman gains nothing by these eulogistic rhapsodies. . . . Eulogies and praises in song, poetry and romance, are lavishly bestowed upon woman in lieu of justice" ("Woman's Dangerous Friends"). One letter reacting to her statement that contented wives did not need the reformers' efforts calls her "truly manlike" (A.C.). The same statement prompted a characterization of White's work as "a queer jumble of contradictory statements" (Austin). She feuded with Victoria Woodhull Martin, whose values of free love and feminism became the foundation for the values of the anarchists who wrote in *Lucifer*. White criticized Woodhull for her turn toward arguments that White believed were "teaching woman her duty" to have children to serve "the community or the good of the race." White writes: "am I nothing in myself? Are my talents and abilities, my understanding and devotion to a useful work, my love of study and achievements of excellence, all of secondary importance to my powers of reproduction? Is that my highest value?" ("The Mother Question").

White's use of biting sarcasm alienated some progressives. Edwin C. Walker, founder of *Lucifer*, criticized White as not having "learned the proper use and relation of words" (qtd. in White, "Charge of Cannibalism"), and she parodied his writing with a sarcastic rant on whether women are free to love whom they wish:

> a woman might choose and be perfectly free to love E.C. Walker, but, should she speak her love in sentences not rounded and polished up to his critical standard of excellence, it is easy to see that, whether she "elect" or not, she would be driven away, for with him personal respect or friendship or love weigh very lightly in the balance against his contempt for people who in his opinion "have not learned the proper use and relation of words."   ("Charge of Cannibalism")

Perhaps the nastiest feud of White's occurs in letters in *Lucifer* and the anarchist periodical *Liberty* with anarchist Victor Yarros over his negative review of a book White had reviewed positively. Yarros calls White "a shrew"—"weak-minded," "frantic and abusive and ridiculous"—whose writings indicate "brainlessness," "stupidity," and the "talk of hysterical imbeciles"; clearly White's anger and sarcasm did not endear her to all progressive men.

I see "The Coming Woman" speech as similar to Elizabeth Cady Stanton's "The Solitude of Self" in many ways. Describing Stanton's speech, Karlyn Kohrs Campbell notes how the speech rejects "progress towards a utopian state" and reveals "an element of absurdity in all reform efforts" (310). White herself said in an 1893 article that "[r]emedies are always impractical and utopian" ("Woman's Work"). White's speech also recalls Campbell's assessment of Stanton's speech as "violating nearly all traditional canons" with its lack of cohesive argument, evidence, or structure (Campbell 305). White, responding to Slenker's praise, admits the flaws of her own argument when she characterizes "The Coming Woman" as possibly lacking an overall point ("Men, Women and Emotions"). White answers criticism that she is inconsistent in her views by affirming that she is in fact inconsistent. She exclaims, "I refuse even to be consistent when consistency stands in the way of my happiness," and adds, "We have discarded obedience, submission, chastity and many other erstwhile virtues from our list of admirable human qualities—there may be more to follow. It is not always wise or best to be consistent" ("Old and the New"). I do, however, see consistency in her work: a refusal to be classified. She is the coming woman she describes, and "[t]he coming woman repudiates spheres, departments, and lines" (*Coming Woman* 19).

"Nevertheless, She Persisted"

"The Coming Woman" is an angry speech. Schilb explains, "By rejecting a procedure that the audience expects, the rhetor seeks the audience's assent to another principle, cast as a higher priority" (3). For White, her repudiations of progressives are more important than unity among radical outliers. Unity was a lofty value of progressives in the 2016 presidential campaign, which led to the dismissal of women's issues as identity politics and the belief that unity is more important than calling out sexism or racism.

Yarros, in a familiar charge, accuses White of trying to silence anyone who disagrees with her (2). White's anger and sarcasm did not spare those who disagreed with her, but I have not found any references to her avoiding printing certain letters when she was editor of *Lucifer* or shouting down or preventing speakers with differing views from making their points. Nor have I seen the kind of insults hurled at her by Yarros used in her own writings; she prefers the thinly veiled "dashing vein of sarcasm" ("Daughters of Cain"). The contemporary charge that criticism equals silencing has a history as well.

The parallels of White's rhetorical situation with contemporary debates on gender, race, "identity politics," and progressive unity reveal qualities of moments of backlash among progressives, from the progressive men who bemoan what they call political correctness to those who insist that all views are needed to create balance (i.e., both-sides-ism) while calling for civility, characterizing justifiable anger, or calling out racism or sexism as impolite. Schilb notes how the rhetorical refusal is especially transgressive in a climate of "openness to debate" (77). But this openness to debate can mean giving equal weight to views undeserving of it. Should the marginalized object to this principle on these grounds and engage in such a rhetorical refusal, they are called out for allegedly violating freedom of speech and contributing to a culture of incivility. Yet, it is often those charging others with incivility who bring the debate down to such levels. Sarcasm can often be the best tool left for these marginalized rhetors: sarcasm can appeal to those audiences who "count on protocols being followed" (Schilb 39) by seemingly accepting the audiences' values while indicting those values and inviting those in the audience who "accept the refuser's break with custom" (Schilb 39) to share in the rhetor's anger.

Anger, then, can be a luxury. Take, for example, the political writer Rebecca Traister's analysis of the demeanor of men and women at the Brett Kavanaugh hearings, noting that Christine Blasey Ford did not appear angry or raise her voice while detailing her sexual assault, while Kavanaugh "bellowed; he snarled; he pouted and wept furiously at the injustice of having his ascendance to power interrupted by accusations of sexual assault." Traister concludes of the distinction, "Fury was a tool to be marshaled by men like Judge Kavanaugh and Senator Graham, in defense of their own claims to political, legal, public power. Fury was a weapon that had not been made available to the woman who had reason to question those claims" ("Opinion"). Traister, the author of *Good and Mad: The Revolutionary Power of Women's Anger*, shows how "[w]hat happened inside the [court]room was an exceptionally clear distillation of who has historically been allowed to be angry on their own behalf, and who has not" ("Opinion").

Traister's historical account of women's anger and Clinton's defiantly calm demeanor indicate that the rhetorical refusal twenty-first-century women perform may not be the refusal to be constrained by feminine speech—White's refusal—but a refusal to be painted with the angry feminist brush or to play into stereotypes of women as too emotional: not getting angry is the twenty-first-century woman's rhetorical refusal. Though anger at women's wrongs, as White calls them, has provoked many feminist movements and reformers, it has also at times set women back or turned to the wrong target, such as when Stanton reached her "boiling point" over suffrage being granted to former male slaves before women ("Letter"). Stanton got angry and turned to racist arguments. White got angry and was forgotten.

Thus, perhaps it is anger that helps women as a group advance and correct their wrongs rather than individual "nasty" women. Traister contrasts the lack of anger expressed by Ford inside the Kavanaugh hearing to the women "incandescent with rage and sorrow and horror" gathering outside the hearing, anger that successfully caused support within the Senate for an FBI investigation of the allegations against Kavanaugh ("Opinion"). On the other hand, Elizabeth Warren's willingness to show anger is part of her populist style: if the masses are angry, she will be angry on their behalf. Yet, as an individual woman, she is portrayed as a "scold" by *The New York Times* (Traister, *Good and Mad* 56) and was told to be silent when speaking on the Senate floor, but "nevertheless, she persisted," an expression originally in reference to Warren that became a rallying cry for feminists' refusal to be silent.

Anger can start the resistance, but individual rhetors from marginalized populations may not always succeed if they allow that anger to dominate their rhetoric. So while anger at injustice was the root of activist rhetorics of the nineteenth century, particularly feminist rhetorics, and it is the cause driving the resistance today, not all are entitled to express that anger and some must mask their rhetoric with "pretty coverings and nice-sounding terms" (White, *Coming Woman* 7). Therefore, as then, so now, women activists can attempt to develop rhetorical strategies that do not call down the criticism leveled at angry hysterics. Or they can take a page from White's book and refuse to abide by the conventions that their righteous anger should not be expressed.

Works Cited

A.C. "Contented Wives—and Others." *Lucifer, the Light Bearer*, vol. 4, no. 13, 7 Apr. 1900, p. 102.

Austin, Kate. "The Uplifting Process." *Lucifer, the Light Bearer*, vol. 4, no. 15, 21 Apr. 1900, p. 115.

Campbell, Karlyn Kohrs. "Stanton's 'The Solitude of Self': A Rationale for Feminism." *Quarterly Journal of Speech*, vol. 66, no. 3, 1980, pp. 304–12.

Clinton, Hillary Rodham. *What Happened*. Simon and Schuster, 2017.

Grube, Melinda. "The Religious Freedom Room." *Matilda Joslyn Gage Foundation*, 2009, matildajoslyngage.org/about-the-gage-home/.

Hayden, Wendy. *Evolutionary Rhetoric: Sex, Science, and Free Love in Nineteenth-Century Feminism*. Southern Illinois UP, 2013.

"Letters from Friends." *Lucifer, the Light Bearer*, vol. 4, no. 40, Jan. 1887, p. 4.

"Light Bearer Library, No. 8." *Lucifer, the Light Bearer*, vol. 4, no. 39, 6 Oct. 1900, p. 39.

McElroy, Wendy. *Individualist Feminism of the Nineteenth Century: Collected Writings and Biographical Profiles*. McFarland, 2001.

McKinley, Blaine. "Holmes, Lizzie May Swank." *Women Building Chicago 1790–1990: A Biographical Dictionary*, edited by Rima Lunin Schultz and Adele Hast, Indiana UP, 2001, pp. 400–02.

"Notes and News." *Woman's Exponent*, vol. 18, no. 18, 1890, p. 140.

Passet, Joanne E. *Sex Radicals and the Quest for Women's Equality*. U of Illinois P, 2003.

Rogness, Kate Zittlow, and Christina R. Foust. "Beyond Rights and Virtues as Foundation for Women's Agency: Emma Goldman's Rhetoric of Free Love." *Western Journal of Communication*, vol. 75, no. 2, 2011, pp. 148–67.

Rowbotham, Shelia. *Dreamers of a New Day: Women Who Invented the Twentieth Century*. Verso, 2011.

Schilb, John. *Rhetorical Refusals: Defying Audience's Expectations.* Southern Illinois UP, 2007.

Skinner, Carolyn. "'She Will Have Science': *Ethos* and Audience in Mary Gove's *Lectures to Ladies.*" *Rhetoric Society Quarterly*, vol. 39, no. 3, Summer 2009, pp. 240–59.

Stanton, Elizabeth Cady. "Letter to Susan B. Anthony, Seneca Falls, April 2, 1852." *Elizabeth Cady Stanton as Revealed in Her Letters, Diaries, and Reminiscences*, edited by Theodore Stanton and Harriot Stanton Blatch, vol. 2, Harper and Brothers, 1922, pp. 38–42. *Internet Archive*, archive.org/details/elizabethcadyst00blatgoog.

———. "The Solitude of Self: Address to the U.S. Congressional Committee of the Judiciary Hearing: January 18, 1892." *Gifts of Speech*, gos.sbc.edu/s/stantoncady1.html.

Traister, Rebecca. *Good and Mad: The Revolutionary Power of Women's Anger.* Simon and Schuster, 2018.

———. "Opinion: Fury Is a Political Weapon. And Women Need to Wield It." *The New York Times*, 29 Sept. 2018, nytimes.com/2018/09/29/opinion/sunday/fury-is-a-political-weapon-and-women-need-to-wield-it.html.

"Various Voices." *Lucifer, the Light Bearer*, vol. 3, no. 30, 5 Aug 1899, p. 239.

White, Lillie D. "A Charge of Cannibalism." *Liberty (Not the Daughter but the Mother of Order)*, vol. 8, no. 3, 30 May 1891, p. 7.

———. *The Coming Woman.* M. Harman, 1900.

———. "Daughters of Cain." *Foundation Principles*, vol. 4, no. 2, Aug. 1893, p. 6.

———. "Love and Finance." *Lucifer, the Light Bearer*, vol. 3, no. 41, 19 Aug. 1899, p. 250.

———. "Men, Women and Emotions." *Lucifer, the Light Bearer*, vol. 4, no. 51, 14 Jan. 1901, p. 4.

———. "The Mother Question." *Lucifer, the Light Bearer*, vol. 9, no. 49, 11 Nov. 1892, p. 2.

———. "The Old and the New." *Lucifer, the Light Bearer*, vol. 4, no. 9, 10 Mar. 1900, p. 70.

———. "Woman's Dangerous Friends." *Lucifer, the Light Bearer*, vol. 9, no. 44, 7 Oct. 1892, p. 3.

———. "Woman's Work." *Lucifer, the Light Bearer*, vol. 10, no. 8, 27 Jan. 1893, p. 2.

Yarros, Victor. "Taming a Shrew." *Liberty (Not the Daughter but the Mother of Order)*, vol. 9, no. 26, 25 Feb. 1893, p. 2.

More Than Mere Display: Susie King Taylor's *Reminiscences of My Life in Camp with the 33d United States Colored Troops*

Patty Wilde

When Susie King Taylor published *Reminiscences of My Life in Camp with the 33d United States Colored Troops* in 1902,[1] the *Boston Sunday Post* declared it to be "a somewhat remarkable book," explaining that "Mrs. Taylor is a colored woman who . . . was a nurse all through the war of the Rebellion and her book, just published, details the story of her experiences during war times" ("Mrs. Susie King Taylor"). Taylor's autobiographical account is indeed unique in that it celebrates the efforts the she and many African Americans made on behalf of the Union during the American Civil War. As Catherine Clinton observes, it is "the *only* published account by a Black woman serving with the military during the Civil War" (ix–x; emphasis added). Although Taylor wrote her narrative at a time when "[b]oth Yankee and Confederate veterans had begun to capitalize on the interest in Civil War exploits, and partisan publications blossomed" (Clinton vii), far different exigencies motivated her to go public with her war experiences. In addition to providing an invaluable written record of her work for the Union, Taylor describes the injustices that people of color experienced post-Reconstruction when their newly acquired rights were rolled back, particularly in the South. Contrasting the sacrifices African Americans made on behalf of the Union with the poor treatment they experienced in postbellum times, she makes visible to her largely northern, white audience the racial hypocrisies of the United States. In this way, as I discuss in this essay, Taylor's memoir participates in the epideictic tradition of rhetoric that mirrors back to audiences their values and beliefs in an effort to transform them.

Although the form precedes him, Aristotle was "the first to isolate the notion of epideictic rhetoric" as one of the three branches of discourse, Laurent Pernot maintains (3). In contrast to the deliberative and forensic modes, Aristotle believed that the epideictic was principally concerned with the present and sought to "prais[e] or censur[e]" to affirm what is honorable or disgraceful (I.3, 1358b 12–18). As its etymological roots suggest, the purpose of the epideictic was to exhibit, to show, to display. Rather than cast a vote or reach a verdict, audiences were called to listen and observe. Because it requires no immediate action, the epideictic has historically been given short shrift. Although such dismissive perspectives still linger today, this rhetorical approach has recently undergone a resurgence that has elevated its status. As Jeffrey Walker explains, the epideictic "shapes the fundamental grounds, the 'deep' commitments and presuppositions, that will underlie and ultimately determine decision and debate in particular pragmatic forums" (*Rhetoric and Poetics* 9). More than mere display, this branch of rhetoric has the power to create, confirm, and disrupt established codes and conventions, as exemplified by Taylor's personal account. In praising the social and martial accomplishments of African Americans, she brings greater attention to the racial discrimination that they experienced in the post-war United States.

Epideictic, Autobiography, and Ethos

While the epideictic is traditionally associated with ceremonial genres such as funeral orations, birth announcements, and wedding speeches, Marjorie O'Rourke Boyle and Kristie Fleckenstein have demonstrated that autobiographical works also share similar rhetorical features.[2] Self-referential texts, Sidonie Smith and Julia Watson explain, "are not merely transparent 'accounts' of some past experience, or exact records of historical events in people's lives or the life of the nation. Rather, they are performances of self-narrating through which the meanings of the past are produced for the occasions and social identities of the present and the future" (*Before They Could Vote* 6). Functioning in the epideictic mode, autobiographical genres invite readers to listen and contemplate the experiences of others, which can be transformative in subtle yet powerful ways. Taylor's first-hand account, which commends the efforts that she and other African Americans made on behalf of the Union, animates this epideictic possibility.

As Fleckenstein observes, there is "a mutual emphasis [on] *ethos*" in both the epideictic and autobiography: "Like memoir," she explains, "a considerable component of epideictic's effectiveness ensues from . . . the authority of the rhetor's 'positive image'" (5). Developing a trustworthy ethos is crucial to the epideictic, as rhetors who are tasked with reinscribing the values of a particular community need to convey a mind similar to that of their constituents. As a Black woman writing in the early twentieth century, Taylor faced significant obstacles in constructing a persona with which her white readers could identify. "Traditionally, [Black] women have come to a rhetorical task with a reputation," observes Jacqueline Jones Royster, "that is, with a situated *ethos* more often than not deeply compromised, especially when they seek as one of their target audiences those outside their immediate home community" (65). Taylor's ethos was further threatened by her critique of the racial inequities that continued to plague the United States. To avoid alienating her audience, she opens her memoir with a letter of support written by Lieutenant Colonel C. T. Trowbridge, the white man who oversaw the 33rd Infantry. Testifying to the veracity of her account and praising her considerable contributions, Trowbridge explains that he has read Taylor's narrative "with much care and interest, and [he] most willingly and cordially indorse[s] it as a truthful account of [her] unselfish devotion and service through more than three long years of war." Many white women who wrote autobiographies of their experiences during the Civil War included a white man's endorsement, but for Taylor, a woman of color, this statement would have been critical to establishing good character. The *Boston Sunday Post* further reported that Taylor's account was endorsed by William Lloyd Garrison, Jr.; Colonel Thomas Wentworth Higginson; and "a number of other White officers of her regiment, who are unstinted in their praise of her heroism and loyalty to the officers and men of the Thirty-third" ("Mrs. Susie King Taylor"). As these testimonials confirm, Taylor was an asset to the 33rd Infantry, and to the Union more broadly, which worked to bolster her credibility in the eyes of her readers.

Following these endorsements, Taylor begins her narrative proper, describing her experiences as a young enslaved girl. In antebellum times, slave narratives were used as powerful rhetorical tools that illustrated the horrors of human bondage. As Frances Smith Foster maintains, "scenes of violence and cruelty . . . could awaken moral outrage against slavery" (19–20). But postbellum slave narratives, William Andrews explains, "argued the readiness of the freedman and freedwoman for full participation in the post-Civil War social and economic order." This shift in purpose required a new rhetorical approach, which can be observed in Taylor's account. Emphasizing fortitude and perseverance, she describes the considerable obstacles that she overcame, particularly in her pursuit of education. Born in 1848 on a plantation in Georgia, Taylor was sent to Savannah at the age of seven to live with her grandmother. In Savannah she attended a secret school, as Georgia law prohibited education for the enslaved. Detailing the extent of her educational efforts, she recounts how she and her brother walked to school every day "with our books wrapped in paper to prevent the police or white persons from seeing them" (5). After she concluded her formal instruction in 1860, when the teacher "had taught [her] all she knew," Taylor sought out lessons from others, including her white peers (6). By describing the effort and risk that she undertook to learn to read and write, she crafts an ethos centered on industry and ingenuity, qualities that would resonate with her readers, helping to bridge the potential chasm between Taylor and her audience.

Taylor further emphasizes personal attributes of strength and resilience as she describes the significant difficulties she endured when the Civil War erupted in 1862. She recalls how she fled to St. Simons Island off the coast of Georgia, a contraband camp where enslaved people gathered in the interim period between slavery and emancipation. While such designated areas were under the protection of the Union, as historian Richard Hall explains, "Food was scarce, disease ran rampant, and the climate was sometimes brutal" (207). Taylor writes that "[i]t was a gloomy time for us all" as rumors circulated about the potential fate of the six hundred men, women, and children who temporarily resided on the island: Would they be returned to life as enslaved peoples? Or sent to Liberia (11–12)? But abduction by rebels was the most significant threat that inhabitants of the contraband camp faced. Taylor explains that Confederates "would capture any persons venturing out alone and carry them to the mainland. Several of the men disappeared, and . . . they were never heard from" (14–15). In recounting the many uncertainties and dangers that she and other residents of St. Simons faced, Taylor illuminates for her audience the significant challenges that people of color weathered on the road to freedom. Deeply committed to emancipation, she withstood these adversities while also supporting the Union cause.

While Taylor would come to assist the Union in a multitude of ways, sharing her literacy skills was one of her first accomplishments, continuing to cultivate an ethos of good will. Her undertaking caught the attention of Union officials, who pledged to support her efforts with books so that she could start a school on the island. "I had about forty children to teach," she recounts, "besides a number of adults who came to me nights, all of them so eager to learn to read, to read above anything else" (11). In teaching others, Taylor highlights her commitment to social progress, emphasizing what African Americans could do when freed from the shackles of slavery. She further underscores this point when she explains to a Union captain that her literacy skills did not make her exceptional. Rather, as she remarks, she was "reared . . . in the city" where she had greater access to educational prospects (9). To successfully acclimate to their new lives as free men and women, people of color needed adequate support, which Taylor helped provide. Lifting as she climbed, she displays her commitment to bettering the lives of the formerly enslaved.

Commemorating African American Contributions to the American Civil War

Peter Wayne Moe contends that "it is through praise and blame that the epideictic realizes its rhetorical potential" (438). These functions communicate values and beliefs, reifying what is revered and rebuked in a given community. As Taylor moves beyond her experiences as an enslaved person, she turns her attention to the efforts that she and other people of color made on behalf of the Union, praising their numerous contributions. Focusing specifically on her involvement with the 33rd Colored Troops, what Colonel Trowbridge declared to be "the first black regiment that ever bore arms in defense of freedom on the continent of America" (qtd. in Taylor 47), Taylor reaffirms the commonplace values of patriotism, courage, and sacrifice. In illuminating these principles, she calls her audience to recognize that African Americans, like their white counterparts, fought on behalf of the Union, and as such deserved to be treated as equals. In this way, Taylor's use of commendation functions as a rhetorical strategy that highlights the need for racial equity.

Providing a rare glimpse into the life of an African American woman who served the Union, Taylor fuses the good character of ethos with the praise of the epideictic, building her credibility by discussing the many adversities that she overcame while concomitantly celebrating her accomplishments and contributions. As she explains, she was not immune to the hardships of the Civil War. At fourteen years old, she "enrolled as company laundress . . . [but] did very little of it, because [she] was always busy doing other things through camp, and was employed all the time doing something for the officers and comrades" (35). Traveling with her regiment, she confronted many of the same risks that soldiers faced. She recalls, for example, how she had to evacuate camp because her unit was under attack. At any moment she "expected . . . to be killed by a shell" (24). Coming to terms with the devastation of war, she later comments on the "many skulls lying about" the battlefield; they "were a gruesome sight, those fleshless heads and grinning jaws, but by this time I had become accustomed to worse things" (31). Through these kinds of revelations, Taylor sheds light on some of the personal traumas that she endured while serving the Union. Exhibiting strength and determination, she continued to support the war effort, despite the many challenges that she faced.

Further detailing her own contributions to the Union, Taylor conveys the great compassion she bestowed upon the sick and wounded soldiers of her regiment, underscoring her efforts to provide care for the troops in need. Illnesses were prevalent during the Civil War, taking many lives. When varioloid, a mild form of smallpox, broke out among the troops, Taylor took it upon herself to tend to those who were diagnosed. She recalls how one soldier in particular was very severely affected by the virus. Only the doctor and camp steward were allowed to see him, but highlighting her devotion, Taylor took her chances and "went to see this man every day and nurse him" (17). In addition to caring for sick soldiers, she also discusses the aid she provided those who were injured in battle, tending to many injuries: "some with their legs off, arm gone, foot off, and wounds of all kinds imaginable" (34). In commenting on these atrocities of war, Taylor reflects on "how strange our aversion to seeing suffering is overcome in war,—how we are able to see the most sickening sights . . . and instead of turning away, how we hurry to assist in alleviating their pain" (31–32). Using the epideictic convention of commendation, Taylor subtly gestures to her own devotion and allegiance.

Moving outward, Taylor also praises the work of the unsung heroes of the Union, specifically commending the labors performed by women of color. "There are many people who do not know what some of the colored women did during the war," Taylor writes; applauding their courage and defiance, she comments that "[t]here were hundreds of them who assisted the Union soldiers by hiding them and helping them to escape" (67). She also recalls how, despite potential threats to their own lives, African American women in Savannah fed Union prisoners who otherwise went without much food. "These things," Taylor emphasizes, "should be kept in history before the people" (68). Extolling the virtues of African American women helped to bring much-needed attention to their war labors while again reaffirming established community codes. In doing so, Taylor reminds her audience that African Americans, too, fought for this country, supporting the North in a range of invaluable ways, and as such they deserved equal treatment.

Building on established themes of bravery, patriotism, and compassion, Taylor devotes considerable attention to describing the troops' valiant efforts. Telling these stories kept African Americans' indispensable contributions in the public eye, which was particularly important at a time in which their rights were regularly degraded. To this end, Taylor describes the battles in which her regiment fought and details the dangerous expeditions on which they embarked. To validate her narrative of these events, she again leans on the ethos of Colonel Trowbridge, including in her memoir a letter that he wrote to his troops at the close of the war: "from that little band of hopeful, trusting, and brave men who gathered at Camp Saxton, on Port Royal Island, in the fall of '62," he writes, "amidst the terrible prejudices that surrounded us, has grown an army of a hundred and forty thousand Black soldiers, whose valor and heroism has won for your race a name which will live as long as the undying pages of history shall endure" (47). In showcasing the troops' loyalty and dedication, Taylor invites readers to identify with their shared values so that they might empathize with the plight of African Americans after the war.

Separate and Unequal

In her work on autobiographies and resistance, Johnnie Stover rightly asserts that "*Reminiscences* represents the voice of an African American woman who cleverly balances her sense of patriotism with her outrage at the inhuman treatment inflicted on America's black citizens" (13). After inviting her audience to contemplate the obstacles that enslaved peoples overcame and then celebrating their fortitude and fearlessness as they fought for the Union, Taylor devotes her last few chapters to discussing life for people of color after the war. Their many contributions starkly contrast with the mistreatment they experienced following the Confederacy's surrender. While the Reconstruction period "saw the passage of a vast array of legislation aimed at transforming the status of the formerly enslaved . . . ," explains Henry Louis Gates, Jr., "[b]y 1890, after a fierce and brave struggle, the momentum had tipped considerably away from advocates of Black equality to the white supremacists' advantage" (7, 28). Making visible the ramifications of this political, social, and legal shift, Taylor deftly moves from praise to blame in her account, participating in the epideictic tradition of what Cynthia Miecznikowski Sheard describes as "addressing private and public 'dis-ease,' discomfort with the status quo" (766).

Taylor highlights several racial inequities in her memoir, but disparities in pay and inadequate employment opportunities for African Americans are a particularly salient theme that emerges. Although the soldiers in her regiment were at first denied pay, the government eventually "granted them full pay, with all the back due pay" (Taylor 16). This situation conspicuously contrasts with Taylor's own financial reality, since she was denied all pay for her war services. Demonstrating an intersectional awareness of her particular plight as an African American woman, she broaches the issue several times in her memoir. Colonel Trowbridge, too, commented on her lack of pay, writing that he "most sincerely regret[s] that through a technicality [she is] debarred from having [her] name placed on the roll of pensioners, as an Army Nurse" (qtd. in Taylor). These kinds of discrepancies in remuneration, Taylor suggests, plagued many African Americans, impeding their ability to successfully transition to life as a free people.

Related to these concerns, Taylor raises questions about viable employment opportunities for African Americans in the post-war United States. She speaks to this particular problem in revealing her own struggle to find work despite her considerable education and experience. She taught for a few years in various parts of Georgia, but soon found herself competing with the "free" school system that was launched after the war. Rather than face financial insolvency, Taylor explains that she "put my baby with my mother and entered in the employ of a family, where I lived quite a while, but had to leave, as the work was too hard." She eventually moved north to Boston, where she secured employment from "a very wealthy lady . . . as a laundress" (55). In sharing these experiences, Taylor exemplifies the employment predicaments that many African Americans faced after the Civil War. Without job prospects and financial security, they were doomed to struggle. Taylor clarifies this issue for readers through her narrative, denouncing the systemic practices that enabled such injustices to flourish.

Flawed economic structures were not the only issues that Taylor condemned in her memoir; she also devotes considerable attention to censuring the Jim Crow South. Shirley Wilson Logan observes a similar trend in her research on nineteenth-century African American women's public, persuasive discourse, noting that African American women were particularly focused on "present[ing] arguments for general assistance to Southern blacks after the Civil War" (18). Participating in this rhetorical tradition through her use of the epideictic, Taylor writes that "the South still cherishes a hatred toward the blacks" (62), offering several anecdotes as evidence of such racial disparities. The circumstances surrounding the death of her son illuminate some of these concerns. When her son became ill, she had to travel from Boston to Shreveport, Louisiana. When her train arrived in Cincinnati, just before crossing the Mason-Dixon line, she and all other African Americans on board were ordered to move to the smoking car, the only one available to them as passengers. Located in close proximity to the coal-burning steam engines, the smoking car exposed its occupants to considerable toxins and debris. This act of segregation was demoralizing, but, as Taylor explains, it also prevented her from taking her son back to Boston. Recovering from a massive hemorrhage, her son was "very anxious to come home," but when she "tried to secure a berth for him on a sleeper . . . they would not sell one to [her], and he was not strong enough to travel otherwise" (71). African Americans were separated from inhabiting the same space as their white counterparts because they were considered biologically inferior. In the case of Taylor's son, this had mortal consequences: unable to get home, he died in Louisiana. Reflecting on the injustice of the situation, Taylor poignantly comments on the tragic situation: "It seemed very hard, when his father fought to protect the Union and our flag, and yet his boy was denied, under this same flag, a berth to carry him home to die, because he was a negro" (71–72). In sharing this personal tragedy, Taylor depicts the Jim Crow South as a harsh, prejudiced place, illustrating for her northern audience how the gross inequities that persisted below the Mason-Dixon line contradicted their own sense of justice.

Amplifying this discrepancy in values, Taylor also confronts readers with the violence she witnessed in the South, as lynching narratives haunt the last chapter of her account. Around the time Taylor published *Reminiscences* in 1902, the lynching of Black men and women was steadily increasing in the United States. The Tuskegee Institute reported that over five hundred African Americans were lynched between 1900 and 1905 (Linder). The threat of lynching is omnipresent as Taylor makes her way to Louisiana. As she recalls, a porter in Chattanooga, Tennessee, tells her, "That is the way they do [it] here" (71). While in Shreveport, she learns that another porter was shot dead by a patron looking for his umbrella, for what was interpreted as a "saucy" response (72–73). She, herself, is privy to such a murder in Clarksdale, Mississippi, when she witnesses the hanging of a Black man. "It was a terrible sight," she reports, "and I felt alarmed for my own safety there" (74). No one was ever tried, let alone convicted, of these atrocities. Contrasting these deplorable events with slavery and the war, Taylor exhibits for her audience the burdens borne by African Americans and asks them to consider the justness of the situation described:

> For two hundred years we had toiled for them; the war of 1861 came and was ended, and we thought that our race was forever freed from bondage, and that the two races could live in unity with each other, but when we read almost every day of what is being done to my race by some whites in the South, I some-times ask, "Was the war in vain? Has it brought freedom, in the full sense of the word, or has it not made our condition more hopeless?"   (61)

Through her narratives describing the violence inflicted upon African Americans in the post-Reconstruction South, Taylor epitomizes the continued problems with racial injustice. Despite their service and sacrifice, "In this 'land of the free,'" Taylor writes, "we are burned, tortured, and denied a fair trial, murdered for any imaginary wrong conceived in the brain of the negro-hating white man. There is no redress for us from a government which promised to protect all under its flag" (61). Exemplifying the potential of the epideictic, Taylor's narrative mirrors the double standards that people of color faced, inviting her largely white audience "to contemplate, evaluate, and judge" (Walker, "Aristotle's Lyric" 8) the impossible position that they inhabited.

Promises Made, Promises Broken

Commenting on the potential of the epideictic, Lawrence Rosenfeld writes that this rhetorical mode has the potential to make apparent "what might otherwise remain unnoticed or invisible" (135). Reading Taylor's memoir as a kind of epideictic rhetoric puts more clearly into focus how her personal account actively calls for greater racial parity. In describing the considerable labors and losses that she and other African Americans endured, she brings the significant contributions that people of color made on behalf of the Union to the attention of her northern, white readers. Contrasting her celebration of these efforts, she describes the discrimination and violence that African Americans continued to endure almost forty years after the war ended, particularly in the Jim Crow South. Taylor's story, shared publicly, reveals the fuller scope of the contradictions of the United States. In reflecting back to her audience these conflicting values, she boldly highlights the flawed system that continually oppresses people of color despite their right to life, liberty, and happiness, a point which she powerfully summarizes in the closing lines of her book:

What a wonderful revolution! In 1861 the Southern papers were full of advertisements for "slaves," but now, despite all the hindrances and "race problems,"
my people are striving to attain the full standard of all other races born free
in the sight of God, and in a number of instances have succeeded. Justice we
ask,—to be citizens of these United States, where so many of our people have
shed their blood with their white comrades, that the stars and stripes should
never be polluted.   (75–76)

In exposing the problematic racial paradigms that prevented African Americans
from fully participating in the freedoms for which they lived and died, Taylor
calls her audience to rectify promises made but broken, time and time again.

Notes

1. The full title of Taylor's text is *Reminiscences of My Life in Camp with the 33d
United States Colored Troops, Late First S.C. Volunteers*. Published in 1902, it could be
purchased for $1.25 at 27 Holyoke Street in Boston or through a bookseller.

2. In contemporary parlance, the definition of *memoir* has been conflated with
autobiography to mean generally "a book that is understood by its author, its publishers, and its readers to be a factual account of the author's life" (Yagoda 1), but
there are some important distinctions. The word *memoir* came into existence in
English almost a century earlier than the word *autobiography*, but the kind of life
writing that it describes has a much longer history—one that some argue extends
back to Old Testament books like Psalms and Prophets (Yagoda 31). Autobiography,
in contrast to memoir, refers to the general practice of life writing, often focusing
on an entire life. In *Reading Autobiography*, Smith and Watson explain that autobiographies were composed during the Enlightenment by "the self-interested individual of property who was intent on assessing the status of the soul or the meaning
of public achievement" (2). Autobiography has historically been considered to be
the more literary mode of life writing. Although there are important distinctions
between the terms *autobiography* and *memoir* and other related terms, I use them
here synonymously for stylistic purposes.

Works Cited

Andrews, William. "North American Slave Narratives: An Introduction to the Slave
      Narratives." *Documenting the American South*. U of North Carolina, docsouth.unc
      .edu/neh/intro.html.
Aristotle. *On Rhetoric*. Translated by W. Rhys Roberts, Modern Library, 1984.
Boyle, Marjorie O'Rourke. "A Likely Story: The Autobiographical as Epideictic." *Journal
      of the American Academy of Religion*, vol. 57, no. 1, Spring 1989, pp. 23–51.

Clinton, Catherine. "Introduction: Let Us Not Forget That Terrible War." Taylor, pp. vii–xl.

Fleckenstein, Kristie. "Epideictic Memories: The Argument for Spatial Agency in Frances E. Willard's *A Wheel within a Wheel*." *Political Women: Language and Leadership*, edited by Michele Lockhart and Kathleen Mollick, Lexington Books, 2013, pp. 1–18.

Foster, Frances Smith. *Witnessing Slavery: The Development of Ante-bellum Slave Narratives*. 2nd ed., U of Wisconsin P, 1994.

Gates, Henry Louis, Jr. *Stony the Road: Reconstruction, White Supremacy, and the Rise of Jim Crow*. Penguin, 2019.

Hall, Richard H. *Women on the Civil War Battlefront*. UP of Kansas, 2006.

Linder, Douglas O. "Lynchings: By Year and Race." *Famous Trials*, famous-trials.com/sheriffshipp/1084-lynchingsyear.

Logan, Shirley Wilson. *We Are Coming: The Persuasive Discourse of Nineteenth-Century Black Women*. Southern Illinois UP, 1999.

Moe, Peter Wayne. "Reading Coles Reading Themes: Epideictic Rhetoric and the Teaching of Writing." *College Composition and Communication*, vol. 69, no. 3, Feb. 2018, pp. 433–57.

"Mrs. Susie King Taylor, Boston's Colored Woman Author—She Was Once a Slave." *Boston Sunday Post*, 4 Jan. 1903. *Newspaper Archive*, newspaperarchive.com.

Pernot, Laurent. *Epideictic Rhetoric: Questioning the Stakes of Ancient Praise*. U of Texas P, 2015.

Rosenfeld, Lawrence. "The Practical Celebration of Epideictic." *Rhetoric in Transition: Studies in the Nature and Uses of Rhetoric*, edited by Eugene E. White, Pennsylvania State UP, 1980, pp. 131–55.

Royster, Jacqueline Jones. *Traces of a Stream: Literacy and Social Change among African American Women*. U of Pittsburgh P, 2000.

Sheard, Cynthia Miecznikowski. "The Public Value of Epideictic Rhetoric." *College English*, vol. 58, no. 7, Nov. 1996, pp. 765–94.

Smith, Sidonie, and Julia Watson, editors. *Before They Could Vote: American Women's Autobiographical Writing, 1819–1919*. Wisconsin UP, 2006.

———. *Reading Autobiography: A Guide for Interpreting Life Narratives*. 2nd ed., UP of Minnesota, 2010.

Stover, Johnnie M. *Rhetoric and Resistance in Black Women's Autobiography*. UP of Florida, 2003.

Taylor, Susie King. *Reminiscences of My Life in Camp: An African American Woman's Civil War Memoir*. 1902. U of Georgia P, 2006.

Walker, Jeffrey. "Aristotle's Lyric: Re-imagining the Rhetoric of Epideictic Song." *College English*, vol. 51, no. 1, Jan. 1989, pp. 5–28.

———. *Rhetoric and Poetics in Antiquity*. Oxford UP, 2000.

Yagoda, Ben. *Memoir: A History*. Riverhead Books, 2009.

Arguing by Numbers: Charlotte Odlum Smith's Fight for Recognition for Women Inventors

Sarah Hallenbeck

In 1883, Mathilda Gage published "Woman as an Inventor," her second tract on what she and others understood as a vital issue of the day: the need for readers to recognize American women's role in the history of invention and to encourage their future inventive endeavors. "The inventions of a nation are closely connected with the freedom of its people," Gage argues (488), adding that any "forms of thought, customs of society, or systems of law" that hamper women's ability to invent also render "the darkness of the world . . . more dense, and its civilization retarded" (489). It is unsurprising that Gage felt so keenly the need to encourage women inventors and honor their past contributions, or that she saw invention more generally as so vital to the nation's future prospects. The second half of the nineteenth century might be understood as a golden age of invention, during which Americans witnessed startling, technology-driven changes in their day-to-day lives, read eagerly in newspapers of new inventions, and tracked the rate at which new patents emerged for evidence of the nation's prosperity or decline.

Perhaps because of the widely perceived significance of invention as an indicator of progress, prosperity, and individuals' intellectual capacities, women's rights activists like Gage seized on invention to support their own arguments about women's legal, educational, and professional rights. Even as these activists sought to recover women's past inventions, they also suggested that women's inventive productivity had been hampered by their second-class societal status. Yet, in an era in which quantitative evidence held increasing sway in public discourse, activists struggled to find concrete data to support their claims. How many women had been issued patents since the first American patent was issued in 1790? What percentage was that number of the whole? And how closely did the number of women patenting inventions correlate to increasing educational opportunities for women?

Attempts to answer these questions were thorny at best. The United States Patent Office did not request the sex of the applicant on the patent application, and it did not keep track of women inventors in its *Official Gazette*, a weekly list of newly granted patents first published in 1872 (Merritt 243). Researchers who sought to count the number of patents issued to women would have had to do so one patent at a time, relying on feminine-sounding names—an overwhelming task when one considers that 600,000 patents were granted in the United States in the years between 1865 and 1900 alone (Merritt 246). Because of social constraints, some women patented under an initial or the name of a husband or brother, while other innovative women did not patent their work at all, daunted by the costs and legal knowledge necessary to do so (Khan 164). So great was the challenge of locating women inventors that the organizers of the 1885 New Orleans World's Fair struggled to recruit exhibitors for their showcase of women's inventive work. The so-called lady managers of the fair complained that "laboriously searching Patent Office records and noting female names" was "a task equivalent to reading a dozen large dictionaries in succession" (qtd. in Macdonald 136).

Although a few journalists and activists undertook research on their own to identify patents granted to women, they generally selected notable innovations to highlight rather than attempting a systematic count of women inventors possessing patents for their work. However, beginning in the early 1880s, Charlotte Odlum Smith—a prominent and controversial advocate for women workers—undertook that project, working for several years to convince the Patent Office to create a list of all patents granted to women in the United States. Smith ultimately appealed to Congress for money to pay Patent Office clerks to create an official list of patents granted to women. Consequently, *Women Inventors to Whom Patents Have Been Granted by the United States Government, 1790–1888* was published in 1888. The list—which I will refer to as the list of women patents, or LWP—contained 5,590 names and took four patent clerks ten days to compile (Smith, "Why I Became Interested"); it was updated twice afterwards, in 1892 and 1895.

Though, as Smith's biographer Autumn Stanley has demonstrated convincingly, the LWP contained significant errors and omissions,[1] it nonetheless circulated widely in various forms, informing public discourse for years to come about women's inventive capabilities and their rightful place in society. Information gleaned from the list appeared in countless articles, in newspapers big and small, across the country. In addition to using the list to shape their own narratives about women's inventive capacities, writers mined the list to create statistics of their own, documenting trends such as increases in women's overall inventive activity over time, stagnation in the realms for which women were inventing, and even differences in women's inventiveness by region of the United States.

The story of the LWP ought to interest feminist rhetoricians because it high-lights the varied ways women can be rhetors—not only by penning argumenta-tive texts or speeches but also by lobbying, over time and in diverse or obscure ways, for the creation and circulation of certain kinds of knowledge that would otherwise not exist to influence public discourse. In the case of the LWP, Smith performed the rhetorical work of marshalling support for a project that never bore her name but that nonetheless reshaped public discussion surrounding women's inventive capacities. She worked to stimulate the circulation and inter-pretation of statistical information about women inventors in an era in which Americans attached unprecedented, for the time, importance to such numerical evidence.

As a rhetor, Smith functioned behind the scenes, as many women have in rhetoric's long history, in the same sorts of "interstitial" spaces as the women pedagogues about whom Tarez Graban and Patricia Sullivan have written re-cently. As Graban and Sullivan suggest, situating such women as rhetors re-quires methods that "better trace women . . . who have otherwise escaped the purview of other landscapes and turns" (189)—that is, we must seek other, more traditional ways of interacting with archives and of understanding and valuing rhetorical activity. Graban and Sullivan offer a framework of "interstitial look-ing" that values circulation and movement over discreet texts or locations. Cit-ing the work of J. Bollen, H. Van de Sompel, and M. A. Rodruiguez, Graban and Sullivan argue that within such a framework, "a subject's importance . . . be-comes assessed according to 'how it is embedded in a network of social relation-ships'" (198). Smith's lobbying to create the LWP, as well as the uptake of the LWP within newspapers around the country, offers an example of how we might recover women rhetors whose virtuosity comes to light only through such widely distributed activity and effects. Additionally, tracing the generation and circu-lation of numerical data within newspapers helps us tap into an important di-mension of nineteenth-century rhetoric that deserves significant attention from rhetoricians, since the field as a whole attends more deliberately to circulation as a historical, and also a contemporary, rhetorical phenomenon.

In what follows, I first offer a brief biography of Smith before examining her role in the creation of the LWP. Next, I consider the circulation of informa-tion gleaned from the LWP via a wealth of newspaper articles I located using the Library of Congress's *Chronicling America* database. I analyze the ways sta-tistics gleaned from the LWP functioned within these articles to shore up par-ticular narratives about women's innate abilities and proclivities. Ultimately, I argue that feminist rhetoricians studying the nineteenth century might recover a broader range of rhetorical activity and activism if we shift our understanding about what it means to be a rhetor to include generating data intended for others to circulate.

Charlotte Odlum Smith's Rhetorical Versatility

Born in 1843 to working-class Irish immigrant parents, Smith's schooling was frequently interrupted by moves and by the need, as the oldest child, to help support her mother and siblings after her father abandoned the family. Before moving to Washington, DC, in 1878, Smith ran several boarding houses with her mother and managed both a dry goods store and an entirely women-staffed magazine called the *Inland Monthly* (Stanley, *Raising More Hell*). Perhaps motivated by her own personal struggles, she advocated for women workers' rights; while living in Washington, DC, she founded the National Women's Industrial League, a union for women who had been excluded from their professional unions. Though the league "never achieved national prominence," as historian Anne Macdonald notes (143), Smith used her capacity as its president to work alongside the presidents of other unions, attend congressional hearings, and petition for jobs and legal protections for women workers ranging from dressmakers to charwomen to dry goods workers.

The range of initiatives in which Smith apparently had her hand is stunning. As Stanley describes her, Smith was "a labor leader, Congressional lobbyist, reformer, iconoclast, and social gadfly—a sort of nineteenth-century Ralph Nader" ("Patent Office Clerk" 128). One particularly effusive 1891 article that appeared in the *Wichita Daily Eagle*, in which it was titled "Help for the Women," and also in the *Wood County Reporter*, titled "Clever Women Inventors," proclaimed of Smith: "There is not a senator or member of the house or public man of any station whatever who does not know her . . . and she has been repeatedly cited on the floor of both the Senate and the House in the last ten years." The same article credits Smith with a dizzying range of accomplishments, including lobbying successfully for the pensioning of Army nurses; securing jobs for one thousand charwomen in Washington, DC; and persuading Massachusetts and New York factory owners to employ women supervisors in their factories. By her own account, she "had more than fifty bills passed by Congress" during her years of greatest political activity ("Like a Knight of Old").

Throughout all of her endeavors, Smith remained convinced of the need to collect and share numerical data to document the labor issues she sought to address.[2] Like other labor leaders of the day, she believed that "accurate statistics would serve the cause of social justice" and that "facts" would provide a better basis for altruism (Grossman and MacLaury 30–31, 25). As president of the National Women's Industrial League, Smith worked alongside other union presidents to lobby Congress for a federal office charged with the official collection of data on issues related to labor and industry. The Bureau of Labor Statistics was authorized in 1884, right around the same time Smith was advocating so fiercely for the creation of the LWP.

Smith's interest in inventors, as she describes in *The Woman Inventor*, had been prompted by the plight of a young woman who died destitute after having patented a highly successful invention under the name of her lawyer. In addition to advocating for the creation of an official list of patents granted to women inventors, Smith published a two-issue newsletter titled *The Woman Inventor*, in which she detailed her own efforts to persuade the Patent Office to publish the LWP. Smith describes appealing to a succession of four patent commissioners over a period of nearly ten years, and she published two letters from commissioners supporting her claim. One notes: "I remember very well the visits which you made [to advocate for the LWP], and how earnest and persistent you were in urging the compilation." The other confirmed, "You are correct, it was during my administration . . . that you suggested to me the necessity of a compilation of the women inventors. I wish also to state that it was done at your suggestion" (qtd. in Smith, "Why I Became Interested"). After being repeatedly told that the work would cost too much money to perform, Smith appeared before the congressional committee on appropriations to gain assistance in paying clerks for their efforts; she was successful, and she received a letter from the Patent Office containing a copy of the LWP and confirming that the work was complete and five hundred copies had been printed for "about $300" (qtd. in Stanley, *Raising* 145). The document itself was forty-four pages in length and contained the names and locations of each inventor, together with the patent number and a brief description of each patent.

It is important that Smith's name is entirely absent from official affiliation with the LWP, other than within the pages of her newsletter. The cover of the list, for instance, notes that the information that follows was "compiled under the direction of the commissioner of patents" (United States Patent Office 1). Similarly, Smith's name is absent from the many newspaper articles in which the LWP is referred to. An 1889 issue of the *St. Tammany Farmer* notes that "the Commissioner of Patents, Mr. Benton J. Hall, has had prepared a list of women inventors, or women to whom patents have been granted" ("Women as Inventors"), while the Washington, DC, *Evening Star* credits "Assistant Chief Alexander Scott of the division of drafting in the patent office" for providing the LWP ("Women Inventors"). Smith's affiliation with the list is invisible to readers, making her role in generating the list difficult to trace.

In general, Smith's rhetorical activity was diverse and highly distributed, both spatially and temporally. Her role involved movement back and forth among private government offices such as that of the Patent Office commissioner, public forums such as Congress, and the homes and workplaces of the women workers for whom she advocated. Her eight-year quest to accomplish the creation of the LWP exemplifies this approach, which I call interstitial in the sense that the significance of her work only emerges in its relation to other parties. Additionally, Smith's personal stamp on the list is limited: despite her efforts in *The Woman Inventor* to assert her role in the LWP's creation, she did not assemble it herself and, as mentioned, her name is not affixed to it in any official way. Yet she did articulate the need for its existence because of her belief in the role of facts in providing useful critiques of existing policy and guiding future changes, which was in keeping with both the emerging progressive climate of the day and, more specifically, with other labor activists' arguments. Next I consider small-town newspapers as one important venue in which the LWP circulated widely in the years following its creation, helping to transform the ways Americans debated and discussed women inventors.

Smith's Numbers in Circulation

Newspapers proliferated in America throughout the nineteenth century, bolstered by new printing technologies, increasing literacy rates, and the emergence of the telegraph as a means to relay news quickly. In addition to time-sensitive news items, these papers frequently included what Ellen Gruber Garvey describes as "fragmented or 'morselized' information" or "tidbits and factoids" (7), and miscellaneous informational texts that lent themselves to reprinting because, as literary historian Ryan Cordell notes, they required "little to no contextual prose and could help compositors fill small gaps on their page" (426). Cordell argues that, because of their wide circulation through reprinting and the care that local editors put into selecting content to reprint, these miscellany are "important to a full understanding of nineteenth-century epistemologies" (425).

Within this print culture context, articles and snippets announcing information from the LWP were well-equipped to circulate widely in one form or another. The topic of American women inventors was not particularly time- or context-sensitive and offered broad appeal to readers in an era of both scientific curiosity and great debate over women's societal roles. The list itself generated provocative statistics as well as brief narratives about interesting inventions. As a result, articles with titles ranging from "Women as Inventors" to "Woman the Inventor" or "The Inventive Genius of Women" circulated widely, usually without clear authorship, in newspapers across the country in the decade following the first publication of the LWP in 1888. These articles often featured a brief reference to the LWP as a news source, commentary containing statistics that characterized women inventors' progress and contributions as a whole, and then specific examples of successful or unusual inventions by women. By searching within the Library of Congress's *Chronicling America* database, I identified both specific articles and instances of reprinting. Similar to the trends that Cordell has investigated (422), individual articles appear to have been reprinted, on average, two or three times in other newspapers, often with minor variations to suit space requirements or individual or regional preferences.

Because of their wide circulation and their importance as a gauge of nineteenth-century culture, these newspaper articles functioned as conduits through which Americans might encounter different facets of the LWP, extensions of the rhetorical work that Smith put into generating the list in the first place. Though, as with the list itself, Smith did not directly author these articles, she intended for the numerical evidence offered by the LWP to be used by others to document the women inventors' progress. Smith's understanding of the usefulness of data—and of authorization of that data by situating it as within the purview of a government office—demonstrate her rhetorical sensitivity to the public moment in which she lived.

Information from the LWP was often used to support the notion that increasing opportunities for education were expanding women's ability to demonstrate their intellectual abilities through invention, and even that this shift would benefit the nation as a whole. An 1888 article printed in the *Bismarck Weekly Tribune* and the Wilmington, Delaware, *Evening Journal*, titled "Women as Inventors" in both, reported as follows: "The patent office shows that the number of inventions presented by women increases as the years go on and as woman's rights increase. The advance of women into the different professions brings another half to the great American mind, and this has already shown itself in patents." Similarly, the *Bryan Morning Eagle* in Texas reported on a talk given by a Reverend Ada C. Bowles in which Bowles traced the correspondence between women's educational opportunities and patent activity ("Women Inventors"). Although in 1809, when the first patent was issued to Mary Klees, the *Morning Eagle* notes that "girls received hardly any education," by 1834 "women had a few more educational privileges, but not many, and in the next twenty-five years women took out patents for thirty-five inventions." Noting that "colleges . . . and manual training are now developing the latent inventiveness of women," Bowles refers to the LWP, according to the newspaper article, in noting that women took out 3,905 patents in the period between 1884 and 1895. Similar numbers are referred to in several articles published in late 1895 and early 1896, ranging from the *Washington Standard* to the *McCook Tribune*: "In 1870 the number of patents issued to women numbered 60, and in each decade the increase was rapid. In 1880 the number was 92; in 1890 over 200, and in 1893 over 300, making it fair to assume that at the close of the present decade the number will be well over 500, if not actually 1,000" ("Women Inventors" [*Washington*]; "Women as Inventors" [*McCook*]). These examples demonstrate how Smith's advocacy for the LWP enabled a new, data-driven basis for some of the claims that Gage had made just a few years earlier that women were becoming increasingly active as inventors as the result of increased educational opportunities.

Articles' authors also drew from the LWP's list of inventors' hometowns to make claims about the relative progress of women in different parts of the country. An article printed in the *Bismarck Weekly Tribune* noted that "the female brain of the United States seems most active in New England, middle and western states. Massachusetts, Connecticut, and New Hampshire have produced quite a number of women inventors, and the patents are of all kinds, from dust pans to fire escapes" ("Women as Inventors"). To this observation the *Omaha Daily Bee* added, "The South has yielded the fewest number, but the Southern women who have entered the field at all have been financially successful" ("Women as Inventors"). These regional assessments correlated to educational opportunities afforded to women, which were more plentiful in the north, so they functioned tacitly to endorse educational opportunity.

Authors did not always understand the LWP as evidence of the benefits of greater educational access for women, however. The *Macon Beacon* noted, for instance, that "the most successful inventions have been to those who had only medium or limited educational advantages, but have been daily toilers in the various lines of industry" ("Women as Inventors"). Similarly, authors would often group inventions into categories to highlight (and thus discredit) the domestic nature of many of women's inventions at the time. For instance, after documenting overall increases in women's inventive activity, one article in the *Southern Herald* announced that "wearing apparel heads the list" of patents granted to women, numbering 160, followed by cooking utensils, with 100 inventions, and other categories—cleaning and household devices, sewing and spinning devices, for instance—behind these ("Women as Inventors"). Similarly, the *Sullivan Republican* and *Scranton Tribune* offered the following judgment: "Women inventors are, according to Patent Office reports, adhering to the lines of the old rather than the new woman. Out of 400 patents granted in 1894, 160 were for wearing apparel and 100 for cooking utensils" ("News and Notes for Women"; "News of Our Industries"). These numbers strengthened the notion that, despite the rise of the "new" woman with her call for educational opportunities, women's inventions remained limited in scope and impact.

In general, the LWP prompted important changes to the ways Americans considered the question of women's inventiveness, and the traces and circulation of these changes are evident in the pages of countless small-town American newspapers. Gage, in her 1883 article, traces women's inventiveness back to ancient times and distant places, and considers unpatented inventive work alongside the modern patents of American women. For instance, she opens her essay as follows: "Isis in Egypt, Minerva in Greece, Surawati in India, the mother of the

Incas in Peru, and several empresses of China, have alike been worshipped because of their inventive genius" (478). In contrast, writers in the aforementioned
newspaper articles focus on patents rather than on inventive work more broadly,
and attend not to women's eternal quality of inventiveness but to the links between education and patents in the nineteenth-century American context. Most
important, they do so with the backing of numbers from the LWP.

Data Collection as a Form of Rhetorical Activism

Clearly, Smith was a prolific public figure in her day. Yet she left behind no private papers and died a pauper in an unmarked grave (Stanley, *Raising* 9–11),
making her a difficult historical rhetor to recover. Additionally, Smith did not
mingle with the suffragists, whose single-minded focus on obtaining the vote,
she believed, was misplaced, and whom she felt, as one article in the *Wichita Eagle*
reported, had "failed to accomplish anything tangible" ("Help for the Women").
Because her network did not include the people with whom we normally associate late-nineteenth-century women's activism, and because her interests were so
broad and diffuse, Smith's contributions are especially difficult to recover.

Yet Smith's labors in advocating for the LWP did result in a flurry of highly
distributed, widely circulated rhetorical activity. As the person who spearheaded
the Patent Office's three installments of *Women Inventors to Whom Patents Have
Been Granted by the United States Government, 1790–1888* (published in 1888,
1892, and 1895), Smith facilitated the circulation of data and statistics that
previously would have been nearly impossible to obtain. Tracing the ripple effects of her rhetorical activity involves what Jacqueline Jones Royster and Gesa
Kirsch call "social circulation"—the prioritizing of "how ideas circulate . . . across
places and regions," and more specifically "how ideas resonate, divide, and are
expressed via new genres and new media" (101). Shaped by widespread reprinting practices and a public with a taste for informational tidbits, the newspapers
of the nineteenth century offered an ideal venue within which statistics drawn
from the LWP might circulate widely in the service of new narratives and arguments about women's inventive activity. These statistics simultaneously sub-
stantiated activists' arguments that an increase in educational opportunities for
women was resulting in more inventions and called into question the value of
women's many domestic inventions. For better or worse, the statistics also con-
tracted the conversation about women's inventions to focus primarily on patent
activity rather than on inventiveness as a human quality. Tracing these shifts in
public discourse back to Smith, as the originator of the data, exposes yet another
robust means by which nineteenth-century women wielded their influence, of-

ten unacknowledged, through the avenues of persuasion available in the world in which they lived.

Notes

1. Stanley recounts the patents from a single year, 1876, finding that within that short time frame the patent office clerks had overlooked thirty-three "unmistakably female names" from the list, out of a total of 157 (the LWP lists 124 names). Although this rate suggests that the clerks omitted "one woman's invention for every four they counted," Stanley's preliminary consideration of a different year, 1890, yields a smaller error rate of only one omission for every twelve patents counted ("Patent Office Clerk" 123, 124).

2. For instance, in 1892 Smith testified to Congress that she spent two months "visiting hundreds of dressmakers, milliners, and merchants" in New York City and surrounding areas to determine the impact of tariffs on these workers' ability to compete with their European counterparts ("Memorial").

Works Cited

"Clever Women Inventors." *Wood County Reporter* [Grand Rapid, WI], 24 Sept. 1899, p. 20. *Chronicling America: Historic American Newspapers*, Library of Congress, chroniclingamerica.loc.gov/.

Cordell, Ryan. "Reprinting, Circulation, and the Network Author in Antebellum Newspapers." *American Literary History*, vol. 27, no. 3, Aug. 2015, pp. 417–45.

Gage, Mathilda Joselyn. "Woman as an Inventor." *The North American Review*, vol. 136, no. 318, May 1883, pp. 478–89.

Garvey, Ellen Gruber. *Writing with Scissors: American Scrapbooks from the Civil War to the Harlem Renaissance*. Oxford UP, 2013.

Graban, Tarez Samara, and Patricia Sullivan. "New Rhetorics of Scholarship: Leveraging Betweenness and Circulation for Feminist Historical Work in Composition Studies." *Circulation, Writing, and Rhetoric*, edited by Laurie E. Gries and Collin Gifford Brooke, U of Colorado P, 2018, pp. 189–98.

Grossman, Jonathan, and Judson MacLaury. "The Creation of the Bureau of Labor Statistics." *Monthly Labor Review*, vol. 98, no. 2, Feb. 1975, pp. 25–31.

"Help for the Women." *Wichita Daily Eagle*, 17 July 1891, p. 6. *Chronicling America: Historic American Newspapers*, Library of Congress, chroniclingamerica.loc.gov/.

Khan, B. Zorina. "Not for Ornament: Patenting Activity by Nineteenth-Century Women Inventors." *Journal of Interdisciplinary History*, vol. 31, no. 2, 2000, pp. 159–95.

"Like a Knight of Old." *Washington Post*, 7 May 1905, p. 12. *ProQuest Historical Newspapers*.

Macdonald, Anne. *Feminine Ingenuity: Women and Invention in America*. Ballantine Books, 1992.

Merritt, Deborah J. "Hypatia in the Patent Office: Women Inventors and the Law, 1865–1900." *American Journal of Legal History*, vol. 35, no. 2, 1991, pp. 235–306.

"News and Notes for Women." *Sullivan Republican*, 13 Dec. 1895. *Chronicling America: Historic American Newspapers*, Library of Congress, chroniclingamerica.loc.gov/.

"News of Our Industries." *Scranton Tribune*, 9 October 1895. *Chronicling America: Historic American Newspapers*, Library of Congress, chroniclingamerica.loc.gov/.

Royster, Jacqueline Jones, and Gesa E. Kirsch. *Feminist Rhetorical Practices: New Horizons for Rhetoric, Composition, and Literacy Studies*. Southern Illinois UP, 2012.

Smith, Charlotte. "Memorial of Mrs. Charlotte Smith, President of the Women's National Industrial League, Praying Congress to Protect by Legislation, the Working Women of the Country." 14 July 1892. *ProQuest Congressional*, congressional-protquest.com.

———. "Why I Became Interested in Women Inventors." *The Woman Inventor*, vol. 1, no. 1, Apr. 1891, p. 2. *Chronicling America: Historic American Newspapers*, Library of Congress, chroniclingamerica.loc.gov/.

Stanley, Autumn. "The Patent Office Clerk as Conjurer: The Vanishing Lady Trick in a Nineteenth-Century Historical Source." *Women, Work, and Technology: Transformations*, edited by Barbara Drygulski Wright et al., U of Michigan P, 1987, pp. 118–36.

———. *Raising More Hell and Fewer Dahlias: The Public Life of Charlotte Smith, 1840–1917*. Lehigh UP, 2009.

United States Patent Office. *Women Inventors to Whom Patents Have Been Granted by the United States Government, 1790–1888*. Government Printing Office, 1888.

"Women as Inventors." *Bismarck Weekly Tribune*, 3 Aug. 1888. *Chronicling America: Historic American Newspapers*, Library of Congress, chroniclingamerica.loc.gov/.

"Women as Inventors." *Evening Journal* [Wilmington, DE], 24 July 1888. *Chronicling America: Historic American Newspapers*, Library of Congress, chroniclingamerica.loc.gov/.

"Women as Inventors." *Macon Beacon*, 13 Jan. 1900. *Chronicling America: Historic American Newspapers*, Library of Congress, chroniclingamerica.loc.gov/.

"Women as Inventors." *McCook Tribune*, 30 Aug. 1895. *Chronicling America: Historic American Newspapers*, Library of Congress, chroniclingamerica.loc.gov/.

"Women as Inventors." *Omaha Daily Bee*, 12 Nov. 1899, p. 5. *Chronicling America: Historic American Newspapers*, Library of Congress, chroniclingamerica.loc.gov/.

"Women as Inventors." *Southern Herald*, 21 Aug. 1896. *Chronicling America: Historic American Newspapers*, Library of Congress, chroniclingamerica.loc.gov/.

"Women as Inventors." *St. Tammany Farmer*, 9 Feb. 1889. *Chronicling America: Historic American Newspapers*, Library of Congress, chroniclingamerica.loc.gov/.

"Women as Inventors." *Washington Standard*, 13 Mar. 1896. *Chronicling America: Historic American Newspapers*, Library of Congress, chroniclingamerica.loc.gov/.

"Women Inventors." *Bryan Morning Eagle*, 3 Sept. 1899. *Chronicling America: Historic American Newspapers*, Library of Congress, chroniclingamerica.loc.gov/.

"Women Inventors." *Evening Star* [Washington, DC], 14 Aug. 1897, p. 11. *Chronicling America: Historic American Newspapers*, Library of Congress, chroniclingamerica .loc.gov/.

Lucy Thompson's Ethos and the Yurok Fish Dam Ritual

Elizabeth Lowry

In 1916, a California Yurok woman named Lucy Thompson published an auto-ethnography entitled *To the American Indian*. The text was intended for both Euro-American and Native American audiences—to teach Euro-Americans about Yurok culture, and to educate a younger generation of Yuroks about Euro-American abuses, exhorting young people not to lose the Yurok's old ways. In this autoethnography, Thompson cites an exigency to preserve Indigenous eco-systems and lifeways, building her ethos through first-person narratives of her experience as a Yurok woman and through her connection to specific sites of Indigenous knowledge and experience. Married to a white man, Thompson lived within both Euro-American and Yurok cultures. This mixed-culture inhabitance was foundational to her ethos in that she believed she could relate to both Yurok and Euro-American perspectives.

Following Kathleen J. Ryan, Nancy Myers, and Rebecca Jones's directive to consider ethos-building as it relates to social justice by focusing on "interruption-interrupting, advocacy-advocating, and relation-relating" (3), this essay examines how Thompson negotiates and builds an ecological ethos that operates effectively across both Euro-American and Native American contexts. Thompson's commentary on resource management marks what would later become a more socially conscious turn in a fledgling environmental movement. When considering sustainability, Thompson is concerned about the environmental and cultural abuses caused by the owners of the salmon cannery on the Klamath River. The Yurok salmon-trapping ritual is given special emphasis in this study because of its profound importance to the Yurok people, salmon being one of their primary means of subsistence.

Ethos is a capacious term, understood in the classical Aristotelian sense as *character*. However, feminist scholarship has complicated this understanding of ethos by linking the term to place—to sites of community and to places where people might gather with the purpose of communicating (Reynolds 329). Scholars such as Nedra Reynolds argue that ethos is fundamentally social and place-based, negotiated across a complex network of relations. I contend that Thompson's descriptions of the Yurok salmon-trapping ritual reveal the scope of such negotiations.

Thompson constructs her ethos by drawing on her stature within the Yurok community as a member of the priest class (known as the *Talth*) and on her work as a cultural liaison. More specifically, Thompson suggests that being married to a white man means that she is able to understand Euro-Americans well and is therefore able to articulate the struggles of the Yurok people in a way that makes sense to Euro-Americans. Further, Thompson is clear about the exigency for her work: the future of her people is imperiled due to unsustainable practices and a series of egregious abuses at the hands of Euro-American colonists. Thompson attempts to appeal to sympathetic Euro-Americans not only on moral grounds but also on the grounds that their actions could harm their own community as well as the Yurok community. In fact, Thompson was able to appeal to sympathetic white people enough to get *To the American Indian* published by Amelia Carson, the daughter of a lumber magnate in Eureka, California. There is no information on the size of the book's original print run, but one imagines that it must have been quite small—intended only for local distribution to interested parties, including anthropologists in the area. Early-twentieth-century anthropologists working in Northern California welcomed the book, seeing it as a valuable contribution to the field; however, after some modest attention in the 1920s, the book quickly slipped into obscurity.

While the publication of *To the American Indian* is certainly an achievement with respect to the cross-cultural dissemination of Indigenous rhetorics, I argue that Thompson's construction of a cross-cultural public ethos can also be considered an exemplar of what Lorraine Code terms "ecological thinking," a model of communication in which "men and women engage purposefully with each other and all aspects . . . of the local and global environment" (qtd. in Ryan et al. 2). Moreover, Thompson's ethos-building demonstrates a model of engagement that "locates inquiry 'down on the ground' where knowledge is made, negotiated, circulated" (Code 5). In the first part of this essay, I discuss Yurok knowledge-making with respect to advocacy. In the second part, I consider how privileged knowledge and access to such knowledge is negotiated by characterizing boundary-setting as a form of resistance to a colonial agenda—a way of disrupting and interrupting Euro-American assumptions of ownership. In the last part of this essay, I conceptualize the circulation of knowledge as a means by which to build on and strengthen relationships within and across communities.

As mentioned earlier, the classical Aristotelian understanding of ethos is *good character*, but feminist scholars such as Reynolds have refashioned the term to emphasize not only place and space but also "custom" or "habit" (327–28). In discussing the Yurok fish dam, Thompson describes knowledges that are made through ritual practice, thereby becoming customs or habits—and rich sites of ethos. When one speaks from a space or place of custom or habit, one must be truthful. For Thompson this is indeed the case; when she speaks from the perspective of a Yurok, particularly as an elite Yurok doctor, or *Talth*, she speaks from her knowledge and experience and, in doing so, commands respect. Moreover, as feminist scholars have also noted, ethos is multiple, mobile, and contextual—hence, Thompson enacts different forms of ethos at varying locations in her text to identify with or relate to both Yurok and Euro-American audiences. Significantly, this relating is predicated on Thompson's advocacy for sustainable lifeways and for her interpretation of European claims to both privileged knowledge and physical domains. That is, Thompson's ethos-building disrupts both material and epistemological Euro-American claims to ownership.

Advocacy: Knowledge-Making

In *To the American Indian* Thompson speaks as an advocate for the Yurok people, making white audiences aware of the kinds of abuses occurring on Yurok land. Thompson works to raise awareness of rampant social and environmental problems and warns audiences of the consequences of inaction in resolving these matters. One of Thompson's most pressing concerns is the environmental degradation caused by the owners of the salmon cannery on the Klamath River. Referencing the "whites and mixed bloods" who fish for the cannery, Thompson describes how the white people established rules about who was allowed to fish and when, and then proceeded to block the river with their nets, "making so complete a network that hardly a salmon can pass" (178). Thompson believes that colonial greed will most likely ensure that the salmon will not be able to pass upstream to spawn and will hence die off. This, Thompson suggests, is an example of the illogic wrought by colonial acquisitiveness. The importance of the salmon to maintaining the health of the ecosystem and the survival of the people within that ecosystem cannot be overemphasized. The Yurok ritual process of installing the fish dam and of calculating how many fish should be allowed to pass upstream and how many can be caught is an example of knowledge built and sustained by the Yurok over multiple generations.

The fish dam ritual therefore promotes knowledge-making in the realms of social stability and environmental responsibility. The dam is installed in the Klamath River as an initiation to what Thompson calls the white deerskin dance (101).[1] Every other year, the Yurok people hold the white deerskin dance to mark a time when all people within the Yurok tribe and other surrounding tribes are meant to come together in peace and harmony to settle old scores and to rebuild broken relationships. Three key roles are played within the fish dam ritual. A high priest (*Talth*) takes the role of Lock, a kind of master of ceremony. Lock selects another *Talth* helper, known as Lock-nee. Then Lock selects the Nor-mer, "one girl of equal high birth"; "the three go to a secluded place out on a high mountain from which place they can have a good view of the surrounding country and there the girl makes a small fire and is given instructions of how and what to do" (Thompson 45). This ceremony emphasizes the idea of the different roles that individuals within a community must play to maintain a functional society. For instance, Lock orders Lock-nee to gather between 100 and 200 healthy young men to help install the fish dam. Thompson goes on to describe in intimate detail how the men cut "small pines" and to explain precisely how the pines are split, woven into mats, and joined with hazel wood—providing enough information that future generations of Yurok might follow her instructions, should the details of this ceremony somehow be lost (45). This ceremony also involves bathing, pipe-making, incense-burning, and prayer. Finally, when the dam is installed, "Lock takes a mallet and as he raises it he talks to God, using words for lots of salmon and to bless all, and at this he comes down with a hard blow, and keeps it up until the first post has been driven to the proper depth, he does not strike his blows fast each blow is struck slowly" (49). Slowness suggests contemplation and deliberation, attention given to each detail. Thompson goes on to describe how "smaller posts are driven at the corners for each trap," as well as the size of the traps and where they are placed in the river (50). Once the dam is complete, its most important features seem to be access and sustainability— room is left on the edges of the river so that people can move up and down the river in their boats, and so that salmon can pass upriver to other tribes. Thompson calls these the "Laws of the Fish Dam," which ensure that there is no waste and that there is enough salmon to go around:

> WHEN the fish dam is put in, they have very strict laws governing it. There are nine traps which can be used, one belongs to Lock and his relatives, one to Lock-nee and his relatives, one to Nor-mer and her relatives, and so on down the line. These families come in the morning and each one takes from the trap that which belongs to them, as many salmon as they need . . . and they must not let a single one go to waste. . . . [T]hen comes the poor class, which take what they can use, some of which they use fresh and the rest they cut up, smoke them lightly then they are dried. . . . . [A]nd then they are put away for the winter. The Indians from up the river as far as they are able to come, can get salmon, and down the river the same. . . . After all have taken what they want of the salmon,

which must be done in the early part of the day, Lock or Lock-nee opens the upper gates of the traps and let [sic] the salmon pass on up the river, and at the same time great numbers are passing through the open gap left on the south side of the river. This is done so that the Hoopa's [sic] on up the Trinity river have a chance at the salmon catching. But they keep a close watch to see that there are enough left to effect the spawning, by which the supply is kept up for the following year.   (136)

This passage is significant in that it highlights the epistemological differences between Euro-American and Yurok social hierarchies. For the Yurok, progress does not mean enriching oneself to the detriment of others; it means maintaining social equilibrium and ensuring the entire community's survival. In explaining the principles according to which Yurok hierarchies operate, Thompson emphasizes that, in contrast to Euro-Americans, the Yurok are always careful to make sure that the supply of fish is "kept up" (136). This contrasts sharply to Western hierarchies in which rich men take over the rivers and deplete the water of resources. Although Yurok laws account for reducing waste, sharing resources, and planning for a future yield of salmon, the white people have set up a cannery on the Klamath, which inevitably leads to an imbalance in resources. Thompson asks: "Will the whites preserve the salmon through all the ages, as the Klamath Indians have done, if they should survive so long?" (137). The question is rhetorical; everyone can see that the Euro-Americans have—thus far—made no attempt whatsoever to preserve the salmon.

In describing the work of knowledge-making, Thompson illustrates how knowledge is made within a community, disseminated across communities, and passed on from generation to generation. Thompson also juxtaposes Euro-American epistemology with Yurok epistemology so that comparisons may be made. Thompson's juxtapositions resonate with the current Indigenous scholarship: Euro-American epistemology tends to be mostly one-dimensional in that it is believed to pertain mainly to the intellect; Indigenous knowledge-making is multidimensional, pertaining not only to the intellect but also to embodiment, collaborative performance, and practice (Todd 9). Such embodiment is accomplished in the white deerskin dance, for instance, through the idea of multiple players who all have specific roles, the importance of slowness and deliberation to each maneuver, and repetitive demonstrative action made sacred by the context of the ritual. Through rituals such as the salmon trapping ceremony at the fish dam, participants are able to teach or transmit specific information to other members of the community. Participants in the fish dam ritual advocate for the significance of their practices on the basis of collaboratively performed embodied knowledge. In this regard, the fish dam ritual emphasizes the cohesiveness within a community as well as ways in which community members are responsible to each other and to their environment. Within the context of the ritual, community members take on different social roles and gradations of power. However, Thompson points out that a community's commitment to sustainability and knowledge-making with respect to resource distribution extends beyond one's own community, to other communities. Hence, ritual practice and its repetition become a kind of advocacy in and of themselves. Through ritual, new knowledge is made and passed on to successive generations. In this manner Thompson suggests that the Yurok can ensure social justice and ecological stability not by adapting to Euro-American lifeways but by preserving the old, Indigenous ways.

Interruption: Negotiating Knowledge

Thompson's work can be interpreted as seeking to disrupt dominant Euro-American historical narratives and epistemologies in that it sets the terms for social exchange, otherwise negotiating the process of knowledge-making and knowledge-sharing. The Yurok people are constructed as knowers to whom outsiders must defer. Euro-Americans may not assume ownership of—or access to—Yurok land, bodies, or epistemologies. For Thompson, negotiation means setting boundaries and deciding what kind of sharing is and is not acceptable in cross-cultural interactions. Some knowledge can be shared, but some should be strategically withheld. The act of negotiating knowledge and how it is shared establishes who is in control of knowledge-making in specific situations and locations. That is, Euro-Americans must establish their bona fides by respecting Yurok cultural values—but even then, Euro-Americans may not qualify to receive certain kinds of knowledge. As Thompson describes how the Yurok people traverse from the fish dam to the site of the white deerskin ceremony, she speaks of how those with privileged or sacred knowledge are separated from the others:

> There are two trails, one goes down next to the river, crossing the creek and up to a small flat just at the foot of the hill, with the large pepperwood trees hanging it [sic], is a place where the dance starts, and this trail and to this place, none can go unless they are born of the highest marriage. The girl and man that are of high birth have already gone and cleaned off the grounds, made the fire and are burning the incense. When the host arrives here they must give all their valuable articles that are to be used at this place, over to the poorest and shabby looking ones, if they have the right birth to take them over this piece of road or trail, to this place, Hel-le-gay-ow, and all from all parts know whether they have the birth, as this is kept close track of by the full blooded Klamath

Indians. And if any persists or offers to go over this trail, to this place, they will
be told very firmly to keep back.   (108)

Simply put, there are people who are eligible to receive sacred knowledge and
people who are not. Thompson explains that the Yurok "do not tell the white man
[about the trail] thinking that they might wish to disobey the rule . . . and of all
the white men that have married the Indian women, we do not think that a single
one of them ever told their husband of this for the reason that they themselves
did not have the birth to pass over this part of the trail" (109). When it comes to
eligibility, no one is permitted a sense of entitlement; the preservation of sacred
knowledge is a means by which the Yurok people can assert their sovereignty. In
this respect, Thompson emphasizes that the localized knowledge the Yurok have
built is immeasurably valuable, because this knowledge has ensured the survival
of their people and the health of their communities for centuries. It is a knowledge that has been won through years of close observation and careful practice.

Thompson's rhetoric, in particular her explanations of the purpose behind
Yurok practices and rituals, appeals to Western audiences because it demonstrates Thompson's understanding of their professed values. Euro-Americans
believe themselves to be logical, practical, and ethical, but Thompson challenges
Euro-Americans to ask themselves if this is indeed true by telling them stories
in which they are forced to reckon with their own unsustainable and destructive
actions. For example, Thompson illustrates Euro-American short-sightedness
and irrationality by describing a couple she once knew—a Native woman and
a white man: "in the fall of the year she would want to gather some pine nuts,
the white man would go with her, taking his axe, and cut down the tree, as he
could not climb it, and told the woman there they are, what are you going to do
about it? At first the woman complained and finally said that the white man
would spoil everything" (31). The idea of cutting down a tree to get to its nuts
is foolhardy. Why would one cut off a future supply of nuts? How can people
this short-sighted be trusted with sacred knowledge? This is where Thompson
begins to draw boundaries between what can be defined as common sense and a
lack thereof. Euro-American readers who claim to have common sense must first
question colonial practices. By juxtaposing Yurok and Euro-American attitudes
toward the environment, Thompson is able to encourage Euro-Americans to interrogate their own practices through vignettes such as that of the white man
and the pine nuts.

Moreover, Thompson points out that Euro-Americans believe themselves to
be civilized, yet there is much evidence that they are not. Thompson discusses
the Euro-Americans' lack of concern for others, their hedonism, and their lack
of morality. As an example, Thompson describes a particular type of man whom

the Yurok community have had the misfortune to encounter: "Fortune-seekers, gamblers and cut-throats" who often "lived with our women in adultery until they grew weary of them and left them with children: poor little children of their own flesh and blood, children without a birth and without a parent to legalize them as his own" (172). Hence, Yurok woman are used for sex—often abused—and then abandoned. This Euro-American is a specific kind of gold-rush-era character, a man who has no sense of shared values, of the sacred, and who, in the pursuit of pleasure, engages in hedonistic and destructive behavior. Much of this behavior arises from the Euro-American man's desire for wealth, which Thompson argues is problematic in that the pursuit of wealth in white culture seems to result in the detriment of both the environment and other people. The Yurok also pursue wealth, but believe that this pursuit must occur while maintaining respect for the environment and for human and nonhuman others. To the Yurok, being civilized means seeking a sustainable and community-minded way of life. They place emphasis on avoiding hedonistic behavior, and they enact civility every day through ritual and prayer.

By emphasizing how Yurok values are explicitly embodied within their practices, Thompson communicates the idea that knowledge-making and -sharing aren't just about holding (or withholding) information—they are ways of life. Thompson invites white readers into her world on her terms, not theirs. She provides readers with a virtual tour of her community, offering up instructions and advice and explaining what specific places mean to her. As a host, she places herself in a position of power, yet, by strategically withholding information, she also explains that Yurok culture does not belong to white people. Some kinds of knowledge must be earned. This withholding prompts sympathetic Euro-American readers to reflect upon their actions and prejudices—to try to understand what it means to be qualified for access to privileged information. Thompson interrupts Euro-American beliefs about Indigenous lifeways by demonstrating how knowledge can be negotiated in terms of determining what is common sense and what is not, what is valuable to the survival of a community and what is not, and which practices should be shared and passed to the next generation.

Sites of Ethos and Circulating Knowledge

Thompson indicates that knowledge is circulated among Indigenous communities through the ethos enacted and reified during ritual practice. As knowledge circulates within (and sometimes across) communities from one generation to the next, Thompson discourages the misuse of power that arises from the occupation of particular social roles. For example, in her references to the ritual of the fish dam, she speaks of the roles of Lock, Lock-nee, and Nor-mer. The girl, Nor-mer, "is a virgin of purity. She goes across the river and bathes herself and dresses her hair, using her Indian knife like a comb, which she carries fastened to her wrist, until her hair is dry and glossy, then she lets it hang loose, wearing a band around her head" (44). That is, Nor-mer is impeccably dressed and groomed, and Lock addresses her as "my child, my daughter, and other endearing terms" (46). When the dam is installed, the ritual significance of Nor-mer, the beautiful young girl, is amplified: "Norm-er [sic] is the absolute ruler of her people as she is the child of God's own purity" (53). Thompson indicates that Nor-mer is at the height of her power during the ritual, but that she'd better not abuse that power: "At this time if Norm-er [sic] was silly enough she could command every man, woman and child to lie flat on their abdomens and go without eating for another twenty-four hours, as all must obey her commands, no matter what they might be" (52). Ordering the people to behave this way would be "silly," Thompson suggests, because power can be felt without having to be exerted—there is no need for Nor-mer to make unnecessary demands. More important, though, Nor-mer will eventually lose her power and may perhaps be at the mercy of someone else. The power of ethos is relinquished with changing social roles and performances. Here, Thompson divulges that when she was a young girl she was a Nor-mer, so she writes from that privileged position—one of knowing.

In their work on Gloria Anzaldúa, Kendall Leon and Stacey Pigg write, "Because we (and ecologies more broadly) evolve and change over time, women's ethos both moves and is multiply located. We need a rhetorical vocabulary to help account for dynamic networks of ethos without overstabilizing locations from which we invent" (237). While the idea of mobility and multiplicity is important to both the construction of ethos and the circulation of knowledge, one should keep in mind that Thompson's ethos as a Yurok woman, a rhetorician, and an advocate for the Yurok people is not restricted only to physical locations but must be constantly renegotiated with each role she adopts for various audiences. For instance, Thompson's use of pronouns in her autoethnography are significant indicators in the shifting of her rhetorical vocabulary along with her ethoic sites or locations. At the beginning of *To the American Indian*, Thompson establishes herself as being part of the white community and friends with Bill McGarvey, the general store owner. She refers to Natives in a distanced manner, speaking of them in the third person. However, when she begins to discuss Euro-American violence against Native women, her language becomes more intimate and direct—she begins to use the word *I* as a way to testify, to bear witness to the atrocities she has seen, and to emphasize what she apparently believes causes the abuse: drunkenness. Toward the end of the first chapter of her autoethnography, Thompson writes:

I have strenuously fought the whisky traffic carried on by the unprincipaled [sic] white men for years and did all that I could to stop it, and made bitter enemies in doing so. Yet it is going on just the same under the very eyes of some of those who are employed by the U.S. Government to put it down. It looks as if they were paid to keep their eyes closed and not see it.   (22)

Thompson is careful about how and where she places her first criticism of Euro-American culture, waiting until she has established herself as a friend to this audience. Possibly, Thompson initially attributes the root problem of the abuse of Indigenous women to whiskey because she does not want to alienate white readers by stating the true problem—that white men evidently feel entitled to Native women's bodies. The *I* that now enters the text is one that circulates back and forth between Euro-American and Native communities. This *I* still does not appear to identify fully with the Yurok people, although Thompson is condemning violence against Native women and critiquing unscrupulous Euro-American men. It is not until a few chapters later, when Thompson begins to use the pronoun *we*, that readers become aware of her deep embeddedness in Yurok culture, particularly when she describes the differences between the *Talth* and ordinary Yurok people: "At every place where my people hold the White Deer Skin Dance (Oh-pure-ah-wah) . . . we separate the Talth and the high birth from the other classes" (108). The use of the pronoun *we* emerges again when Thompson describes the construction of the fish dam and various other instructions pertaining to cooking, building, and healing, narrating as if she is in the process of collaborating with these makers, having been a maker herself—offering step-by-step instructions. The use of the first person plural, Beth Daniell and Letizia Guglielmo argue, can be "either inclusive or exclusive, and sometimes both. . . . Women rhetors, especially those writing or speaking to other women about issues of particular concern to women, often use the first-person plural not just to identify with their audiences of women but to speak for that audience as well" (71). Hence, as an advocate for the Yurok people, Thompson's use of *we* becomes central to establishing her ethos. She circulates knowledge by building her ethos as a friend of various Euro-Americans, as a young Nor-mer in the fish dam festival, as an older Yurok woman, as a collaborator in constructing essential technologies for Yurok life, and as a cultural liaison.

In *To the American Indian*, Thompson calls on white people to recognize the Yurok epistemic community. That is, she seeks to "ensure and secure their recognition as knowers" (Code 165). The act of making Yurok people recognizable as knowers is a rhetorical move that is both a form of advocacy and a transformative practice. In representing Yurok people as knowers, Thompson builds relationships that support advocacy, invites white readers into Yurok lifeways, and explains Yurok logics, providing clear evidence of the Yurok community's progressive thinking and community-mindedness. Significantly, however, in emphasizing the existence of privileged spaces, epistemological and material, Thompson draws boundaries. There are private spaces that Euro-Americans may not enter. In this respect, Thompson communicates that *relating* means knowing how, when, and why to draw boundaries as a means of self-preservation. (This perhaps is a rhetorical move intended for an audience of younger Yurok readers since Thompson models when and how to share access and when not to). Choosing what to share and what not to share thus becomes a way of demonstrating sovereignty and expressing agency. In this manner, Thompson creates a shared community between Euro-Americans and Yuroks by asserting the possibility of building positive cross-cultural relationships based on mutual respect, but she simultaneously disrupts Euro-American assumptions of ownership and access to Yurok culture. Hence, Thompson's descriptions of Yurok ceremonial dances and their ritual purpose serve to interrupt Euro-American concepts of ownership, to advocate for more sustainable practices, and to relate not only to other Yurok people but also to Euro-Americans.

Note

1. Thompson calls this the white deerskin dance, although others have referred to it as the antelope dance or world renewal ceremony.

Works Cited

Code, Lorraine. *Ecological Thinking: The Politics of Epistemic Location.* Oxford UP, 2006.

Daniell, Beth and Letizia Guglielmo. "Changing Audience, Changing Ethos." Ryan et al., pp. 67–86.

Leon, Kendall and Stacey Pigg. "Conocimiento as a Path to Ethos: Gloria Anzaldúa's Networked Rhetoric." Ryan et al., pp. 235–56.

Reynolds, Nedra. "Ethos as Location: New Sites for Understanding Discursive Authority." *Rhetoric Review*, vol. 11, no. 2, Spring 1993, pp. 325–38.

Ryan, Kathleen J., et al. Introduction. *Rethinking Ethos: A Feminist Ecological Approach to Rhetoric*, edited by Ryan et al., Southern Illinois UP, 2016, pp. 1–22.

Thompson, Lucy. *To the American Indian by Mrs. Lucy Thompson (Che-na-wah Weitch-ah-wah)*. Cummins Print Shop, 1916.

Todd, Zoe. "An Indigenous Feminist's Take on the Ontological Turn: 'Ontology' Is Just Another Word for Colonialism." *Journal of Historical Sociology*, vol. 29, no. 1, Mar. 2016, pp. 4–22.

Indigenous Speakers: "Race Traitors" or Rights Activists?

Megan Vallowe

On 23 May 1826, the *Vermont Watchman and State Gazette* reprinted a review from the *Recorder and Telegraph* of a lecture given by a Cherokee man named Elias Boudinot. According to the review, Boudinot's speech focused on Cherokee population growth, as well as certain civilized aspects of the Cherokee Nation, including its Anglo-American agricultural practices; its vast numbers of livestock, mills, and industrial shops; and its constitutional government and mission schools. Such strong evidence of civilization among the Cherokee led the editor of the *Recorder and Telegraph* to conclude his review by saying:

> We could wish that instead of removing them into the wilderness beyond the Mississippi (according to the project recently broached by the Secretary of War, but which we are happy to say has been put to rest in the House of Representatives) they might be organized into a separate State, possessing the same privileges as the twenty-four already constituted. ("Cherokees")

Boudinot, through engaging in transpositional discourse, or an equalizing rhetoric of comparison, convinced this newspaper editor, and perchance other like-minded audience members, that the United States would be better served by adding a Cherokee state to the Union rather than moving the Cherokee Nation west (Walker 17). To make such a claim in an increasingly divided United States was risky for the *Recorder and Telegraph*'s editor, and it still reads as incredible today. Why? Because Boudinot is infamous for signing, along with other powerful men in the Cherokee Nation, the Treaty of New Echota in 1835. That treaty exchanged Cherokee homeland in the southeastern United States for land west of the Mississippi River and guaranteed Cherokee removal from their homeland.

Boudinot's signing of this treaty sealed his fate; he was murdered four years later by Cherokees who opposed the treaty. Indigenous leaders like Boudinot, and the two other orators discussed in this essay, Ely Parker and Charles Eastman, have often drawn the accusation of "race traitor" from scholars and Native communities since.[1] However, their speeches often required these men to show-case their assimilation into Anglo-American culture. Through the language of assimilation, they were often able to present themselves and their Indigenous communities as intelligent and worthy of respect and basic human rights to predominantly white audiences. To this end, Boudinot, Parker, and Eastman, while separated by decades, shared common oratorical rhetoric and used simi-lar themes to persuade their white audiences when advocating for Indigenous rights and tribal sovereignty. Connecting the rhetorical nuances of these three Indigenous orators, I examine the ways their speeches juxtapose the discourse of *civilized* with the discourse of *savage* and demonstrate how the rhetors critiqued the hypocrisy of religious assimilation practices done in the name of civilizing the Indian. Highlighting these two common themes exposes how each of these men worked within the language of assimilation through using equalizing and subjugated discourses to critique violent, unjust, and hypocritical actions com-mitted by their colonizers.

From Race Traitors to Rights Activists

Primary criticisms of Boudinot, Parker, and Eastman as inauthentic, both during their time and after, place great weight on their Western educations, their con-versions to and advocacy of Christianity, and their marriages to white women. For instance, many of Eastman's writings present a highly assimilated narrative, an issue that often brought Eastman and others like him heavy criticism.[2] This criticism has not escaped its own rebuke. For example, Erik Peterson critiques other scholarship on Eastman for what he calls "essentialisms of cultural au-thenticity," which do not accept the differences that occur between people of multiple cultures (174). Keri Holt, James Parins, Maureen Konkle, and I make similar points about the need to avoid arguments of authenticity and recognize the significance of hybridity in the works of both Boudinot and Parker (Vallowe). This essay takes up this ongoing push for recognition of nineteenth-century In-digenous hybridity among activists who fought for Indigenous sovereignty while simultaneously having assimilated in certain respects to white society.

   While Boudinot might be most known for his role in signing the Treaty of New Echota, his influence on the Cherokee Nation and white perceptions of Cherokees should not be limited to that one action. Born Gallegina Uwati, Boudi-not was educated at several mission schools, as was common for Cherokee elites of the time. While at school in Connecticut, he met and married Harriet Gold. After the townspeople burned effigies of the interracial newlyweds, Boudinot and Gold returned to the Cherokee Nation, where Boudinot worked to improve the lives of his people, which included advocating against their removal from the land. Boudinot's stance on removal only changed after the Indian Removal Act's passage in 1830, the Marshall Court Trilogy, and Andrew Jackson's refusal to accept such rulings. Such events, along with Georgian military threats, convinced Boudinot that the removal of the Cherokee Nation was inevitable. Before he changed his stance on removal, Boudinot served as editor in chief of the *Cherokee Phoenix*, the first bilingual, Indigenous-produced newspaper in North America; and before that, he raised funds for the Cherokee Nation's printing press through his 1826 speaking tour, which included his speech "An Address to the Whites."

Roughly thirty years after Boudinot's speaking tour, Parker entered the national stage, largely through his close friendship with Civil War general Ulysses S. Grant. Parker was born to a prominent Seneca family, studied law and engineering as a young man, and was named a sachem, or paramount chief, of the Seneca. Over the course of his life, Parker befriended Grant, eventually becoming Grant's military secretary and commissioner of Indian affairs. Scholarly works on Parker's life and his influence on nineteenth-century Indian affairs and Indigenous nationalism are easily accessible.[3] However, unlike Boudinot or even Eastman, Parker's speeches have largely been ignored. Boudinot's and Eastman's speeches exist in one printed form or another; the speeches' preservation allows for scholars to readily engage with them (even if, as I contend, Indigenous oratory at large deserves more scholarly attention). Most of Parker's speeches exist only in manuscript form, in nondigitized archives scattered across the country. Moreover, most of those manuscript speeches exist today in fragments. As such, engaging with Parker as an Indigenous orator, in addition to his many other roles, has proven difficult. For that reason, I've looked at similar rhetorical patterns from several partial lecture notes as a way of beginning to think about how Parker as an orator might complicate our understanding of an otherwise well-known Indigenous leader.[4]

Sixty years after Boudinot's prominence and thirty years after Parker's, Eastman, a Santee Dakota physician, became a leading figure in the national conversation about Indigenous peoples. Eastman, originally named Ohiyesa, converted to Christianity at a young age after being reunited with his father, Jacob Eastman. Eastman left the Dakotas to study at institutions in Wisconsin, Illinois, New Hampshire, and Massachusetts before returning to South Dakota reservations, namely Pine Ridge, to work as a physician. He wrote a number of books and essays about Dakota life, including the most well-known of his many autobiographies, *From the Deep Woods to Civilization*. Around the turn of the twentieth century and for several decades thereafter, Eastman frequently went on speaking tours. Some of these tours were related to his books and his work with the YMCA, but a good number were associated with events, like the "Friends of the Indian" Lake Mohonk Conference, organized by the Indian Rights Association, a predominantly white social rights group dedicated to the well-being (via assimilation) of Indigenous peoples. Throughout the late 1800s and early 1900s the association was an influential lobbying group that worked to shape policy and social beliefs. A key component of that effort was conferences that often included leading Indigenous activists and orators of the day. As a highly acculturated and well-known Indigenous man, Eastman fit well within the Indian Rights Association's goals of advocating for Indigenous rights via the adoption of Anglo-American cultural norms.

By engaging in public advocacy via the genre of the lecture circuit, Boudinot, Parker, and Eastman illustrate the importance of nineteenth-century speaking tours as an activist venue. These tours, due to their ephemeral nature, often leave present-day scholars with little to read or interpret. Piecing together an archive that demonstrates the rhetorical nuance of these men's speeches requires careful attention to the time period's print culture. Since both Boudinot's and Eastman's speeches considered here were printed conjointly with their lecture tours, I pair them with additional sources that indicate the moment of performance, like the review that opens this essay. By placing these speeches within a rhetorical context that emphasizes their predominantly white audiences, I argue that, by virtue of their fluid manipulation of equalizing and subjugated discourses, Boudinot, Parker, and Eastman navigated changing racial politics throughout the nineteenth century in continual pursuit of improving the lives of Indigenous peoples in the United States.

While lecture circuits were immensely popular throughout the nineteenth century, and issues like slavery, women's suffrage, and Indigenous rights were consistently featured, the dominant voice in the room remained wealthy, white, and male. These affluent white men controlled who accessed the lecture stage and what was lectured about, and typically occupied the roles of lecturer, audience, and organizer. Limited scholarly attention exists on this widely popular media form, and such attention tends to focus on prominent white men like Ralph Waldo Emerson. Tom Wright explains that such scholarship tends to forward ideas that the lecture was a way to help build and spread a national identity (2). In this way, the nineteenth-century lecture was very much a critical part of popular patriotic media. In her important discussion of the American Lyceum, Angela Ray illustrates that after the Civil War, lectures engaged heated political issues of the day more frequently. Ray notes that writers of the 1860s and later often described such lectures "as a site for agitators and reformers" (41).

Boudinot, active several decades before the Civil War, would have fallen in the period of lecture circuits during which speakers tended to make use of the more restrained, if still activist, style associated with ideas of popular education via the lecture hall. Boudinot's lectures followed the format of the early-nineteenth-century lecture, which was a space for both education and intellectualism (Bradbury 30). Because he was appealing to audiences interested in how he was like them and could educate them, it follows that Boudinot would have made more consistent use of transpositional discourse: a mode that allows for both parties of the comparison to imagine themselves as part of an equal relationship. In contrast, Parker and Eastman, who gave lectures nearly thirty to eighty years later, would fall more in line with the post–Civil War lecture style of direct critique and reform, which was more easily conveyed via rhetorical subjugation, or descriptions of the unequal relationship between Indigenous nations and the United States.

Following Scott Lyons's view that rhetorical imperialism "set[s] the terms of debate" (452), my readings show that such speakers navigated rhetorical imperialism via debates that occurred in the language of assimilation. These readings reexamine Indigenous orators' use of assimilationist language, what Lyons calls "contact-zone rhetoric" (453), as a means of achieving what Malea Powell might term "rhetorical survivance" (400). By interrogating Boudinot's, Parker's, and Eastman's use of equalizing and subjugated discourses, I, like Powell, understand Indigenous orators' "use" of assimilationist language as part of the consumption and reproduction process by which Indigenous activists project and perform nineteenth-century "beliefs" about Indigenous peoples to a predominantly white audience (Powell 404). For Boudinot, Parker, and Eastman, acts of rhetorical survivance include speaking directly to that audience's assimilationists beliefs.

Civilized or Savage?

Boudinot, Parker, and Eastman engaged in equalizing and subjugated discourses to juxtapose stereotypes of what is considered civilized and savage. For instance, despite his eventual support for Cherokee removal, Boudinot presented quite the opposite stance on the policy before the passage of the Indian Removal Act of 1830. The *Vermont Watchman*'s affirmative review of his lecture tour offers a prime example of Boudinot's strong opposition to removal in the years leading up to the Removal Act's enactment. That lecture referred to by the *Vermont Watchman* editor was most likely Boudinot's "An Address to the Whites." Aimed at predominantly wealthy, white, and progressive northern audiences, the speech was designed to raise money to start a Cherokee newspaper, which offered further evidence for the claim made in the article, published originally in the *Recorder and Telegraph*, that the United States should "acknowledge them [Cherokees] as fellow-citizens and friends" who would encourage other Indigenous peoples to adopt the "ways of civilization" ("Cherokees"). Boudinot's efforts were ultimately successful in raising money to purchase a printing press for the Cherokee Nation.

What about Boudinot's speech made it such a success? Based on reviews like that above, Boudinot's success came primarily from his emphasis on defining citizens of the Cherokee Nation as equal to citizens of white America. Through questions such as "What is an Indian? Is he not formed of the same materials with yourself?" Boudinot emphasizes his stance on the shared qualities between his people and his audience early and often in his lecture (3). For much of the speech, Boudinot proceeds systematically, showing how Cherokee people meet the assumed qualities of civilization with their system of government, adoption of Anglo-style agriculture, participation in capitalism, devout Christian belief— including an emphasis on the Christian chastity of Cherokee women—and the drastic rise in literacy rates after the creation of the Cherokee syllabary. Boudinot is also sure, however, to allude to the savagery of the United States in its interactions with Indigenous peoples. Whether by referencing the Gnadenhutten massacre or drawing his audience's attention to common idioms of the day, like "[d]o what you will, an Indian will still be an Indian" or "it is the purpose of the Almighty that the Indians should be exterminated," Boudinot reminds his audience that stereotypes of Indigenous savagery often neglect the numerous savage actions taken by white Americans (4–5). Boudinot's primary use of an equalizing discourse, in conjunction with references to the misapplication of savagery onto his people rather than the United States, made the speech a success; it raised enough funds to produce the *Cherokee Phoenix*, which made it possible to present expressions of Indigenous nationhood as equal to United States nationhood to a much larger audience.

Over the course of the century, the critique of the United States' savagery became increasingly apparent. These later, more pointed critiques of white savagery emerged with orators like Parker and Eastman, who witnessed nineteenth-century federal Indian policy play out in the United States, largely through the continued breaking of treaties, the ongoing reduction of Native land through reservation and then allotment, and the systematic genocide carried out on the frontier. Like Boudinot before him, Parker engages with ideas of civilized and savage in a lecture given in New York around 1850. Parker uses subtle rhetorical shifts to point out wrongs done to Indigenous peoples at the hands of the United States. After a short introduction, Parker explains, "I have appeared before you, as an isolated fragment of that once powerful and magnanimous, but now feeble, scattered and nearly extinct race" ("Lecture Notes"). In these lines, Parker plays to his white audience's belief in the myth of the vanishing Indian, emphasizing Indigenous power and graciousness in the face of his people's presumed mass extinction. Parker spends most of his lecture on this last idea. The reference to Indigenous power works in two ways. On one hand, it connects to the popular ethnographic modes of the latter half of the nineteenth century, which sought to preserve knowledge of Indigenous communities before they went extinct. On the other, it allows Parker to set up his predominantly white audience to pay close attention to the cultural traditions that make up the bulk of the lecture's content.

Parker follows up these references to Indigenous power among his "nearly extinct race" with several rhetorical questions, such as: "when I have heard of their heroic deeds, their patriotism, their multitudinous hearts, the extent and support of their 'Long House,' I have inquired with an anxious and swelling heart 'Where are they all now'? Wither have they fled" ("Lecture Notes"). All of his questions refer to qualities revered by the largely white audience sitting before him. Parker describes his ancestors as heroic, patriotic, glorious, mighty, and supportive of their government. Here, Parker mirrors the language he used at the start of his speech to refer to great men of history like Alexander the Great, Philip of Greece, and George Washington. To all his questions, Parker hears the reply, "[Y]ou will never see such mighty hearts." Why not? Parker provides that answer, too: "By the coming of the Pale Face among us we are dissolved. Our hunting grounds are turned into open and cultivated fields, our fishing streams are dried up, the sound of the axe have driven before it the animals of the chase, to seek refuge in depths of remoter forests" ("Lecture Notes"). Parker equates the coming of his audience's ancestors to the eradication of his own people's livelihoods, culture, and foodways. In this manner, Parker switches from an equalizing stance that replaces rhetoric of "noble Indian warriors," who are similar to men whom his audience applauds, with a subjugated rhetoric. It is not some other savage Indigenous group that erases the Seneca Nation's civilized stance, but the savage hostilities of Parker's audience's forebears.

Parker's direct critique of white savagery is not confined to his circa 1850 speech. In another fragmentary speech from circa 1878, Parker again directly criticizes the government of his predominantly white audience. In this speech, Parker takes up multiple issues regarding forced assimilation strategies, including religious conversions that I discuss in my next section. He also spends time discussing the reservation system and violence committed by the United States military. In one such passage, Parker contends:

> But let me ask how long have these poor Indians been permitted to learn the ways of a civilized life upon these reservations? Only until the avarice and cupidity of the white man required these reservations for his own use, then the strong arm of the government was invoked to move the poor Indians farther towards the setting sun. If they aren't willing, well and good, if they refused they were crushed as an obstruction in the path of progress. But I was speaking of the error in the method of Indian civilization. ("Speech")

In this passage, Parker explains that any resistance to such land reduction resulted in violent responses by the United States military. Parker actively tracked such responses through extensive newspaper clippings in scrapbooks, which reached twelve volumes before the end of his life.[5] In outlining the violence used by the United States government to civilize Indigenous Americans, Parker plays with subjugated discourse. He drives home this critique through his ironic line, "But I was speaking of the error in the method of Indian civilization." Ending his critique in this way, Parker highlights his true purpose in bringing up the failings of civilization practices: to point out the hypocrisy of the belief that Indigenous Americans are uncivilized or incapable of governing themselves, as judged by white America. Parker's use of subjugation to illustrate the United States' savagery rather than Indigenous savagery encourages his white audience members to entertain the proposition—based on their own definitions of *civilized* and *savage*—that they are as uncivilized and equally incapable of governing themselves or others as they believe Indigenous Americans to be. Parker's background in the United States military and his intimate role in the Civil War lends itself to such a reading. After all, Parker witnessed the fight to end slavery and watched the United States rip itself in half over one such savage practice.

Eastman, another thirty years after Parker, uses subjugation to even more directly critique his white audiences' presumed stance of civilized superiority. In his 1907 Lake Mohonk address, Eastman encounters an audience supportive of Indigenous rights but also supportive of rights via assimilation. Taking up the topic of religion and civilization, Eastman makes multiple reversals in subjugated rhetoric regarding Indigenous and white Americans throughout the speech. Roughly halfway through the relatively short address, Eastman speaks of "converted savages" returned to the reservation as "wonderful preachers" and "wonderful Christians" (177). In these phrases, Eastman subjugates non-Christian Indigenous Americans, playing into stereotypes of civilized and savage. The following lines continue this subjugation by referencing the boarding school system and listing the oft-lauded benefits given to Indigenous peoples by the United States, explaining that "he is clothed and fed; he has seen everything that is good. He has been in your society and seen everything" (177). Throughout this section, Eastman leads his audience members through their assumptions about the benefits of assimilation, playing into the benevolent attitudes of groups like the so-called Friends of the Indian that make up his audience. After he reassures his white audience members of their superior position, Eastman quickly reverses subjugation. Following his explanation that the converted, educated, Indigenous man returns to the reservation, Eastman reflects that the returnee has become a profane man, the same man about whom Eastman began his speech. Further, it is this man "who influences the others to believe that there is no God in the white man's soul" (177). Eastman reminds his audience that it is education, conversion, and immersion in the civilized society of white America that has caused the Indigenous man to draw such a conclusion.

Pious or Heathen?

Over the course of the century, Indigenous orators like Boudinot, Parker, and Eastman would pair their critiques of the United States and stereotypes of civilized and savage with critiques of religious conversion, as seen in Eastman's 1907 address. As the century wore on, Indigenous orators also began to emphasize the way Christianity was weaponized against Indigenous Americans.

Unlike Parker and Eastman, who both make pointed critiques of Christianity's use in contrast to its teachings, Boudinot makes a different use of religion in his "Address to the Whites." Rather than critiquing Christianity or even dismissing his own people's religion as they convert—a tactic he does employ at other times in this same speech and in his *Cherokee Phoenix* editorials—Boudinot draws parallels between his people's spirituality and that of his Anglo-American audience. He does so by explaining, "They cannot be called idolators; for they never worshipped Images. They believed in a Supreme Being, the Creator of all, the God of the white, the red, and the black man" (9). Here Boudinot positions a Christian God and an Indigenous Supreme Being as one in the same. Boudinot continues such equalizing rhetoric when he adds that "when the ancient customs of the Cherokees were in their full force, no warrior thought himself secure, unless he had addressed his guardian angel; no hunter could hope for success, unless before the rising sun he had asked the assistance of his God" (9). By speaking of his people's piety in these lines, Boudinot forwards an equalizing argument that denounces the treatment of Indigenous people by white Americans who consider themselves followers of a benevolent faith.

In contrast, Parker engages in direct criticism of civilization and its enforcement on Indigenous Americans in the latter half of the nineteenth century. In a speech circa 1878, Parker states that Indigenous Americans did not cultivate logical thought, did not practice advanced agriculture, and followed only rudimentary religious practices. Parker explains that civilization methods always failed because civilization practices started with religious conversion rather than agricultural changes. The Indigenous American learned "first to walk before he had learned to creep." Several lines later, however, Parker uses the same logical argumentation that he claimed Indigenous people did not possess to point out the peculiarity of Pilgrims in the Americas. Parker argues that the Pilgrims "themselves leaving the old country by reason of religious intolerance they in turn in the new country become intolerant, and attempted the introduction of the enforced religion" ("Speech"). In this speech, Parker plays with subjugated discourse by reinforcing stereotypes that his people are incapable of logical reasoning and possess deficient religious and farming practices. Almost immediately, however, Parker flips Indigenous and Anglo subjugated positions by pointing out the hypocrisy of Pilgrims' religious intolerance. In this instance,

Pilgrims, and by extension white Anglo-Americans, are incapable of engaging in civilized behavior but rather enact the exact behavior of religious persecution from which they fled.

Parker does not stop with this one critique. He continues by stating that when these earlier attempts at religious conversion failed, the United States government stepped in to "aid the religious organizations in civilizing the Indians" through the reservation system. Parker critiques that system, too, when he asks, "[H]ow long have these poor Indians been permitted to learn the ways of a civilized life upon these reservations?" ("Speech"). In answering this question, Parker points out the hypocrisy of using reservations for religious conversion. He argues that Indigenous Americans were sent to reservations to expedite religious conversions until the United States government wanted that land, too. In other words, religious conversion was not done to improve the lives of Indigenous Americans, as so much of white America presumed, but as a way to acquire land and capital for a burgeoning empire.

Eastman's 1907 address to the Lake Mohonk Conference similarly critiques assumptions about Indigenous religious sincerity. Eastman starts his address by introducing his topic, "the religious apathy of the Indian to-day" (176). Here, Eastman subjugates Indigenous religious practice through the language of apathy under the assumed religious superiority of Christian Americans. Then Eastman quickly flips subjugation in a similar manner to Parker but in much more rapid succession. He does so by explaining the religious characteristics of Indigenous Americans, stating: "there is scarcely a thing he says or does publicly but he looks up first in silent prayer. There is not a time when he is entering upon his daily chase but he has first held his pipe to the Great Mystery in a silent prayer" (176). In these lines, Eastman purposefully contradicts his prior claim of religious apathy among Indigenous Americans. He continues in discussing the Great Mystery and the religious reverence given to this mystery by his people. Here, Eastman emphasizes the embedded nature of religion and spiritual belief in all actions of Indigenous life. Like Boudinot nearly seventy years earlier, Eastman quickly moves to the crux of the problem as rooted within a critique of the United States' treatment of Native peoples. Like Parker, Eastman will make that critical shift through the use of a rhetorical question, asking, "[W]hat is my Indian to-day?" His answer: "He is a profane man." Eastman continues by stating that "he never knew the devil or hell until the missionary came to him" (176). Through the rhetorical question and answer, Eastman reverses the Indigenous-settler placement within the subjugated discourse that started his speech. By the speech's close, it is the Indigenous man who is pious and civilized, and the Christian man who is corrupt and savage.

Eastman's rhetorical reversal leads into a more direct critique of his white audience, a feature among Indigenous oratory whether focused on stereotypes

of civilized and savage or on religious conversion. For Eastman, the critique typically concerns Christianity as used by white America, as opposed to the religion
itself. In his 1907 Lake Mohonk address, Eastman explains:

> To-day he looks at the white religion as a mere business, as a profession, one
> of the professions of the white man that must be practiced just so; a salary is
> attached to it; a collection must be taken; everything must be paid for; if you
> pray loud, if you have a good voice to pray with you get more pay; he who can
> entertain the audience best gets more pay. This is the position of my Indian to-
> day who is educated, who has been all over Europe, all over this country, and
> has taken an external view of you, just the same as your snap-shot judgment of
> his knife and his tomahawk.   (176)

In this explanation, Christianity as used by white America is not a religion that
practices morality, ethics, or even a spiritual alignment, but a capitalist venture.
Preachers are paid entertainers instead of spiritual guides. The well-educated,
well-traveled Indigenous American (i.e., Eastman) has judged Anglo-Americans
much like Indigenous Americans were judged by "his knife and his tomahawk"
as uncivilized. Through pointing out similarities in judgment, Eastman returns
to a transpositional, or equalizing, rhetoric between both white and Indigenous
Americans. For Eastman, neither people is fully civilized or uncivilized, and
therefore they are rendered equal. This return to an equalizing discourse, if not
every equalizing turn by Indigenous orators, makes a case for tribal sovereignty
by rhetorically positioning Indigenous peoples and Indigenous nations as equal
to the United States and its citizens.

Oration and Rhetorical Survivance

Indigenous orators like Boudinot, Parker, and Eastman engaged hybrid rhetorical strategies in their pursuit of tribal sovereignty and Indigenous rights. Framing this analysis with Lyons's concepts of rhetorical imperialism and contact-
zone rhetoric showcases the orators' definitional push and pull of terms like
civilized, savage, and spiritual. My reading of these orators, mirroring Powell,
focuses on the rhetorical context of the audience as a method to tease out these
men's use of the language of assimilation as a complex and often overlooked act
of rhetorical survivance. Their acts of redefinition on stages cultivated by and for
predominantly white, imperial audiences should be read not as traitorous acts
but as sovereign ones. More than simply constructing their lectures around their
white audiences' expectations, these orators manipulate such codified assimilationist terms, like *civilized* and *savage*, to speak back to that white audience and
to show the hypocrisy of the language of assimilation itself. I build here on Lyons

and Powell to demonstrate that Indigenous orators' rhetorical survivance is one that uses the language of assimilation to redefine the very words so often used against Indigenous peoples in lecture halls controlled by affluent white men. In the case of the orators discussed in this essay, such redefinition deconstructs false dichotomies of civilized and savage, pious and heathen, race traitor and rights activist.

Over the course of the nineteenth century, Boudinot, Parker, and Eastman navigated advocacy, sovereignty, and survivance by redefining core assimilationist beliefs. While their rhetorical strategies shifted across the century depending on the speaker and his rhetorical situation, consistent use of equalizing and subjugated discourses allowed for such activists to advocate for equality and to engage in resistance. For Indigenous activists then and now, such rhetorical moves imply a richer expression of tribal sovereignty than hitherto recognized in studies of nineteenth-century Indigenous rhetoric. Such acts of rhetorical sovereignty and survivance for Boudinot, Parker, and Eastman, as well as many other Indigenous orators like them, ultimately produce nuanced performances of the hybridity embodied in the so-called civilized Indian.

Notes

1. For scholarship critical of Boudinot's assimilation, see Carstarphen; Luebke; Perdue, esp. 3–38. For scholarship critical of Eastman's assimilation, see Bess; Carlson; Eick; Ellis; Robbins; Clark. And for scholarship that criticizes Parker's assimilation, or that asserts that Parker is anti-assimilationist and racist due to his critique of white America, see Michaelsen.

2. For additional scholarship that disagrees with Eastman's easy acceptance of assimilation, see Bayers; Pripas-Kapit.

3. See, among others, Parker; Genetin-Pilawa.

4. The partial lecture notes used in this essay can all be found in the Edward Ayer Collection held by the Newberry Library in Chicago.

5. Parker's extensive scrapbook collection can be found in the Edward Ayer Collection held by the Newberry Library in Chicago.

Works Cited

Bayers, Peter L. "Charles Alexander Eastman's *From the Deep Woods to Civilization* and the Shaping of Native Manhood." *Studies in American Indian Literatures*, vol. 20, no. 3, Fall 2008, pp. 52–73. *JSTOR*, www.jstor.org/stable/20737424.

Bess, Jennifer. "'Kill the Indian and Save the Man!'" *Wicazo Sa Review*, vol. 15, no. 1, 2000, pp. 7–28. *JSTOR*, www.jstor.org/stable/1409586.

Boudinot, Elias. *An Address to the Whites.* W. F. Geddes, 1826. *HathiTrust*, hdl.handle
.net/2027/loc.ark:/13960/t6sx6dh4s.

Bradbury, Kelly Susan. *Reimagining Popular Notions of American Intellectualism: Literacy,
Education, and Class.* Southern Illinois UP, 2016. *EBSCO eBooks.*

Carlson, David J. "'Indian for a While': Charles Eastman's *Indian Boyhood* and the
Discourse of Allotment." *American Indian Quarterly*, vol. 25, no. 4, 2001,
pp. 604–25. *Project Muse*, doi:10.1353/aiq.2001.0033.

Carstarphen, Meta G. "To Sway Public Opinion: Early Persuasive Appeals in the
Cherokee Phoenix and *Cherokee Advocate.*" *American Indians and the Mass Media*,
edited by Carstarphen and John P. Sanchez, U of Oklahoma P, 2012, pp. 56–60.

"The Cherokees." *Vermont Watchman and State Gazette*, issue 1022, 23 May 1826, p. 4.
Gale Nineteenth Century U.S. Newspapers.

Clark, Carol Lea. "Charles A. Eastman (Ohiyesa) and Elaine Goodale Eastman: A
Cross-Cultural Collaboration." *Tulsa Studies in Women's Literature*, vol. 13, no. 2,
1994, pp. 271-80. *JSTOR*, http://www.jstor.org/stable/464110.

Eastman, Charles. "Indian Affairs—Address." *Proceedings of the Twenty-Fifth Annual
Meeting of the Lake Mohonk Conference of Friends of the Indian and Other Dependent
Peoples*, edited by Lilian D. Powers, 1907, pp. 176–77. *HathiTrust*, catalog
.hathitrust.org/Record/100150784.

Eick, Gretchen Cassel. "U.S. Indian Policy, 1865–1890 as Illuminated through the
Lives of Charles A. Eastman and Elaine Goodale Eastman." *Great Plains Quarterly*,
vol. 28, no. 1, Winter 2008, pp. 27–47. *JSTOR*, www.jstor.org/stable/23534183.

Ellis, Reuben. "'Events Threw Us Together': Intercultural and Interpersonal Dialogue
in the Autobiographies of Elaine Goodale Eastman and Charles A. Eastman
(Ohiyesa)." *MAWA Review*, vol. 11, no. 2, 1996, pp. 76–83.

Genetin-Pilawa, C. Joseph. *Crooked Paths to Allotment: The Fight over Federal Indian
Policy after the Civil War.* U of North Carolina P, 2012. *EBSCO eBooks.*

Holt, Keri. "'We, Too, the People': Rewriting Resistance in the Cherokee Nation."
Mapping Region in Early American Writing, edited by Edward Warts et al., U of
Georgia P, 2015, pp. 199–225.

Konkle, Maureen. *Writing Indian Nations: Native Intellectuals and the Politics of
Historiography, 1827–1863.* U of North Carolina P, 2004. *ProQuest Ebook Central.*

Luebke, Barbara F. "Elias Boudinot and 'Indian Removal.'" *Outsiders in Nineteenth-
Century Press History: Multicultural Perspectives*, edited by Frankie Hutton and
Barbara Straus Reed, Popular Press, 1995, pp. 115–44.

Lyons, Scott Richard. "Rhetorical Sovereignty: What Do American Indians Want from
Writing?" *College Composition and Communication*, vol. 51, no. 3, Feb. 2000,
pp. 447–68. *JSTOR*, www.jstor.org/stable/358744.

Michaelsen, Scott. *Limits of Multiculturalism: Interrogating the Origins of American
Anthropology.* U of Minnesota P, 1999. *ProQuest Ebook Central.*

Parins, James W. *Literacy and Intellectual Life in the Cherokee Nation, 1820–1906.* U of
Oklahoma P, 2013.

Parker, Arthur Caswell. *The Life of General Ely S. Parker: Last Grand Sachem of the Iroquois and General Grant's Military Secretary.* Buffalo Historical Society, 1919. *Internet Archive*, archive.org/details/lifeofgeneralely00parkrich/page/n8/mode/2up

Parker, Ely Samuel. "Lecture Notes, ca. 1850." Ely Samuel Parker Papers, Newberry Library, Chicago, Ayer MS 674, folder 1.

———. "Speech, ca. 1878." Ely Samuel Parker Papers, Newberry Library, Chicago, Ayer MS 674, folder 2.

Perdue, Theda, editor. *Cherokee Editor: The Writings of Elias Boudinot.* U of Tennessee P, 1983.

Peterson, Erik. "'An Indian . . . An American': Ethnicity, Assimilation, and Balance in Charles Eastman's *From the Deep Woods to Civilization.*" *Early Native American Writing: New Critical Essays*, edited by Helen Jaskoski, Cambridge UP, 1996, pp. 173–89.

Powell, Malea. "Rhetorics of Survivance: How American Indians *Use* Writing." *College Composition and Communication*, vol. 53, no. 3, Feb. 2002, pp. 396–434. *JSTOR*, www.jstor.org/stable/1512132.

Pripas-Kapit, Sarah. "'We Have Lived on Broken Promises': Charles A. Eastman, Susan La Flesche Picotte, and the Politics of American Indian Assimilation during the Progressive Era." *Great Plains Quarterly*, vol. 35, no. 1, Winter 2015, pp. 51–78. *Project Muse*, doi:10.1353/gpq.2015.0009.

Ray, Angela G. *The Lyceum and Public Culture in the Nineteenth-Century United States.* Michigan State UP, 2005.

Robbins, Sarah Ruffing. "The 'Indian Problem' in Elaine Goodale Eastman's Authorship: Gender and Racial Identity Tensions Unsettling a Romantic Pedagogy." *Romantic Education in Nineteenth-Century American Literature: National and Transatlantic Contexts*, edited by Monika M. Elbert and Lesley Ginsberg, Routledge, 2015, pp. 192–207.

Vallowe, Megan. "The Long Arm of the *Phoenix* in Nineteenth-Century Political Reprinting." *American Periodicals*, vol. 28, no. 1, Apr. 2018, pp. 41–55.

Walker, Cheryl. "The Subject of America: The Outsider Inside." *Indian Nation: Indigenous American Literature and Nineteenth-Century Nationalisms*, Duke UP, 1997, pp. 1–24.

Wright, Tom F., editor. *The Cosmopolitan Lyceum: Lecture Culture and the Globe in Nineteenth-Century America.* U of Massachusetts P, 2013.

Put It in the Papers: Rhetorical Ecologies, Labor Rhetorics, and the Newsboys' Strike of 1899

Brian Fehler

On the evening of 24 July 1899, Lower Manhattan's Irving Place Theatre did not host its usual production of a German-language play or a vaudeville sketch. It hosted, instead, a strike rally composed of newsboy youths whom the New York papers described as "fleet-footed urchins," or "keen, and sharp and quick" ("Newsboys Act and Talk"; "New-York Newsboys" 2). Orators such as Frank Wood, the voice of the famous baseball field the Polo Grounds, addressed the crowd, but the young newsboy leaders, themselves possessors of "no little oratorical ability," earned the rowdiest applause ("Newsboys Act and Talk"). Just one day earlier, "Kid Blink and his Strike Committee had sent the call for the meeting from the Bronx to the Battery, and from Brooklyn to Jersey City, and the arriving delegations choked Broome Street . . . and drove the neighborhood indoors. By 8 o'clock there were 5,000 boys on the block" ("Great Meet"). The newsboys—their headline-hawking voices loud and clear—were not, for once, calling the headlines written by others; that night they, themselves, became the news and told their story.

That story, however, turned on a dime. For, as the *New York Times* reported:

> The strike of the newsboys was due to the fact that *The Evening World* and *Evening Journal* would not reduce their price from 60 to 50 cents per hundred. The price was raised to 60 cents at the outbreak of the [Spanish-American] war when papers were in great demand, and the newsboys thought it time it was lowered. Word was circulated Wednesday night that there was to be a general strike the next morning, and before noon the fun had begun in earnest. Cries of "Scab! scab!" followed the few who dared to handle the forbidden papers, and before long few of them were to be found on the streets.
>
> ("Newsboys Go on Strike")

Strikes were not uncommon by the end of the nineteenth century in the United States. Neither were strikes involving children and young people uncommon, as national child labor laws did not yet exist and would not until the twentieth century. In fact, the first national effort to introduce child labor legislation formed five years after that night in Irving Place Theatre.[1]

Strikes had become so commonplace by the end of the nineteenth century that workers were not guaranteed much public attention. Workers' ability to be visible and vocal was vital for the success of any strike, and newsboys were certainly both visible and vocal. First, the newsboys were massively visible, ubiquitously so, on the streets of New York and other cities, large and small. When they struck, as they rather frequently did, they made news simply because there were so many of them, crowding and joking in the streets; theirs, as Vincent DiGirolamo writes, was a "masculine work culture untroubled by fighting, gambling, or sleeping out" (42). Second, the newsboys were, of professional necessity, vocal. Sometimes called "little merchants," they were little orators, too (DiGirolamo 4). In an era that valued oratory so highly—an era Lawrence Buell describes as having a "cult of oratory" (153)—workers gathered; and when they did, they made speeches, maybe impromptu, perhaps unpolished ones, but speeches that stirred comrades to solidarity and the public to support. Newsboys were eminently public fixtures, living their lives out in the open, on the streets, and, thus, public figures were often happy to be seen lending the boys support. At Irving Place that night in 1899, Jon Bekken writes, "Representatives of the Newsdealers' Association and several local politicians attended to express their support" (209). Newsboys were by no means the only workers to strike in the nineteenth century—certainly not even the only child laborers to strike—but their big voices and big personalities endeared them to the public.[2]

Big voices and big personalities were indeed on display at Irving Place. Marilyn Cooper has helped us think of rhetorical agency as emergent, and agents emerged that night, fellows who bore piquant sobriquets such as Racetrack Higgins, Spot Conlon, Crazy Arburn, and Kid Blink. The boys appreciated prowess, be it physical or oratorical, and that night wished to reward both—and charismatic newsie Kid Blink possessed both. Though the *New York Times* described Blink as both "undersized" and partly "blind" (he had a glass eye), a peer admiringly called him "a bully boy" ("Newsboys Act and Talk").

"Yer know me, boys," Blink, identifying with his audience, begins his first rally speech, and the newsboys respond with greetings and calls of "yer bet we do." "I'm telling the truth," continues Blink, "I'm trying to figure how ten cents on a hundred papers can mean more to a millionaire than it does to a newsboy. And I can't see it" ("Great Meet"). Despite the rowdiness of the proceedings, a newsboy rally was incomplete without probably its most charming feature, the awarding of a horseshoe of flowers to the best orator.[3] The newsboys, many of them, spent time at the races; in their world, a winner received a floral horseshoe. On that night marked by "glowing flights of youthful oratory," Blink, already a favorite with newsboys and soon to be with newsmen as well—whose columns his name would grace for two weeks—walked away with the prize ("Boys Foresee a Victory").

In this essay I argue for the importance of ecologies for rhetorical historiography and demonstrate the ways labor rhetorics, in particular, can be understood ecologically as we work toward better telling the stories of those laborers who have historically been uncast and miscast.

Ecologies and Rhetorical Historiography

For the past thirty years, especially, historians of rhetoric have resisted and revised what Patricia Bizzell called in 1992 the "very traditional 'rhetorical tradition'" (50). As part of this ongoing revision and reframing of our tradition, scholars along the way such as Cheryl Glenn have offered new ways to look at our history and to map it: "by constructing our map by means of angular as well as linear measurements, we can chart and account for previously unseen and unmeasured contours of the landscape. Through angular lenses we catch fragmentary glimpses of the previously unconsidered variations that had been smothered over by the flat surface of received knowledge" (289). This essay advocates the use of ecological methodologies to "unsmooth" those surfaces, to unflatten them, and to retell our history.

As scholars were calling us to rethink our canon, other calls, though not always in the same conversations, sounded to embrace and investigate rhetorical ecologies. Gaining momentum especially after Jenny Edbauer (who now goes by Jenny Rice) published "Unframing Models of Public Distribution," what Joe Edward Hatfield has recently called "the ecological turn in rhetorical studies" reconsiders old sender-receiver models, in favor of multivariant rhetorical maps (29).[4] In an ecology, Edbauer points out, "a given rhetoric is not contained by the elements that comprise its rhetorical situation (exigence, rhetor, audience, constraints). Rather, a rhetoric emerges already infected by the viral intensities that are circulating in the social field" (15). Considering these intensities, this circulation within a social field can "unsmooth," uncover, labor rhetorics— since labor is so often concealed by the very products it produces, the systems it supports. Labor is everywhere present, but so often unseen, necessary but unnoticed.[5]

Introducing Ecological Terminologies

To reveal an ecological methodology's usefulness for reframing our tradition, particularly in considering labor rhetorics, I introduce three terms to tell the story of the newsboys' strike of 1899—*rhetorical relatedness, interinanimation,* and *circulators.* First, *rhetorical relatedness* refers to the cast of characters, human and material, that hold relatively stable roles in a given ecology. Rhetorical relatedness should be thought of in relation to mappings, lines from one thing to another.[6] Such maps show not just the expansion of territory, as when new characters are added to the list, but also, most important here, the ways in which rhetorical players are connected.

Second—not a new word, obviously, for rhetorical studies—*interinanimation* refers to a word's changing meaning as it interacts with other words in a discourse (Richards 55). I. A. Richards's term is useful here as we move from considering words alone to considering bodies in an ecology. Andrea Lunsford first noted the embodied potential of interinanimation, as she "enriches I. A. Richards's notion of the 'interinanimation of words'" by arguing: "It is not only that individual words shift meaning given their context within a sentence, but also that words shift meaning given their embodied context and their physical location in the world" (170). Though not writing of ecologies, Lunsford makes an important contribution to the rhetorical study of ecologies as we consider how words and bodies (can) change purposes and potentialities in a particular ecology.

Finally, *circulators,* as a term, a new one here, is most useful in revising nineteenth-century rhetoric, rhetorical history generally, and particularly labor rhetorics. While the newsboys' strike receives our attention, that year, 1899, exhibited what the *New York Times* called a "strike fever" and what the *Sun* called a strike "bacillus," as freight workers, messenger boys, boot blacks, and others all attempted to negotiate with management, failed, and, as a result, struck ("Strike of the Newsboys"; "Newsboys 'Go Out'"). What did all these striking groups have in common? They understood the power of circulation—the circulation of products and people—and the power, too, of stopping circulation. When movement—of people, of production—was stalled, laborers knew, the capitalists who sat atop a system suffered. Newsboys were, unsurprisingly, uniquely situated to understand circulation and the power of holding the presses.

Rhetorical Relatedness

Our map of rhetorical relatedness, for this study, must consider the city of New York itself, that teeming, towering metropolis, and its newspapers, which told the story of the city. The newspapers, like the newsboys themselves, both grew up with and reported on their dynamic city. Newspapers emerged from the ecology of a city, and, in Gilded Age America, robber barons emerged from the consolidation of newspaper syndicates. Just as their peers—Carnegie or Rockefeller or Clark—exploited natural resources, newspaper titans Joseph Pulitzer and William Randolph Hearst exploited news—exploited truth—and exploited labor, too, to build their empires. Ecologically, we can see the rhetorical relatedness of the strands of exploitation, as Hearst advocated for the Spanish-American War in order to sell more newspapers, and in doing so increased the price newsboys paid for the *Evening Journal.*

Our ecological map of rhetorical relatedness must also consider the newsboy myth that was well established by the time of the strike of 1899. Stories and novels about enterprising newsboys proliferated in the nineteenth century; Horatio Alger, alone, wrote five popular newsboy novels. All these tales featured independent, street-smart, clever young boys navigating a new urban capitalism. The newsboy myth was so widespread and cherished, David Whisnant writes, even reformers "treated symptoms rather than the social problem" of exploited child labor (289). Newsboy charities and lodging houses emerged to ensure some of the boys were fed and clothed, but few of those charities wanted to see the scrappy newsboys disappear from the streets. The myth, despite its drawbacks, provided a framework for the quick ascendancy of someone like the strike leader Kid Blink.[7] Blink rose so high so quickly in the public imagination, in our ecology, because readers already knew him, characters like him, from Alger's novels and a multitude of other cultural sources.

Blink, whose agency emerged most colorfully during the short strike, embodied all these various strands of rhetorical relatedness: the myth and reality of the newsboy, an understanding of New York's streets and circulation, a desire to join in strike fever. Blink kept his message simple, kept the lines of rhetorical relatedness clear. He missed no chance to repeat his refrain of relating newsboys to millionaires: "Ten cents in the dollar is worth as much to us as it is to Mr. Hearst the millionaire," he proclaimed at a rally; "We can do more with ten cents than he can with twenty-five" ("Newsboys Act and Talk"). Kid's message quickly circulated through the ecology as other newsboys took up his theme.

Blink understood, too, the power of a united front, both for internal morale and external visibility. During the first few days of the strike, he possessed an almost obsessive desire for a newsboys' parade. Blink held a rally in front of the *New-York Tribune* building (a paper sympathetic to the newsboys). Blink's desire for a perfect parade makes sense when ecologically considered. The newsboys associated parades with winners: the jockeys and prizefighters so many of them admired receive parades. An evening parade, a great one across the Brooklyn Bridge with a big bass brand, desired by Brooklyn leader Spot Conlon, would show the loyal newsboys, the scabs, New Yorkers in general, and Pulitzer and Hearst that the united newsboys of New York could win, were winners.[8] Blink, facing a crowd of five hundred newsboys and many reporters and police, and loving the attention, took up Conlon's proposal. "Some of the boys thought the parade ought to be in the evening," the *Sun* reported, "but Kid Blink is a far-seeing leader" who addressed the boys as follows:

> "De bigger dis parade is," he said, "de bigger de success it is. If we p'rade in de morning we kin all go out, 'cause it's before de evening papes come out and nobody can't be detained by business. Den again, d'yer remember what happened when a few of us [actually several hundred] went down into Wall Street de oder day. Didn't we get more nickels and dimes in since we've had since? We want de businessmen with us if we're goin' ter keep this fight up, and to get 'em we must p'rade down deir way. So I say we start out from here about 8 or 9 o'clock and go all t'rough the lower part of de city. If we want to p'rade again uptown where de loidies kin see us, we kin do it in de evening."   ("Plan to Down Newsboys")

The *Sun* further reported that "Mr. Blink's reasoning found universal favor." And why not? In the short speech, Blink brought together so many strands of importance in our ecology: the life of the streets; visibility; a gendered understanding of support (coins from the Wall Street men, sympathy, and likely coins, too, from their uptown wives); circulation. Blink succeeded, while he succeeded, in propagating a map of rhetorical relatedness of these various ecological threads of his time because he embodied these threads as he integrated and represented viral concerns of the era into a crowd-pleasing production—one that exploited the long-circulated newsboy myth to his own and the strike's advantage.

Ecological Interinanimation

In a rhetorical ecology, though, no single message-sender controls a message; no single, initial, set of constraints inhibits the message. Rather, ecological conditions are in flux, elements bumping up against each other and changing in doing so. Blink had a strong message, to be sure, and a grasp of relevant strands of rhetorical relatedness—but he could not, nor could anyone, control the interinanimation of those threads. Since the ecology is not a snapshot but rather is moving, is virally infecting and infected, our rhetorically related elements can, and do, change shape and form. Just as the emergent agency of Blink well represents the rhetorical relatedness of viral strands infecting the strike, so too does his fall from favor demonstrate the workings of interinanimation in that ecology as the strike, once born, progressed.[9]

Blink's longed-for, mass-visibility parade, in which "Blink and his colleagues" would show the strength of their numbers and of the sympathy they had won, never took place ("Plan to Down Newsboys"). The newspaper publishers did not want the parade, that much is certain. And while newsies had many rank-and-file police officers on their side—regular cops who were apt to "look on the newsboys with amusement"—the publishers had the "brass" on their side, leading the *Sun* to label the police, whose chief would not issue a strike permit, "blue-coated servants of capital" ("Plan to Down Newsboys").

In the face of this resistance, Blink did what he did best: he rallied his boys. Calling upon "me nobul men," his "good and loyal" peers, he told the boys a braggadocious story of personally bypassing the police entirely, of going straight to the mayor and obtaining from him a special permit ("Newsboys' Word"). In that rousing moment, another one of his oratorical triumphs, Blink demonstrated his understanding of what his boys wanted, what his readers—his public—wanted, and what Pulitzer and Hearst absolutely did not want. Only: it was not true. The *Sun* reported later that Blink's speech had been a "song and dance"; this was an accurate expression because the speech was just that—not just a lie but a performative one ("Newsboys Get New Leader").

Things unraveled, or not, depending on the angle of our ever-shifting ecological map, for Blink pretty quickly. Always featured in the strike stories, he soon had headlines all to himself, such as the *New York Times*'s "'Kid' Blink Arrested." Blink, it seems, had taken a bribe from either the *Evening World* or the *Evening Journal* or both; or he had approached the papers himself and had extorted them; or maybe the headlines were not of his doing and he had been framed in some way. What we do know: Blink's story about meeting with the mayor was untrue. What else we know: just after the parade did not take place, Blink appeared on the streets among his peers in new clothes. News of his new suit and frustration over the unmaterialized parade circulated quickly in this ecology. Did Blink think his "loyal" and "nobul" fellows would follow him anyway, when he was literally wearing a sign of (alleged) disloyalty? When Blink made an appearance in the new suit at an informal gathering of two thousand newsboys, in fact, "some of the boys cheered him and others hooted" ("Newsboys Get New Leader"). Maybe Blink counted on his charisma to carry the day; maybe he was right to do so. For the boys chased him, but the boys were always chasing, raring to fight somebody daily, hourly. But when Blink ran, lots of boys pursued, and the police finally had a reason to restrain him: as a public nuisance—inciter not of a rally this time but of a riot ("Newsboys Get New Leader").

Not really a trial, just a court appearance, Blink's presence in the courtroom drew plenty of attention, and the legend of Kid Blink certainly went on trial. And the legend took a little bit of a bruising, a "soaking," as the newsboys would say (see "Newsboys' Strike"). The courtroom was full of reporters, as Blink would have liked; less desirably, image-wise, his mother was also there, and the bail bondsman she brought along, and Blink had to reveal his real, less romantic, name: Louis Baletti ("Newsboys Get New Leader").

In perhaps the most dramatic and appropriate image that illustrates the principle of ecological interinanimation so well, we are presented with the picture of

Blink running to and from the courthouse. Running, initially, to get away from the police, who caught him, fleet-footed though he was; after the proceedings, Blink, confident as always, returned to Park Row, the heart of newspaper distribution and newsie loitering. His brash return, the *Sun* reported, transformed the street into a "theater for incursions and alarums [alarms]. The boys chased him, the police chased him, and there was a noisy time" ("Newsboys Get New Leader).

The rise and fall of Blink reveals three ways in which interinanimation works in an ecology. First, Blink was a sender of a message, to be sure, but that message changed as he interacted with the elements of the ecology. As he interacted with his peers, Blink was a labor leader, loyal to the cause. As he interacted with the press, police, and publishers, he gained notoriety enough to either demand or be offered bribes. Secondly, in this dynamic ecology, Blink never experienced either a pure rise or fall. In terms of his rise, when Blink won his floral horseshoe, plenty of boys wanted to award the prize to someone else (to Racetrack Higgins); while the boys as a whole appreciated Blink's oratory and charisma, they were most loyal to the leaders of their own boroughs, blocks. In terms of his fall, the image of Blink pursued by peers is colorful but not complete. Some boys actually pursued Blink because they still supported him. After the court date, Blink still moved among the newsboys, part of the strike ecology, as a "walking delegate" of their "Newsboys' Protective and Benevolent Union" ("Parade To-Night"). Within the short span of the strike, many boys showed their status as interinanimators, cheering or chasing their leader, as the argument of the day held sway.

Ecological Circulators

This consideration of interinanimation in terms of rhetorical ecology reveals something special about the case of the newsboys and their strike: circulation is better considered in our scholarship than circulators are, and who are circulators but the embodiments of circulation? And who knew circulation better than newsboys? For labor rhetorics, in particular, recognizing circulators is essential for expanding our disciplinary map. Edbauer writes, metaphorically, that ecologies "simply bleed" (9). They do, certainly, in an intellectual-metaphorical way, and sometimes literally and profusely, as in the newsboys' strike. "The first blood in the strike goes to the newsboys," the *Sun* reported, unmetaphorically ("Newsboys 'Go Out'"). Few stories of the strike omitted descriptions of brawls and blood, the "red blood from many a juvenile nose" ("Only Tie-Up"). Circulation was embodied by these young circulators, soaked scabs and each other alike, and police sometimes, and even men on the streets or streetcars who carried a copy of the *Evening Journal* or the *Evening World*. This ecology indeed did bleed, and the bright newsboy blood was a signal of the spreading of the message, at the level of the streets—hand-to-hand, fist-to-nose, physical, embodied circulation of an ecology of labor.

As the embodiment of circulation, the newsie circulators wore the messages they circulated, quite literally, on their sleeves—and on their hats and heads. Kid Blink's strike committee raised the eleven dollars necessary for printing thousands and thousands of flyers, flyers which the newsboys, ingeniously, inserted into the newspapers they were still selling. Were you to buy a paper—the *Times*, say, or the *Sun*, or the *Tribune*—from a newsboy on the streets of New York in late July 1899, you would have received one of these flyers as well as a verbal plea not to buy the struck *World* or *Journal*. The text of the flyer, as reported by the *Times*, read: "Help us in our struggle to get fair play by not buying The Journal or World. Help us! Do not ask for The World or The Journal. Newsboys Union" ("Striking Newsboys"). As an added visual touch, the *Times* tells us, probably with competitive satisfaction, "the words *Journal* and *World* are printed in yellow"—yellow for coward/traitor ("Striking Newsboys"). Newsboys also pinned phrases such as "Please don't buy the *Evening Journal* and *World*" and "I ain't a scab" onto their "hats and coats," as they walked "from the Battery to the Bronx, and even across the Brooklyn Bridge" ("Strike of the Newsboys").

It is essential that, as rhetorical historians embracing the ecological turn, we not ignore the body and embodied rhetorics. In "Octalog III," Jay Dolmage reminds us: "Rhetoric is always embodied. When I say this, I mean, first, that all meaning issues forth from the body, and that second, communication reaches into the body to shape its possibilities" (114). The newsboys, through their bloodied and embodied arguments, reveal that circulation, too, should be considered as carried by and through the body. Newsboys were often disabled bodies, and their nicknames—Crutchy or Stubby or Blink—often referred to bodily characteristics. The newsboys were poor bodies too, embodying the poverty of the Gilded Age, a poverty that required their messages to sometimes be of the found variety. Enterprising newsboys, for example, took special revenge on Pulitzer's *World*. The *World*, refusing ever to mention the newsboys' strike, continued to report on the trolley strike. The paper's competitor the *Sun* reported, with some glee:

> Several hundred printed signs will be carried by the boys. These were contributed by the *World*, although that newspaper never thought of their being put to such use when it printed them. Several days ago the evening edition of the *World* came out with an account of the Brooklyn strike, headed in letters six inches long, "Strikers Still Firm." Underneath, in tiny letters, it continued, "but cars still running." The newsboys have secured a lot of these papers, cut out the big head[line]s, pasted them on cardboard, and nailed them to sticks.
>
> ("Plan to Down Newsboys")

The boys, physically circulating their message—because they were poor, because they embodied poverty—found ways to use the *World*'s words, and resources, against itself.

If the newsboys embodied circulators and well understood circulation, they knew, too, the power of circulation's opposite: blockage, stoppage. In the parlance of the day, the newspapers regularly referred to the strike by the term *tie-up*, and the strike was just that. Just as the boys embodied circulation they also embodied stoppage. The boys were so successful at these sorts of stoppages of circulation that the *Sun* reported that the newsboys' actions resulted "in a tie-up so tight as to make the street car strikers ridiculous in comparison" ("Only Tie-Up"), all this despite the *World* and *Journal* hiring "muscle" to intimidate the boys and "untie the tie-up" ("Newsboys' Strike"). Ecologically, we can see that the newsboys were certainly influenced in their decision to strike by the presence in the city of other, adult strikers, no doubt principally the streetcar workers. In their fill-the-streets enthusiasm, though, in their circulatory expertise, the newsboys possessed skills that other labor groups may not have; their youthful, sympathy-inspiring, very visible bodies also gave them an edge.[10]

The newsboys of New York, in that summer of 1899, acted agentially, conducting forces and viral energies at play to correct a wrong. Their stories were presented heroically, admiringly; they were thought to be "as full of fun as fight" ("New-York Newsboys" 2). The *Tribune* compared the stand of the newsboys to the actions of "many great men" and its leaders to "heroes of old" ("Boys Foresee a Victory"). So should we now praise those (momentarily, some of them) famous (young) men? After all, even after more than a century, the newsboy myth is still appealing. Whisnant writes of the power of that myth in the late nineteenth, and even into the early twentieth, century: "To question the newsboy as an institution was to undermine the economic and ideological foundations of the republic" (273). Ecologically, now, we have the opportunity to see beyond, or into, the institution, to consider newsboys as laborers, as interinanimators, as circulators. Even today, the myth relies on charm and physicality. The *Newsies* musical, based on a 1992 film by the same name, presents the vigor and physicality, the embodiedness, of the strike, winning an award for choreography, and featuring what critic Andrew Boynton describes as "fearless, athletic movement that perfectly conveyed their rough-and-tumble world" and "boyish charm."

What's more, as historians of rhetoric, we have an opportunity to seize upon ecological approaches to tell our stories, to enliven and expand our tradition. The story of the newsboys certainly lends itself to a heroic approach: a group (albeit a sizable group) of rough-and-ready urchins take on terrible titans Pulitzer and Hearst. Undoubtedly, Hearst and Pulitzer were pretty awful—withholding that dime from their labor force, influencing the police against the boys, hiring strong arms. And what's more, Hearst and Pulitzer, in their own newspapers, silenced the newsboys. Not a word of the strike found publication in the *World* or the *Journal*. Undoubtedly, too, the newsboys accomplished much. Circulation of the struck papers fell by two-thirds and worried advertisers and publishers alike ("Exploited Children"). As the strike ended, incidentally, the newsboys did not see the price return to fifty cents for a hundred papers: the price remained at sixty cents. Newsboys won another concession, though. The *World* and *Journal* agreed to buy back any papers at the end of the day that the newsies did not sell, a new practice, and one that saved the newsies both anxiety and money, and with which they were satisfied (Nasaw 176).

After the strike, the newsies went back to peddling headlines rather than creating them. The *World* put a few of the boys on trial for extortion, and one or two made headway in the profession so many newsies seemed to dream of entering: prizefighting. Kid Blink eventually became a saloonkeeper, later was acquitted in a murder trial, and died young of tuberculosis, a disease that was the ultimate circulator in the nineteenth century, taking the lives of high and low.

The story of the newsies, then, is not, finally, necessarily, a heroic one—nor does it need to be. It is a story of circulation in an ecology of human, embodied circulators, ones who sought a change, who fought for a fair deal. Theirs is the story of laborers laboring together, laborers who were not revolutionaries, who were not, really, even activists. They lived and worked—circulated—within systems that they did not wish to overthrow. They lived and worked and achieved as so many countless laborers in any age have done, people whose stories sender-receiver models tend to fail but which ecologies can capture.

Notes

1. Even earlier, though still after the newsboys' strike considered here, efforts were made at the state level to curtail child labor. Lee Polansky writes: "In 1901, Edgar Gardner Murphy, an Episcopalian minister from Arkansas, founded the Alabama Child Labor Committee, the first organization specifically devoted to ending child labor" (504). For the larger story of the National Child Labor Committee, see Trattner.

2. From the 1870s on, newsboys were frequently infected with so-called strike fever. DiGirolamo's recent book "places newsboys at the center of the social upheavals of the Gilded Age," including such upheavals as the "mass strikes of the 1870s and 1880s" (7).

3. On the occasion of another rally, the floral arrangement was purchased by African American lemonade and pretzel vendor William Reese, whose Printing Square stand was a gathering place of newsboys ("Striking Newsboys").

4. Sender-receiver models such as Lloyd Bitzer's rhetorical situation. Bitzer's "The Rhetorical Situation," of course, has been oft cited, extended, and disputed. From Richard Vatz's and Scott Consigny's critiques in the 1970s, however, Bitzer's article has been a continual touchstone for the discipline.

5. So far, ecological studies have tended to focus primarily on fairly recent events, such as Edbauer's own example of the "Keep Austin Weird" slogan, though works such as Nathaniel A. Rivers and Ryan P. Weber's analysis of the Montgomery Bus Boycotts demonstrate historians' increasing acceptance of ecological models.

6. We only rarely see the term *rhetorical relatedness*—and in disciplines other than our own, such as graphic design. In the late 1990s, for example, Stephan Kerpedjiev, Giuseppe Carenini, Nancy Green, Johanna Moore, and Steven Roth use the term *rhetorical relatedness* to refer to two graphics, on the same page, that share a goal of relaying like information (4).

7. The myth lives on. Blink's character seems to be at least one inspiration for the character in the Disney musical *Newsies* (film and Broadway) named Jack, a charismatic, oratorically gifted newsie. A version of Blink's story, and the newsboys' strike generally, is presented in Don Brown's charming children's book *Kid Blink Beats the World!*

8. The newsboys, masters of circulation, were the first group to seize upon the potential of using New York's still-new engineering marvel, the Brooklyn Bridge, as a point of protest.

9. An example of interinanimation from the other side: to curry favor, Pulitzer's *World*, previously critical of the police in the trolley workers' strike, published only laudatory articles about the police during the duration of the newsboy strike.

10. On another dramatic occasion, the boys acquired so many struck papers from printing offices that, when they shredded the pages to bits, the "sweepers of the Street Cleaning Department were called out to clean up the street. The torn papers filled Frankfort St. from Park Row to William St. to a depth of six inches" ("'Kid' Blink Arrested").

Works Cited

Bekken, Jon. "Newsboys: The Exploitation of 'Little Merchants' by the Newspaper Industry." *Newsworkers: Toward a History of the Rank and File,* edited by Hanno Hardt and Bonnie Brennen, U of Minnesota P, 1995, pp. 190–225.

Bitzer, Lloyd F. "The Rhetorical Situation." *Philosophy and Rhetoric*, vol. 1, no. 1, Jan. 1968, pp. 1–14.

Bizzell, Patricia. "Opportunities for Feminist Research in the History of Rhetoric." *Rhetoric Review*, vol. 11, no. 1, 1992, pp. 50–58.

Boynton, Andrew. "Boyish Charm: The Dancing in 'Newsies.'" *The New Yorker*, 26 Mar. 2012, www.newyorker.com/culture/culture-desk/boyish-charm-the-dancing-in-newsies.

"Boys Foresee a Victory." *New-York Tribune*, 25 July 1899, p. 1. *Chronicling America: Historic American Newspapers*, Library of Congress, chroniclingamerica.loc.gov/.

Brown, Don. *Kid Blink Beats the World!* Roaring Brook Press, 2004.

Buell, Lawrence. *New England Literary Culture: From Revolution through Renaissance.* Cambridge UP, 1986.

Consigny, Scott. "Rhetoric and Its Situations." *Philosophy and Rhetoric*, vol. 7, no. 3, Summer 1974, pp. 175–86.

Cooper, Marilyn M. "Rhetorical Agency as Emergent and Enacted." *College Composition and Communication*, vol. 62, no. 3, Feb. 2011, pp. 420–49.

DiGirolamo, Vincent. *Crying the News: A History of America's Newsboys.* Oxford UP, 2019.

Dolmage, Jay. "The Circulation of Discourse through the Body." *Rhetoric Review*, vol. 30, no. 2, 2011, pp. 113–15.

Edbauer, Jenny. "Unframing Models of Public Distribution: From Rhetorical Situation to Rhetorical Ecologies." *Rhetoric Society Quarterly*, vol. 35, no. 4, Fall 2005, pp. 5–24.

"Exploited Children Organize, Defeat Newspaper Titans." *APWU*, 30 Apr. 2012, apwu.org/news/exploited-children-organize-defeat-newspaper-titans.

Glenn, Cheryl. "Remapping Rhetorical Territory." *Rhetoric Review*, vol. 13, no. 2, Spring 1995, pp. 287–303.

"Great Meet of Newsboys." *The Sun* [New York], 25 July 1899, p. 2. *Chronicling America: Historic American Newspapers*, Library of Congress, chroniclingamerica.loc.gov/.

Hatfield, Joe Edward. "The Queer Kairotic: Digital Transgender Suicide Memories and Ecological Rhetorical Agency." *Rhetoric Society Quarterly*, vol. 49, no. 1, 2019, pp. 25–48.

Kerpedjiev, Stephan, et al. "Saying It in Graphics: From Intentions to Visualizations." *Proceedings of the IEEE Symposium on Information Visualization*, 1998, pp. 97–101, www.cs.cmu.edu/Groups/sage/PDF/piv98.pdf.

"'Kid' Blink Arrested." *The New-York Tribune*, 28 July 1899, p. 2. *Chronicling America: Historic American Newspapers*, Library of Congress, chroniclingamerica.loc.gov/.

Lunsford, Andrea A. "Writing, Technologies, and the Fifth Canon." *Computers and Composition*, vol. 23, no. 2, 2006, pp. 169–77.

Nasaw, David. *Children of the City: At Work and Play.* Oxford UP, 1985.

"Newsboys Act and Talk." *The New York Times*, 25 July 1899, p. 3. *ProQuest: New York Times Archive (1857–1922)*, proquest.com.

"Newsboys Get New Leader." *The Sun* [New York], 28 July 1899, p. 2. *Chronicling America: Historic American Newspapers*, Library of Congress, chroniclingamerica.loc.gov/.

"Newsboys Go On Strike." *The New York Times*, 21 July 1899, p. 2. *ProQuest: New York Times Archive (1857–1922)*, proquest.com.

"Newsboys 'Go Out.'" *The New York Sun*, 20 July 1899, p. 3. *Chronicling America: Historic American Newspapers*, Library of Congress, chroniclingamerica.loc.gov/.

"Newsboys' Strike Swells." *The Sun* [New York], 23 July 1899, p. 2. *Chronicling America: Historic American Newspapers*, Library of Congress, chroniclingamerica.loc.gov/.

"Newsboys' Word Stands." *The New-York Tribune*, 23 July 1899, p. 3. *Chronicling America: Historic American Newspapers*, Library of Congress, chroniclingamerica.loc.gov/.

"New-York Newsboys: The Kind of Stuff the Strikers Are Made Of." *The New York Tribune Illustrated Supplement*, 30 July 1899, pp. 1–2.

"The Only Tie-Up in Town." *The Sun* [New York], 21 July 1899, p. 2. *Chronicling America: Historic American Newspapers*, Library of Congress, chroniclingamerica.loc.gov/.

"Parade To-Night, Sure." *The Sun* [New York], 27 July 1899, p. 3. *Chronicling America: Historic American Newspapers*, Library of Congress, chroniclingamerica.loc.gov/.

"Plan to Down Newsboys." *The Sun* [New York], 24 July 1899, p. 3. *Chronicling America: Historic American Newspapers*, Library of Congress, chroniclingamerica.loc.gov/.

Polansky, Lee. "National Child Labor Committee." *Encyclopedia of the Gilded Age and Progressive Era*, edited by John D. Buenker and Joseph Buenker, M. E. Sharpe, 2013, pp. 504–05. *EBSCOhost*, ebscohost.com.

Richards, I. A. *The Philosophy of Rhetoric*. 1936. Oxford UP, 1965.

Rivers, Nathaniel A., and Ryan P. Weber. "Ecological, Pedagogical, Public Rhetoric." *College Composition and Communication*, vol. 63, no. 2, Dec. 2011, pp. 187–218.

"Strike of the Newsboys." *The New York Times*, 22 July 1899, p. 4. *ProQuest: New York Times Archive (1857–1922)*, proquest.com.

"Striking Newsboys Are Firm." *The New York Times*, 23 July 1899, p. 3. *ProQuest: New York Times Archive (1857–1922)*, proquest.com.

Trattner, Walter. *Crusade for the Children: A History of the National Child Labor Committee and Child Labor Reform in America*. Quadrangle, 1970.

Whisnant, David E. "Selling the Gospel News; or, The Strange Career of Jimmy Brown the Newsboy." *Journal of Social History*, vol. 5, no. 2, Spring 1972, pp. 269–309.

Vatz, Richard E. "The Myth of the Rhetorical Situation." *Philosophy and Rhetoric*, vol. 6, no. 3, Summer 1973, pp. 154–61.

Affection, Intimacy, and Labor Organizing: Queering Public Activism in the Long Nineteenth Century

Brenda Glascott

The fire that consumed the Triangle Shirtwaist Factory and killed 146 people—mostly women, mostly Jewish and Italian immigrants—on 25 March 1911 in New York City has been characterized as "the worst industrial factory fire in the history of American capitalism" (Greider xi). Many died jumping out the windows from the eighth and ninth floors to get away from the flames. Others succumbed to smoke or fire on the factory floor. The people who escaped had dramatic stories of trying to survive a factory that seemed almost specifically designed to keep anyone in it trapped. Public servants, including various inspectors and the fire chief and fire commissioner, had been trying to get factory owners to adopt protections such as sprinklers even just a few weeks before the fire. The owners responded with alarmist rhetoric that they were being forced to take on an unfair expense that trespassed on their property rights (Stein 25). To make matters worse, the fire department didn't have ladders that could reach past the Triangle Shirtwaist Factory's seventh floor (the three-floor factory started on the eighth floor).

A week and a day after the fire, the Women's Trade Union League (WTUL), an organization founded to create a coalition among working-class and elite women, rented out the Metropolitan Opera House to bring together labor, government, and religious leaders; while the opera house balconies were filled with working-class men and women, the orchestra seats were reserved for the upper classes. Major community leaders spoke at this memorial meeting, including a former district attorney, the director of charities for the Catholic Diocese of Brooklyn, a bishop, a rabbi, and a Columbia University economist. The proposal offered during the meeting to create a bureau for fire prevention provoked an angry response from the working-class audience, who feared a committee would fail to provide concrete action. One of the leaders of the WTUL, Rose Schneiderman, a young, Jewish immigrant from Poland who was both a garment worker and union organizer, interrupted the proceedings and delivered an uninvited speech that harshly criticized the "allies" in the audience.[1] She said:

I would be a traitor to these poor burned bodies if I came here to talk good
fellowship. We have tried you good people of the public and we have found
you wanting. . . . This is not the first time girls have been burned alive in the
city. . . . We have tried you citizens; we are trying you now, and you have a
couple of dollars for the sorrowing mothers, brothers and sisters by way of a
charity gift. But every time the workers come out in the only way they know
to protest against conditions which are unbearable, the strong hand of the law
is allowed to press down heavily upon us. . . . I can't talk fellowship to you who
are gathered here. Too much blood has been spilled. I know from my experience
it is up to the working people to save themselves. The only way they can save
themselves is by a strong working-class movement.   (qtd. in Argersinger 107)

Despite her position as an officer for the cross-class organization that arranged
this public meeting, Schneiderman conveys deep skepticism about the intentions and reliability of "you good people of the public." She critiques the "good
people" for empty sympathy and calls them out for ineffectual activism. She invokes "burned bodies" and spilled blood as obstacles to "fellowship." And, finally,
she appeals to other members of the working class to do what needs to be done
without concern about gaining allies or building coalitions. She creates a trope of
having "tried" these "good people" and good "citizens," and having found them
"wanting." The elite women, who formed part of the leadership and membership
of the WTUL—including Mary Dreier, president of the New York WTUL—were
not spared by Schneiderman's speech.

Despite, or perhaps in part because of, Schneiderman's vocal skepticism
about and rejection of committees as a response to the Triangle fire, the committee that did emerge from these meetings ended up being extraordinarily
influential.[2] In June, three months after the fire, the state legislature formed
the Factory Investigating Commission. Leon Stein writes that "[t]he four-year
term of the Commission marks the beginning of what is generally recognized as
'the golden era in remedial factory legislation,' in the state of New York" (210).
Significantly, this nine-member commission included Dreier, the upper-middle-
class president of the WTUL, as a commissioner. The commission hired Schneiderman, Clara Lemlich, and Pauline Newman, all three of whom were Jewish
immigrant garment workers, labor activists, and members of the WTUL, as factory investigators; Frances Perkins, future secretary of labor, was also hired.[3]
Far from alienating powerful allies with her speech, Schneiderman was put in a
position to directly affect legislation through the patronage of Dreier.

What made this coalition at the heart of the New York WTUL resilient was
the ties that bound women across class and ethnic boundaries and through
difficult times. These bonds were particularly strong between Dreier and the

working-class activists Schneiderman, Newman, and Leonora O'Reilly. Relationships in the WTUL were nurtured by the intimate relationships between specific pairs of women—several of which were recognized as couplings within the activist circle—and the affectional rhetoric the women used in their interpersonal communication regarding their activist work. The centrality of personal relationships and affectional rhetorics to the WTUL's successful public activist work erases distinctions between the private and the public and exists as a trace of nineteenth-century women's literacy practices. Moreover, these women's affectional rhetoric and intimate relationships built, sustained, and queered their public activist work. In the following pages, I outline the ways class conflicts and personal relationships challenged and maintained the WTUL, examine examples of affectional rhetorics, and discuss to what extent this historical example offers a queer example of public activist rhetoric.

Cross-Class Tension and the Women's Trade Union League

The National Women's Trade Union League of America was founded in Boston in 1903 as a coalition of white working-class women; white middle-class, university-educated New Women; and white women from wealthy and prominent families. According to the league's unpublished records, located at Radcliffe College's Schlesinger Library, the purpose of the league was to "assist in the organization of women wage workers into trade unions and thereby to help them secure conditions necessary for healthful and efficient work and to obtain a just reward for such work." The league emphasized the importance of having working-class women in leadership positions from its founding. However, the cross-class coalition project of the WTUL was never without complications. William English Walling, founder of the WTUL, "envisioned an organization in which 'women of college education were to give ideas, women of social position to use their influence to create social sensitiveness and the women in the trades to supply the practical information'" (Dye 34). Especially in the early years, the middle- and upper-class women outnumbered the working-class women in the organization (Dye 28). Historian Annelise Orleck claims that "[d]espite their genuine commitment to trade unionism, League leaders [upper-class women] had credibility problems among women workers" (43).

The WTUL was strained by cross-class frustrations and cross-class disagreements about rhetorical choices, about strategy, and about desirable alliances. Orleck writes that "[t]he League women [elites] often seemed to Schneiderman and O'Reilly to act out of a patronizing benevolence that had little to do with real coalition building" (43). Another source of tension was socialism. The two most prominent working-class leaders in the New York WTUL, Schneiderman and O'Reilly, were members of the Socialist Party, which discomforted the middle- and upper-class progressives (Orleck 43). Many of the middle- and upper-class members of the WTUL originally gravitated to the organization because the focus on union-building seemed poised to make more direct and systematic change than other progressive outlets, such as the settlement house movement. The upper- and middle-class members also saw this coalition as a way to recruit working-class women into the movement for suffrage, but "were surprised and offended when the organizers they had helped used the language of class struggle to argue for their right to vote" (Orleck 92).

Despite the class stressors on the WTUL, it remained an influential organization through the 1920s, when its leaders, including Schneiderman, became personal friends of the Roosevelts and helped develop the vision of the New Deal. Interestingly, what helped hold the coalition together was affectional bonds. Dreier had close friendships with O'Reilly and Schneiderman, and the social bond between these women meant that even though O'Reilly, for instance, resigned from the organization in disgust multiple times, she was welcomed back. Personal relationships increased the resilience of the organization. Nancy Dye explains that "[c]lass and ethnic conflicts explain much of the league's factionalism, policy disputes, and difficult personal relationships . . . [although] social relationships among league members sometimes tended to mitigate serious class conflict" (52). These social relationships were built on intimacy. Dye further explains that "allies and workers vacationed together, concerned themselves with one another's families and finances, and generally shared day-to-day life experiences" (57). Although the women worked within an organizational structure with hierarchical roles, structured meetings, and a national umbrella organization, their professional lives blended into their personal lives.

The importance of intimacy for the public work of the WTUL is further evidenced by the close relationships between key activists. Dye writes that many of the women in the WTUL chose to "establish their closest emotional ties with other women" and that "[a] number maintained permanent households with one another" (56, 57). Several of the women whose letters I examine in this essay had long-term same-sex partnerships: Dreier with Frances Kellor, a "social investigator" with a law degree from Cornell and graduate work in sociology at the University of Chicago (Dye 36); Helen Marot with Caroline Pratt, an influential educator and theorist of progressive pedagogy; and Schneiderman and Newman, as detailed below.

Orleck provides more information about these emotional ties, writing that "Mary Dreier . . . was very close to Newman, Schneiderman, and O'Reilly. Her friendship with O'Reilly was particularly strong and over the years would come to include financial support. . . . Newman later said of Dreier, 'Mary was loved, deeply loved by everybody'" (44). Newman, who went by "Paul" and was known for "eschew[ing] conventional feminine dress, favoring suits and short, slick-backed hair" and smoking cigars (310, 3), had an intense relationship, accompanied by passionate letters, with Schneiderman before a fifty-six-year-long coupling with Frieda Miller, with whom Newman raised a child.[4] Newman's relationship with Miller was a cross-class partnering. Miller came from a mill-owning family and was a "research assistant in the economics department at Bryn Mawr College" before leaving academia and going to work for the Philadelphia WTUL. Newman and Miller's daughter, Elisabeth Burger, said in a 1986 reflection that "the home that I grew up in was in some respects a harbinger of things to come—a female-headed household made up of two employed women and a child" (qtd. in Orleck 311).

For her part, Schneiderman had a lifelong partnership with another working-class activist, Maud O'Farrell Swartz; these two women were "partners in work and in their travels . . . they were invited places together and gave gifts together" (135). By the mid-1920s Schneiderman and Swartz had become close friends with Eleanor Roosevelt, who had them to her New York City apartment for "scrambled egg suppers" and to "the cottage at Val-Kill that FDR had constructed for Eleanor, [Blanche] Cook, and [Marion] Dickerman" (144).[5]

Affectional Rhetoric

In their letters, the WTUL women frequently mix comments about personal life with news or plans for organizing, they use terms of endearment, they clearly state their affection for one another, and they do emotional labor on one another's behalf. To illustrate what I mean by affectional rhetoric, I will analyze three letters sent to Schneiderman during her vacation in the summer of 1910 by three different colleagues in the WTUL, Dreier, Alice Bean, and Marot.

At the time she wrote the following letter, Dreier was president of the New York WTUL and Schneiderman was one of its two vice presidents. Dreier writes:

> Rose dear: —
> Your letter was such a dear one, and I thank you more than I can say for it! How glad I am that you are in that lovely spot in Mass among the hills,—and I hope you'll stay there just as long as possible.
> I can't tell you Rose what a surprise it was to me when I found that great bunch of American beauties from my Executive Board—I can't tell you how deeply I was touched by it—and then when several days later I opened a little package Leonora gave me and discovered that that too came from all you dear

people. . . . I can't tell you what this means to me—this [word unclear] from the dearest group of fellow workers and friends I have ever known.

Dear Rose—I hope for goodness sake, you won't all be worn to a frazzle if this cloakworkers strike comes off. . . . This prospective strike strikes terror to my heart—and I hope we have all gathered [two unclear words] learned at great cost from the other strike to apply it here . . .

Drier then goes on to discuss other organizing plans and WTUL news before signing off: "Good luck and blessings to you dear—+ I'll be back before you know it—Lovingly dear Rose[,] Mary."

This letter illustrates the affectional rhetoric that stabilized the WTUL. The message here is intimate: Dreier demonstrates emotional vulnerability with her gratitude and surprise at gestures of care from her comrades. There are dual, but not dueling purposes, in the letter: it is written to both provide caretaking and to conduct the business of the WTUL. In urging Schneiderman to rest on her vacation and expressing worry about the toll the activist work takes on her, Dreier evokes "that lovely spot in Mass among the hills," which strikes a pastoral tone contrasted with the "frazzle" of organizing strikers in the city, an echo of nineteenth-century values in this letter. Drier's phrasing—her characterization of Schneiderman's letter as "such a dear one" and her colleagues as "the dearest group" as well as her hyperbolic description of the upcoming strike as "strik[ing] terror to my heart"—not only creates an intimate voice but also resonates with the representations of women's talk in sentimental literature.

We can see a similar pattern in another letter Schneiderman received from a colleague at the WTUL in June 1910. By 1912, Bean, a member of the WTUL, would also be secretary for the New York branch of the Bookkeepers, Stenographers, and Accountants Union. According to an October 1912 article in *Life and Labor* (Marot, "Organizing Stenographers"), Bean did this union work from the offices of the WTUL. Bean's 1910 letter to Schneiderman begins:

Dear Rosey Rosey[,]

It was nice to have a letter from you + to know you are enjoying the holidays so much. The League, has still head-quarters at 4th & 22nd in spite of the fact that the Organizer, President Secretary and Chairman of Educational Committee also Label [unclear mark] a valuable member of the Finance Committee are away + what do you think those of us are left find to do. Why = the Corset Workers at Bridgeport Conn., have been on strike and there seems a good field for organizing among them and Melinda Scott goes up, probably Leonora also tomorrow. Leonora is the mainstay of the poor Cordage Strikers in B'klyn and if she does not put in an appearance + try to collect money to scratch up $1.00 a day for them to live on for a week—, why I don't know what would happen.

So far the Shirt Waist Mtg's have not succeeded in trying to upset or grab our treasury, or at least the contents, but there's no telling what may happen to it, or us. I guess the Mtg Ass is back of this pending lawsuit and think they will bust us, but I guess they will find out when they try that it will be as good an advertisement for us as "The Shirt Waist Strike.". . . Now you all have your restful vacation + may kind providence send you many warm sunny days and when August 1st comes perhaps I too may fly away to the Berkshire, if not to Canada, since I have not heard of that rogue of a brother of mine. However there are some nice Brothers + Sisters in the U.S.A. and I'm as well + happy as the days are long. Much love to you all[.]

Although Bean's letter is less intimate than Dreier's, it still carries the dual purpose of building affectional bonds and conducting organizing business. The affectional rhetoric here is notably playful, from the salutation, "Rosey Rosey," to the mention of "that rogue of a brother of mine." Like Dreier, Bean makes a point of urging Schneiderman to rest and enjoy her vacation, exhibiting the caretaking of affectional rhetoric. Even the business-focused parts of the letter are playful, with Bean joking about most of the leadership being away and using equal and plus signs to add rhythm and voice to the letter. Both Dreier's and Bean's letters include phrases that create an almost embodied voice, and looking at the phrases in contrast, we can begin to get a sense of the women's different personalities. While Dreier sounds a bit more formal, Bean's phrases "why I don't know what would happen" and "bust us" are more informal, if not slangy; both women, however, pen letters that convey personality and do work to maintain an intimate relationship with Schneiderman.

The third letter I include here is the most formal, although it also demonstrates the affectional rhetorical moves of the previous two. This 25 August 1910 letter addressed to Schneiderman from Marot, secretary at the WTUL, is written on WTUL letterhead. Marot, like Dreier, was an educated, upper-middle-class ally (she was the daughter of a Philadelphia publisher and Quaker) who moved from other efforts for social reform into the WTUL. Like many of the "allies," Marot had started in the settlement movement, although she had been "working as a child-labor investigator for the New York Child Labor Committee" before she joined the WTUL (Dye 39). Like several other women in the leadership of the WTUL, Marot never married; she spent her life with a female companion, Caroline Pratt (Dye 39). Marot writes:

Dear Rose: —
I have been restraining myself for two weeks, but I can't keep to my resolution to leave you undisturbed. There is a critical turn in affairs down in the Shirt Waist Makers Union which none of us can manage but you. We have been

needing you all through the month, and now I fear must have you. Could you possibly come back next Wednesday and see us at the League on Thursday and be ready for a meeting of the Shirt Waist Makers Thursday night. This leaves your month uncompleted, and I am terribly sorry to bring you back a day earlier than you feel like coming, but I don't see what we are going to do without you. Love from us all, Helen.   (Letter)

Marot adds this postscript in handwriting: "I hope, pray dear that you are rested and have had a chance for rest. The work ahead of you is so appalling! You must-must leave straight or what should we do?"

The body of Marot's letter is much more formal than the previous two letters; Marot also carefully sections off her affectional rhetoric into the postscript. Nonetheless, there are slippages even within the body with Marot "fear[ing]" that she must recall Schneiderman, feeling "terribly sorry," and signing off, "Love from us all" (Letter). Her postscript, however, is performatively affectional with the exclamation about the "appalling" work coming and the hyperbolic expression of being lost without Schneiderman. Like Dreier and Bean, Marot uses a term of endearment in addressing Schneiderman and expresses concern about the amount of rest she has been able to get during her vacation. From all three examples, there are consistent features of affectional rhetoric: terms of endearment, explicit concern about Schneiderman's well-being, and performative emotions.

Interestingly, Marot alienated herself from Schneiderman and Newman a year later when she publicly argued that the WTUL should abandon trying to work with the "East Side unions," particularly the Jewish members of those unions, whom she criticized for not following the WTUL's "methods" (qtd. in Dye 99). Instead, she argued, the WTUL should turn its attention to "American" women workers.[6]

A Queer Rhetorical History?

The contrast between the fiery activist public rhetoric Schneiderman uses to confront and chasten her allies and the affectional rhetoric her comrades use in their correspondence is intriguing. Both rhetorical strategies point to the centrality of relationships to this activist rhetorical strategy; after all, for it to be effective for a rhetor to tell listeners that they have been "found . . . wanting" relies on a belief that the listeners are invested in the rhetor's good opinion. The blurred boundaries between the personal and the public in the relationships among these activists, the overlap between their organizational titles and interpersonal roles, and the correspondence that mixes affectional rhetoric with union and strike planning can be understood as feminist practices. Can we also think of these practices as queer? What advantages, if any, are there in also naming these blurred boundaries and affectional rhetorics as queer, and not just feminist?

The term *queer* has been under continual (re)definition in rhetoric studies. It has been defined as expansively as "a broad critique of normativity along many different axes of identity, community, and power" (Morris and Rawson 75). In contrast, a more restrictive understanding of *queer* as embodied can be found in Jacqueline Rhodes and Jonathan Alexander's definition in *Techne: Queer Meditations on Writing the Self*, where they write that queer rhetoric is "a self-conscious and critical engagement with normative discourses of sexuality in the public sphere" tied to how sexual and sexualized bodies "disrupt and reroute the flows of power, particularly discursive power."[7] The continuum along which the term *queer* is defined seems to allow us to identify the activist leaders of the New York WTUL as engaging in queer activist rhetorics in potentially two ways.

Jean Bessette argues that we need to refine how we deploy "normativity" as a proof of queer or not queer, writing that her reworking of queer rhetoric "attends to the historical specificity of an act, and examines with nuance the complexity of power relations within what seems to be normal and what seems to be queer. It allows, and even assumes, that a rhetorical act can be both queer and normative, depending on how it is read, when, where" ("Queer Rhetoric" 161–62). Bessette's caution about paying attention to the historical specificity of a rhetorical act, for instance, allows us to see that it isn't the affectional rhetoric in these women's correspondence that is queer. Indeed, two centuries of letter-writing conventions in English position the caretaking, terms of endearment, and intimate voice in correspondence among women as normative. Instead, it is the strategy for activist organizing, the planning for upcoming strikes, and the commenting on the organization they are running that is antinormative—or queer—for women in this context. Bessette's reframing, then, also allows us to see how these letters include both normative and queer rhetorics.

The question remains, at least for me, about what is to be gained in identifying this specific case of affectional rhetoric as an example of queer rhetoric as opposed to feminist rhetoric, which also encompasses the antinormative work of challenging conventional ideologies and ways of being. An argument could be made that, particularly considering the coupling up of these activists in same-sex relationships, identifying theirs as a queered rhetoric is an important act of recovery, an act that "queers the archive" to reverse "longstanding and ongoing contexts of erasure" (Morris and Rawson 77). The problem with recovery projects, about which many queer studies scholars have written, is how to identify queer people and contexts, considering that sexuality and sexual identity is a discursive and changing category and that the history of sexuality and sexual identity is both made visible and obscured to us by powerful institutions that generate the changing discourse about sexuality, gender, and identity (religious institutions, medicine and psychiatry, the state, educational institutions, etc.). Despite K. J. Rawson's caution that "we may label anachronistically, use history for our own agenda, distort the historical record, dig up materials that were never meant to resurface, and violate a person's right to self-identification" (247), it may be worth these risks so that current and future readers see a useable past for themselves. Bessette refers to this use of the past as "retroactivism," a "replacing . . . of pejorative accounts of lesbianism with new versions of the past . . . to effect change in the present and, as Michel de Certeau maintains, 'a fashion of *making a place for the future*'" (*Retroactivism* 10).

I hesitate to characterize any of these women's relationships beyond labeling them as partnerships and couplings, particularly considering Rawson's warning. As a cis, gay, white woman from a working-class family, I need to consider my personal interest in identifying these women as part of a queer rhetorical history. Historians have noted Schneiderman's and Newman's discomfort with what the historians see as offensive suggestions regarding the women's intimate relationships and sexuality. Famously, Schneiderman "destroyed almost every piece of evidence about her personal life" (Orleck 300) when working on her memoir, and Newman reacted angrily to an interviewer who characterized her as a lesbian in the 1980s (310).

Eric Darnell Pritchard offers a more productive framework through which we can see the women's relationships as a queer rhetorical history. In *Fashioning Lives: Black Queers and the Politics of Literacy*, Pritchard constructs a theory of what he calls "restorative literacies," which he describes as a way

> to codify the diversity of methods Black LGBTQ people use to create and sustain their identities and environments in ways that demonstrate and engender self- and communal love. This self- and communal love takes various shapes, such as writing for empowerment, justice, self-care, healing, truth-telling, and community formation. (246)

Pritchard's theory of restorative literacy is rooted in Black LGBTQ "identities and environments" and is inextricable from the unique experiences of Black LGBTQ people and their work to "create a space outside of oppressive institutional structures and individual acts of violence" (34). Indeed, he connects restorative literacy to Elaine Richardson's theory of African American "survival literacies" (34). This specificity is integral to Pritchard's framework, and therefore the framework cannot be adopted wholesale for this WTUL context.

However, Pritchard's work is extremely generative; although the WTUL activists I look at here were not and cannot be identified as practicing restorative literacies, Pritchard's discussion of Black LGBTQ literacies prompts new ways to analyze the WTUL case study as queer. I am struck by Pritchard's identification of the composing of self- and communal love as a Black queer modality, and I see resonance between his location of this modality in Black LGBTQ experiences and the significance of intimacy and performative affection in the relationships between the WTUL activists I investigate here. Pritchard's connection between this composing of self- and communal love and the specific literacy actions of "writing for empowerment, justice, self-care, healing, truth-telling, and community formation" is especially rich. Pritchard allows us to see how "truth-telling" and "community formation" can coexist as part of an active composing of self- and communal love. The emphasis on love as a goal is particularly queer. Pritchard explains that this construction of self- and communal love is tied to efforts to effect broader social change when he identifies his study participants as using "literacy as an act of self- and communal love that contributes to broader quests for social and political change to disrupt normativity" (246). What Pritchard allows me to see about the women activists from the WTUL I look at in this essay is that the construction of communal love is a queer, purposeful literacy and rhetorical activity and goal. The women's affectional rhetoric and intimate relationships built, sustained, and queered their public activist work.

Notes

1. Annelise Orleck explains that the middle- and upper-class women in the WTUL had "dubbed themselves 'allies' of the working class" (43).

2. The Factory Investigating Commission, in Jo Ann Argersinger's words, "triggered the passage of over thirty statutes on workplace safety, child labor, and protective legislation for women. . . . Many of the laws became models for other states" (31).

3. Orleck attributes much of the labor activism that would emerge from this setting to the Jewish women's origins in Russia and eastern Europe, where the girls who would become major labor activists and, much later, advisors to Roosevelt grew up excited about "Socialism, Zionism, Russian revolutionary populism, and Yiddish cultural nationalism" (17). Orleck claims, "[T]he changes sweeping the Russian Empire toward the end of the nineteenth century shaped the consciousness of a generation of Eastern European Jews who contributed, in wildly disproportionate numbers, to revolutionary movement in Russia and to the labor and radical movements in the United States" (17).

4. For more on these relationships, see Orleck.

5. Through Eleanor Roosevelt, the activists also became friends with Franklin Delano Roosevelt, and "Frances Perkins would later argue that FDR's ideas about the labor movement and about government's proper relationship to workers were crystallized and fleshed out during the conversations he had with Swartz and Schneiderman from 1925 to 1928" (Orleck 148).

6. Dreier echoed this anti-Jewish sentiment in a 1911 letter to her sister, writing, "The girls are bitter toward the union and also to the Jews, whom they say have not treated them fairly. Yet the girls are good stuff—we are pining to get ahold of the American girls" (qtd. in Dye 115).

7. See also Bessette, "Queer Rhetoric," for an excellent overview of queer as antinormative in queer rhetorical studies.

Works Cited

Argersinger, Jo Ann E. *The Triangle Fire: A Brief History with Documents*. Bedford / St. Martins, 2016.

Bean, Alice. Letter to Rose Schneiderman. 20 June 1910. James, collection VI, Rose Schneiderman papers, reel 1.

Bessette, Jean. "Queer Rhetoric in Situ." *Rhetoric Review*, vol. 35, no. 2, 2016, pp. 148–64.

———. *Retroactivism in the Lesbian Archives: Composing Pasts and Futures*. Southern Illinois UP, 2018.

Dreier, Mary. Letter to Rose Schneiderman. June 1910. James, collection VI, Rose Schneiderman papers, reel 1.

Dye, Nancy Schrom. *As Equals and as Sisters: Feminism, the Labor Movement, and the Women's Trade Union League of New York*. U of Missouri P, 1980.

Greider, William. "Introduction: 'Who Will Protect the Working Girl?'" Stein, pp. xi–xxii.

James, Edward T., editor. *Papers of the Women's Trade Union League and Its Principal Leaders*. Research Publications, 1979. Collection VI, Rose Schneiderman papers, reel 1. Microfilm.

Marot, Helen. Letter to Rose Schneiderman. 25 Aug. 1910. James, collection VI, Rose Schneiderman papers, reel 1.

———. "Organizing Stenographers." *Life and Labor*, Oct. 1912, pp. 292–94.

Morris, Charles E., III, and K. J. Rawson. "Queer Archives/Archival Queers." *Theorizing Histories of Rhetoric*, edited by Michelle Ballif, Southern Illinois UP, 2013, pp. 74–89.

Orleck, Annelise. *Common Sense and a Little Fire: Women and Working-Class Politics in the United States, 1900–1965*. U of North Carolina P, 1995.

Pritchard, Eric Darnell. *Fashioning Lives: Black Queers and the Politics of Literacy*. Southern Illinois UP, 2016.

Rawson, K. J. "Archive This! Queering the Archive." *Practicing Research in Writing Studies: Reflexive and Ethically Responsible Research*, edited by Katrina M. Powell and Pamela Takayoshi, Hampton Press, 2012, pp. 237–50 .

Rhodes, Jacqueline, and Jonathan Alexander. *Techne: Queer Meditations on Writing the Self.* Computer and Composition Digital Press, 2015.

Stein, Leon. *The Triangle Fire.* Centennial ed., IRL Press / Cornell UP, 2011.

Part Two

Locating Rhetorical Activities

Caricatures versus Character Studies: Helen Potter's Mimetic Advocacy for Women's Rights

Angela G. Ray

Traveling the lyceum circuits of the 1870s and 1880s from Maine to California, the costumed impersonator, dramatic reader, and elocutionist Helen La Dite Potter (1837–1922) advanced the canonical status of nineteenth-century orators and actors. Performing in the guise of celebrities of the lecture platform and the theatrical stage, this white woman from upstate New York was lauded for artistry and accuracy as she minutely re-created public personae through costume, comportment, vocal tones, gestures, and distinctive linguistic patterns. In the last section of an evening's program, following her dramatic readings and then a musical interlude performed by others, Potter presented four or five excerpts from well-known speeches and theatrical scenes. She might offer the temperance orator John B. Gough decrying demon rum, or the tragedienne Adelaide Ristori performing as Queen Elizabeth. She might mimic Charlotte Cushman in her signature role as Sir Walter Scott's Meg Merrilies or sermonize as the Presbyterian divine T. De Witt Talmage. She might appear as Sarah Bernhardt in a sumptuous gown by Charles Frederick Worth or as Lawrence Barrett in a Roman toga. The spectacle entertained, yet with an earnest tone. Potter's contemporaries repeatedly insisted that her impersonations were "not caricatures or burlesques, but living pictures," significant for their "exquisite fidelity" to the originals (Kimball).

Among the oratorical celebrities whom Potter regularly impersonated were several white northeastern women involved in the early women's rights movement. Whether performing the courtroom speech that Susan B. Anthony delivered during her 1873 trial for illegal voting; presenting comments on American art by Julia Ward Howe; declaiming, in the guise of Elizabeth Cady Stanton, the Declaration of Rights of the Women of the United States that was prepared for the centennial of national independence; or delivering selections from Anna Dickinson's lyceum lecture on women's labor, Potter represented white feminists of the post–Civil War period in a resoundingly positive light, as worthy of sustained, serious attention. Challenging circulating claims about women activists as "unsexed monstrosities" ("Silks and Speeches"), she proffered her mimetic art as public argument.

Potter's performances can be seen as an example of the strategy that Stuart Hall describes as the effort to reverse stereotypes through a "positive regime of representation" (20). In the face of parody, Potter promised authenticity; in the face of caricature, she presented character study. Hall, however, is not sanguine about the capacity of positive representations to destabilize negative ones. Instead, he recommends "occupy[ing] the very terrain" of the negative representations, to "turn the stereotypes . . . against themselves" and expose their fabrication (21). Adapting this advice for Potter, Hall might have suggested that she personify a shrill, man-hating woman activist and then step outside that caricature to mark the impersonation's deceptive, oppressive qualities.

Yet if the two strategies—presenting a positive alternative and exposing the architecture of the negative image—are understood as points on a continuum rather than a binary, then Potter's artistry, I argue, lies between these points. Even as she invited respect for the impersonated figures, Potter borrowed formal features of caricature, especially the emphasis on bodily idiosyncrasies. The legibility of both caricature and character study requires that audiences possess cultural knowledge sufficient to recognize who or what is being represented and to identify the semblance. Indeed, despite claims that "the audience often forgot [that Potter's performance] was a personation" (Pond 171), responses in the aggregate suggest that spectators took pleasure in assessing the quality of the renditions as renditions. Playing with truth and illusion had further potential: spectators' capacity to suspend disbelief made the impersonations feasible as advocacy. Amid the play, audiences heard arguments for gender justice in the words of the represented characters, and performances could serve as cultural pedagogy and persuasive invitation.

In this essay I investigate the complexities and contradictions of Potter's mimetic advocacy. As she publicized a major strand of nineteenth-century feminism and honored its advocates as oratorical luminaries, she performatively disavowed caricatures of these women even while adapting caricature's techniques. At the same time, alongside the sincere character studies, Potter embraced an exaggerated, pernicious caricature, especially in her dramatic readings, vocalizing common stereotypes of racial, class, regional, and national differences. Thus Potter's presentations illustrate the capacity of nineteenth-century aesthetic entertainment to advocate for the women's rights cause and also embody the failures of alliance and inclusion that characterized white feminism of the post–Civil War period.

To elucidate this complexity, I show how Potter's persuasive efforts for women's rights were implemented and interpreted, based on more than eighty thousand words of my transcriptions of commentary about her work as well as archival evidence of her performances. First, I rehearse Potter's impersonation of Anthony, as a representative illustration and as an invitation to imaginative reflection. Then I explicate Potter's involvement in lyceum culture and in women's rights before exploring the interactions of character study and caricature in her impersonations and dramatic readings. Through performance and analysis, I posit the potential for Potter's work to speak conceptually across time about entertainment and social action.

On Trial for Voting

It is an evening in 1877, 1879, or 1881. Perhaps we are at Chickering Hall in New York City, or Central Music Hall in Chicago, or the opera house in Golden, Colorado. Newspaper advertisements have promised ingenuity and novelty. The assembled audience has paid fifty cents apiece or, for reserved seats, seventy-five cents or a dollar.

An anticipatory hush heralds the performer. From the wings strides a white woman of middle age, "a trifle above medium height and weight." She is dressed soberly and with middle-class respectability, in a "dark silk or wool walking dress" with "point lace at the throat and wrists." She carries "a shawl or wrap over the left arm." Her "dark brown hair" is combed smoothly, and she sports "gold spectacles." She takes "short steps upon entering" the stage, tosses the shawl over the back of a chair, and sits down without leaning back (Potter, *Helen Potter's Impersonations* 15–16). Someone in the audience remarks, "Why, that must be the original Susan B. Anthony herself" ("Pleiades"; see fig. 1).

A flat, apparently disembodied voice—produced through ventriloquism—sets the scene: "Has the prisoner anything to say why sentence shall not be pronounced?" The seated woman rises and begins to speak, sharply and emphatically, in language redolent of American revolutionary precept and founding documents alike: "Yes, your honor, I have many things to say; for in your ordered verdict of guilty, you have trampled under foot every vital principle of our government." She develops the thesis: "My natural rights, my civil rights, my political rights, my judicial rights, are all alike ignored. Robbed of the fundamental privilege of citizenship, I am degraded from the status of a citizen to that of a subject; and not only myself individually, but all of my sex, are, by your honor's verdict, doomed to political subjection under this, so-called, Republican form of government." Then she frames the case in broad terms: "Your denial of my citizen's right to vote, is the denial of my right of consent as one of the governed; the denial of my right of representation as one of the taxed; the denial of my right to a trial by a jury of my peers as an offender against law, therefore,

Figure 1. Helen Potter as Susan B. Anthony, ca. 1876. *Helen Potter's Impersonations*, 1891, facing p. 12.

the denial of my sacred rights to life, liberty,—property" (Potter, *Helen Potter's Impersonations* 12–13).

The judicial voice interrupts, commanding the prisoner to sit down, but she continues to stand and speak, detailing the "high-handed outrage" against her and other disenfranchised women and condemning the legal prohibitions against women that leave all men their "political sovereigns." Reminded by the judge that she has been tried for illegal voting according to established procedure, the woman responds by rhetorically destabilizing the law, casting it not as holy writ but as a collection of edicts that are "made," "*interpreted*," and "*administered*" by men . . . and against women." She introduces a historical analogy, protesting that only a few years earlier "the same man-made forms of law, declared it a crime" for anyone to assist a fugitive slave seeking to escape from the United States to Canada. Elaborating the analogy, she legitimates her own opposition to current law: "As then," she says, "the slaves who got their freedom had to take it over, or under, or *through* the unjust forms of law, precisely so, now, must *women,* to get their right to a voice in this government, *take it; I have* taken mine, and *mean* to take it at every possible opportunity." The judge requires her to pay a fine. She states her refusal to pay "this unjust penalty" and concludes with a promise to incite rebellion in other citizens: "I shall earnestly and persistently continue to urge all women to the practical recognition of the old revolutionary maxim, that *'Resistance to tyranny is obedience to God.'*" Immediately after speaking, the performer leaves the stage, still defiant. She returns upon the audience's applause only to "bow abruptly and retire" (Potter, *Helen Potter's Impersonations* 13–16).

Music plays, and minutes later the performer reenters in a new guise, maybe as a bearded Gough declaiming the gospel of temperance or as a toga-clad Barrett as Cassius inciting Brutus to the assassination of Julius Caesar. The next day a journalist records that "the *vraisemblance* was undeniable, and the applause was hearty" ("Readings and Personations").

The Lyceum and Women's Rights

Like other American women from the early republic through her own time, Potter combined teaching with platform performance (Ganter 42–43; Lampert 138). A teacher of elocution and a dramatic reader of prose and poetry, Potter added costumed impersonations to her repertoire in 1874 (Wilbor 114; "Miss Helen Potter"). She would later credit the lyceum manager James Redpath with the suggestion to "take a ten-minute extract from the text of ten of our best lectures and give it in one evening" (Smith 3). Potter performed four or five extracts rather than ten, blended oratorical star turns with famous theatrical scenes, and raised the stakes for renown by impersonating in costume, inviting spectators to evaluate her appearance against their experience watching the people represented or seeing photographs of them.

The entertainments were a hit. Potter's fame as an impersonator quickly overshadowed her repute as a dramatic reader, and she purportedly earned over twenty thousand dollars in her second season (Pond 171). Her carefully fashioned public identity had important class and racial dimensions: as Potter enacted a woman's professional competence, she crafted a remunerative vocation that permitted scope for personal choice while sustaining a white, middle-class respectability (Lampert 139). Related to this respectability was the venue. Despite their theatricality, Potter's impersonations appeared on lyceum platforms, conventionally understood as more reputable than the stage. The historian Stacy Roth notes that performing in the lyceum allowed Potter to avoid the taint of scandal associated with actors (33).

Potter came to the lyceum at a time of transition. The lyceum had developed in the mid-century United States as a loose network of local organizations often sponsoring instructional, entertaining public lectures on topics ranging from popular science to international travel. Circuits of traveling lecturers grew alongside European settlement and the transportation infrastructure. After the Civil War the lyceum lecture circuit became more professional and commercial, with the advent of lecture-management bureaus like Redpath's in Boston. Whereas lyceum courses across the fall-to-spring season continued to present lectures as their chief staple, they increasingly included musical and theatrical offerings (Ray, *Lyceum* 13–47; McKivigan 113–52; Lampert 131). Further, although many antebellum lyceums had repressed controversy, postwar lyceums sought reformist lecturers who could draw crowds of the committed and the curious. Several women identified with the women's rights movement—including Anthony, Stanton, Dickinson, Frances Ellen Watkins Harper, Mary Livermore, and Olive Logan—found remunerative employment as traveling lyceum lecturers (Ray, "What Hath She Wrought").

The term lyceum always connoted learning; even as lyceums changed, the venues continued to promote cultural knowledge valued by the communities that sponsored and supported them—often, though not always, the white, native-born, Protestant professional class. Audiences were demographically broader, and recent scholarship emphasizes the significance of lyceums for women audiences, as well as women's active interest in assessing the quality and content of presentations (Zboray and Zboray). As Granville Ganter notes, "Lecture culture was shared, exchanged, and lived, not just passively heard" (42). In such a milieu, Potter's impersonations, while unique in form and style, resonated with existing impulses for learning combined with pleasure. In 1903 one commentator listed Potter as one of the major figures from "the lyceum in its palmiest days," alongside orators Edward Everett, Charles Sumner, Wendell Phillips, Gough, Livermore, and Dickinson (Willets 2: 979). Potter's impersonations thus condense various postwar phenomena: the lyceum platform as popular education and commercial entertainment, evolving discourses of social change, and celebrity culture.

Potter chose her focal characters to attract an audience, but her selections of avowed reformers also meshed with her beliefs. She was deeply committed to fostering temperance, to alleviating the plight of the urban poor, and to promoting opportunities for women. The latter effort engendered personal connections between Potter and major women's rights activists. In 1873 Potter delivered a lecture of her own at the Woman's Congress in New York, advocating women's education in industrial art and design as a means to national advancement (Potter, "Woman in the Industrial Arts"). Her delivery impressed Stanton, who recorded a hope that "every woman who proposes to read at our next Congress will begin at once to study elocution" and to practice "vocal gymnastics" ("Woman's Congress"). Stanton sustained her views of Potter's elocutionary skills. In 1895, at a public celebration honoring Stanton on her eightieth birthday, the venerable leader, weak in body and voice, invited Potter to read the speech Stanton had prepared for the occasion ("Elizabeth Cady Stanton"). Here Potter provided not mimicry but a mouthpiece.

Long before these birthday festivities, in August 1876, Potter spent a day at Stanton's home in Tenafly, New Jersey, where Anthony was also present. Anthony noted in her diary that Potter "personates me in her entertainments this season—my answer to Judge Hunt, why sentence should not be pronounced" (Diary for 1876). Stanton later recalled "the merry day we had together at my home" (Letter to Helen Potter). During this visit Potter likely attended carefully to "the minutiae" of the appearance and comportment of the two leaders (Wilbor 114), who seem to have responded collaboratively. The next year, after Stanton delivered a lyceum lecture in Hazleton, Pennsylvania, she wrote to Potter, presenting herself as a character and even adopting the role of costume designer:

> As you are to imitate Mrs. Stanton here I thought I would tell you how I was dressed last night that you may come as near as possible. Well, I did not wear a black lace on my head, simply my hair nothing more. Black satin train one skirt plain waist with standing ruffle, & a piece of soft blond lace round the neck & running to the waist with a large cameo pin, the lace puffed a little round the pin.   (Letter)

The detailed letter reveals not only the women's camaraderie but also Stanton's endorsement of Potter's work and her keen awareness of the impersonator's goals for aesthetic precision.

Caricature as Form and Foil

Such interactions as those among Anthony, Stanton, and Potter support claims that Potter's impersonations were not sardonic or satirical but scrupulously sincere. Repeatedly praised in newspapers of the 1870s and 1880s for originality "without a single harsh line of caricature" ("Miss Helen Potter" 11), Potter would be remembered later for the "restrained and sustained fidelity of her impersonations" (Smith 4) and for "scorn[ing] caricature as a business man would scorn forgery" (Wilbor 114). Yet the recurrent emphasis on caricature in reports of Potter's performances—typically in statements of denial—suggests the proximity of Potter's work to that other mimetic art. Both caricature and character studies rely on mimicking distinctive "peculiarities" (Potter, *Helen Potter's Impersonations* xi–xiv), and writers who puffed Potter in print recognized the potential for a reproduction that aimed at faithfulness to shade into exaggeration. Nearly all commentators of the time defended Potter against this charge. For example, one Boston reporter wrote in 1874 that "the peculiarities of the different lecturers were not in the least exaggerated, but rather understated just a trifle" ("Miss Helen Potter" 9). Even in Philadelphia in 1877, when Dickinson objected to Potter's plan to portray scenes from her playwrighting and acting debut, *A Crown of Thorns*—the only instance I have found of a complaint from an impersonated subject—reports focused on Dickinson's purported fear of "ridicule" and said that Potter claimed "that she never caricatures anybody in public" ("Anna Dickinson's Troubles"). Whereas Dickinson's financial insecurity—and concerns about controlling her work and image—precipitated the objection, reporters' comments again revealed the unstable line between caricature and characterization that Potter's art accentuated.

The exaggerated hyperbole of widely circulating caricatures of women's rights activists created a foil for Potter's artistic opposition. In her 1891 book, part career chronicle and part instruction manual, Potter condemns cartoons of Anthony from the 1870s and '80s, as well as the beliefs that such images cultivated:

> There is a prevailing idea among people who have no acquaintance with Miss Anthony, that she is hard and unwomanly, with little claim to personal attraction. This is an erroneous notion obtained through efforts at raillery and derision of the cause she advocates. Pen and pencil caricatures of this noble champion of woman's rights were formerly industriously circulated to dismay the weak and amuse the crowd; but the exponent of "equal rights" has lived to see an unpopular subject command the respectful thought of the world's great and gifted ones.   (*Helen Potter's Impersonations* 15–16)

Potter's description well fits images like Thomas Wust's cover cartoon for the New York *Daily Graphic* in 1873, showing Anthony as a gargantuan "woman who dared," glowering in a star-spangled top hat while men attend to babies and women shout from the hustings (see Wust). Images like this affected opinions so much that Anthony once joked at a St. Louis suffrage convention: "She would never forget, she said, the casual remark she overheard of a lady who had just heard her lecture: 'Why, I had no idea that Miss Anthony was a decent-looking woman'" ("Silks and Speeches"). Even before the Civil War, women's rights lecturers sometimes viewed their own public appearance as refuting the belief "that all women's rights women are horrid old frights with beards and mustaches" (qtd. in Ray, "What Hath She Wrought" 203). Potter's impersonations, emphasizing meticulous reproduction, similarly participated in an embodied refutation.

Texts as Advocates

Exactitude in a character study for Potter involved not only reproducing appearance and manner but also selecting texts. Lyceum audiences had long preferred celebrated lecturers who spoke on the subjects that had made them famous (Ray, *Lyceum* 101), and an art of impersonation that expected audiences to assess accuracy had to rely on scripts consistent with public personae, whether orators delivering stirring passages or actors performing their most famous scenes. In Potter's impersonations of Stanton and Anthony, her choice of texts not only showed her ability to assess public expectations of these speakers but also underscored the advocacy function of her mimetic art. Stanton's own lyceum audiences were familiar with her "comfortably feminine" self-presentation as a sausage-curled, matronly figure who lectured on topics like child-rearing and told stories that gently undermined gender biases (Ray, "What Hath She Wrought" 203; Strange). Whereas Potter sometimes presented Stanton in this guise—delivering excerpts of her popular lyceum lecture "The Coming Girl"—she also represented Stanton reading the 1876 Declaration of Rights of Women of the United States, a document rendered in legal prose that "arraign[ed]" the nation's rulers for women's political and legal "degradation" (Potter, *Helen Potter's Impersonations* 91–94). The National Woman Suffrage Association, over which Stanton presided, had generated the centennial declaration's unequivocal demand for justice. Potter's artistry thus brought Stanton's most forceful public persona directly into the lyceum venue. As Potter performed an impersonation of Stanton assertively making political demands, she reproduced a text whose planned delivery to the president of the United States (in writing) had been suppressed by the government officials who were organizing the centennial celebrations. Instead, on the Fourth of July, Anthony read the text aloud on the grounds of Philadelphia's Independence Hall, and Stanton read it at a suffragist meeting (Stanton et al. 27–36). Activists then distributed the declaration in print, but Potter dispersed its contents in an oral, embodied form beginning in the autumn of 1876 (see, e.g., "Lyceum"). Further, in Potter's 1891 book she preserved an excerpt of the declaration, not of "The Coming Girl," to exemplify her impersonation of Stanton, thus continuing to recirculate the declaration's powerful text.

   In the lyceum season of 1876–77—the first one after the "merry day" in Tenafly (Stanton, Letter to Helen Potter)—Potter also began impersonating

Anthony. Although the centennial declaration stated live issues and marked a recent event, Anthony's trial had occurred three years before. Anthony was the best known among hundreds of postwar women who had participated in a national campaign of direct action to seize a citizen's right to vote. Motivated by a compelling legal argument, these women showed up at registry offices and polling places, demanding political participation (Ray, "Rhetorical Ritual"). By the time Potter began delivering the excerpt from Anthony's 1873 statement to Judge Ward Hunt, however, the Supreme Court had decisively ruled in the *Minor v. Happersett* case in 1875 that citizenship did not entail voting rights. The court decision curtailed the practical promise of the strategy of direct action but not the rhetorical power of the suffragists' claims. Many persistently kept the arguments alive long after the *Minor* decision (Ray and Richards 394–95), and Potter's art participated in this perseverance. Potter's impersonation not only made the implicit claim that Anthony's trial was a major event and that Anthony was an oratorical celebrity, but it also repeated to audience after audience an argument for women's legitimacy as political actors and invited consideration of that logic. Potter's impersonation of Anthony was a regular feature on her programs from 1876 through the early 1880s, and she delivered the impersonation as late as 1895 ("National Woman's Christian Temperance Union" 15). Time after time, in place after place, Potter, echoing Anthony, endorsed a gender revolution to citizen-spectators momentarily reconfigured as legal authorities.

Refuting Caricature, Practicing Caricature

Potter's impersonations of Stanton and Anthony subsumed legal argument within performance, inviting a judicial response along with the spectatorial. Through her own body, elaborately costumed and thoroughly practiced in gestural characteristics, attitudes, movements, vocal inflections, tones, and pacing, Potter mediated the words, actions, and attitudes of the activists. Offering ostensibly neutral, artistic description, she could avoid the contempt heaped on the women themselves and could produce sympathetic renderings of their arguments and refutations of public censure. She presented a positive representation to rebut the caricature.

At the same time, Potter's artistic techniques in developing character studies approximated caricature's methods of emphasizing distinguishing traits. She and her admirers in the press denied the links so often and so emphatically that their commentary accentuates the parallels. Furthermore, on many evening programs, Potter's respectful impersonations accompanied her own practice of distorted exaggeration. Preceding the impersonations, Potter read popular prose and poetry. In addition to texts like an excerpt from Charles Dickens's *Pickwick*

Papers or a poem by George Bungay mimicking the tones of church bells, she offered dialect readings of the "Negro, Scotch, and Yankee." For example, her rendering of the prose piece "Brother Anderson," by the white Congregational minister Thomas K. Beecher, simulated Beecher's impression of a "Negro preacher." Dialect markers—"I tell you, brudders an' sisters, dat heaven's a mighty big place"—relentlessly fixed the character as exotic and grotesque yet with primitive insight, much like Beecher's sister's character Uncle Tom (Beecher 2). Such stereotyped texts, widely reprinted and common on readers' platforms and in schoolrooms alike, normalized malign assumptions of reality, such that a Boston reporter could imagine having heard an "illustration of the negro dialect" ("Miss Helen Potter" 9; see Wilson and Patia 81). The presentation of such vocal material preceding Potter's impersonations—despite the musical interlude, the addition of costumes, and the shift to celebrities—highlights interpretive challenges in the event as a whole. Did audiences understand different portions of the program as discrete, or as gradations of truth claims? Historian Sara Lampert notes distinctions between nineteenth-century perceptions of dramatic reading and acting, with the former offering "an array of moods and characters" and the latter "an illusion of total transformation" (145). As Potter moved from one mode to another, her performance could reinforce distance from characters caricatured, represent affinity with individuals impersonated, and, through it all, implicitly assert who and what should be susceptible to caricature and who and what should not. The presentation policed communal boundaries, and prevalent supremacist ethics—of race and class and national origin, if not gender—remained intact (see Cobb 115–16).

Yet the two parts of the program did not exhaust Potter's range of caricature and character study. A more thorough blending came in her costumed impersonation of a Chinese singer and actor called Chin Foo (not the writer and lecturer Wong Chin Foo). The Redpath Lyceum Bureau advertised the character as "Heathen Chinee" (see Baker), and in 1891 Potter would preserve her impersonation not of an individual but of a type, a "Chinese sketch" (*Helen Potter's Impersonations* 47–49). This impersonation, comparatively sympathetic for the time, is still perceptible as yellowface, authorizing the white North American performer to inspect, assess, and produce the presumptive truth of a Chinese identity (Ray, "How Cosmopolitan" 37).

Since the time of Plato, Western writers have expressed misgivings about the power of representation to influence beliefs about reality (Wilson and Patia 84), and scholars have long noted the didactic character of caricature (Curtis xvi). Potter's character studies and caricatures, with the imprimatur of the lyceum, were culturally marked as edutainment a century before the term arose. Simultaneously generating positive and negative representations, endorsements and stereotypes, Potter's performances challenged prevailing assumptions about white feminists while reproducing privileged distortions of other forms of difference. Potter thus generated both celebration and denigration, supplied implicit lessons about classification, and inadvertently provided living pictures of the hope and the failures of the postwar women's rights movement.

Works Cited

"Anna Dickinson's Troubles." *Philadelphia Times*, 25 Apr. 1877, p. 2.

Anthony, Susan B. Diary for 1876. Holland and Gordon, reel 18, frames 516–702.

Baker, Joseph E. *Miss Helen Potter, in Her Personations of Celebrities*. Ca. 1875. American Antiquarian Society, catalog.mwa.org/vwebv/holdingsInfo?bibId=148299. Lithograph.

Beecher, Thomas K. "Brother Anderson." *Herald and Presbyter* [Cincinnati], 19 Sept. 1872, p. 3.

Cobb, Jasmine Nichole. *Picture Freedom: Remaking Black Visuality in the Early Nineteenth Century*. New York UP, 2015.

Curtis, L. Perry, Jr. *Apes and Angels: The Irishman in Victorian Caricature*. Rev. ed., Smithsonian Institution Press, 1997.

"Elizabeth Cady Stanton." *The New York Times*, 13 Nov. 1895, p. 1.

Ganter, Granville. "Women's Entrepreneurial Lecturing in the Early National Period." Ray and Stob, pp. 41–55.

Hall, Stuart. *Representation and the Media*. Directed by Sut Jhally, Media Education Foundation, 1997, mediaed.org/transcripts/Stuart-Hall-Representation-and-the -Media-Transcript.pdf. Transcription of filmed lecture.

Holland, Patricia G., and Ann D. Gordon, editors. *Papers of Elizabeth Cady Stanton and Susan B. Anthony*. Scholarly Resources, 1991. 45 microfilm reels.

Kimball, John C. "A Word for Miss Helen Potter." *Hartford Daily Courant* [Connecticut], 4 Nov. 1879, p. 2.

Lampert, Sara E. "The 'Perfect Delight' of Dramatic Reading: Gertrude Kellogg and the Post–Civil War Lyceum." Ray and Stob, pp. 130–49.

"The Lyceum: Miss Helen Potter's Entertainment in Music Hall." *Boston Daily Advertiser*, 11 Oct. 1876, p. 4.

McKivigan, John R. *Forgotten Firebrand: James Redpath and the Making of Nineteenth-Century America*. Cornell UP, 2008.

"Miss Helen Potter." *Redpath's Lyceum: Season of 1875–76*, pp. 9–12. American Antiquarian Society.

"National Woman's Christian Temperance Union: Twenty-Second Annual Convention." *Union Signal and World's White Ribbon*, 7 Nov. 1895, pp. 2–22+.

"The Pleiades." *Colorado Transcript* [Golden, Colorado], 29 June 1881, p. 3.

Pond, James B. *Eccentricities of Genius: Memories of Famous Men and Women of the Platform and Stage*. G. W. Dillingham, 1900.

Potter, Helen. *Helen Potter's Impersonations.* E. S. Werner, 1891.

———. "Woman in the Industrial Arts." *Papers and Letters Presented at the First Woman's Congress of the Association for the Advancement of Woman,* pp. 105–09. Mrs. Wm. Ballard, 1874.

Ray, Angela G. "How Cosmopolitan Was the Lyceum, Anyway?" Wright, pp. 23–41.

———. *The Lyceum and Public Culture in the Nineteenth-Century United States.* Michigan State UP, 2005.

———. "The Rhetorical Ritual of Citizenship: Women's Voting as Public Performance, 1868–1875." *Quarterly Journal of Speech,* vol. 93, no. 1, Feb. 2007, pp. 1–26.

———. "What Hath She Wrought? Woman's Rights and the Nineteenth-Century Lyceum." *Rhetoric and Public Affairs,* vol. 9, no. 2, Summer 2006, pp. 183–213.

Ray, Angela G., and Cindy Koenig Richards. "Inventing Citizens, Imagining Gender Justice: The Suffrage Rhetoric of Virginia and Francis Minor." *Quarterly Journal of Speech,* vol. 93, no. 4, Nov. 2007, pp. 375–402.

Ray, Angela G., and Paul Stob, editors. *Thinking Together: Lecturing, Learning, and Difference in the Long Nineteenth Century.* Pennsylvania State UP, 2018.

"Readings and Personations." *The New York Times,* 13 Nov. 1877, p. 5.

Roth, Stacy F. *Past into Present: Effective Techniques for First-Person Historical Interpretation.* U of North Carolina P, 1998.

"Silks and Speeches." *St. Louis Globe-Democrat,* 8 May 1879, p. 2.

Smith, G. Paul. "Helen Potter." *Talent,* Jan. 1906, pp. 1–4.

Stanton, Elizabeth Cady. Letter to Helen Potter. 21 Oct. 1877. Holland and Gordon, reel 19, frames 570–71.

———. "The Woman's Congress." *Golden Age,* 25 Oct. 1873. Holland and Gordon, reel 17, frame 394.

Stanton, Elizabeth Cady, et al., editors. *History of Woman Suffrage.* Vol. 3, Rochester, 1886.

Strange, Lisa S. "Dress Reform and the Feminine Ideal: Elizabeth Cady Stanton and the 'Coming Girl.'" *Southern Communication Journal,* vol. 68, no. 1, Fall 2002, pp. 1–13.

Wilbor, Elsie M. "Helen Potter." *Werner's Voice Magazine,* May 1890, pp. 113–14.

Willets, Gilson. *Workers of the Nation.* P. F. Collier and Son, 1903. 2 vols.

Wilson, Kirt H., and Kaitlyn G. Patia. "Authentic Imitation or Perverse Original? Learning about Race from America's Popular Platforms." Ray and Stob, pp. 72–94.

Wright, Tom F., editor. *The Cosmopolitan Lyceum: Lecture Culture and the Globe in Nineteenth-Century America.* U of Massachusetts P, 2013.

Wust, Thomas. "The Woman Who Dared." *Daily Graphic* [New York], 5 June 1873. *Library of Congress,* www.loc.gov/pictures/item/95512461/. Cartoon.

Zboray, Ronald J., and Mary Saracino Zboray. "Women Thinking: The International Popular Lecture and Its Audience in Antebellum New England." Wright, pp. 42–66.

Acting Like Rhetors: Women's Rights in Amateur Theatrical Performances

Lisa Suter

> Stories repeat themselves and become accepted history.
>
> —Carol Mattingly

Historians of rhetoric who study the last quarter of the nineteenth century may easily observe the proliferation of amateur theatrical activity in this period: the wide variety and seeming ubiquity of dramatic offerings in newspaper reviews, ads for dramatic entertainments, sections of plays in parlor rhetorics, acting courses at colleges of oratory, and more. For nearly forty years, we have read the theater as rhetorical space (Campbell); however, our field has not yet attempted any systematic analysis of the rhetorical function of this plethora of nonprofessional dramas—many written by women, acted by women, produced by women, and subsequently attended, viewed, and reviewed by women. The popularity of amateur drama in this period arises from multiple factors, but none, I will argue, more important than the simple exigency of women's urge to be heard in a society that wished them to remain silent. These collaborative rhetorical forums comprised one of the few platforms where women's voices could be raised and where women's issues could be discussed without censure.

In a variety of social venues, amateur theatrical productions afforded women the opportunity to speak in a welcoming space about the concerns that mattered most to them. With women restricted from most platforms of the day, a dramatic production at the local women's college, high school, or community hall offered not just a safer space in terms of maintaining women's social standing but also, crucially, the chance for women to compose their own persuasive scripts, to adapt scripts written by others, and to direct and star in their own persuasive productions. Moreover, instead of facing a hostile audience unwilling to hear lecturing arguments for greater opportunities for women, these dramas often attracted an audience of more amenable viewers—family members, friends, classmates, members of women's clubs—who would come to see a friend or daughter perform, and would listen appreciatively.

Why has this rich site of rhetorical activity been so long overlooked? In "Telling Evidence: Rethinking What Counts in Rhetoric," Carol Mattingly observes that while feminist historians assiduously dig in archives, looking for proof of women's rhetorical endeavors, many also unconsciously reinscribe canonical definitions of rhetoric that shape what we believe that proof ought to look like. Prejudiced, too, by our own academic style of "confrontational and assertive" argument and hoping to "prove the credibility" of the women we study, we often prefer to examine individuals engaging in agonistic and logical forms of persuasion. Meanwhile, Mattingly asserts, we've ignored many "more rhetorically effective" methods employed by female rhetors of the past: for example, the strategic use of humor (101). The collaborative nature of theatrical productions is likely the second reason why historians have not recognized such productions' rhetorical efficacy. Barbara Biesecker rightly comments that "the rhetorical canon is . . . predicated on and celebrates the individual." Therefore collaborative rhetorics, which Biesecker reminds us "have been the most common form of women's intervention in the public sphere," are often left out of our scholarly conversations (157).

Almost all theatrical performance is collaborative, but I take as my focus the genre of the dialogue: a short, easy-to-stage performance piece attractive to amateur actors and fun to write and act out in costume, making this genre wildly popular with girls and young women in this era. Because these short pieces were relatively easy to stage, they made ideal vehicles for almost any persuasive content, as I will show. Crucially, the dialogue allowed young women a space in which to forward their own opinions: a place to speak out freely in public, where no one would tell them to be quiet or that they had no right to speak (a recurring thematic complaint in the dialogue below). When they wrote dialogues of their own, girls often wrote about the lives of strong and powerful women, even socially transgressive women, and then acted out those roles on stage in view of others. One scholar has suggested that performing male roles on stage may have had an empowering effect on college girls in this period, since the girls also "learned how to act as a man" in society (Horowitz 163). In my own research, I have observed how girls composed and enacted dramatic stories of female scholars, artists, wives, and warriors—the whole spectrum of powerful womanhood—and I am similarly drawn to speculate how this role-playing may have helped girls learn to act like confident women in the public sphere.

This focus on women's lives is vividly evident in the dialogue that I analyze here. *The Chronothanatoletron; or, Old Times Made New* was written by girls at a college preparatory school in Massachusetts in 1887. The script concerns a female inventor who has created a time machine and uses it to talk to women who have lived in different eras. I look at how this dialogue was staged at a women's college in Ohio in 1892. It was significantly adapted from the original published work; the second set of students altered the women brought through the time machine for their own persuasive purposes. My analysis of this adaptation is intended to underline the importance of analyzing both the rhetoric of the text and also, when possible, the rhetoric of production.

The Nineteenth-Century Dialogue as Collaborative, Conversational Rhetoric

Dialogues were a popular performance genre in the last quarter of the nineteenth century. A steady stream of staged productions of these amusements was announced weekly in the society pages of newspapers (often featured as part of a larger theatrical or musical program), and many of the elocution anthologies published in this era contained a section devoted to dialogues, offering a variety of dramatic and comic pieces that a group could perform.

The scripts within these anthologies offer only half of the rhetorical value of any dialogue, however; the other half always lies within the dialogue's performance, as Paul Newell Campbell argues. He names "three rhetorics of theater," two of which are always present when a play is staged. The first rhetoric is "the rhetoric of the text." The second and third rhetorics that Campbell names are different varieties of "the rhetoric of production": one that tries to enact the original meaning of the text faithfully and one that attempts to alter or overthrow the script's meaning (13–19). These rhetorics of production emanate from the choices made by cast and crew—actors, costumers, music designer, prop master, director—decisions which translate the text into a three-dimensional, living performance.

To assist groups engaged in producing a dialogue, parlor rhetorics with dialogue texts often contained a section on how to stage these short performances: for example, how to create a stage from "stout boards" and how to rig a stage curtain out of a bolt of cloth, some small rings, and a wire (Stratton and Stratton 398). Clearly, these production instructions indicate that dialogues were intended to be performed by amateurs in whatever space was available, not by professional actors in a traditional theater. Other such instructions are similarly addressed to amateurs, such as notes that "[a]lmost any household contains a sufficient variety of furniture and 'properties' for any indoor scene, and a little ingenuity will produce a fair theatrical wardrobe from very common material" (Northrop 438).

The dialogue's dramaturgical constraints—a one-act play whose action usually takes place within a single physical setting (e.g., a schoolroom or a town square) and within a single period of time—made dialogues convenient for amateurs to stage without the benefit of many props, sets, or stagehands. Unlike a traditional three-act play running a hundred pages or more in print and requiring several hours to perform, the dialogue is far shorter, with far fewer pages of lines for would-be actors to memorize. Most dialogues have between two and ten characters—though some have more, as seen below—and they were categorized in lists of published plays by the number of male and female roles each required, to help groups decide which works to purchase. The name of the genre reflects the fact that the lion's share of the action of the piece is the conversation occurring between the multiple characters.

The conversational nature of the genre may have made these pieces attractive to female rhetors. Jane Donawerth's *Conversational Rhetoric: The Rise and Fall of a Women's Tradition, 1600–1900* examines how women have theorized communication across three centuries, contending that female rhetoricians have valued both different strategies and different outcomes than their male counterparts. Donawerth finds that, based on their different positioning in society, women have repeatedly used conversation as an analogy to explain how (ideally) rhetoric should work (11). She shows that, time and again, women counseled ". . . speaking and writing that is collaborative, not antagonistic in relation to the audience, seeking consensus, not domination as the goal of communication" (16). It therefore seems reasonable that nineteenth-century female playwrights might have enjoyed writing theatrical dialogues designed to woo audience members around to the playwrights' positions with wit and humor, rather than attempting to dominate listeners with sterile logic and cold facts. Unlike the rhetoric of a speech or lecture by an individual, in a dialogue an audience will hear a wide variety of positions relating to a given topic as different characters take turns speaking. The characters' back-and-forth debate is often quite lively and, within the comic dialogue, quite humorous; most important, however, is that all of the positions are presented as entertainment for the audience's enjoyment. Instead of a lecturer taking an assertive position on an issue—one she believes the audience disagrees with—and insisting that she is right, in the dialogue, a group of thespians provides the playful spectacle of how the debate looks from both sides, and all to comic effect.

Besides their conversational structure, other elements may have made dialogues a desirable genre for female rhetors. The collaborative nature of the production—both in staging and acting out the play—meant that a girl did not have to brave the censure of disapproving society as she walked out onto a platform alone; instead she would go onto the boards with a large band of her fellow actors. (There is aptness here in the adage *safety in numbers*.) Play-making also highlighted gendered female strengths: sewing costumes, applying stage makeup, painting pieces of the set, and decorating a stage, for example. In this way, each member of the production could contribute her unique skills to the success of the piece. Last but not least, in a time when entertainment amounted to little more than reading or needlepoint, townspeople were often willing to shell out a small sum to see whatever was on offer, especially if it looked like a good time. Women, who had fewer legitimate means of making money, used the production of theatrical performances to raise money for a wide variety of causes, from charity work to buying new equipment for a school or a college. The transgressive act of women speaking publicly in this era may have been more defensible, too, when couched in terms of fundraising for a good cause.

Amateur Theater as Rhetorical Space for Women in the Late Nineteenth Century

In "On Gender and Rhetorical Space," Roxanne Mountford theorizes the connection between physical space and the production of meaning in rhetorical performance. She also examines cultural judgments inherent within geographical space, taking up Susan Riddick's notion of the "social imaginary," described as a culture's notion of "where people . . . ought to be" (qtd. in Mountford 48–49), and how that preconceived concept affects an audience's reception of a rhetor and her argument.

Newspaper ads and reviews suggest that much of women's amateur theater took place on stages in community halls where women's organizations met, in parlors in women's own homes, or on school or college grounds where women were professors, teachers, and administrators, and where young girls were students: in other words, places where one might already expect women to be in this period. Indeed, Shirley Wilson Logan asserts that it is more accurate to see parlors as "alternative public spheres" than as domestic spaces (89), noting that this phrasing "resists the notion of one privileged white male-dominated public and recognizes instead the always already existence of many publics" (152n108). I find value in this insight and would add that other spaces, such as the auditoriums, stages, platforms, and grounds of girls' schools or colleges, should also be counted among the multitude of public forums in the late nineteenth century. These spaces, while public, had the advantage of being already gendered female in the audience's mind; therefore, it stands to reason that a female rhetor did not provoke the same level of threatening gender anxiety when she voiced her opinions in such spaces.

This line of reasoning may help explain Helen Horowitz's striking observation in *Alma Mater* that dramatics "dominated" women's college life in this period, and that "almost universal participation" obtained in theater productions in the ten girls' colleges she researched (159, 162). Horowitz details how at Vassar, the three literary societies on campus all transformed into dramatic societies, presenting "plays to other chapters, the preparatory students, and eventually the faculty" (63); and at Smith College, the frenzy of students' nonstop participation in their own theatrical productions made the school calendar "so crowded . . . that the college continually tried to limit student participation" (162).

Logan documents that the societies created by African Americans in the nineteenth century "paralleled but rarely intersected with" similar societies formed by white Americans at this time. She states that both movements "had a community orientation, in that lectures, *plays*, and debates were held in public spaces" (58; emphasis mine), but her analysis centers on the lectures and oratory offered by these groups. It is difficult to estimate how many amateur theatricals may have been produced and enjoyed by marginalized communities, since these groups may not have thought it useful to place ads for their entertainments in white newspapers; likewise, said newspapers might have declined to run those ads. My research to date has uncovered evidence of only one production of *The Chronothanatoletron* by any organization of women of color—an African American women's church group—which I also discuss below.[1]

A Dialogue of Their Own: Dana Hall School Students Write and Publish *The Chronothanatoletron*

On 18 June 1887, the sixteen seniors of Dana Hall School in Wellesley, Massachusetts, were two days shy of graduation. These girls had successfully finished the four-year preparatory program that Dana Hall had been providing since it opened in 1881, and their graduation from the program guaranteed their admission into nearby Wellesley College "without further examination" ("Catalog").[2] It seems likely that the girls felt triumphant and ready to celebrate. But before they mounted one platform to receive their diplomas, they would take to another platform for the ritual of Class Day: the public exhibition of their educational achievements. To highlight their collective accomplishments, several students coauthored a dialogue with sixteen characters. This script granted each scholar a speaking role and allowed each girl the chance to address the audience of instructors and friends gathered to congratulate them. The girls titled their dialogue *The Chronothanatoletron*, and while they had no way of knowing it, their short play articulating woman's worth in the world was about to become a long-running hit. Groups of women would produce it all across the United States for twenty-five years.

Records differ in the matter of who authored the dialogue. The cover of the play's original 1887 program, maintained in the Dana Hall School archives, says it was written "by Elizabeth Stewart and Maud M. Taylor"; however, two published, hardbound copies of the 1889 play, held by the Library of Congress and

Harvard's Widener Library, list the author as "M.A. Greely and others" or "M.A. Greely," respectively.[3] What is certain is that all three girls—Stewart, Taylor, and Greely—were Dana Hall students in 1886–87. Stewart and Taylor were traditional students who graduated on 20 June 1887. Mary Ann Greely had only just matriculated in 1886 as a "special" student—in other words, she was older than her classmates—and never graduated, according to school records, but left the school in 1888 (DeSimone).[4] She went on to study at the Emerson College of Oratory, graduating in 1893 (Greely, "Spirit" 106).

More important than whose hand, or hands, held the pen is the matter of what issues these young scholars were interested in, and that these girls were writing with the intent of expressing their thoughts publicly. Written for their Class Day, this twenty-three-page dialogue offered the entire graduating class the opportunity to voice its belief in woman's worth, "before members of the school and their friends," as mentioned on the title page (Greely, *Chronothanatoletron*). As further evidence of the graduating class's intent to forward the argument in the public sphere, shortly after staging the work, one of the girls submitted the play to a well-known drama publishing house for publication.

The Chronothanatoletron centers on a fantastic new invention, the so-called Time-and-Death Annihilator, also known as the Chronothanatoletron. The machine has just been created by the Inventress, who is showing it to her friend the Genius of Nineteenth Century. Proudly the creator exclaims, "Long have I waited for some soul capable of comprehending the stupendous powers of my *production!*" (Greely, *Chronothanatoletron* 6). Numerous double entendres are deployed in the play for comic effect, such as this one: clearly the speaker is referring to the time machine, but the italics in the text suggest that she also refers to the "stupendous" theatrical "production" the actors are in the midst of collectively creating.

The time machine device itself is ingeniously simple. In the instructions at the beginning of the play, it is described as "a large cabinet arranged with doors in front . . . so contrived that one can enter it from behind the scenes without being seen." Additionally, "to one side is attached a large crank" which the Inventress turns before each character appears. Then, "at a given signal," the doors open and the summoned character steps down out of the machine (6).

The Inventress tells the Genius that they can summon any famous personage desired, from any era of history: all they need do is speak the person's name. Calling forth the first historical figure—Sarah, the biblical wife of Abraham—the Genius tells Sarah that she has been "summoned from the tomb to join the most illustrious women of all time" (7). The young playwrights' phrasing suggests that they hoped to represent all women in their short drama; however, most of the characters deemed "most illustrious" are white and of European or

American origin. The few figures drawn from outside those boundaries—Sarah, Cleopatra, Pharaoh's Daughter, and Pocahontas, in this iteration of the play— can be seen to reflect the prevailing racial stereotypes of the day.

In this, the original Dana Hall School production, fourteen famous women are summoned: Sarah, Pharaoh's Daughter, Cornelia, Cleopatra, Queen Elizabeth, Mother Bickerdike, Saint Cecilia, the Abbess Hilda, Hypatia, Agnes of Bologna, Joan of Arc, Sappho, Martha Washington, and Priscilla (Stewart and Taylor).[5]

The play functions as an encomium to women's unheralded contributions to the world and as such enters into the literary genre of the women worthies argument, also known as the *de claribus* tradition, after Boccaccio's *De Claris Mulieribus*, or *Concerning Famous Women*. Many classical authors wrote on the subject of woman's worth: Boethius, Chaucer, Virgil, Ovid, and more (King and Rabil xxi), often including some subset of the same honorable women, but treating them in different ways, to buttress the author's unique argument about the putative worth of the entire female sex (McMillan). Scholars have noted the curious fact that a work in the *de claribus* tradition, ostensibly written in praise of good or virtuous women, could in fact be unfriendly to women, for the tradition generally singles out for praise only those women who possess the traditional virtues of chastity, obedience, and, notably, silence. Women active in the public realm—for example, rulers and warriors—are usually depicted as being lascivious and suffering terrible punishments for entering into the masculine sphere (King and Rabil xxi).

The genre may deserve such criticism when authored by male writers; however, the Dana Hall students who authored this play not only included rulers and warriors without focusing on their occasionally tragic ends, they also chose to include women whose claim to fame was speaking up for themselves or for others. Most important, the dramatic medium used to present this catalog of women worthies allows its writers and actors to perform the opposite of what society expected of them; in producing their play, they were literally bespeaking their own values: notably, the value not of silence but of a woman's right to speak in public.

The figures the Dana Hall School girls chose to represent women's contributions to society span many of the life choices possible for women in history. Three characters are notable for being mothers (and for raising famous men): Sarah, Isaac; Pharaoh's Daughter, Moses; and Cornelia, the Gracchi; other characters were famous and powerful in their own right, as in the case of Cleopatra and Queen Elizabeth. Several were the wives of famous men, including Martha Washington and Priscilla, though the figure of the pilgrim Priscilla Alden (née Mullins) is included not because she is married but because she spoke up for her own desires. Priscilla is famous for asking, when the Plymouth colonist John Alden came to ask for her hand in marriage for his friend Captain Miles Standish,

"Why don't you speak for yourself, John?" In thus prompting the man she hoped to marry to ask for her hand himself, Priscilla determines her own life's course and future happiness.

Other characters in the dialogue were chosen not merely to represent women's potential life choices but to showcase the schoolgirls' recently completed education and newfound erudition. It is no accident that they include Saint Cecilia, the patron saint of music, who comes on stage to sing a hymn in Latin; or Hypatia, who delivers a short (and comically lugubrious) discourse on philosophy; or Agnes of Bologna,[6] the first-known woman professor of mathematics at a university, who spends her time on stage talking of polygons, parallelograms, and proofs (Greely, *Chronothanatoletron* 16). As students who had been fighting through challenging academic classes but were now on the eve of graduation, it seems evident that they wished to celebrate their mastery of difficult curricula. Some of these sections could also be read as a subtle argument in favor of young women studying course material often reserved for young men. When a character asks Agnes a question about the eponymous witch of Agnesi curve, Agnes replies, "Ah! You are acquainted with that? I am glad to see that you have had mathematical training" (16).[7]

Finally, some characters were included for their bravery or outspokenness, such as "Mother" Mary Ann Bickerdyke. An Ohio woman, Bickerdyke served as a Civil War nurse on nineteen battlefields, created many field hospitals, and later became chief of nursing under General Ulysses S. Grant. Still, Bickerdyke is perhaps best known for bucking military orders to do what she believed necessary for the safety of the soldiers in her care, and for publicly challenging any authority figure standing in the way of that mission. In the dialogue she is depicted as blunt and largely unconcerned with others' opinions; she is not impressed with Hypatia and Agnes's pedantic discourse and tries to move the conversation along. When she does, the two former rulers attempt to silence her:

> ELIZ. Zounds, woman! What mean you by these unmannerly interruptions? Stand aside, while your superiors converse!
> MOTH. B. My superiors!
> CLEO. Such effrontery passes all belief. Who is this woman?
> MOTH. B. Now, just see here: you needn't come that bossin' act over me. I won't stand it. Why, you folks seem to have a deal o' trouble about lettin' a free-born American speak her mind. Now just take my advice and settle down, for this one thing is certain. When anybody gets into a quarrel with me, somebody always goes to the wall, and it ain't never me. (16)

According to the *Oxford English Dictionary*, the old phrase "to go to the wall" means "to give way" or "to succumb in a conflict" ("Wall," def. P1.c). Mother

Bickerdyke is letting her interlocutors know that she will not be cowed by any so-called superiors who believe she has no right to speak. In another scene near the end of the dialogue, Mrs. Washington criticizes Priscilla for the unseemly act of prompting John to ask for her hand. Mother Bickerdyke responds, "I say, if you've got anything to say, say it, and what's the difference whether it's the man or the woman?" Sarah interjects, "My lord Abraham was wont to say that woman should hold her peace," but the Inventress has the last word: "You will pardon my saying that as your lord Abraham is rather antiquated, his opinions are a little out of date" (21).

In writing about historical female figures who were undaunted by societal mores that advised them to "hold [their] peace," these young rhetors showed their own courage and also their intention to speak out in life, just as they were speaking from the Dana Hall School platform that was their stage. Once their dialogue was published in 1889, other girls' schools and women's groups around the country began to purchase the script and stage it. Newspaper archives online show the dialogue's steady popularity for over twenty years across a sizable section of the United States. As the *Newark Daily Advocate* noted on 4 June 1890:

> Everyone was anxiously waiting for the second part of the program which was called "The Chronothanatoletron." After a short interval, the curtain at the rear of the stage was drawn aside and the audience beheld a tall cabinet neatly draped with lace curtains in front, with a large crank on one side which betrayed its nature. At the top across the front appeared in large silver letters the mysterious word which had excited so much curiosity.   ("Unique Affair")

From Massachusetts, it was performed as far west as Iowa, Oklahoma, and Utah. It was put on by Sunday school classes and Epworth Leagues. Many of the troupes that performed the script were Christian; almost all were white. One African American group, the Young Women's Club of the Methodist Church in Reidsville, North Carolina, produced the dialogue in 1912 at the opera house in town. One review states that the club's "excellent" performance was full of "wit and humor" and was presented to "a large and appreciative audience" ("Colored People").

Some of the groups altered the play slightly or significantly in production to offer a different cast of characters. For example, in 1900, a high school in Pennsylvania added five additional characters: "Xantippe, Wife of Socrates; Noah's Wife, Mistress of the Ark; Tsi An, Empress of China; Mrs. Dewey; and Queen Victoria" ("Chronothanatoletron"). It is likely that these additions were born of a simple exigency: there were more would-be actors in the group than there were roles, so a few more worthy women needed to be added. This is known to be the case in the production at an Ohio women's college in 1892, described below.

They Added More Geniuses: Oxford College Students Produce and Adapt *The Chronothanatoletron*

Like the original Dana Hall School production, the performance of *The Chrono-thanatoletron* undertaken at Oxford College in Oxford, Ohio, was planned for Class Day: 7 June 1892. The June edition of the student newspaper, the *Oxford Ladies Collegian*, states that the play was put on by the seniors who comprised the graduating class of '92, and features a lengthy, glowing review of the entertainment. As in the Dana Hall School premiere, all of the class's seniors, nineteen of them, appear on stage and have a speaking role.[8] To make this possible, a few new characters had to be added (and two were dropped): the Oxford girls chose to add an Operator to work the time machine, a Genius of '92, a Genius of the Twentieth Century, Helen of Troy, and Sairy Gamp ("Class Day" 110).

As in the Dana Hall School production, the Inventress explains that from this "product of her fertile brain . . . could be ground out . . . women of all ages, ranks, and nation," and begins "grinding" this character and that. The *Oxford Ladies Collegian* reviewer notes that "[a]gain and again the audience was convulsed with laughter" as they viewed "good-natured 'hits' and 'grinds' on local characters. . ." ("Class Day" 110). The triple entendre intended here may no longer be familiar to today's readers. To *grind* in modern dictionaries still means "to operate . . . by turning a crank" ("Grind *v.*" [*Merriam-Webster's Collegiate Dictionary*] def. 5) and "to study hard" ("Grind *v.*" [*Merriam-Webster's Collegiate Dictionary*] def. 4) but formerly it also meant "to subject to ridicule or to satirize" ("Grind *v.*" [*Webster's New International Dictionary*] def. 7). In this last sense, *grinding* was close to the meaning of *roasting* someone today, as in the "hits and grinds" remark, which suggests that their characterizations were intended to tease one another in some way. The play's adaptors seem to have had great fun with the three semantic levels of the word at play in these lines.

In addition to new characters, the Oxford College women added new elements to the play. The review documents that the Genius of the Nineteenth Century spoke on the "growing popularity of women's colleges" (although there are no details of this discourse), and that the Genius of '92 delivered "a brilliant paper written in the biblical chronicle style, [giving] an excellent history of the class of '92" ("Class Day" 110). This history of the students' four years at the college is quite witty, as in this scene:

> This class goeth forth to battle with Philosophy, with the kings of the Hedonites and the Kantianites and the Deweyites. And they are weak and these kings are strong and '92 despaireth for its life. But truly, a great leader is sent unto them who verily knoweth the way of the enemy and she leadeth them

through the "slough of despond" and into the fair country beyond. And for this that she hath done for '92 they do emblazon her name on their banner and shout, honor and blessing and power be unto her and hers from this time forth and forevermore . . . ("Class Day" 111)

Sadly, this redoubtable leader's name might have been emblazoned on their banner, but it was not recorded in the review and thus is lost to history—a professor? A fellow student? What is evident in this lengthy drama within a drama is that the Oxford College students wished to celebrate the humorous and exciting details about their own lives and college experiences, as well as to act out the lives of famous women from history.

At the end of the production there was one final adaptation as the Inventress, "to display all the powers of her invention," ground out the Genius of the Twentieth Century. Coming back from the future, this new genius tells the audience "the prophetic history" of their class from her future vantage point. No details of this future history were recorded, except to say that "it made mirth over each one," leaving no one out, and "[a]s the prophecy ended, the class closed this delightful exercise with their Class Song." They closed the dialogue singing about leaving their "dear" college "forever" ("Class Day" 112).

In the late nineteenth century, the dialogue performance genre provided girls and women with a forum that served their need to speak about pressing matters in public. Published dialogues were widely available in the elocutionary handbooks of the period and, as I have argued, were popular for a multitude of reasons: they allowed girls to speak in front of a crowd but to not have to do so alone, they drew on feminine-gendered artistic strengths, and they were useful as fundraisers for charitable causes. Furthermore, young female rhetors sometimes wrote their own dialogues to address their concerns (e.g., being silenced) more directly, using brains and humor to win over their audiences. In this way, the stage became a staging ground for girls' first rhetorical forays into the public arena: groups worked together, with every member getting her turn in the spotlight, and everyone getting in on the fun of a theatrical production.

The Dana Hall School students of 1886–87 provide modern-day scholars with an exceptional example of the fervency of young girls' rhetorical aspirations and how those aspirations took shape within this genre. The Dana Hall School girls both wrote history and made history when they composed and published the dialogue known as *The Chronothanatoletron*, which "excited so much curiosity" across the country, as the *Newark Daily Advocate* reported ("Unique Affair"), that it played to packed houses around the United States for over two decades. Already a crowd-pleasing hit, the play was later adapted by many young women's groups who were eager to add their own innovations to the piece: they added new songs and stories, and they added more geniuses. These rhetors were eager to rewrite history, to focus on women's accomplishments—including their own. Now that their time machine has finally reached the twenty-first century, perhaps we can play the geniuses who hear what they had to say.

Notes

1. Future archival work might turn up documentation confirming more productions of *The Chronothanatoletron* by minority women's groups; however, it is also possible that this dialogue's rhetorical focus and its predominantly white cast of characters made it less appealing to more marginalized women. The issue of women's access to higher education, for example, might not have seemed worth the trouble of staging publicly to women of color in an era when education remained overwhelmingly segregated and restricted.

2. I am deeply indebted to Dorothy DeSimone, the archivist at the Dana Hall School archives, for her help in finding, scanning, and e-mailing to me copies of the original documents referred to in this section.

3. In the digitized Library of Congress copy, the faint, handwritten note "by Miss M.A. Greely and others" can be discerned on the copyright page, but Miss Greely's name has been incorrectly transcribed into the corresponding *HathiTrust* catalog entry as "Greedly." To eliminate this potential source of confusion, I refer throughout this essay to the Harvard University copy, also digitized by *HathiTrust*, instead.

4. Both are among the graduates listed in the Dana Hall School "Graduating Exercises" program, dated 20 June 1887.

5. This list is taken from the Stewart and Taylor program and is nearly identical in the published play: Agnes of Bologna becomes Agnesi, and Mother Bickerdike's name becomes Bickerdick (the correct spelling is Bickerdyke). The one significant change is that the character of the Abbess Hilda in the Dana Hall School premiere is replaced with Pocahontas in the published version. There is no author's prologue or critical prolegomenon in either text that explains the change, but it's possible to imagine that the students of a Christian preparatory school thought it prudent to include more figures from the Christian faith tradition to give their play-acting a more defensible ethos.

6. Donna Maria Gaetana Agnesi was professor of mathematics at the University of Bologna in the eighteenth century. In a math handbook she wrote—the first-known math textbook by a woman—she discusses an equation for a curve that became known as the witch of Agnesi curve.

7. The four-year Dana Hall School "course of study" from the school's catalog the year the play was produced lists arithmetic in the first year, algebra in both the second and third years, and geometry in the fourth year ("Catalog").

8. The number of seniors appears prominently in their class song, which they weave into their production of the dialogue: "In the College, in the College, Dwelt the seniors, ten and nine, Who are leaving Oxford College—Oh the glorious ten and nine!" ("Class Day" 112). (It was surely sung to the tune of folk song "Oh, My Darling Clementine.")

Works Cited

Biesecker, Barbara. "Coming to Terms with Recent Attempts to Write Women into the History of Rhetoric." *Rethinking the History of Rhetoric: Multidisciplinary Essays on the Rhetorical Tradition*, edited by Takis Poulakos, Westview, 1993, pp. 153–72.

Campbell, Paul Newell. "The Rhetoric of Theatre." *Southern Speech Communication Journal*, vol. 48, no. 1, 1982, pp. 11–21, doi:10.1080/10417948209372549.

"Catalog, 1886–87." Nina Weald Webber '49 Archives Room, Helen Template Cooke Library, Dana Hall School, Wellesley, MA.

"Chronothanatoletron." *The Bradford Era* [Bradford, PA], vol. 23, no. 278, 17 Nov. 1900, p. 1. *Newspaper Archive*.

"Class Day." *Oxford Ladies Collegian* [Oxford, OH], June 1892, pp. 109–12. *Newspaper Archive*.

"Colored People Give Play at Opera House." *The Reidsville Review*, 28 June 1912, p. 2. *Newspapers.com*, www.newspapers.com/clip/6935153/the_reidsville_review/.

DeSimone, Dorothy. "One More Dana Hall Research Question." E-mail message received by Lisa K. Suter, 12 Mar. 2019.

Donawerth, Jane. *Conversational Rhetoric: The Rise and Fall of a Women's Tradition, 1600–1900*. Southern Illinois UP, 2012.

"Graduating Exercises." 20 June 1887. Nina Weald Webber '49 Archives Room, Helen Template Cooke Library, Dana Hall School, Wellesley, MA. Commencement program.

Greely, M[ary] A[nn], [et al.]. *The Chronothanatoletron; or, Old Times Made New: An Entertainment for Female Characters Only*. Walter H. Baker, 1889. *HathiTrust*, babel .hathitrust.org/cgi/pt?id=hvd.hx5a4e;view=1up;seq=7.

Greely, Mary Ann. "The Spirit of Emerson College." *The Emerson College Magazine*, vol. XIX, no. 1, Nov. 1910, pp. 106–09.

"Grind, *v.*" *Merriam-Webster's Collegiate Dictionary*. 10th ed., Merriam-Webster, 1998, p. 513.

"Grind, *v.*" *Webster's New International Dictionary of the English Language*. 2nd ed., unabridged, G & C Merriam, 1956, p. 1103.

Horowitz, Helen Lefkowitz. *Alma Mater: Design and Experience in the Women's Colleges from their Nineteenth-Century Beginnings to the 1930s*. Alfred A. Knopf, 1984.

King, Margaret L., and Albert Rabil, Jr. "The Other Voice in Early Modern Europe: Introduction to the Series." *The Story of Sapho*, by Madeleine de Scudéry, translated by Karen Newman, U of Chicago P, 2003, pp. xi–xxxi.

Logan, Shirley Wilson. *Liberating Language: Sites of Rhetorical Education in Nineteenth-Century Black America*. Southern Illinois UP, 2008.

Mattingly, Carol. "Telling Evidence: Rethinking What Counts in Rhetoric." *Rhetoric Society Quarterly*, vol. 32, no. 1, Winter 2002, pp. 99–108. *JSTOR*, www.jstor.org/stable/3886308.

McMillan, Ann. "Chaucer and the Legend of Good Women." *The Legend of Good Women*, by Geoffrey Chaucer, Rice UP, 1987, pp. 3–62.

Mountford, Roxanne. "On Gender and Rhetorical Space." *Rhetoric Society Quarterly*, vol. 31, no. 1, Winter 2001, pp. 41–71. *JSTOR*, www.jstor.org/stable/3886401.

Northrop, Henry Davenport, editor. *The Delsarte Speaker, or Modern Elocution Designed Especially for Young Folks and Amateurs*. Chicago, 1895.

Stewart, Elizabeth, and Maud M. Taylor. "The Chronothanatóletron: A Farce Written for the Class of '87, Dana Hall." Nina Weald Webber '49 Archives Room, Helen Template Cooke Library, Dana Hall School, Wellesley, MA. Class Day program.

Stratton, Josephine W., and Jeanette M. Stratton. *The New Select Speaker: Together with Rules and Exercises for Physical Culture and Elocution*. 1902.

"A Unique Affair: The Annual Commencement of the Literary Societies." *Newark Daily Advocate*, 4 June 1890.

"Wall, *n.1*." *Oxford English Dictionary*, Oxford UP, 2020, www.oed.com/view/Entry/225282?redirectedFrom=to+go+to+the+wall#eid15264580.

Embroidering History:
The Gendered Memorial Activism of
the Daughters of the American Revolution

Jessica Enoch

> There is much work to be done by American women of the present and
> future, not alone in inculcating patriotism, the chief mission of this orga-
> nization [the Daughters of the American Revolution], but as collectors, and
> even as writers of American history. . . . To woman, in a peculiar sense,
> belongs the embroidering of history.
>
> —Jane Meade Welch

In 1892, during the opening days of the First Continental Congress of the Daughters of the American Revolution (the DAR), Jane Meade Welch of the New York
DAR chapter identified the related missions of this new organization: encouraging American patriotism and composing the nation's history and public memory.
In making this claim, Welch confirmed the prime work outlined in the DAR's
"Act of Incorporation" set out just two years earlier at the organization's inception. As this act states, the objects of the DAR are:

> To perpetuate the memory of the spirit of the men and women who achieved
> American independence by the acquisition and protection of historical spots
> and the erection of monuments; by the encouragement of historical research
> in relation to the Revolution and the publication of its results; by the preserva-
> tion of documents and relics, and of the records of the individual services of
> Revolutionary soldiers and patriots, and by the promotion of celebrations and
> all patriotic anniversaries.

This more developed description gives a clearer sense of the DAR's historical, memorial, and patriotic agenda. Along with the quotation from Welch in this essay's
epigraph, the description additionally indicates the DAR's multilayered gendered
imperatives: this all-women's group was to "perpetuate the memory of . . . men
and women" by crafting history and public memory in a way that was metaphorically engendered as and equated with the feminine practice of embroidery.

In this essay, I define the DAR's work as a form of gendered memorial activism
that enabled this women's organization to shape the American public consciousness about the Revolution within the volatile context of the 1890s. My arguments
reveal that the memorial efforts of DAR members were directed in equal measure

to both the Revolutionary past and their sociopolitical present, since they sought to speak to and change their contemporary moment through their remembrance just as much as they worked to recover those memories of one hundred years previous. It is critical to recall that at the close of the nineteenth century, the civil rights project of the Reconstruction period (1863–77) had largely failed, and the country had embarked on what became known as the nadir of race relations in the United States when virulent racism targeted Black Americans, evidenced through overt segregation, lynchings, and Jim Crow laws. Concurrently, due to increased labor opportunities brought on by the Industrial Revolution, an un-precedented number of immigrants came to the United States looking to take advantage of new work options: between 1890 and 1920, 18.2 million people em-igrated from southern and eastern Europe, Asia, and Mexico (Archdeacon 113). At this time, too, the government prioritized settlement throughout the Great Plains and West. The first transcontinental railroad was completed in 1869, and the Homestead Act of 1862 offered potential farmers (almost) free land, mainly west of the Mississippi. Meanwhile, off-reservation boarding schools and legisla-tion like the Dawes Act (1887) worked forcefully (and violently) to assimilate Na-tive Americans into the society of the United States by breaking up tribal lands and reallocating those lands to individual Native citizens, as well as by working to erase Native language and culture through education.

The DAR inserted itself into this precarious moment through its gendered memorial activism. The society's project was to stabilize the country in the way this organization's members saw fit by turning attention to the Revolution and asserting that the white, Anglo world that they were purposefully recovering should set the course for the American future they wanted to inhabit. For read-ers familiar with the DAR, it should come as no surprise that the organization's patriotic and memorial project was a deeply conservative one that reflected the interests of the dominant white, patriarchal culture—a culture that, DAR members believed, was under threat due to immigration, tense race relations, and an American citizenry disconnected not just by cultural ties but also by geo-graphic distance.[1] The organization's own requirements for membership reveal its white, Protestant exclusionary politics: to be a member, a would-be daughter had to trace her bloodlines back to a patriot of the Revolution—and a patriot, the DAR made clear, was a white patriot, even though Black and Native people participated in the conflict. In this essay, I explore how the DAR initiated and sustained its public memory campaign in a way that specifically responded to its 1890 moment by working to focus national attention on an idealized (and largely fictional) white, Protestant American past.

Following the arguments of feminist rhetoricians Charlotte Hogg and Carol Mattingly, I turn to the DAR to interrogate the rhetorical complexity of the organization's memorial project, of which its conservatism was part and parcel. The DAR was an immensely popular, and even powerful, women's group that wielded a rich repertoire of rhetorical resources aimed to inform the public imagination at the century's turn. By 1898, the DAR boasted 23,000 members who participated in 444 chapters across the nation.[2] This essay considers how the DAR crafted its gendered memorial activism by leveraging the twin rhetorical practices of remembering and forgetting. As public memory scholars such as Bradford Vivian, Barbie Zelizer, and Kendall Phillips assert, forgetting and remembering are intertwined: the call to remember is often made in response to the impending danger of forgetting. This essay examines how the DAR's memorial activism was catalyzed by the possibility of the American public forgetting specific (that is, white, patriotic) aspects of the Revolution. However, the DAR's moves to remember white patriotism in the colonial period hinged on the need to forget another period: the nation's more recent past. The DAR thus worked toward what Vivian defines as "communal forgetting": the organization purposefully directed attention away from recent sociopolitical strife and toward the Revolution. In this case, then, forgetting does not mean that a memory falls into oblivion (41). Rather, forgetting can happen through replacing one memory with another (Zelizer 220). By looking to the Revolution, the DAR prompted its publics to forget the complexity of the recent past and present moment. The group's memorializations erased the presence of Black, Native, and immigrant populations, as well as these populations' claims on citizenship. In exchange, the DAR asked the public to celebrate what member Mrs. Hugh Hagan called the "colonial simplicity" of the Revolution (242).

Critical to the work of this essay is to highlight the gendered memorial strategies the DAR developed to persuade its publics toward remembering and forgetting. As my opening epigraph indicates, the DAR saw its work to be that of memorial embroidery. At the close of the nineteenth century, DAR members themselves were not fully enfranchised, and, as a conservative group, its intention was not to cast itself as an organization arguing for women's rights. Yet, even though they were not full citizens in terms of their voting rights, I see that members were, in the words of Kristy Maddux, "practic[ing] alternate modes of citizenship" through their memory work (106). That is, the DAR crafted its memorial activism in a way that enabled members to direct the nation's attention and identify the nation's priorities. The organization's unique approach to memorialization reveals how the DAR envisioned memorial work as an opportunity for women to shape the public consciousness and point the country toward a version of patriotism its members believed was best: it was the duty of DAR women to embroider the history they wanted the nation to remember. On a more particular level, I argue that the DAR's gendered memorial activism involved three distinct embroidery projects: remembering the local patriot and everyday patriotism, using Revolutionary memory to unite the country geographically, and memorializing women. Together, these projects prompted the public to forget the recent past and remember instead an idealized version of the colonial period. To take up this analysis of the DAR's work, I call on the organization's magazine, the *American Monthly*, which began in 1892, and the organization's meeting reports, as well as smaller publications produced by the DAR and its chapters.

Local Patriot and Everyday Patriotism

The prime catalyst that prompted women to create the DAR was their anxiety that the American public at the turn of the twentieth century had forgotten or would never know what members saw as the most important moment in the history of the United States: the Revolutionary War. The DAR's 1899 report recalls the exigencies that inspired the organization's genesis: "There was great danger that coming generations would utterly forget the purposes and ideals that gave strength and unity to the nation. It was felt that the old landmarks must be rescued from oblivion before it was too late, and that the young must be taught a reverence for the past" ("Work of the Continental Congress" 35–36). This concern for forgetting was specifically exacerbated by the influx of immigrants coming to the United States during this period; the DAR feared that these disparate groups would have little attachment to or knowledge of this important historical moment. As member Mrs. Charles W. Fairbanks recalls in the 1903–04 DAR report, "Our founders realized that with the steady immigration of foreigners . . . something must be done to foster patriotism and love for our country and our flag and to make Americans of them, or there was danger of our being absorbed by the different nationalities among us" (qtd. in "Daughters of the American Revolution" 92). To speak to these concerns, the DAR devised its memorial project. But a key concern for this women's group was to consider what to remember and how, for if women were to generate patriotism by composing history and public memory, the DAR had to identify the memorial possibilities open to them.

One key decision was to memorialize local acts of everyday patriotism enacted by those who were often DAR members' ancestors. As member Mrs. Lindsay makes clear at the thirteenth national meeting of the DAR: "We have monuments to illustrious statesmen and to the famous generals of Revolutionary times" but yet the "men who stained the snow with their blood from their shoeless feet, who starved at Valley Forge, languished and died as martyrs on prison ships, . . . these men have been neglected" (qtd. in "Evening Session" 239). Writing the history of the forgotten soldier and memorializing his dedication to American ideals thus became a key point of the DAR's activism that enabled the members to fend off

Figure 1. "Olde Letters and Historie of Firesides." *American Monthly*, vol. 2, no. 1, p. 63.

what they saw as the dangers of immigration. Through this grassroots effort, members recalled local acts of patriotism by accessing genres available to them: essay contests, pageants, relic displays, and of course memorial creation. Not competing with massive monuments such as the Washington Monument, which was completed in 1884, more modest memorials were within individual DAR chapters' purview. For instance, the Norwalk, Connecticut, chapter installed a small stone marker outside the town that reminded residents of their local history. On the marker is written: "from the summit of this hill, Major General William Tryon witnessed the burning of NORWALK by the British Troops during the engagement of July 11 & 12 1778" (DAR Norwalk Chapter Marker).

The DAR's periodical *American Monthly* also became a prime rhetorical space for members to publish their local memorial work. Articles such as "Incidents in the Life of a Colonial Family," by Mrs. James B. Taylor, and "Bombardment of Bristol, Rhode Island," by Emma Wescott Bullock, are just two representative examples of such publications by DAR members. But even more than the periodical as a site for publication, *American Monthly* also functioned as an archival space for members to showcase their local and familial research. One section of the publication was titled "Olde Letters and Historie of Firesides" (see fig. 1), and it was based on the DAR belief that "the real causes of the American Revolution could be disclosed by a true history of early American firesides." This section displayed "domestic letters and other memoranda" that offered readers memorial access to correspondence between husbands and wives, brothers and sisters, mothers and sons. These personal and intimate artifacts endowed patriotic value to familial relationships, for they evidenced the smaller acts of bravery, fortitude, and care that also contributed to the Revolution.

By archiving and displaying these artifacts, the DAR engendered public memory and asserted the civic significance of the group's work. Figure 1 corroborates and adds dimension to the DAR's mission, as it pictorially represents and reveres the work of those women who remember by their firesides the families that helped the nation come to be. Both visually through the image and textually through the letters themselves, the domestic scene and familial relationships are highlighted as valid sites for patriotic expression and examination as well as public memory production. Within these sites too, women are central characters as both the subjects for and producers of public memory.

Memorialization for National Unity

A second way DAR members achieved their patriotic memorial project was by prompting local chapters throughout the United States to join forces to remember the Revolution. This kind of unifying and collaborative work was often praised, especially by those noting how the chapters in the North and South worked together in this post–Civil War context. For instance, one observer commented, "[I]f this Society of the Daughters of the American Revolution had existed then [during the antebellum period] there would have been no civil war." This person continued, "You are doing more to draw together the union of this country than all the men have been able to do from Washington's time down" (qtd. in "Evening Session" 236). DAR member Mrs. Hugh Hagan from an Atlanta chapter elaborated on this point, asserting that the uniting work of the DAR functioned not just to mend the strife of North and South but also to close the distance between the eastern and western shores of the nation. She states, "[C]ommingling we may prove the southern sister as sincere and loving as she of colder climes, and our country shall gradually unite in colonial simplicity and confidence, 'No North, no South, no East, no West, but one grand Union'" (242). As Hagan articulates and as DAR practices exemplified, the way toward national unity was to forget present-day diversity and divides by remembering "colonial simplicity" (242). Instead of dwelling on the Civil War, the presence of slavery and its aftermath, or immigrant-related differences, the DAR called the public to remember the Revolution. Of course, contemporary readers will notice that the DAR was misremembering what the group cast as a homogenous white colonial period. But for DAR members, the idea was to resurrect a white, patriotic, Anglo world that they wanted to recreate.

As much as unification was a priority for the DAR, however, there were real problems with its grassroots public memory strategy that the organization had to address. Prime among these problems was that, for chapters beyond the Eastern Seaboard and original colonies, there were few opportunities to conduct local research or to produce memorializations dedicated to the Revolution. For example, a Minnesota DAR chapter reports that the state is "poor in historic landmarks" (Leggett 228); similarly, Nebraska members had the "impression that there were [no landmarks] of national importance within the state" (Allee 241). In response, the DAR crafted unique rhetorical strategies for members in these regions to feel included in the organization's memorial and patriotic mission, and these strategies enabled members in such states as Texas, Florida, and California to connect not only to the Revolution but also with one another. The DAR report that reviewed activities from 1890 to 1897 outlines the "work of the chapters" and cites the following common features:

> Each chapter possesses a gavel made of some historic material. Almost all have their charters framed in woods connected with some famous event. Many have made the exhibition of historic heirlooms a specially instructive part of their work. Entertainments have been given at which members clad in costumes of old have dispensed hospitality with the grace of ancient days. In all such ways the facts of history have been made to educate each member, while at the same time they have roused the interest of the public at large.
>
> ("Work of the Chapters" 53)

As an even more detailed example, the Sequoia chapter in San Francisco celebrated its commitments to the Revolution and connection to other DAR chapters by planting what it called a "liberty tree." The process through which the tree was planted reveals the chapter's intention to connect its California land to revered Revolutionary space. This chapter's 1894 publication *Ceremonies at the Planting of the Liberty Tree* recounts the ceremony for the planting and also explains that the planting gained Revolutionary significance by virtue of the fact that chapters from the East Coast sent soil for the planting from key locations. Spanning over seventy-seven pages, the text lists all the chapters that donated soil from sites such as Jefferson's grave at Monticello and the Yorktown battlefield in Virginia to the "trenches of Valley Forge" and "earth from the Bunker Hill Monument in Charlestown, Mass." (7). Each listed entry, too, was accompanied by short notes about the DAR contributor and the historic site from which the soil was donated.

The DAR's memorial activism in these instances makes real Kenneth Burke's rhetorical theories of identification and consubstantiality. As Burke explains, interlocutors in a rhetorical situation who are, of course, different, identify with one another by "joining interests" and "acting together," and through this work they share substance or become "consubstantial"—united in their identified commonality (20–21). Members in DAR chapters identified with one another

and created unity across the nation by literally sharing substance with one another through the materiality of gavels, frames, and relic displays. For the Sequoia chapter in particular, the sacred ground from sites such as Jefferson's
grave consecrated California land and, in so doing, made it into a site of Revolutionary significance.

Remembering Women

When the DAR turned attention to everyday acts of patriotism, members capi-
talized on the opportunity to include women in this memorial project. Over and
again, DAR publications asserted that women had been erased from Revolutionary history and public memory with comments such as these:

> In the days of the Revolution, we well know that woman's courage and endur-
> ance were called into action as inevitably as were those of the stronger sex,
> but, alas! the records of her individual performances are very meagre, told only
> incidentally, and facts concerning her are to be gleaned only here and there by
> careful search of histories, diaries, old letters and biographical sketches widely
> scattered, in many cases only accidentally preserved.   (Smith 252)

A priority for the DAR was not just to point to this absence but also to do the
work of making women's Revolutionary presence known. It was their members'
duty to remember. As Janet Elizabeth Richards explains in her 1892 address to
the DAR, "To the women of '76, no less than to its men, belongs the honor of
achieving this great gain for liberty. And to us, the daughters of these honored
dames, does it particularly pertain to gather and preserve the records, honor the
deeds, and cherish the memory of the Women of the Revolution!" (292).

The DAR took up this gendered recovery work by naming its chapters (for
example, the Hannah Winthrop chapter of Cambridge, Massachusetts, and
the Anna Warner Bailey chapter of New London, Connecticut); by publishing
magazine articles such as Mrs. Mary Stuart Smith's "The Virginia Women in
the Revolution"; and by helping to fund public memorials dedicated to figures
like Mrs. Kerenhappuch Turner of Guilford, Maryland, and "the heroic women
of Bryan's Station" in Lexington, Kentucky ("Kentucky"). The DAR cast light on
women who were likely seen as more famous, like Abigail Adams, Dolly Madison, and Mary Washington, as well as more ordinary women such as the wives
of Valley Forge soldiers, those who boycotted British goods after the Stamp Act
was imposed, and women who created and wore "homespun" clothing to show
their allegiance to the colonies and Revolutionary ideals.[3] While the DAR often
remembered women whose gendered performances were normative, such as

women supporting their soldier husbands or even politicizing domestic tasks like purchasing and making domestic goods, the DAR also highlighted women who tested gendered boundaries. *American Monthly* readers learned about Mercy Warren, who composed protest poetry; Molly Pitcher, who took her injured husband's place at the cannon; and Deborah Samson, who gender-bended her way into the military (see Richards). The examples of women's bravery were not only many and diverse but purposeful. As Richards asks, "What are the lessons to be drawn from these instances of feminine patriotism, these pictures of woman's heroism?" (291). The implicit yet obvious response to this question was that DAR members and their publics were to learn that women patriots had been and continued to be critical players not just in the Revolutionary past but also in the tumultuous present. The DAR called members to draw strength from these Revolutionary-era women and activate similar kinds of patriotism at the turn of the twentieth century.

Yet another obvious strategy the DAR deployed to create these connections to the past and assert members' critical importance in the present was to consistently publish members' genealogical records—records that made clear how DAR women were inheritors not just of their ancestors' blood but also their patriotism. For example, in its October 1892 issue, the *American Monthly* published "Mrs. A.S. Hubbard," an article that traces DAR member Sarah Isabelle Sylvester Hubbard's ancestry to her grandfather Valentine Holt, who at thirteen years old fought in the battle of Bennington, Vermont. Hubbard's claim to fame, though, goes beyond her bloodline: the male soldier Valentine Holt is not the main character in this article. Rather, as the title of the piece makes clear, DAR member Hubbard—not Holt—is the central figure, with the article highlighting her patriotism instead of his. Presiding officer of the Sequoia chapter in California, Hubbard is described as "strong in character and fearless in expression." (L.M.B. 327). Hubbard takes on the uniting work described above by attempting to create, in Hubbard's own words, "one undivided sisterhood from the Atlantic to the Pacific shores" (qtd. in L.M.B. 327). Here, especially, readers of the *American Monthly* learn how DAR members like Hubbard practice alternative modes of citizenship and see themselves as active agents in shaping their vision of the nation.

Embroidering History

In this essay I have set out three unique practices—the remembrance of everyday patriotism, the use of memorial unification, and the imperative to remember women—that played key roles in the DAR's gendered, and in large part conservative, memorial activism. Yet it should be clear that DAR members were not just

Report of D. A. R., 1890–97.   PLATE 3.

SEAL OF 1890.

Figure 2. DAR Seal. 1890. Daughters of the American Revolution. *Report of the Daughters of the American Revolution, 1890–1897.* Government Printing Office, 1899, p. 41.

remembering their preferred forms of "feminine patriotism" (Richards 291) but also performing them: members' commemorative work enabled these women to shape public discourse and identify their preferred vision for the nation. Their memorializations, then, substantiate Carole Blair's claim about the political nature of public memory: "struggle over symbolism in the past is just as surely a struggle over power in the present" (57). The DAR intervened in the complex sociopolitical scene at the turn of the twentieth century by remembering and revering a white, Anglo, patriotic past—one that DAR members were attempting to invent for themselves in their current moment.

It is important to note, however, that this "struggle" was not only evidenced in the ways the DAR was working to shape raced, cultured, and spatial politics on the national scene. The DAR's struggle also pertained to the gendered politics of public memory and civic engagement. Returning to the epigraph that opens this essay, I want to emphasize that Welch's statement about the DAR's imperative to "embroider history" was not a singular claim. Instead it was a representative metaphor for the organization: this sentiment was expressed and repeated through the use and circulation of the DAR's seal (fig. 2). This seal conveys the image of a woman at the spinning wheel, equating the key practice of the organization—memorialization—with that of threadwork, a feminine activity that would not traditionally be endowed with civic importance. But yet, we might also read in this image the DAR charging its form of feminized gendered activity with power. For here the woman, and by extension the DAR, weaves together her vision of the nation through her local, domesticated memorial activism—work that remembers the everyday patriotism of women and asserts their presence on the historical and political landscape.

Notes

1. The DAR's activities and politics have been marked by racism against African Americans as well as by anti-Semitism. One of the more significant instances of the organization's racism was its 1939 decision to bar the African American singer Marian Anderson from performing at Constitution Hall; protesting this decision, then First Lady Eleanor Roosevelt revoked her membership in the organization.

2. As Julie Des Jardins's work makes clear, the DAR was not the only "women's preservationist" group of this period (68). The Society of the Colonial Dames, the Mount Vernon Ladies' Association, and the United Daughters of the Confederacy were contemporaneously building their memberships and taking on the work of historiography and public memory.

3. For an extended discussion of the relevance of "homespun," see Ulrich.

Works Cited

"Act of Incorporation." Daughters of the American Revolution, *Report*, p. 115.

Allee, Mrs. Abraham. "Nebraska." Daughters of the American Revolution, *Seventh Report*, pp. 241–51.

Archdeacon, Thomas J. *Becoming American: An Ethnic History*. Free Press, 1983.

Blair, Carole. "Collective Memory." *Communication as . . . Perspectives on Theory*, edited by Gregory J. Shepherd et al., SAGE, 2006, pp. 51–59.

Bullock, Emma Wescott. "Bombardment of Bristol, Rhode Island." *American Monthly*, vol. 1, no. 3, Sept. 1892, pp. 207–11. *Daughters of the American Revolution Digital Magazine Archive*, services.dar.org/members/magazine_archive/download/?file =DARMAG_1892_09.pdf.

Burke, Kenneth. *A Rhetoric of Motives*. U of California P, 1969.

Ceremonies at the Planting of the Liberty Tree in Golden Gate Park. Sequoia Chapter Daughters of the American Revolution of San Francisco, 1894. *Google Books*, books.google.com/books?id=sgMRAQAAMAAJ.

DAR Norwalk Chapter Marker. Daughters of the American Revolution, *Seventh Report*, pp. 165.

Daughters of the American Revolution. *Report of the Daughters of the American Revolution, 1890–1897*. Government Printing Office, 1899. *HathiTrust*, babel .hathitrust.org/cgi/pt?id=mdp.39015070206068.

———. *Seventh Report of the National Society for the Daughters of the American Revolution*. Government Printing Office, 1905. *HathiTrust*, hdl.handle.net/2027/ nyp.33433081811006.

"Daughters of the American Revolution at the Louisiana Purchase Exposition, October 11, 1904." Daughters of the American Revolution, *Seventh Report*, pp. 88–117.

Des Jardins, Julie. *Women and the Historical Enterprise in America: Gender, Race, and the Politics of Memory, 1880–1945*. U of North Carolina P, 2003.

"Evening Session, Tuesday, April 19, 1904." *American Monthly*, vol. 25, 1904, pp. 230–56. *Google Books*, www.google.com/books/edition/Daughters_of_the_ American_Revolution_Mag/tcYWAAAAYAAJ?hl=en&gbpv=0.

Hagan, Mrs. Hugh. "The Daughters of the American Revolution as Represented in Georgia." *American Monthly,* vol. 1, no. 3, Sept. 1892, pp. 239–44. *Daughters of the American Revolution Digital Magazine Archive*, services.dar.org/members/ magazine_archive/download/?file=DARMAG_1892_09.pdf.

Hogg, Charlotte. "Including Conservative Women's Rhetorics in an 'Ethics of Hope and Care.'" *Rhetoric Review*, vol. 34, no. 4, 2015, pp. 391–408.

"Kentucky." Daughters of the American Revolution, *Seventh Report*, p. 62.

Leggett, Mrs. M. R. B. "Minnesota." Daughters of the American Revolution, *Seventh Report*, pp. 228–40.

L.M.B. "Mrs. A. S. Hubbard." *American Monthly*, vol. 1, no. 4, Oct. 1892, pp. 325–27. *Daughters of the American Revolution Digital Magazine Archive*, services.dar.org/ members/magazine_archive/download/?file=DARMAG_1892_10.pdf.

Maddux, Kristy. "Without Touching upon Suffrage: Gender and Economic Citizenship at the World's Columbian Exposition." *Rhetoric Society Quarterly*, vol. 47, no. 2, 2017, pp. 105–30.

Mattingly, Carol. "Telling Evidence: Rethinking What Counts in Rhetoric." *Rhetoric Society Quarterly*, vol. 32, no. 1, 2002, pp. 99–108.

"Olde Letters and Historie of Firesides." *American Monthly*, vol. 2, no. 1, p. 63. *Daughters of the American Revolution Digital Magazine Archive*, services.dar.org/ members/magazine_archive/download/?file=DARMAG_1893_01.pdf.

Phillips, Kendall R. "Introduction." *Framing Public Memory*, edited by Phillips, U of Alabama P, 2004, pp. 1–16.

Richards, Janet Elizabeth. "Heroic Women of the American Revolution." *American Monthly*, vol. 1, no. 3, Sept. 1892, pp. 278–92. *Daughters of the American Revolution Digital Magazine Archive*, services.dar.org/members/magazine_archive/download/ ?file=DARMAG_1892_09.pdf.

Smith, Mrs. Mary Stuart. "The Virginia Women in the Revolution." *American Monthly*, vol. 1, no. 3, Sept. 1892, pp. 252–57. *Daughters of the American Revolution Digital Magazine Archive*, services.dar.org/members/magazine_archive/download/?file =DARMAG_1892_09.pdf.

Taylor, Mrs. James B. "Incidents in the Life of a Colonial Family." *American Monthly*, vol. 1, no. 4, Oct. 1892, pp. 356–61. *Daughters of the American Revolution Digital*

Magazine Archive, services.dar.org/members/magazine_archive/download/?file =DARMAG_1892_10.pdf.

Ulrich, Laurel Thatcher. *The Age of Homespun: Objects and Stories in the Creation of an American Myth*. Vintage, 2009.

Vivian, Bradford. *Public Forgetting: The Rhetoric and Politics of Beginning Again*. Pennsylvania State UP, 2010.

Welch, Jane Meade. "American History for American Women." *American Monthly*, vol. 1, no. 2, Aug. 1892, pp. 128–32. *Daughters of the American Revolution Digital Magazine Archive*, services.dar.org/members/magazine_archive/download/?file =DARMAG_1892_08.pdf.

"Work of the Chapters." Daughters of the American Revolution, *Report*, pp. 53–55.

"Work of the Continental Congress and National Board of Management." Daughters of the American Revolution, *Report*, pp. 35–50.

Zelizer, Barbie. "Reading the Past against the Grain: The Shape of Memory Studies." *Critical Studies in Mass Communication*, vol. 12, no. 2, 1995, pp. 214–39.

Beginning Again, Again: Monument Protest and Rhetorics of African American Memory Work

Shevaun E. Watson

"Statue vandalized following shooting," reads the headline on 22 June 2015, in Charleston, South Carolina's, *Post and Courier*. The newspaper reports that vandals spray-painted the word "racist" on the John C. Calhoun statue located in Marion Square, part of the city's popular historic tourist district. The words "and Slavery" were added to "Truth, Justice and the Constitution," a list of Calhoun's purported legacies inscribed on the base of the statue (Elmore). The gruesome murder of nine Black parishioners by an avowed white supremacist in Charleston's historic Mother Emanuel AME Church just a few days earlier, on 17 June, shocked the nation and sparked weeks of vandalism of white supremacist monuments, and ensuing debate across many southern states (Boughton; Holley). In Charleston, authorities put large orange barricades around Calhoun's statue, only to have vandals return days later to deface the statute once again with balloons filled with red paint. Another monument struck by protesters after the church slaying was the Fort Sumter memorial, which was spray-painted with "This is the problem #racist" and "[Mayor Joe] Riley and [Governor Nikki] Haley—Why defend this evil—This is the root of our evil" (Tyson; see also "Vandals"; Munday). The defaced monument, located in White Point Garden in the Charleston Battery, created a bloody-looking gash in the elegant charm of Charleston's most iconic neighborhood, whose row of colorful, lavish homes overlook the Ashley River.

There is much to say about these incidents; indeed, much ink has been spilled in public and scholarly venues about the meaning of Confederate heritage in light of the church massacre, many noting Charleston's peaceful, unifying, and forgiving response to the tragedy and others underscoring that the vandals in Charleston and elsewhere were not exclusively African American. One important fact, however, remains largely unacknowledged: the summer of 2015 was not nearly the first time that white supremacist monuments in Charleston were vandalized.

There is a long and complex history of Black protest against such monuments and specifically against the memorialization of Calhoun, the nation's most ardent champion of slavery, who famously argued that slavery was "a positive good" (Calhoun).[1] Black Charlestonians and their allies have been fighting for over 150 years to shape the cultural meaning and memory of this South Carolina politician, the war he portended, and the institution he defended. These rhetorical acts of resistance exist in a telling chronology that illuminates the key role that Black protest played in remembering American slavery, and thereby adds to our deepening understanding of African American agency in nineteenth-century rhetorical history. The constant furor over the Calhoun monument provides the most probing example of this resistance, in part because of what Calhoun came to represent but also because this protracted public-memory drama plays out in Charleston, a city that has masterfully commodified particular memories of slavery and the Civil War, and has packaged them into one of the most alluring tourist destinations in the United States (Yuhl; Estes; Poirot and Watson).

Using Bradford Vivian's framework of the potentially restorative power of "public forgetting," I argue that Black Charlestonians have attempted at two distinct points in time—at "transformative junctures"—to use monument protest as a specific rhetorical strategy to "begin again," to "reject normative perceptions of the past . . . [to] inaugurate a new era of qualitatively transformed sociopolitical relations" (Vivian 58–60). African Americans have used vandalism rhetorically to urge white Americans to abandon sentimental memories of slavery, which was crucial for egalitarianism to take hold. African Americans' first bid to establish a new accord, which I focus on here, transpired during the Reconstruction era. These early efforts, which included both protest and commemoration, drove the public memory narrative about slavery. In other words, white Americans' "lost cause" account (Glymph 116), which ultimately came to dominate public remembering of the Confederacy, was originally created in response to freedpeople's concerted rhetorical actions right after the war. Black Charlestonians focused their ire on Calhoun as a way to aggregate and forward their own memories of the very evils of slavery that white Americans wanted to forget.

The second attempt to begin again, and hopefully the more lasting one, since we know that Jim Crow crushed that initial effort, was the official deposal of the Confederate flag from the South Carolina statehouse in the aftermath of the Charleston church shooting and renewed vandalism of white supremacist monuments. Just as their emancipated counterparts 150 years earlier knew that certain versions of the past could set race relations on better or worse footing, many African Americans and their allies returned in 2015 to sites of slavery and Civil War memory, such as the Calhoun monument, to call again for a kind of public forgetting, a laying to rest of some memories—memories which, in their dogmatic preservation, have become politically debilitating and socially impracticable.

In elucidating the details of nineteenth-century African Americans' efforts to shape public memories of slavery, I propose that monument protest is in itself an important kind of rhetorical memory work. Vandalism in particular is a rhetorical strategy that makes the remonstration highly public while allowing individual protesters anonymity, which is an important combination of effects. Such an argument extends current scholarship on monuments and memorials to encompass the responses to them as a form of collective re-remembering that needs to be accounted for (Blair and Michel; Dickinson et al.). Following Vivian, I do not intend for my rhetorical analysis merely to fill in historical gaps to counter collective amnesia or historiographical neglect. Instead, the larger aim is to use this nineteenth-century instance of monument protest—vandalism as rhetoric—to reconsider what it means to do rhetorical history and public memory work in our age of mass shootings and incessant violence against Black Americans within a national landscape marked by symbols of racist heritage. We have to find a way to forget some things, to "strategically excise" (Vivian 9) parts of our collective past that have become hindrances to beginning again.

Prelude to the Possibilities

Even though Calhoun predates the Civil War, he is one of the war's central ideological figures, arguing throughout the early nineteenth century that the South should protect slavery at all costs. A master of two plantations and more than a hundred slaves, Calhoun understood slavery to be the bedrock of southern civilization, and in 1837 he presaged the Civil War for what it truly was, a choice between slavery and secession: "Abolition and the Union cannot coexist . . . I openly proclaim it—and the sooner it is known the better. . . . By the necessary course of events . . . we must become, finally, two people" (Calhoun). Calhoun was one of the most influential politicians in nineteenth-century America, rising from powerful local statesman to representative, senator, secretary of war, secretary of state, and vice president. He imbued national politics with his fervent commitments to slavery and what became a doctrine of states' rights, advocating for slavery to accompany westward expansion and facing off against his own president, Andrew Jackson, in the nullification crisis over federal tariffs. For Calhoun, any whiff of federal overreach presented an existential threat to the South's way of life, which he defended indefatigably. As historian Walter Edgar explains, by the mid–nineteenth century South Carolinians, and Charlestonians in particular, came to feel uniquely vulnerable to national incursions: with a native-born Black majority and a smaller, homogenous white population, "South Carolina had become a closed society," whereas in the colonial era the state "welcomed new people and new ideas as vital to its growth and development, antebellum South Carolina viewed these as potential threats" (323). No one embodied or articulated this concern more cogently than Calhoun, so it is not surprising that efforts to memorialize him began in earnest while he was still alive. Sculptures and portraits and gold-embossed copies of his speeches were commissioned as early as the 1840s; his birthday was an occasion for elaborate parades and his funeral in April of 1850 a mammoth, star-studded affair (Wiltse; Meigs).

Yet, still in the grips of bondage in the heart of American slavery, African Americans openly, if intermittently, demonstrated their disdain for Calhoun. When all South Carolinians were invited to visit Calhoun laying in state, Black Charlestonians arrived in "considerable numbers," not to mourn his passing but to celebrate his demise ("South-Carolina Mourns"). One witness to this event, Fredrika Bremer, reported that "a whole crowd of negroes leaped about the streets, looking quite entertained," with some openly declaring that "Calhoun was a wicked man, for he wished that [they] might remain slaves" (305). Later, a bust of Calhoun adorning the office of the proslavery newspaper the *Charleston Mercury* was destroyed by a freedwoman once she realized what the statesman stood for (Floyd 2; see also Jenkins 30–45). In 1863 Calhoun's tomb was being vandalized so often that his remains were disinterred under the cover of night and placed in an unmarked grave "for fear that local blacks . . . might dig them up" (Kytle and Roberts, *Denmark Vesey's Garden* 98–99; see also Gregg). Though somewhat scant, archival evidence does suggest that Black Charlestonians held Calhoun and his legacy in some contempt.

Among Black Charlestonians' white counterparts, however, there were "extraordinary initiatives to enshrine Calhoun in the civic landscape" (Brown 133). In 1843, a small group of local merchants and planters commissioned the first statue of South Carolina's beloved son. After much delay, the statue was shipped in 1850 from Italy but sank in the infamous wreck of the *Elizabeth* off the coast of New York.[2] As the *Elizabeth* struck a sandbar, the enormous marble likeness of Calhoun ripped through the hold, bringing the ship down (Capper 505–12; see also "Wreck"). After months of intense labor, the damaged statue was located, raised from the ocean floor, and installed in Charleston's City Hall, where it stood prominently, though damaged and stained, for fifteen years. During the war, it was moved to Columbia for safe keeping, only to be destroyed by one of the countless fires marking General Sherman's sack of the capital.

In 1853, on the third anniversary of Calhoun's death, local men's organizations created the Calhoun Monument Association, began raising private funds, and identified space in the Battery overlooking Fort Sumter for another statue.

The Ladies' Calhoun Monument Association formed the next year as a separate benevolent society equally committed to cementing Calhoun's place in the city's memoryscape. The women selected the Citadel Green, which later became Marion Square, as a more appropriate setting for Calhoun's memorial. The Ladies' Association ultimately outmaneuvered the men's group in gaining public favor and the necessary funds to erect their statue.[3] The association laid the cornerstone for its monument in 1858, but construction was significantly delayed not only by the war, Reconstruction politics, and a massive earthquake that levelled the city in 1886 but also by Black residents who rallied to make the evils of slavery, not the political triumphs of Calhoun, the locus of public memory about the war.

African American Memory Work, 1865–96

Emancipation, Appomattox, and Reconstruction ushered in a kairotic phase of the cultural and political war over Calhoun's memory. After the war, freedwomen and men made every effort to change Charleston from the cradle of the Confederacy into the gravesite for the nation's paramount sin. This did not mean the freedpeople wanted to forget slavery, however; quite the opposite. Joined by abolitionists and Republican allies, Black Charlestonians seized the moment of newfound freedom and sociopolitical power to articulate the meaning of emancipation for their lives and to reverse the city's racial politics by casting Calhoun's legacy in their own light. They feared what ultimately did come to pass, that "slavery [understood as inhumanity] fell into the trashheap of history" (Savage 129), but they tried to prevent this outcome by placing their individual experiences of slavery at the center of collective memory practices in the years after the war. Vivian's important distinction between "commendable and condemnable forms of public forgetting" pertains here (8), in that the "Jubilee Year" and Reconstruction-era memory efforts of freedpeople united around the conviction that some forms of human persecution and violence should never be forgotten. Black Charlestonians and the thousands more African Americans who flocked to slavery's old capital to celebrate emancipation knew they "were obligated to remember [these] past atrocities in reflective and constructive ways because the consequences of forgetting them [were] too appalling to tolerate" (Vivian 12; see also Zelizer).

Beginning in 1865, former slaves and their Republican allies were the first to claim center stage and interpretive control in what would become the American saga of clashing postbellum memories. About a month after the Union Army seized Charleston, and twenty-two years before Calhoun would come to dominate the city's memorial landscape, enormous crowds of jubilant African Americans congregated in the Citadel Green, so named after the nearby military academy founded to quell slave rebellions. Citadel Green was also the site where Calhoun's body was ceremoniously received fifteen years earlier and where his lengthy funeral procession began. Aiming to mark a new beginning for their community, the city, and the country, the group marched through the city's streets in a boisterous parade miles long, enacted a mock slave auction and coffle to symbolize the depravity from which they were now free, and held a grandiose funeral for the institution of slavery (Kytle and Roberts, *Denmark Vesey's Garden* 42–44; Jenkins 36–42). In a letter of 12 August 1865, Elias H. Dees observed that "Charleston saw freedmen . . . promenading on King Street . . . while black schoolchildren sang 'John Brown's Body' within ear-shot of Calhoun's tomb" (Dees; see also Foner 94). From freedom festivals such as this one to flag-raising ceremonies, Emancipation Day celebrations, Independence Day festivities, church anniversaries, political rallies, and Union grave decoration days, African Americans gathered regularly in Charleston and urban centers throughout the South for decades after the Civil War to articulate their own interpretation of the war and to put slavery at the center of Civil War commemoration.

This rhetorical memory work among African Americans developed as a powerful, if short-lived, political tool to compel white Americans to never forget the wickedness so many died defending. Their message was helped along by the many financial, social, political, and symbolic losses facing former slave-holders. Reconstruction created a moment of powerlessness that forced white Charlestonians to stand back as African Americans actively coalesced to pronounce their individual memories of slavery and build the memories into more potent, collective ones. This rhetorical activism of African Americans was not, as many assume, a counternarrative to white southern authority. As historian Thavolia Glymph argues, "Black people's Civil War memory shaped the white South's own memory and the precise ways in which southern history came to be produced. The Lost Cause movement stands as an explicit rejoinder to the memory work of black southerners, not the other way around" (116). African Americans controlled the slavery and Civil War narratives until southern white Americans regained enough power to begin the lasting work of uncoupling slavery from the Confederate cause in a manner that still dominates commonplace understandings of slavery and the war (Horton and Horton; Savage 129–61; see also Duggan).

Since Calhoun had so pointedly and presciently intertwined slavery and secession, white Americans' memorialization of him required strategic reinterpretation and sustained misremembering of his deeds and words, which is why African Americans protested his monument so vehemently. Commemorating not just Confederate heroes but also the "political architects of disunion" like Calhoun was of the utmost importance to white Charlestonians, as the historian

Thomas Brown notes, and freedpeople wholly understood the stakes of such commemoration (130). Brown writes, "The Charleston [Calhoun] project demonstrates that even in a tribute to an antebellum icon identified with the origins of the war, white Southerners preferred to recall their wartime experience and assert a broad claim of regional achievement rather than describe their shattered dreams of a separate nation" (132). By the time the Ladies' Association unveiled its monument in 1887, the excitement and political momentum of Reconstruction had waned considerably, and white narratives disassociating slavery from the Confederacy were taking hold. The Calhoun monument was the apotheosis of these efforts. The Ladies' Association's location for Calhoun's memorialization turned out to be remarkably farsighted; in the intervening years while construction was stalled, the city annexed several additional wards on the neighborhood's northern edge, thereby "asserting full control over an area disproportionately populated by free blacks deemed threatening. . . . Placement of the Calhoun monument in [what is now] Marion Square reinforced this extension of racial authority" (Brown 138). Depicted in classical oratorical style, Calhoun towered literally and ideologically over his city once more.

For many Black Charlestonians, Calhoun's imperious stance, his right finger outstretched and upturned, symbolized a particularly galling invitation to restore white supremacy. As historians Ethan Kytle and Blain Roberts explain, "Calhoun was represented as the South's iconic figure of defiance: standing up . . . for his regions' interests. . . . The Calhoun Monument thus signaled an attachment to the racial ideology of the Old South . . . harken[ing] back to a time before the war, when its precipitating cause occupied the energies of the state's politicians" (Denmark Vesey's Garden 102–03). It seemed that slavery's most notorious champion was being summoned to shepherd Reconstruction out and usher segregation in. One Black woman living in Charleston at the time remarked, "I believe white people were talking to us about Jim Crow through that statue" (Fields 57).

To honor the man who considered slavery an inevitable, unequivocal good, without any reference to the institution he thought southerners should die to protect, marked a rhetorical coup that Black Charlestonians could not abide. "Presumably the monument fostered some admiration for Calhoun and his principles, but few records of its impact are as vivid as local African Americans' testimony that they saw the statue as an emblem of white supremacism and the possibility of black resistance," notes Brown (149). Once installed, the monument became the primary target for the disdain of former slaves, their descendants, and their allies. Originally, the Ladies' Association planned for four allegorical figures—Truth, Justice, the Constitution, and History—to be part of the statue's granite base. Only Justice was figured in the final monument, a woman in classical garb seated directly below Calhoun, and it was widely known that Afri-

can American residents derisively referred to the monument as "Mr. Calhoun an'
he Wife" ("Vandal's Work"). The daily happenings section of the *Charleston News
and Courier* regularly reported on the rebukes and pranks "Old Calhoun" was sub-
jected to. The Justice figure was painfully ironic to be paired with Calhoun, and
this part of the monument, being low to the ground, was also much easier to
reach. Over the years, some vandals "placed a tin kettle in her hand and a cigar in
her mouth," making her look "as if she had been on a spree," while others painted
her stone complexion "lily white" ("All about Town"; see also "Vandal's Work" and
"All around Town"). There are other records of Black Charlestonians regularly using the monument for target practice, resulting once in an African American boy
injuring a white toddler while shooting at Lady Justice ("Dangerous Toy Pistol").
The young man insisted to police that he never intended to "shoot the chile, I
shoot at Mr. Calhoun wife" ("Caught").

The Calhoun monument, or this particular version of it, did not last long.
It soon became the locus of incessant outcry and mockery. Publicly citing widespread disappointment with the statue's aesthetic shortcomings, while privately
bemoaning that their considerable female influence to get the statue built had
been reduced to an "image of subservient womanhood" in countless parodies of
"He Wife," the members of the Ladies' Association had the monument removed
in 1895, sold for scrap metal, and a new one commissioned and installed in 1896
(Brown 148). Yet there is much to suggest that the real reason for the demise
of the first Calhoun monument was the constant ridicule and damage heaped
on it by African Americans, suggesting that their rhetoric of vandalism worked.
The newspapers recorded much of this in bits and pieces as noted above, but
memoirs of Black Charlestonians living at the time, like Mamie Garvin Fields's
Lemon Swamp and Other Places, provide some detailed accounts of the communal
outrage and protest:

> Since we thought like Douglass, we hated all what Calhoun stood for. . . . When
> I was a girl, they put up a life-size figure of [him]. . . . Blacks took that statue
> personally. As you passed by, here was Calhoun looking you in the face and tell-
> ing you, 'You may not be a slave, but I am back to see you stay in your place'. . . .
> We used to carry something with us, if we knew we would be passing that way,
> in order to deface the statue—scratch up the coat, break the watch chain, try
> to knock off the nose. . . . Children and adults beat up John C. Calhoun so badly
> that the whites had to come back and put him way up high, so we couldn't get
> to him. (57)

Indeed, the effects of African Americans' remonstrations were manifest
in the design of the second Calhoun monument, which boasted a much taller
column so that, with the statue atop, it stretched more than one hundred feet

high, and it retained a much smaller, simpler base. The decommissioning of the first memorial was marked by large crowds of Black onlookers, with children reportedly crawling on the discarded statue as it lay on the ground, "heap[ing] all sorts of indignities upon him"; as many more people came the next day to bear witness to the removal of "Missis Calhoon" ("Calhoun Monuments").

It is clear that monuments like Calhoun's and all the others defaced of late have not been deemed racist only recently, as if contemporary concerns have been applied to Confederate memorials anachronistically or unfairly. The Calhoun statue and many like it were considered from the outset to be white supremacist in purpose and scope, and were from the beginning contested by African Americans as such. Further, these protests—some visible and documented, some of which I've shared here, others ephemeral and unspecified (such as all the acts of vandalism that have been erased as property destruction and dismissed as juvenile crimes)—served not just as unflagging resistance to white supremacy but as deliberate memory-creation and memory-sharing practices in their own right.

This accumulated history of protest as a crucial form of African American rhetorical memory work recalls cultural theorist Michael Taussig's remarks in *Defacement* that "there exists a sort of death wish deep within the monument, something in the monumentality of the monument that cries out to be toppled, besmirched, desecrated" (20–21). This inherent "death wish" is borne of the paradox or admixture of selective remembering and strategic forgetting that necessarily animates all memorializations. Extending Taussig, Sabine Marschall's work on cultural preservation argues that forgetting is inexorably built into any monument itself: "The repressed history is always already installed in the statue—like a hidden flaw waiting to be revealed. The more monumental, imposing, conceited the statue, the more alluring, inviting, beckoning it presumably becomes as a target for expressions of discontent in times of contestation and sociopolitical change" (204). The mass "oblivion," as Vivian would call it (7), regarding slavery that undergirded the lost cause, in addition to freedpeople's rhetorical actions that inadvertently provoked such willed amnesia, and the largely unacknowledged history of Black protest to racist heritage merge to form the repressed history, the deep and fatal flaw, that lies within both Calhoun monuments.

From this vantage point, we should not be surprised or offended that the monuments have been constant targets of legitimate outrage, whether in 1865 or 2015; they are an open provocation. In clearing some conceptual space to contemplate positive forms of forgetting in public culture, Vivian acknowledges that reprehensible forms of cultural forgetting, such as those embodied in the Calhoun monuments, "resemble a forcible and potentially unhealthy repression of the past, not its erasure, and that which is repressed may return in forms more intense than before" (50). Though the wretched "He Wife" was destroyed, perhaps even as a result of early African American campaigns against whitewashed slavery and Civil War commemorations, the rhetorical opening for beginning again, the possibility of public deliberation about "adapting collective remembrances in light of emerging social, political or ethical dilemmas" (Vivian 9), was closed shut. At least for a time. Another equally problematic monument was put in its place, one that until recently loomed high above Charleston's quaint skyline. After the war Charlestonians lacked the political will to "interrupt customary patterns of communal memory" (Vivian 50) to create more just racial relations, and, indeed, there was a deliberate tack in the opposite direction.

Beginning Again, Again: Charleston in 2015 and Beyond

The transformation of Charleston from the physical and economic ruination of the Civil War to one of America's top tourist destinations is an incredible, though ultimately cautionary, tale about the power of nostalgia, the romance of decay, and the commodification of white Americans' Civil War memories. Histories and analyses of this unparalleled example of urban renewal abound (e.g., Bures; Estes; Hicks; Kytle and Roberts, "Is it Okay"; Poirot and Watson; Yuhl). In sum, beginning in the early twentieth century, an array of social and political forces conjoined to stake Charleston's economic future on its place in history through heritage tourism. The municipal government worked with the highest echelons of local society to cordon off and forge part of the city into Historic Charleston, a gleaming, intoxicating version of certain parts and views of the city's antebellum history that perhaps symbolize the epitome of modern "revivals of communal heritage" for "escapist entertainment and consumerism" (Vivian 4). Charleston has become a strange, unrecognizable version of its true antebellum self; the city has exercised and profited handsomely from "a hypertrophy of memory," an overactivity of nostalgia bordering on obsession (qtd. in Vivian 4). In this way, Charleston's rise from the postbellum ashes was not so much beginning again as doubling down on what some saw as the city's "unalterable historical obligations" (Vivian 50). It is worth noting that the young man who murdered the nine people at the AME church went on six trips to Historic Charleston and from there determined his target (Gillespie 11–12).

In arguing for the value of some forms of forgetting, Vivian highlights the radically contingent nature of forgetting: "Public forgetting arises from uncommonly pivotal moments in the evolution of communal time, history and memory" (14). After 17 June 2015, we seemed to be in a different discursive and deliberative moment, where old arguments against symbols of racist heritage like the Confederate flag and the Calhoun monument took on new relevance and urgency. What had been politically and rhetorically impossible for generations happened on 9 July 2015, when the South Carolina General Assembly voted overwhelmingly to remove the Confederate flag from statehouse grounds. The next day, the South Carolina poet Nikky Finney published the poem "A New Day Dawns" in Columbia's newspaper, which appeared next to a picture of the empty flagpole. "I have been writing these 230 words all my life," she remarks in an accompanying video. One indication that we may be beginning again, taking up the rhetorical memory work African Americans began in 1865, is Finney's introduction in her poem of a new cultural idiom, which Vivian asserts is crucial to "calling into being a new, politically and morally transformative historical consciousness" (52). Finney writes:

> We are not free to go on as if nothing happened yesterday, not free to cheer as if all our prayers have finally been answered today. We are free, only, to search the yonder of each other's faces . . . asking silently who are we now?. . . What new human cosmos can be made of this tempest of tears, this upload of inconsolable jubilation? In all our lifetimes, finally, this towering undulating moment is here.

The moment is here not just for African Americans, Charlestonians, South Carolinians, or Americans but also for us as humble scholars of rhetoric, history, and memory who want to demand something more from the work we do.

Notes

1. See Roberts-Miller for analysis of Calhoun's and others' proslavery rhetoric.

2. The import of this shipwreck can be attributed to the fact that Margaret Fuller was among those who perished. See Barnes in this volume.

3. For details on the way the ladies' organization claimed a central role for women in this public commemoration, see Brown.

Works Cited

"All about Town." News and Courier [Charleston], 12 Feb. 1888, p. 8. Post and Courier Historical Archive.

"All around Town." News and Courier [Charleston], 2 Jun. 1887, p. 8. Post and Courier Historical Archive.

Blair, Carole, and Neil Michel. "Civil Rights Tactics: The Rhetorical Performances of the Civil Rights Memorial." Rhetoric Society Quarterly, vol. 30, no. 2, 2000, pp. 31–55.

Boughton, Melissa. "Confederate Monument a Focus of Debate after Graffiti Appears People Then Cover Words with Tarp, More Messages." *The Post and Courier* [Charleston], 20 June 2015, www.postandcourier.com/archives/confederate -monument-a-focus-of-debate-after-graffiti-appears-people/article_d53542c2 -1200-56ef-9afe-2238b348dd4d.html.

Bremer, Fredrika. *The Homes of the New World; Impressions of America.* Vol. 1, Harper and Brothers, 1853. *University of Wisconsin, Madison, Digital Collections*, digital .library.wisc.edu/1711.dl/History.BremrHemme.

Brown, Thomas J. "The Monumental Legacy of Calhoun." *The Memory of the Civil War in American Culture*, edited by Alice Fahs and John Waugh, U of North Carolina P, 2004, pp. 130–56.

Bures, Regina M. "Historic Preservation, Gentrification, and Tourism: The Transformation of Charleston, South Carolina." *Research in Urban Sociology: Critical Perspectives on Urban Development*, edited by Kevin Fox Gotham, vol. 6, Emerald Group, 2001, pp. 195–209.

Calhoun, John C. "Slavery a Positive Good." 1837. *Wikisource*, 6 May 2016, en .wikisource.org/wiki/Slavery_a_Positive_Good.

"The Calhoun Monuments." *Harper's Weekly*, vol. 41, 3 Apr. 1887, p. 343.

Capper, Charles. *Margaret Fuller: An American Romantic Life.* Vol. 2, Oxford UP, 1992.

"Caught the Little Rascals." *News and Courier* [Charleston], 15 Dec. 1894, p. 12. *Post and Courier Historical Archive.*

"A Dangerous Toy Pistol." *News and Courier* [Charleston], 14 Dec. 1894, p. 12. *Post and Courier Historical Archive.*

Dees, Elias H. Letter to Anne Dees. 12 Aug. 1865. Elias Dees Papers, South Caroliniana Library, University of South Carolina, Columbia.

Dickinson, Greg, et al., editors. *Places of Public Memory: The Rhetoric of Museums and Memorials.* U of Alabama P, 2010.

Duggan, Paul. "Sins of the Father." *The Washington Post*, 28 Nov. 2018, www .washingtonpost.com/news/magazine/wp/2018/11/28/feature/the-confederacy -was-built-on-slavery-how-can-so-many-southern-whites-still-believe -otherwise/?utm_term=.810ff53a4510.

Edgar, Walter. *South Carolina: A History.* U of South Carolina P, 1998.

Elmore, Christina. "Second Charleston Statue Vandalized Following Shooting at Emanuel AME Church." *The Post and Courier*, 22 June 2015, www.postandcourier .com/archives/second-charleston-statue-vandalized-following-shooting-at -emanuel-ame-church/article_1c05aa04-b2d7-5e26-ba08-4d3162cd00c5.html.

Estes, Steve. *Charleston in Black and White: Race and Power in the South after the Civil Rights Movement.* U of North Carolina P, 2015.

Fields, Mamie Garvin. *Lemon Swamp and Other Places: A Carolina Memoir.* Free Press, 1983.

Finney, Nikky. "A New Day Dawns." *The State*, 9 July 2015, www.thestate.com/living/ article26928424.html.

Floyd, Viola Caston. "The Fall of Charleston." *The South Carolina Historical Magazine*, vol. 66, no. 1, Jan. 1965, pp. 1–7. *JSTOR*, www.jstor.org/stable/27566552.

Foner, Eric. "The Meaning of Freedom." *Radical History Review*, vol. 39, 1987, pp. 92–114, doi:10.1215/01636545-1987-39-92.

Gillespie, J. David. *The Trial of White Nationalist Dylann Roof: Killer of Nine Black Christians in Their Charleston Church*. Edwin Mellen, 2017.

Glymph, Thavolia. "'Liberty Dearly Bought': The Making of Civil War Memory in Afro-American Communities in the South." *Time Longer Than Rope: A Century of African American Activism, 1850–1950*, edited by Charles M. Payne and Adam Green, New York UP, 2003, pp. 111–40.

Gregg, John N. "Exhumation of the Body of John C. Calhoun 1863." 1901. *South Carolina Historical Magazine*, vol. 57, 1956, pp. 57–58. *JSTOR*, www.jstor.org/stable/27566042.

Hicks, Brian. *The Mayor: Joe Riley and the Rise of Charleston*. Evening Post Books, 2015.

Holley, Peter. "'Black Lives Matter' Graffiti Appears on Confederate Memorials across the U.S." *The Washington Post*, 23 June 2015, www.washingtonpost.com/news/morning-mix/wp/2015/06/23/black-lives-matter-graffiti-appears-on-confederate-memorials-across-the-u-s/?utm_term=.0de4424ed961.

Horton, James Oliver, and Lois E. Horton, editors. *Slavery and Public History: The Tough Stuff of American Memory*. New Press, 2006.

Jenkins, Wilbert L. *Seizing the New Day: African Americans in Post–Civil War Charleston*. Indiana UP, 1998.

Kytle, Ethan J., and Blain Roberts. *Denmark Vesey's Garden: Slavery and Memory in the Cradle of the Confederacy*. New Press, 2018.

———. "'Is It Okay to Talk about Slaves?' Segregating the Past in Historic Charleston." *Destination Dixie: Tourism and Southern History*, edited by Karen L. Cox, UP of Florida, 2012, pp. 137–59.

Marschall, Sabine. "Targeting Statues: Monument 'Vandalism' as an Expression of Sociopolitical Protest in South Africa." *African Studies Review*, vol. 60, no. 3, Dec. 2017, pp. 203–19. *Project Muse*, muse.jhu.edu/article/679569.

Meigs, William. *The Life of John Caldwell Calhoun*. Vol. 2, Neale, 1917.

Munday, Dave. "Vandal Quotes Obama with Spray Paint on Confederate Memorial Statue." *The Post and Courier*, 9 July 2015, www.postandcourier.com/archives/vandal-quotes-obama-with-spray-paint-on-confederate-memorial-statue/article_979c7e8c-9a9f-5c8f-8a41-be661efd095b.html.

Poirot, Kristan, and Shevaun E. Watson. "Memories of Freedom and White Resilience: Place, Tourism and Urban Slavery." *Rhetoric Society Quarterly*, vol. 45, no. 2, 2015, pp. 91–116.

Roberts-Miller, Patricia. *Fanatical Schemes: Proslavery Rhetoric and the Tragedy of Consensus*. U of Alabama P, 2009.

Savage, Kirk. *Standing Soldiers, Kneeling Slaves: Race, War, and Monument in Nineteenth-Century America*. Princeton UP, 1997.

"South-Carolina Mourns for Her Dead." *News and Courier* [Charleston], 27 Apr. 1850, p. 1. *Post and Courier Historical Archive.*

Taussig, Michael. *Defacement: Public Secrecy and the Labor of the Negative.* Stanford UP, 1999.

Tyson, Charles. "Statue of John Calhoun Vandalized in Downtown Charleston." *ABC News 4* [Charleston], 21 June 2015, abcnews4.com/news/emanuel-ame-shooting/confederate-statue-vandalized-downtown.

"Vandals Paint 'Black Lives Matter' on Confederate Monument in Half-Dozen States." *MassLive,* 26 June 2015, www.masslive.com/news/index.ssf/2015/06/vandals_paint_black_lives_matt.html.

"A Vandal's Work." *News and Courier* [Charleston], 5 Sept. 1983, p. 8. *Post and Courier Historical Archive.*

Vivian, Bradford. *Public Forgetting: The Rhetoric and Politics of Beginning Again.* Pennsylvania State UP, 2010.

Wiltse, Charles M. *John C. Calhoun.* Vol. 3, Bobbs-Merrill, 1944.

"The Wreck of the *Elizabeth.*" *National Park Service,* 22 Dec. 2015, www.nps.gov/fiis/learn/historyculture/wreck-of-the-elizabeth.htm.

Yuhl, Stephanie E. *A Golden Haze of Memory: The Making of Historic Charleston.* U of North Carolina P, 2005.

Zelizer, Barbie. *Remembering to Forget: Holocaust Memory through the Camera's Eye.* U of Chicago P, 1998.

Archiving Our Own Historical Moments: Learning from the Disrupted Public Memory of Temperance

Jessica A. Rose and Lynée Lewis Gaillet

> The dogma of woman's complete historical subjection to men must be rated as one of the most fantastic myths ever created by the human mind.
> —Mary Ritter Beard

While we now have extensive scholarship recovering the memory of nineteenth-century feminist activists working in sociopolitical spheres, many of these early protest efforts become two-dimensional once passed through the lens of history. Consequently, numerous women's social movements have been reduced to footnotes, with members often disrupted, erased, silenced, or worse—recast as stereotypes, as in the case of the "teetotalers and prudes" of the temperance movement (Stansell 112). Some critics might push back against this characterization of the state of American women's history, citing the lauding of early suffrage efforts in the movement, from the 1979 minting of the Susan B. Anthony dollar coin to the recent act of American congresswomen wearing white at formal functions in commemoration of their foremothers. However, while memorialization is important for materializing a strong legacy, it is not the same as preservation, which, when accessible, can establish and advocate for more exact cultural memory.

In *Rhetorical Feminism and This Thing Called Hope*, Cheryl Glenn explains that "rhetorical feminism," as opposed to feminist rhetoric, "is a conceptual action, a trope that can be used to help negotiate cross-boundary mis/understandings and reconciliations; illuminate rhetorical theories . . . and secure our hope for the future." She explains that "rhetorical feminism works in the service of and to advance feminist rhetoric," a term that Glenn associates with advocacy and that focuses on "rights, contributions, expertise, opportunities, and histories of marginalized groups and supports coalition across and among these groups" (3–4). Through an examination of the Woman's Christian Temperance Union (WCTU) and temperance memorials, we wish to offer another view of the WCTU, articulating ways in which the organization's primary mission may have been disrupted and in some cases erased. Furthermore, we wish to take up Glenn's call to look beyond "the stubborn belief to which rhetoricians seem to hold fast . . . that rhetorical practices should do something" and reexamine the work of temperance women "to redefine rhetorical history, theory, and praxis to the end of representing and including more users and uses of rhetoric; to represent more ethically and accurately the dominant and the marginalized alike . . . and to prepare the next generation of rhetorically empowered scholars, feminists, teachers, and citizens" (4). How might we engage in archival coalition-building to meet Glenn's challenges?

Looking back at the WCTU's early preservation efforts can offer some guidance. The nineteenth century was the organization's golden era in which members most effectively fundraised, lobbied, and advocated for a variety of efforts beyond combating the ills of drinking. The temperance movement constituted the largest organization of women in the nineteenth century and boasted an impressive number of active orators and rhetors as well (Blocker 460). Archived WCTU meeting minutes reveal consistent, rhetorically driven conversations about the union's actions at both local and national levels; the WCTU's sociopolitical capital cannot be discounted. Deanna Beard, in researching the power of the WCTU, identifies a "rich oral and visual rhetoric" developed by members across multiple platforms, including temperance and social justice music, plays, and pamphlets (59). She claims that the WCTU "succeeded because its leadership effectively articulated the need for public female activism," employing a rhetoric of "social housekeeping" and predicting a peaceful "future American society" (53–54).

Carol Mattingly's "Woman's Temple, Women's Fountains: The Erasure of Public Memory" explores the WCTU's rhetorical power, viewing the organization's monuments and archives as spaces of public memory. Yet Mattingly, who has written extensively about the WCTU, does more than recover the WCTU's rhetorical power: she also uncovers the networks that women had to develop to effect change, given their social and legal limitations. Mattingly emphasizes that although the WCTU is largely remembered today for the organization's efforts to bring sobriety to the nation, most of the organization's women saw the effects of alcohol consumption as directly connected to all aspects of women's lives, making the WCTU an active arm of the early women's movement—not a single-issue mission. In fact, enrollment statistics and meeting minutes demonstrate just how diverse the WCTU causes were, and just how consequential a body of mobilized women could be (Mattingly 133).

The WCTU's second president, Frances Willard, is still a highly memorialized American whose name graces statues and memorial halls, although most people no longer recognize the figure behind the name. The historian Catherine Murdock, interviewed for the documentary miniseries *Prohibition*, remarks that "there was a time when every school child in America knew [about Willard], and she was sort of on par with Betsy Ross. She was that important to American history" ("Nation" 00:35:59). Willard saw the WCTU as a vehicle for social justice. Drawing from the WCTU's founding principles and "Plan of Work," which included education, social work, and legal reform, Willard developed an even stronger focus on "Prohibition, Woman's Liberation, and Labour's Uplift" as a "blessed trinity of movements" and envisioned the WCTU's structure as promoting a "Do-everything" policy (2). In her address to the WCTU for the World's Columbian Exposition in Chicago, Willard calls this policy a natural consequence of "woman's genius for details, and her patient [steadfastness] in following the enemies of those she loves 'through every lane of life,'" which resulted in "an all-around movement . . . carried forward by all-around advocates" (1–2). "Do everything" became a call to action, wherein members worked diligently for temperance reform but also loudly called for women's suffrage and expanded property rights, children's health education in schools, and labor reform, injecting "temperance in everything" (Willard 3).

Although the WCTU held some measure of ascendancy, its diligent efforts to capture and preserve the organization's work for posterity failed to secure an accurate historical foothold, being not only "largely forgotten," as Mattingly contends (133), but also inaccurately remembered, despite the organization's meticulous record keeping. These records of meetings, resolutions, and accounting reveal just how effective the WCTU was in the waning twenty-five years of the nineteenth century. The minutes note that, through lobbying, the WCTU helped pass school curriculum laws in fourteen states, requiring that all students receive health and hygiene instruction alongside courses on the effects of alcohol (*Annual Minutes* 41). Of suffrage, national meeting minutes exclaim, "Let women everywhere distribute suffrage literature," and encourage the women of New York to "make a test of this question for woman's full ballot" (cxxv). Adopting this practical philosophy of activism and philanthropy, the WCTU aggressively fundraised for each branch of Willard's trinity.

The WCTU was so successful at lobbying and fundraising that it independently paid for the construction and implementation of a significant number of freshwater fountains and monuments across major American cities, including an early skyscraper, known as the Woman's Temple, in Chicago (fig. 1). Although these monuments and the temple were built with the newest technologies, by respected architects and expert engineers, the structures no longer stand, the result of systematic acts of undoing and erasure of public memory. This loss exemplifies how precarious the fleeting nature of power by historically marginalized groups is, especially when those groups are attempting to steward public space.

The strength of the WCTU in Chicago coincides with the rise of Chicago itself, whose identity was recrafted after the great fire of 1871. The city shifted from prairie town to Midwestern metropolis with an explosion of innovation and commerce, and a modern social scene, inviting clear conversations about social reform. Alcoholism reached epidemic proportions by 1830, as per capita consumption peaked at 7.1 gallons per year (O'Brien). Though women were pub-

Figure 1. Woman's Temple, Chicago. Reprinted by permission of the Center for Women's History and Leadership, WCTU Archives.

licly drinking alongside men by the mid–nineteenth century, discussions concerning alcohol's effect on families and communities formalized, and in 1874 the newly formed WCTU joined a growing movement that saw social value in prohibition (Remus). For the WCTU members, however, the focus remained squarely on men's sobriety, which they connected to issues of food insecurity, poverty, abuse, and even deaths of women and children.

One popular justification for increased alcohol consumption was the insistence that cities, like Chicago, did not have consistent access to clean drinking

Figure 2. WCTU fountain, Pen Argyl, Pennsylvania (postcard). Reprinted by permission of the Center for Women's History and Leadership, WCTU Archives.

water, which drove workers into bars throughout the day. During the organizing convention for the national WCTU, members responded with plans to erect conveniently placed public drinking fountains, some so that men could bypass saloons to quench thirst, others for horses and dogs (see Mattingly for images). These fountains were not merely troughs, though; they were classically designed sculptures with well-constructed plumbing, adopting the latest technologies to deliver cold water (fig. 2). Fountains ranged in size from simple sipping spots to elaborate statues with chilled faucets; however, all featured WCTU branding to commemorate the efforts of union members. Fountains were strategically placed in valued public spaces, like city epicenters and central parks, to stake their position in the public sphere (Mattingly 140).

After the passage of prohibition and suffrage, and beyond the era of WCTU power, these fountains lost their cachet, and few community stakeholders advocated to keep them in place. While several WCTU fountains remain in some form, most have been decommissioned and removed from their original locations. Despite recent restoration efforts in select cities, most fountains have systematically become divorced from their original homes, victims of destruction, storage, and relocation. Other fountains have been dismantled and rebuilt, stripped of identifying marks and their WCTU signatures, becoming anonymized in the process.

The Woman's Temple met a similar fate. Opening in 1892 at a cost of $1.5 million, the magnificent structure was destroyed in 1925, just three decades after its erection, to make room for the State Bank of Chicago ("Women's Temple"). The destruction of the temple resulted from a series of unfortunate circumstances, both financial and social. Following the passage of prohibition, and with the retirement of many of its original leaders, the WCTU lost ownership of the building as the union's finances dwindled. Furthermore, the Woman's Temple occupied one of the most desirable corners of downtown Chicago, the corner of Monroe and LaSalle, making the location attractive to buyers and developers, but the style of the building was dated and had fallen out of contemporary favor. The temperance movement, which had gathered steam at the time of the temple's construction, had lost its luster as society grew disenchanted with prohibition as a social cure. Ultimately, while the WCTU had negotiated a ninety-nine-year lease on the building's site, the union's purpose fell radically short of that time span ("Woman's Temple").

The physical constraints of the building made it vulnerable to the wrecking ball. Once hailed as a skyscraper, the Temple was eclipsed by thirty subsequent years of vertical construction. And, although it was fireproof, built of steel, granite, brick, and terracotta, modern advances in construction and architecture made a case for the building's destruction. The skyscraper, a focus of Chicago School architecture, required lighter construction materials to achieve height, and favored simple, functionalist façades with delicate details (Miller). Inside the temple, novel features once touted as "modern domestic" marvels—Edison lights, modern plumbing, mail-chutes, hot and cold water—had grown commonplace, and in many instances improved upon ("Woman's Temple").

Yet, when the temple was first erected, it stood as evidence of the success of temperance rhetoric and the value of women in public life. The temple served multiple functions, like the fountains, offering a majestic place for the WCTU's national offices, a storage location for papers and archives, and retail space for restaurants that did not offer alcohol. But, visually, the temple also memorialized the women of the movement and the causes for which they fought, rendering the building a consummate shrine to nineteenth-century women's activism. The temple encouraged local chapters to begin building places they also could call their own (Mattingly). While we establish that the opulence and elegance of the building was expensive to maintain, we suggest that the choice to demolish it was complicated by the fact that the new century found society moving beyond the relevance of WCTU reforms, many of the union's names and efforts becoming flattened in modernization. As a result, the larger cultural interest in memorializing these earlier voices diminished, and the building found no architectural or ideological savior.

The fate of the Woman's Temple makes it clear that the public, decorative memorials indicate, for all social groups, not only who is responsible for the writing of shared historical stories but also who is denied credit of authorship. What we choose to erase is as vital to the cultural record as what we choose to preserve and codify. Collective memory, the social knowledge that is passed between generations, manifests not only in formal histories but also through the physical landmarks in quotidian spaces. Americans may read about the Puritans' city on a hill, but a preponderance of churches demonstrates current traditions of faith; students learn from textbooks factual accounts of a war, but public statues signifying the war's heroes signal who and what future generations should value. Thus, the material culture left behind reifies select ideals within the collective memory and obscures others for future generations.

Mary Ritter Beard, the daughter of a Methodist temperance advocate, also understood this idea of erasure and its consequences and sought to organize a World Center for Women's Archives (WCWA) dedicated to the achievements and contributions of women. Beard, an early-twentieth-century women's rights advocate, historian, and influential author, worked to reconfigure historical narratives to include women's contributions and achievements, most notably through her numerous publications and sponsorship of an archival collection, an act she saw as especially important as late-nineteenth-century feminists began to pass away. Beard succinctly summed up these concerns about the documentary exclusion of women's contributions in the WCWA's choice of motto, first coined by the French historian Fustel de Coulanges: "no documents, no history" (Voss-Hubbard 20).

We introduce Beard's efforts herein as a monument to nineteenth-century women's work—highlighted in Beard's feminist textbook, *Woman as Force in History: A Study in Traditions and Realities*—and as a call to map the work of modern feminism onto earlier temperance activism. Despite Beard's extensive collaborative efforts to champion the WCWA's efforts to keep alive the work of fore-mothers, the project ultimately fell short. The WCWA failed to materialize as Beard envisioned but provided both inspiration and resources for subsequent noteworthy collation projects, including the women's archives at the Arthur and Elizabeth Schlesinger Library on the History of Women in America and the Sophia Smith Collection of Women's History at Smith College, which still provide rich resources for studying nineteenth-century women's accomplishments. We link the fate of the WCWA and temperance memorials, whose destinies largely mirror that of the Woman's Temple. With the passage of laws regarding suffrage, prohibition, and women's rights, narratives and artifacts were retired as part of strategic efforts to close doors on a contentious past. While the temperance women's historical legacy is largely lost, Beard's vision and collected works spark subsequent successful archival initiatives for retaining and mapping earlier women's sociopolitical activities. Feminist recovery efforts rely upon access and upon our ability to trace the circulation of ideas and feminist practices. As Tarez Graban and Patricia Sullivan tell us, historians must look to records of "women's performances—including the places where their documents are kept, the definitions that make them obscure, the disciplines through which they are noticed, and the cultural or ideological reasons why historians fail to notice them" (189).

Why these two efforts—Beard's attempt to archive and the WCTU's attempt to memorialize—face such different fates is a question that merits a second glance, especially as modern women struggle to identify how women's accomplishments and stories are to be both preserved and amplified in the shifting current moment. Adopting Jacqueline Jones Royster and Gesa E. Kirsh's conception of social circulation, feminist rhetorical history scholars are asked to examine "complex rhetorical interactions across space and time . . . to enhance the capacity to reimagine the dynamic functioning of women's work in domains of discourse, re-envision cultural flow in specific localities, and link analyses of these phenomena in an informative and compelling way in support of amplifying and magnifying the impacts and consequences of women's rhetoric" upon public memory (*Feminist Rhetorical Practices* 98). In using social circulation to trace the fates of earlier attempts to reify women's contributions, we begin to contemplate opportunities for both creating and integrating archival systems that honor earlier achievements while capturing and mapping our own.

The Worth of a Physical Space

Social circulation works to close the gap of the "public domain of men" and the "private domain of women" through the social networks and circles in which women travel, which is precisely what the WCTU—and later Beard's work to remember late-nineteenth-century women's activism—hoped to accomplish by establishing monuments, memorials, and archives within public, concrete spaces (Royster and Kirsch, *Feminist Rhetorical Practices* 98). In combining and linking architectural elements through social circulation, we can begin to see how disruption was socially met, tolerated, or vanquished. Public monuments, memorials, and museums are often rhetorically chosen, lobbied for, and constructed. These structures embody deeper meaning and represent large, abstract ideas. Like signposts, the structures speak to what is important, to what should be remembered and also accepted as part of a community's heritage. Australian geographic scholar D. N. Jeans refers to such spaces as "centres of meaning in the landscape," elaborating that "every aspect of landscape is loaded with meanings, meanings of home and history, scientific interpretation and personal histories" (qtd. in Auster 219). As part of topography, monuments act as material support for oral histories and visual mnemonics that reinforce a community's history, ideals, and ethics.

In fact, by preferencing certain historical elements over others, monuments do more than suggest what is important to remember—they also demand that future generations continue to identify with and elevate certain roles, behaviors, and ideologies over others. By taking up residence in vernacular spaces but acting as ceremonial markers that privilege through commemoration, monuments and memorials suggest the importance of keeping certain people and events in the sphere of public memory, while actively embodying, internalizing, and modeling the ethics and tenets associated with these artifacts. Circulation, defined by Laurie E. Gries as "spatiotemperal flow as well as a cultural-rhetorical process" (3), is a central component of remembering; social circulation, which Kirsch and Royster define as part of feminist research practices, likewise "invokes connections among past, present, and future in the sense that the overlapping social circles in which women travel, live, and work are carried on or modified from one generation to the next and give rise to changed rhetorical practices" (660). By applying notions of social circulation and archival collection practices to the study of temperance women's memorials, we can better understand these nineteenth-century women's "presence, impact, movement, and patterns of migration as we bring visibility to continuities, connectivity, and sociopolitical change over time" (Royster and Kirsch, "Social Circulation" 171), just as Beard attempted to do in her early-twentieth-century archival efforts to collate and record these women's acts.

Publicly accessible archives for specific groups or purposes can also reiterate what is socially and culturally relevant. The Woman's Temple and the women's archives sought space in the historical cultural narrative through a physical presence. Critics who in the past may have dismissed these structures as un-necessary or as merely decorative didn't recognize that such spaces rhetorically participate in the long-term spatial mapping of memory through architecture by materializing value, power, and knowledge. Jessica Enoch (referencing the work of Graban and Sullivan) asks feminist scholars to engage in feminist circulation methodology by considering "how stakeholders well beyond the artifact's origi-nary moment have propelled that artifact forward or even stalled its movement" (297). To engage in this kind of mapping or circulation work, we need a compre-hensive and longitudinal project like the women's archive initiative sponsored by Beard.

Speaking for Oneself

The WCTU made full use of its limited resources by designing its fountains to serve a dual purpose: to offer a ready source of clean water for communities in need and to publicize the union's organizational mission. Similarly, the Woman's Temple also served multiple functions. As a structure, the temple simultaneously visually memorialized the WCTU's legendary founders and functioned as public offices for national union leaders. Yet the temple also assumed the role of archi-val repository for papers and ephemera linked to the organization's projects and public works to preserve materials that would secure the WCTU's legacy in the future. Promoting the temple to WCTU constituents, Willard remarked that, as a seat, the Woman's Temple would act as the temperance reformers' "Westmin-ster Abbey, its West Point, and its gold mine, all in one" (qtd. in Bohlmann 110). Yet, when the walls came down twenty-six years later in the name of civic and architectural progress, many of the documents and ephemera were misplaced, mishandled, or destroyed.

The destruction of the Woman's Temple and the decommissioning of lo-cal public water fountains catalyzed a radical misunderstanding of the WCTU and the breadth of its mission. Although the WCTU was once understood as a women- and family-focused group that addressed issues of domestic violence, social inequality, and suffrage, often the founders and pre–Nineteenth Amend-ment members are now remembered only through the documents and images that oppose, exaggerate, and mischaracterize them as mere prudes and radical prohibition church ladies. Mattingly notes that after the passing of the Eigh-teenth and Nineteenth Amendments, the power of the WCTU, which had felt like a freight train, began to lose steam ("Woman's Temple"). Despite the temper-ance movement's internal image as one that had political legs and social longev-ity, externally the movement was ultimately treated as a temporary one whose problem had been fixed.

While this perception that the WCTU had ameliorated a single, serious social problem can be traced back to the organization's successful focus on temperance, what is historically significant is the swiftness with which the WCTU's
reputation subsequently diminished and its opponents' caricatures further prevailed. Moreover, the way in which the Woman's Temple was destroyed, as if it
were abandoned, serves as a cautionary tale about how momentary movements
and institutional movements are treated differently. This fate requires us to
ask: Who chose what was to be saved and why were so many of the documents
discarded? Part of the answer is readily available: the movement had limited
capabilities by 1926, both financially and physically, and had limited available
space beyond the Woman's Temple, which acted as the main archival storehouse.
Additionally, no national archives building existed in the United States at the
time, and it was another ten years before Beard would initiate a collaboration to
build a woman's archives. In fact, the same year the temple fell, Congress passed
the Public Buildings Act, which authorized the construction of the National Archives, among other much-needed government office spaces. Despite the social
power and political influence the WCTU wielded during this historical moment,
the preservation of its documents was left up to who was left—regional chapters with little to no practical experience, money, womanpower, or space. Lacking a strong documentary presence in the national narrative and with a limited
physical presence in the communities where local chapters were most rooted, the
WCTU lost more than the temple: it lost its voices, too. The moral of this cautionary tale is, therefore, that modern memory is temporal and short on record keep-
ers; without a systematic way of capturing and recording archival records (both
historical and those of our own cultural moment), public memory runs the risk
of being erased, disrupted, or critically revised.

"No Documents, No History"

The story of Mary Ritter Beard's attempts to create a World Center for Women's
Archives in the 1930s offers one model for how we might gather, organize, and
access women's records. Beard envisioned an archive of women's papers and records that would both provide a foundation for (particularly nineteenth-century)
women's history as an academic field and serve the public good. Beard's guiding principle as she gathered oral histories, cataloged records of women's accomplishments, and searched for artifacts and ephemera in basements and attics
was to focus on women's work in public venues. She wanted work and acts (not
personal stories) to speak for women. According to Nancy F. Cott, the former director of the Schlesinger Library, "Beard's history writing began from the premise that 'everything is related to everything else,' that it was essential to see the

'interplay of government, politics, economics, modes of the living and working schools of thought, religion, power, class, society and family, the arts and ambition, and the biological and cultural aspects of sex'" (1); the WCTU case study illustrates this interplay of demographic and cultural components.

Without a searchable past, including documents and artifacts to research and map, women's accomplishments often become polarized; some individuals and movements are valorized while others are overlooked or dismissed, or the women are reductively viewed as victims. Rather than concentrating on grievances and questions of the subjugation of women, Beard's work promoted women's contributions to the formation of society and brought to light a long-neglected past. In 1935, Beard asked, in a letter to Rose Arnold Powell, "Reverencing our pioneers is important. But work in our own time for our own time is equally vital, is it not?" (Cott 132). Beard's question rings true today. Her plans for a World Center for Women's Archives are yet to be realized but dovetail with our present moment. Moving our attention to the present, we need to overtly attempt to capture recent women's events and movements—seeking ways to collect voices, ephemera, and artifacts into a collective archive. Many local organizations and libraries are trying to do just that, but we need a more cohesive and integrated system of digitally documenting world marches and events, so that we might engage in "'circulatory looking' by attending to the spaces in which [historical women's] intellectual capital can be traced and reflecting on how historians' ideas of women are institutionally documented or disciplinarily formed" (Graban and Sullivan 190). For example, in the case of temperance women, we know that WCTU membership numbers (larger than National American Woman's Suffrage Association membership numbers) argue for the influence of temperance women in the passage of the Nineteenth Amendment. As Mattingly explains, "The WCTU supported suffrage for women, and the suffrage amendment was passed within a year of the eighteenth amendment, the prohibition amendment; this was not simply coincidental" (150). Revisiting temperance women's work through the lens of social circulation provides an opportunity to chart the fuller story of their nineteenth-century activism and subsequent (largely unrecognized) influence.

Implications

Perhaps it is time to review not only who will archive these modern movements but also how the movements will be archived. Mattingly's and Beard's cautionary tales pose questions about how we might consider our own contexts and media— and what archival lessons we can take from temperance women. Both the WCTU and Beard made good use of networks in their initial efforts to commemorate;

both required a skilled understanding of what we may call, today, crowdsourcing. If rhetorical feminism "is in a constant state of response, reassessment, and
self-correction" (Glenn 4), then how do we engage in building archival preservation coalitions that leverage what we can learn from our ancestors in a contemporary context that feels even more demanding and scattered?

In addition to the examples of collecting and collating women's work mentioned above, plans are currently in the works for a National Women's History
Museum, a comprehensive archival plan that promises an infrastructure and
funding model for taking archival collation to the next level. The mission of the
National Women's History Museum is "to tell the stories of women who transformed our nation . . . through a growing state-of-the-art online presence and a
future physical museum to educate, inspire, empower, shape the future, and provide a complete view of American history" ("Mission and Vision"). This current
project begins to enact Beard's 1935 insistence upon both immediate preservation and historical consideration. Likewise, the WCTU called for self-archiving
through its creation of the Women's Temple. The WCWA and the WCTU both
looked to create a base of legacy, but their efforts were necessarily built in real
time through crowdsourcing, dwelling within and dependent upon physical
spaces. We now have both momentum and technologies that allow us a greater
chance at diverse archival preservation.

The Women's March on Washington archives (as well as other initiatives)
have begun documenting events by gathering oral histories and digitizing images of often fragile ephemera (signs, posters, flyers, clothing, and other tex-
tiles) similar to the artifacts associated with nineteenth-century women's activist efforts. Digitizing in connection with a physical building, as the National
Women's History Museum proposes, is important, but how might we create more
comprehensive networking efforts and crowdsourcing? How might we build a
network of efforts, where sources from a wide range of local venues are digitally
searchable? How can we connect places and sites of rhetorical and public action
to one another in ways that make communication about civic efforts, successes,
and programming shareable and trackable?

We need a women's network clearinghouse that can capture work in local,
national, and international regions—big and small—to encourage and promote
both historical and contemporary research that is sociopolitically and civically
engaged. We need to look to current moments to begin to do so. For example,
the Schlesinger Library, one recipient of Beard's records and materials, planned
to celebrate the library's seventy-fifth anniversary and the suffragist centennial
of the passing of the Nineteenth Amendment in 2020 by supporting interdisciplinary scholarship in the form of grants, fellowships, programming, exhibits,
undergraduate courses, and an international conference designed to promote

understandings of "American women's citizenship, past, present, and future" (Ware). This initiative—labeled The Long Nineteenth Amendment, sponsored by an $870,000 grant from the Andrew W. Mellon Foundation, and relying on the Schlesinger Library's archival holdings—was planned to intersect with many other planned research opportunities connected with suffrage celebrations and may serve as a springboard for us to examine ways in which suffragists, temperance women, and nineteenth-century women who were working for women's rights before the Seneca Falls Convention intersect and diverge. By creating an integrated, organic archive of women's work, we can honor the legacy of nineteenth-century forebears and earlier archivists, tracing and giving voice to their work and our own.

Works Cited

Annual Minutes of the Women's Christian Temperance Union at the Twelfth Annual Meeting. Martin and Niper, 1885.

Auster, Martin. "Monument in a Landscape: The Question of Meaning." *Australian Geographer*, vol. 28, no. 2, 1997, pp. 219–27.

Beard, Deanna M. Toten. "'The Power of Woman's Influence': Nineteenth-Century Temperance Theatricality and the Drama of Nellie H. Bradley." *Theatre History Studies*, vol. 26, June 2006, pp. 52–70. *EBSCOhost*, ebscohost.com.

Beard, Mary R. *Woman as Force in History: A Study in Traditions and Realities.* Macmillan, 1946.

Blocker, Jack S., Jr. "Separate Paths: Suffragists and the Women's Temperance Crusade." *Signs*, vol. 10, no. 3, Spring 1985, pp. 460–76. *EBSCOhost*, ebscohost .com.

Bohlmann, Rachel E. "Our 'House Beautiful': The Woman's Temple and the WCTU Effort to Establish Place and Identity in Downtown Chicago, 1887–1898." *Journal of Women's History*, vol. 11, no. 2, Summer 1999, pp. 110–34, doi:10.1353/jowh.1999.0001.

Cott, Nancy F., editor. *A Woman Making History: Mary Ritter Beard through Her Letters.* Yale UP, 1991.

Enoch, Jessica. "Archival Problems, Circulation Solutions." Gries and Brooke, pp. 289–99.

Glenn, Cheryl. *Rhetorical Feminism and This Thing Called Hope.* Southern Illinois UP, 2019.

Graban, Tarez Samra, and Patricia Sullivan. "New Rhetorics of Scholarship: Leveraging *Betweenness* and *Circulation* for Feminist Historical Work in Composition Studies." Gries and Brooke, pp. 189–207.

Gries, Laurie E. "Introduction: Circulation as an Emergent Threshold Concept." Gries and Brooke, pp. 3–24.

Gries, Laurie E., and Collin Gifford Brooke, editors. *Circulation, Writing, and Rhetoric.* Utah State UP, 2018.

Kirsch, Gesa E., and Jacqueline J. Royster. "Feminist Rhetorical Practices: In Search of Excellence." *College Composition and Communication*, vol. 61, no. 4, June 2010, pp. 640–72. *EBSCOhost*, ebscohost.com.

Mattingly, Carol. "Woman's Temple, Women's Fountains: The Erasure of Public Memory." *American Studies*, vol. 49, nos. 3-4, Fall-Winter 2008, pp. 133–56, doi:10.1353/ams.2010.0040.

Miller, Hugh. *The Chicago School of Architecture: A Plan for Preserving a Significant Remnant of America's Architectural Heritage.* Department of the Interior, 1973. *National Park Service History eLibrary*, npshistory.com/publications/chicago-school -of-architecture.pdf.

"Mission and Vision." *National Women's History Museum*, www.womenshistory.org/ about-us/mission-vision.

"A Nation of Drunkards." *Prohibition*, directed by Ken Burns and Lynn Novick, episode 1, PBS, 2011.

O'Brien, Jane. "The Time When Americans Drank All Day Long." *BBC News Magazine*, 9 Mar. 2015, www.bbc.com/news/magazine-31741615.

Remus, Emily A. "Tippling Ladies and the Making of Consumer Culture: Gender and Public Space in *Fin-de-Siècle* Chicago." *Journal of American History*, vol. 101, no. 3, Dec. 2014, pp. 751–77, doi:10.1093/jahist/jau650.

Royster, Jacqueline Jones, and Gesa E. Kirsch. *Feminist Rhetorical Practices: New Horizons for Rhetoric, Composition, and Literacy Studies.* Southern Illinois UP, 2012.

———. "Social Circulation and Legacies of Mobility for Nineteenth-Century Women: Implications for Using Digital Resources in Socio-Rhetorical Projects." Gries and Brooke, pp. 170–88.

Stansell, Christine. *The Feminist Promise: 1792 to the Present.* Modern Library, 2011.

Voss-Hubbard, Anke. "'No Documents—No History': Mary Ritter Beard and the Early History of Women's Archives." *American Archivist*, vol. 58, no. 1, Spring 1995, pp. 16–30. *EBSCOhost*, ebscohost.com.

Ware, Susan W. "The Long Nineteenth Amendment." *Schlesinger Newsletter / Radcliffe Institute for Advanced Study at Harvard University*, Presidents and Fellows of Harvard College, 2018, www.radcliffe.harvard.edu/news/schlesinger-newsletter/ long-19th-amendment.

Willard, Frances E. *Address before the Second Biennial Convention of the World's Woman's Christian Temperance Union, and the Twentieth Annual Convention of the National Women's Christian Temperance Union.* White Ribbon Publishing, 1893. *Library of Congress*, www.loc.gov/item/93838352/.

"Woman's Temple." *Chicagology*, chicagology.com/goldenage/goldenage100/.

Aesthetic Daughter and Civic Mother: Collective Identity and the Visual-Verbal Rhetorics of the New Negro Woman

Kristie S. Fleckenstein

With the National Association of Colored Women as her exemplar, Fannie Barrier Williams, in "The Club Movement among the Colored Women," celebrates her peers' ability to "organize and remain organized for practical usefulness in the social uplift of the Negro race" (99). Williams's explicit verbal praise of the club women's activism—characterized as a part of a "heart movement" (99) that contributes to "the lesson of citizenship" (102)—configures the identity of the New Negro Women as "civic mothers" (101): agents who, by taking action in "municipal life," seek to improve home and race (102). Five months after the publication of Williams's article, in "Rough Sketches: A Study of the Features of the New Negro Woman," author and artist John H. Adams, Jr., designs a very different identity for the twentieth-century African American woman. Relying on a combination of words and images, Adams rejects the figure of the civic mother for the mien of the aesthetic daughter, one valued for her beauty, grace, and intelligence.

Though both Williams's and Adams's articles were published in the 1904 volume of *The Voice of the Negro,* a monthly periodical judged as "the most promising, eclectic magazine of that period and one of the best published in the United States" (Daniel and Huber 23), these two very different articles, with their very different visual-verbal dynamics, highlight a tension within the efforts of Black elites to craft a group identity for collective action. Construed as a crucial element of activism, one that implicates resources, strategies, and affective motivations (Polletta and Jasper 284), collective identity serves as my focus here. Examining the rhetorical efforts of African Americans to forge and maintain group cohesion in the service of racial uplift, I argue that the struggle to configure the New Negro Woman played out rhetorically through the joint auspices of the printed word and image, two means of persuasion afforded by the burgeoning fin de siècle Black public sphere. In addition, the ways in which image-word resources were transformed into rhetorical strategies reflect not only contrasting views of the New Negro Women but also contrasting views of collective identity:

as solidarity, or a fixed meaning that is stable across time, place, and people (Polletta and Jasper), and as "fluidarity," negotiated meanings that shift in response to internal and external pressures (Maruggi; SinghaRoy).

Collective Identity and the Black Public Sphere

Writing in 1896, Williams encourages African American women's participation in the public sphere by applauding the "new usefulness" of the New Negro Woman, who is a force for the evolution of a "pure and strong and beautiful" home and race ("New Colored Woman"). Through such advocacy, Williams contributes both to the constitution of the New Negro Woman identity and to the reconstitution of a collective identity for those pursuing racial uplift. Since the mid–twentieth century, rhetorical scholars have increasingly attended to the phenomenon of collective identity, attending to the vital role such identity plays in group activism as a crucial element affecting the success or failure of a social movement. Although suffering from a "definitional catholicity," collective identity, with its web of cognitive, emotional, and moral connections between individual and broader community, is imagined and articulated through visual and verbal cultural materials, such as names, narratives, symbols, linguistic styles, rituals, and so forth (Polletta and Jasper 285). The constitution of collective identity, then, requires spaces for invention and delivery of those cultural materials. Defined as a "critical social imaginary," the Black public sphere, a resource Williams expertly employed, provided just those spaces in the post-Reconstruction era (Black Public Sphere Collective 2).

Influenced by rising literacy rates and composed predominantly of flourishing print publications, from newspapers to periodicals to books (Danky 341, 345), the late-nineteenth-century Black public sphere offered an unprecedented opportunity for Black Americans to seize the tools of discursive and visual representation as a means to invent a collective identity and pursue collective action. Print publications opened up a "'universe of discourse' for the black middle class," through which African Americans debated issues, protested injustice, and imagined avenues to uplift (Fultz 130). Beyond this, however, publications also served an epideictic function. Within print venues, African Americans praised individual and joint achievements, victories, and accomplishments to promote shared values and shared communal identities. Thus, the molding of a collective identity designed to combat racial injustice relied on the existence and health of the Black public sphere. But the Black public sphere, in turn, relied on the existence and health of Black print culture.

Black print culture served as the material matrix for the flowering of the Black public sphere in the late nineteenth century, an era marked by three radical transformations in the print industry. First, technological innovations—including steam-powered rotary presses, new typesetting processes, cheap wood pulp paper, and improved ink—increased output and reduced costs, bringing print publishing within the reach of African Americans (Ivins; Kaestle and Radway, "Framework" 11). Second, the explosion of photography in 1839, coupled with the invention and refinement of the halftone process—an innovation that facilitated the inexpensive reproduction of photographs—revolutionized publishing (Ivins 137; Kaestle and Radway, "Framework" 12). Photography provided a means for African Americans to tap into visual images as a method to refute the "codified racist debris of centuries of representations of blacks" (Gates, "Face and Voice" xxix). Finally, training in print technologies facilitated the emergence of a cadre of African Americans proficient in the mechanics of print production and photography. These factors combined to ensure that Black printers, publishers, papermakers, and book binders could prosper. However, even as the collaboration of Black print culture and the Black public sphere provided fruitful ground for generating Black collective identity, this collaboration also provided fruitful ground for generating multiple fault lines in that collective identity, such as the threat presented by the rise of the New Negro Woman that Williams celebrates.

For many in the Black community, the New Negro Woman portended an unwelcome change. Until the emergence of women's organizations, Black women, beyond a few luminaries, "had never been thought of as a significant factor in the racial struggle," Paula Giddings notes (31). Race men, not race women, led the fight for equality, dominating the public and political scenes. However, with the rise of the National Colored Women's Association in 1896, the insignificant gender became significant, presaging a potential shift in the traditional gender dynamic. "African American women's struggles assumed unprecedented visibility in the years 1890–1920," James P. Danky asserts, to the extent that "[b]lack intellectuals labeled the period 'the Woman's Era.'" A major point of contestation was the effort of women to enter the Black public sphere "to push for social change and racial justice" (349). T. Thomas Fortune implicitly gestures to the gender realignment such entry presages. In an 1896 article praising the reform efforts of the "new Afro-American woman," Fortune fans the flames of gender anxiety by soundly criticizing the "Afro-American as a man and citizen" for his failure across political, civil, and business venues. Fortune then praises the New Negro Woman, suggesting that she replace the Afro-American man on the public stage. The Black public sphere thus constituted itself out of multiple voices and perspectives, exposing asymmetrical power dynamics within the African American community. This public sphere afforded African Americans not only the resources to form a collective identity out of those multiple voices but also the resources to fracture that identity. The conversation concerning the New Negro

Woman illuminates both those voices and rhetorical strategies as well as the tug
of solidarity and fluidity in collective identity.

The Aesthetic Daughter as Solidarity

Standing in a formal pose with her body in profile, Gussie tilts her head and
gazes with assurance at the viewer (fig. 1). A proficient violinist and pianist as
well as a "sweet singer" and talented writer, Gussie is a "home making girl," the
caption under her full-length portrait confides (Adams 326). The image, along
with the accompanying article's verbal narrative, spotlights both the operation
of conjunctive visual-verbal rhetoric in defining the New Negro Woman as the
aesthetic daughter and the force of solidarity in a community's collective identity. I identify Adams's approach in this article, "Rough Sketches," as conjunctive
visual-verbal rhetoric because, first, it privileges the processes of linking people,
beliefs, values, and so forth in an array of reinforcing relationships. Second, that
process of relationship building serves as the heart of coalition building. "Solidarity," theologian Matthew Maruggi contends, "affirms a human interconnect-
edness while at the same time challenging each person to assume responsibility
for the other," revealing the concept's significance in collective action (309). Conjunctive rhetoric that is also visual-verbal creates solidarity through relations by
aligning word and image to reinforce a particular connective relation. As a result, conjunctive visual-verbal rhetoric operates as a centripetal force that pulls
and organizes elements, including those on the periphery, into a cohesive—a
fixed and stable—center. In Adams's hands, conjunctive visual-verbal rhetoric,
literally and figuratively, drew a *we* for the Black middle-class community that
tapped into a core of beliefs and aspirations revolving around the New Negro
Woman as the aesthetic daughter.

The definition of the New Negro Woman as the aesthetic daughter anchors
itself in the most important component of Adams's conjunctive visual-verbal
rhetoric: the illustrations. Consisting of portrait studies of seven winsome and
attractive females (one adolescent and six young adults) scattered across every
page of the article, the sketches dominate Adams's short piece, almost exceed-
ing in column inches the eight paragraphs of narrative text. Accompanied by
captions detailing the name of the subject as well as a set of her achievements
and traits, the illustrations derive their unifying power from their status as high
art. As William Ivins indicates, a hierarchy of art governed print media in the
late nineteenth century, with human-crafted pictures, such as illustrations and
paintings, on the highest level of the hierarchy (114). Illustrations as high art operated in Adams's conjunctive visual-verbal rhetoric to solidify collective identity
by satisfying two communal aspirations: the desire among African Americans

An admirer of Fine Art, a performer on the violin and the piano, a sweet singer, a writer—mostly given to essays, a lover of good books, and a home making girl, is Gussie.

Figure 1. "Gussie." *The Voice of the Negro*, vol. 1, no. 6, June 1904, p. 326. *HathiTrust*, hdl .handle.net/2027/inu.32000013344009.

for control over their own visual representations and the desire for recognition of their contributions to cultural enrichment. The sketches of the New Negro Woman as the aesthetic daughter assuaged both needs, reifying values along with gender asymmetry.

The existence of illustrations qua illustrations encouraged unity within Black enclaves by feeding the longing for control over self-representation. As early as the seventeenth century, African Americans had recognized the necessity of refuting the dominant images of themselves as "devoid of all the characteristics that separate the lower forms of human life from the supposedly higher forms" (Gates, "Trope" 131). Thus, African Americans sought control over their own verbal and visual images, commissioning, when financially feasible, "paintings, and later photographs, of themselves, so that they could metaphorically enshrine and quite literally perpetuate the example of their own identities" (Gates, "Face and Voice" xxix). Art, then, served its own unifying function by emphasizing African American aesthetic agency. Adams's seven illustrations embodied evidence of that agency on two fronts. First, by the criteria of the time, the illustrations constituted Black self-representational agency, with favorable depictions of African American features affirming individual and collective worth. Second, the illustrations constituted Black artistic agency because they were created by a Black artist who not only taught art but also contributed illustrations to periodicals such *The Voice of the Negro* and later the *Crisis*. The seven sketches of the New Negro Woman as the aesthetic daughter testified to the ability of African Americans to create—as well as to commission—art, underscoring that they, too, possessed the higher forms of human life. Thus, the seven illustrations reproduced in the pages of *The Voice of the Negro* served solidarity by satisfying the longing among African Americans to be recognized not only as self-selected subjects of high art but also as producers of high art. The illustrations incarnated the existence of a "new Negro visual aesthetics" (Willis 53), an accomplishment intimately intertwined with a New Negro politics.

In addition to satisfying aesthetic-political needs, and thus cementing collective identity around that satiation, the illustrations qua illustrations also supported group cohesion by configuring the content of the illustrations as abstractions rather than representations. Ivins explains that, in the wake of photography, especially portrait photography, the illustration "lost its place as a means of representing concretions" but "maintained its place as a means of making abstractions" (137), or symbols. Adams makes explicit the symbolic meaning of the New Negro Woman: she is the aesthetic daughter who adorns the home, gaining salience as an art object that is seen but does not act. Instead, valuable for her inner and outer beauty, she is to be displayed, revered, and protected. Captions under each sketch focus attention on aspirational qualities manifesting beauty of body and soul: "an uncommon sweep of kindness and affection" in one face and the "lofty impulses" of a poetic soul in another (Adams 323, 325). Blessed with beauty, the young women are also graced with intellect, moral stamina, loftiness of purpose, and sober consciousness (325), all gifts enriching the home. Situated on the pedestal, as appropriate to art rather than the public stage, Adams's New Negro Woman denotes an ideal rather than an actuality, a hopeful goal around which the entire community—men and women—could rally in shared enthusiasm.

Finally, Adams's conjunctive visual-verbal rhetoric matches image with word, constructing through narrative a verbal image of the aesthetic daughter's partner: the new Negro male, who, as an adoring connoisseur of high art, gazes upon the aesthetic daughter, esteems her for her inner and outer beauty, and vows to protect both. Because imagery and story share the same narrative core, as well as significant structural parallels and functions (Fleckenstein 924), the two can operate reciprocally, with each reinforcing the force of the other. Such is the situation in Adams's article, where the narrative unfolds in the first paragraph with the setting (business section of Atlanta), the characters (the narrator and Alford, an "innocent companion"), and the initiating incident—the sight of two young women, one white and one Black, chatting together in an open carriage. The article then proceeds with the conflict (determining which woman is prettier) and the denouement with "young Alford" committing himself to the protection of the New Negro Woman, a "real, pure, substantial beauty" who touches his soul and "inspires him to love" (324). A poetic celebration of the New Negro Woman's virtue and loveliness as well as a celebration of the birth of the New Negro man as one who recognizes, appreciates, and safeguards this treasure, the two semiotic streams conspire to assert the same aspirational reality: the passive ornamental New Negro Woman configured by the active male eyes, male hands, and male words. The semiotic reciprocity thus sets out the steps for communal unity via a gendered contract stipulating with remarkable clarity roles, spaces, activities, and behavior of men and women.

Through word and image, conjunctive visual-verbal rhetoric creates the New Negro Woman as the aesthetic daughter and the New Negro man as the connoisseur tasked with her blossoming. However, that rhetoric hides the fragility of solidarity, for collective identity demands constant remaking (SinghaRoy). The disjunctive visual-verbal rhetoric of a group of African American women both challenges and negotiates the aesthetic daughter, endorsing the centrifugal force of fluidity in collective identity.

The Civic Mother as Fluidarity

The African American community, Williams writes, is learning that only through the New Negro Woman's domestic and social activism will the race progress

("Club Movement" 102). In making such bald and bold claims, Williams challenges what Giddings calls attempts by Black men during the turn of the century "to vindicate their manhood largely through asserting their authority over
women" (61). As Williams confronts the asymmetrical power dynamic in the
Black community's gender relations, she highlights the importance of a particular definition of the New Negro Woman—the civic mother—a role seemingly
at odds with Adams's aesthetic daughter. Simultaneously, Williams highlights
the importance of fluidarity in constituting collective identity, an attitude and
practice which "invokes partial knowledge, placing value on being incomplete,
vulnerable, and never totally fixed" (Maruggi 310).

While solidarity accentuates the vital importance of a cohesive identity
within a social movement, it also hides the degree to which the drive for cohesion
"homogenizes" members by ignoring the presence of "difference and oppression"
(Maruggi 308). Henry Louis Gates, Jr., indirectly gestures to the problem posed
by solidarity for elite African Americans. He argues that the New Negro man and
woman at the turn of the century had to "transform themselves from objects
to subjects, a process that was essential to effect before they could assume the
prerogatives of full American citizenship" ("Face and Voice" xxix). However, as
the aesthetic daughter, the New Negro Woman is object first and subject second,
reinstating within the Black culture the objectification dominant in the white
culture. To redress the limitations of that symbol, African American women
writers in *The Voice of the Negro* employ a disjunctive visual-verbal rhetoric that,
like fluidarity, embraces "the complexity of engaging the other in pluralized and
ever changing struggles" (Maruggi 308). The rhetoric embraces this complexity by courting the differences always already at play in any collective, opening up a social movement to the rejuvenating power of new identity formation
(SinghaRoy 7).

A key step in reformulating the New Negro Woman as civic mother necessi-
tated delinking, or separating, the New Negro Woman from the aesthetic daughter, a task that foregrounds differences in ethics, politics, and ways of knowing.
A primary tactic of delinking for National Association of Colored Women club
women consisted of privileging word over image, a rhetorical choice that defined
the New Negro Woman in terms of rationality rather than aestheticism. That
reformation of the New Negro Woman operated through the dual affordances of
the word as synonymous with rationality and the word as a performative site of
propositional logic. To begin, word qua word taps into the belief prevalent at the
fin de siècle that only the rational human could read and write with facility. "To
many, it [print literacy] was the most visible embodiment of reason itself, and if
one were 'reasonable,' then one's humanity could not easily be denied" (Gates,
"Face and Voice" xxxi). Mastery of the printed word, apart from the content of

that word, then, signals mastery of rationality, the tools of higher-level thinking long denied to African Americans. The radical uptick in African American
authorship—the rise of the Black public sphere itself—reflects a move on the
part of the Black community, especially its male members, to "metaphorically
[write] themselves to freedom by articulating the complexity of their human
subjectivity" (Gates, "Face and Voice" xxxi). The almost exclusive reliance on
word, rather than image, by African American women writing in the July 1904
issue of *The Voice of the Negro* manifests their effort to claim the mantle of rationality for the New Negro Woman.

The most obvious sign of word's domination is the sheer number of women
authors—eight—featured in this single issue of the periodical, a departure from
previous issues where male authors overwhelmed women's perspectives. *The
Voice of the Negro* made visible women's linguistic authority in a variety of ways,
beginning with the teaser in the June 1904 issue. Appearing on the last page,
this preview of the forthcoming issue advertises that "the women will occupy the
greater portion of the magazine," underscoring the importance of their words to
the public conversation. The teaser further commends the women by listing six
contributors by name and introducing each with adjectives such as "eloquent,"
"scholarly," "versatile," "erudite," and "wisely conservative." The descriptors spotlight not the authors' beauty but their status as gifted intellectuals and writers,
an impression reinforced by the inclusion of positions of responsibility, such as
"Corresponding Secretary of the Woman's Auxiliary to the National Baptist Convention" and "President of The National Association of Colored Women." Thus,
before the July issue even appears, the New Negro Woman, as exemplified by
these contributors, distinguishes herself—her behavior, thinking, and areas of
expertise—from the aesthetic daughter. That delinking via word qua word is
further endorsed by the parsimonious use of images within and across the eight
articles, a tactic that provides a subtle reinforcement of word with its entail-
ments. *The Voice of the Negro*, like other periodicals of the era, enthusiastically in-
corporates images, many times three or four in a single article (Ivins). However,
the presentation of the eight articles, one after another, interrupted only by the
occasional discreet photographic portrait, departs from that style. This devia-
tion signals the ability of the New Negro Woman to achieve recognition through
the rationality of her words, not through her physical beauty. Thus, without even
considering the content of the articles, word qua word enables the New Negro
Woman to emerge as a rational citizen prepared to work in public with her peers
for racial uplift. The logic of the New Negro Woman's words in action furthers
the delinking process.

Starting in 1880, "the printed word became the sine qua non of influence and
organization," acting as "an instrument and an expression of change" (Kaestle

and Radway, "Framework" 8), and *The Voice of the Negro*, with its fifteen thousand subscribers (Fultz 132), offered a stage for women's printed word to effect that change. The traditional site of argumentation since Aristotle, the word and its propositional logic of claim and support increased the separation between the New Negro Woman and the aesthetic daughter. For, by deploying arguments, especially arguments that highlighted fluidity in her identity as well as, by extension, the movement's collective identity, the New Negro Woman performed rationally. Two examples demonstrate that double move of logic and fluidity in delinking the civic wordsmith from the parlor ornament. First, a major claim-support structure that circulated across articles concerned individual agency in gender uplift as a necessary ingredient to racial uplift. The New Negro Woman exists not as an object acted upon but as a subject acting, a primary characteristic of fluidity in which movement members exercise their autonomy even as they embrace "fluidity in their identity" (SinghaRoy 67). Mary Church Terrell asserts this claim to agency, contending that African American women are, in their own lives, "rendering valiant service to their race . . . struggling and striving and hoping" (294). The contention that women can act as individual agents is then backed up with evidence that women do act and act publicly. From helping each other buy homes (Washington 288) to establishing kindergartens (Silone-Yates 284) to protesting Jim Crow Car Laws (Terrell 293), women find in their agency a "public experience of self" (McDonald 111) that feeds sustained personal and group activism. Second, delinking the New Negro Woman from the aesthetic daughter operates through word's propositional logic by seizing particular sites of agency: local sites. An essential trait of fluidity consists of its incarnation as pockets of solidarity for the-moment (Maruggi; SinghaRoy). Actions emerge, form, and circulate in response to the needs unique to each municipality, each neighborhood, each home. Williams presages such pockets in her March 1904 article, advising each National Association of Colored Women club "to work out its own individuality, know its own needs and find its own work" ("Club Movement" 102). Margaret Murray Washington especially supports this declaration, providing a list of specific community-based activities that women individually and jointly pursue in their "efforts aimed at local needs" (290). The reliance on word's propositional logic thus construes the New Negro Woman not only as a rational agent but also as a rationally flexible agent.

Disjunctive visual-verbal rhetoric's emphasis on word illuminates the importance of delinking in articulating what the New Negro Woman is not: the aesthetic daughter. But equally important to her identity is articulating what the New Negro Woman is: the civic mother. The act of counter-narrating aims for exactly that. In the July 1904 issue of *The Voice of the Negro*, disjunctive visual-verbal rhetoric counter-narrates the civic mother especially through the

MRS. JOSEPHINE SILONE-YATES, A. M.
Professor of English of Lincoln Institute, Jefferson City, Mo., and President of
The National Association of Colored Women

Figure 2. "Josephine Silone-Yates." *The Voice of the Negro*, vol. 1, no. 7, July 1904, p. 266. *HathiTrust*, hdl.handle.net/2027/inu.32000013344009.

play of photographic images operating as "subversive resistance" (Willis 55). Perhaps the most dramatic performance of that subversive resistance occurs with the juxtaposition of two photographic portraits: one of Josephine Silone-Yates, which serves as the frontispiece for the July 1904 issue (fig. 2) and one of Washington, which appears as a full page at the end of Washington's article (fig. 3).

MRS. BOOKER T. WASHINGTON
Wife of the Distinguished Principal of Tuskegee Institute

Figure 3. "Margaret Murray Washington." *The Voice of the Negro*, vol. 1, no. 8, Aug. 1904, p. 289. *HathiTrust*, hdl.handle.net/2027/inu.32000013344009.

The effectiveness of visual counter-narrating ensues, first, from the nature of the images as photographic portraits and, second, from the content of the images, gesturing, by turn, to the New Negro Woman as civic agent and then to the New Negro Woman as mother.

Visual counter-narrating draws on the medium and genre of photographic portraiture, a ubiquitous form of photography that, by the turn of the century, operated as "powerful[ly] as the written word" for refuting racist attitudes and realities (Willis 54). Central to visual counter-narrating was the informational function of photography, including portrait photography. Supplanting illustrations, photographs were perceived as providing "factual detailed informational pictures" possessing greater detail and accuracy than that endowed by the human hand (Ivins 136–37). The informational function thus emphasized the truth-value of a photograph, including photographic portraits. Unlike sketched illustrations, then, that presented the subject as an abstraction or an aspirational symbol, photographic portraits presented the subject as an actuality, a concrete reality. In the July 1904 portraits, the actuality of the New Negro Woman as the civic mother took shape at the interface of two portraits, bringing into alignment the different but compatible identities of the New Negro Woman as civic mother.

Visual counter-narrating configures the civic and maternal aspects of the New Negro Woman through the details—the information—of the image itself: props, apparel, and pose, all signifiers of status and sources of empowerment (Willis 52). As the sitting president of the National Association of Colored Women, Silone-Yates actualized the civic aspect of the New Negro Woman, one ready to step out of the parlor and onto the dais with middle-class gentility. With her full face turned to the viewer, body at a quarter turn to the right, and a slight smile at the lips, Silone-Yates conveys through her erect posture her confidence and her readiness to act. In addition, her dark dress with its discreet pattern, high collar, and puffed sleeves as well as her Gibson-Girl-like bouffant hair arrangement evoke the fashion of the period but shorn of its excesses. These conservative stylistic choices convey Silone-Yates's commitment to professionalism rather than the extremes of aestheticism, a commitment that the portrait's caption—a list of her professional positions—endorses. Here is the quintessential race woman, who justifies the activism of the New Negro Woman because of such activism's "well-defined aim for the elevation of the race" (283). However, juxtaposed to the civic face of the New Negro Woman is her maternal face, incarnated by Washington. The full-page portrait of Washington delivers that identity dramatically. Seated in a spindled chair, perhaps even a rocker, with her face averted from the viewer, Washington leans back at her ease, relaxed in a casual pose that seemingly offers a lap for the pleasure of a small child, an interpretation reinforced by the caption that identifies her simply as the wife of Booker T. Washington. Washington's single prop—her purse hanging from her waist—signifies her devotion to the wifely domestic sciences, establishing her authority over home management. Thus, Washington partners Silone-Yates as the civic mother who enters the public sphere because of her commitment to family as a means to lift the race. Neither the civic nor the maternal, the New Negro Woman is both: the civic mother.

Visual counter-narrating provided "African Americans with the opportunity for reinvention" (Willis 67), and the July 1904 portraits, in partnership with delinking, configure the New Negro Woman not as a single treasured identity, holding all accountable to that identity, but as the necessary play of multiple identities, multiple sites of action, and multiple forms of agency. The portraits highlight the crucial role of fluidarity in collective identity secured through the auspices of disjunctive visual-verbal rhetoric.

Whether the aesthetic daughter or the civic mother, the construction of the New Negro Woman through conjunctive and disjunctive visual-verbal rhetorics contributed to and honored "a spirit of self-awareness, artistic consciousness, and racial pride" (Willis 52), characterizing the Black elite community at the turn of the century. At the same time, the rhetorics and the New Negro Woman they advocated underscored the importance of neither solidarity nor fluidarity in collective identity. Rather, the fault line created by the New Negro Woman and the visual-verbal discourses she generated highlight that collective identity is not a being but a becoming, one that undergoes "frequent processes of construction, transformation and reconfiguration," expressing itself in "diverse modes of solidarity, fuzziness, and fluidity" (SinghaRoy 11). After all, the civic mother is what the aesthetic daughter, if she is lucky, will grow up to be. As this examination of the debates around the New Negro Woman reveals, the important question in collective identity and in social movement theory rests neither on the creation and adherence to a single, fixed identity nor on the celebration of fluidarity's fragmentation. The question rests, instead, on both: the need for fluidarity to ensure attention to peripheral voices and the need for solidarity to ensure unity for the moment. In turn, a collective identity as a becoming requires the resources of the Black public sphere and Black print culture. Without rich spaces for speaking and seeing available to all members of an enclave, spaces within which differences are articulated, respected, and negotiated, a social movement risks its resilience, sustainability, and, ultimately, its effectiveness. There is not only room at the table for the daughter and the mother but also a need for the voices—and the faces—of both.

Works Cited

Adams, John H., Jr. "Rough Sketches: A Study of the Features of the New Negro Woman." *The Voice of the Negro*, vol. 1, no. 8, Aug. 1904, pp. 323–26. *HathiTrust*, hdl.handle.net/2027/inu.32000013344009.

The Black Public Sphere Collective, editor. *The Black Public Sphere: A Public Culture Book*. U of Chicago P, 1995.

Daniel, Walter C., and Patrick J. Huber. "*The Voice of the Negro* and the Atlanta Riot of 1906: A Problem in Freedom of the Press." *Journalism History*, vol. 17, no. 1, 1990, pp. 23–28. *Humanities Full Text (H. W. Wilson)*, accession number 509493219.

Danky, James P. "Reading, Writing, and Resisting: African American Print Culture." Kaestle and Radway, *Print*, pp. 339–58.

Fleckenstein, Kristie S. "Images, Words, and Narrative Epistemology." *College English*, vol. 58, no. 8, Dec. 1996, pp. 914–33. *JSTOR*, www.jstor.org/stable/378229.

Fortune, T. Thomas. "Afro-American Women." *The Sun* [New York], 5 July 1896. *Chronicling America*, chroniclingamerica.loc.gov/lccn/sn83030272/1896-07-05/ed -3/seq-1/.

Fultz, Michael. "'The Morning Cometh': African-American Periodicals, Education, and the Black Middle Class, 1900–1930." *Print Culture in a Diverse America*, edited by James P. Danky and Wayne A. Wiegand, U of Illinois P, 1998, pp. 130–48.

Gates, Henry Louis, Jr. "The Face and Voice of Blackness." *Facing History: The Black Images in American Art 1710–1940*, by Guy C. McElroy, edited by Christopher C. French, Bedford Arts, 1990, pp. xxxix–xliv.

———. "The Trope of a New Negro and the Reconstruction of the Image of the Black." *Representations*, vol. 24, no. 24, Autumn 1988, pp. 129–55. *JSTOR*, www.jstor.org/ stable/2928478.

Giddings, Paula. *When and Where I Enter: The Impact of Black Women on Race and Sex in America*. Amistad, 1984.

Ivins, William M., Jr. *Prints and Visual Communication*. MIT Press, 1953.

Kaestle, Carl F., and Janice A. Radway. "A Framework for the History of Publishing and Reading in the United States, 1880–1940." Kaestle and Radway, *Print*, pp. 7–21.

———, editors. *Print in Motion: The Expansion of Publishing and Reading in the United States, 1880–1940*. Vol. 4, U of North Carolina P, 2009.

Maruggi, Matthew. "Through Solidarity to 'Fluidarity': Understanding Difference and Developing Change Agency through Narrative Reflection." *Teaching Theology and Religion*, vol. 15, no. 6, Oct. 2012, pp. 307–22.

McDonald, Kevin. "From Solidarity to Fluidarity: Social Movements beyond 'Collective Identity'—The Case of Globalization Conflicts." *Social Movement Studies*, vol. 1, no. 2, 2002, pp. 109–28, doi:10.1080/1474283022000010637.

Polletta, Francesca, and James M. Jasper. "Collective Identity and Social Movements." *Annual Review of Sociology*, vol. 27, 2001, pp. 283–305. *JSTOR*, www.jstor.org/ stable/2678623.

Silone-Yates, Josephine. "The National Association of Colored Women." *The Voice of the Negro*, vol. 1, no. 6, June 1904, pp. 283–87. *HathiTrust*, hdl.handle.net/2027/inu .32000013344009.

SinghaRoy, Debal K. *Identity, Society and Transformative Social Categories: Dynamics of Construction, Configuration and Contestation.* SAGE, 2018.

Teaser. *The Voice of the Negro*, vol. 1, no. 6, June 1904, p. 262. *HathiTrust*, hdl.handle .net/2027/inu.32000013344009.

Terrell, Mary Church. "The Progress of Colored Women." *The Voice of the Negro*, vol. 1, no. 6, June 1904, pp. 291–94. *HathiTrust*, hdl.handle.net/2027/inu .32000013344009.

Washington, Mrs. Booker T. "Social Improvement of the Plantation Woman." *The Voice of the Negro*, vol. 1, no. 8, Aug. 1904, pp. 288–90. *HathiTrust*, hdl.handle.net/ 2027/inu.32000013344009.

Williams, Fannie Barrier. "The Club Movement among the Colored Women." *The Voice of the Negro*, vol. 1, no. 3, Mar. 1904, pp. 99–102. *HathiTrust*, hdl.handle.net/ 2027/inu.32000013344009.

———. "The New Colored Woman." *The Freeman*, 19 Dec. 1896, p. 7. *Google News*, news .google.com/newspapers?nid=FIkAGs9z2eEC&dat=18961219&printsec =frontpage&hl=en.

Willis, Deborah. "The Sociologist's Eye: W. E. B. Du Bois and the Paris Exposition." *A Small Nation of People: W. E. B. Du Bois and African American Portraits of Progress*, compiled by the Library of Congress, HarperCollins, 2003, pp. 51–78.

Crypto-Feminist Enthymemes in the Periodical Texts of Louise Clappe and Fanny Fern

Suzanne Bordelon and Elizabethada A. Wright

As Anne Firor Scott observed in 1979, many nineteenth-century American women were neither feminists nor antifeminists; most were somewhere between, "often holding some part of each set of values simultaneously . . . [accommodating] those who were in motion, moving toward the feminist end of the spectrum" (4). How these women who were uncertain about feminism promoted activism has not been fully considered. Instead, most groundbreaking research on nineteenth-century American rhetoric has tended to view the term activist writ large, highlighting broad political movements (Campbell; Mattingly, *Water* and *Well-Tempered Women*). Though scholars have recently considered sites beyond public and political discourse, locations, and genres and thus have reframed previous assumptions (Enoch; Johnson; Mountford), little scholarship examines women who are between feminist beliefs and disbeliefs.

We explore the rhetoric of these women, arguing that carefully structured pedestrian views have the ability to disrupt the hegemony via the enthymeme. To make such a claim, we analyze the rhetoric of Louise Clappe and that of Fanny Fern, popular nineteenth-century writers, both of whom appear to have "[held] some part of each set of values simultaneously" (Scott 4). Extending the scholarship on indirect critique (Barrett-Fox, "Posthuman Feminism" and "Rhetorics"; Bordelon; Kates), we demonstrate the ways Clappe and Fern (and perhaps others) used the enthymeme as a tool to bring unexamined suppositions to the public's attention. With both women originally publishing their work in periodicals, a medium that has the potential to resist the status quo (Beetham; S. Smith), we consider the ways Clappe and Fern maneuvered their audiences "to consider" how accepted practices often violated social norms (Burnyeat 92). More specifically, we examine the ways the enthymeme structure itself proved useful to Clappe and Fern because it allowed them to slip in controversial ideas without stating them openly.

In examining Clappe's *The Shirley Letters from the California Mines, 1851–1852*, we draw on recent scholarship, given that Clappe often uses words to create visual enthymemes that problematize gendered assumptions and everyday practices in the mining camps. Through these portrayals, Clappe directs her audience to consider the situation from her perspective. In analyzing Fern's writing, we use postmodern considerations of the enthymeme to understand how she manipulated contradictory audience assumptions regarding her columns' true meanings. Because her audiences came to expect a mix of earnestness and wit, Fern could say whatever she desired—and audiences interpreted her words with similar variations. If condemned for what she said, Fern would claim humorous ironic intentions. The humor and critique in both Clappe's and Fern's writing often emerge from the audience-supplied assumptions evident in their texts. Instead of making direct claims, with the potential risk of being held accountable for those claims, both women draw upon shared visual and cultural norms that encourage their audiences to participate in the completion of the enthymemes.

Defining and Contextualizing Enthymemes

Within rhetoric and communication, the enthymeme has conventionally been described as a truncated syllogism (McBurney; V. Smith). However, Aristotle's description of the enthymeme as "the 'body' of persuasion" (1354a) suggests a more substantial role. Scholars have responded by positing more complex understandings of the enthymeme (Fredal; Gage; Grimaldi, *Aristotle* and *Studies*; McBurney; Poster; Walker). Although scholars have noted that various definitions of the enthymeme exist (Harper; Madden; Poster), we build on explanations offered by M. F. Burnyeat and Roger Aden. According to Burnyeat, the cognate verb for enthymeme means "to think about something, consider it"; thus, Burnyeat views enthymemes as "considerations one is swayed by when reflecting on an issue where conclusive argument is not to be had" (92, 93). Given the constraints they faced as women in the middle to late nineteenth century, Clappe and Fern could not typically state their critiques directly. Instead, they urged their audiences "to think about something," to consider the different aspects of life that they highlight for consideration. To be persuasive, then, Clappe and Fern needed to create enthymemes that "identif[ied] with the common opinions of their intended audiences" (V. Smith 120). Although successful enthymemes are based on discovering these common opinions, both women allow for audience members' interpretations. As Aden observes, in contemporary society enthymemes are useful since postmodernism itself suggests conclusive arguments rarely exist within postmodernism's proliferation of discourse, reconstruction of previous discourses, and constant construction of new interpretations. With this lack of certain conclusions, Aden argues, the probabilities of the enthymeme become useful, encouraging individual interpretations. This use of the enthymeme is particularly evident in Fern's work.

More recently, scholars have extended the concept of the enthymeme to the analysis of visual arguments (Birdsell and Groarke; Blair; Finnegan; V. Smith; Young). Valerie J. Smith discusses how Aristotle's more complex view of the enthymeme applies both to visual and verbal arguments. Smith asserts that visual enthymemes "involve probable premises and conclusions" that accommodate audiences' different interpretations, they "accommodate ethical and emotional dimensions of argument," and they "depend on agreement between messenger and audience" (120). We draw on Smith's understanding of the concept, given that Clappe's and Fern's visual and verbal enthymemes involve not only logical reasoning but also appeals to emotions and character. However, Clappe's visual enthymemes typically depend on identifying with the common assumptions of her audience, while Fern's draw on claims and reasons that "accommodate differences among audience members' interpretations" (V. Smith 119).

While J. Anthony Blair, Cara Finnegan, Valerie Smith, and David Birdsell and Leo Groarke discuss the enthymeme in terms of pictorial images, Clappe and Fern evoke the visual through their vivid language, or ekphrasis. Clappe often uses narrative forms of visual enthymemes to highlight incongruities, what Kenneth Burke calls "perspective by incongruity" or "verbal 'atom cracking.'" As Burke explains, "[A] word belongs by custom to a certain category—and by rational planning you wrench it loose and metaphorically apply it to a different category" (308). According to Sonja Foss, "juxtaposing incongruities" is a "strategy of disruption" used by feminists to "disrupt established hegemonies and, in turn, create new ways of thinking, acting, and being" (147). Although Clappe was not a feminist per se, she frequently practiced the tactic of juxtaposing incongruities in her narratives to encourage her audience "to think about something, consider it" (Burnyeat 92). Fern uses enthymemes in both texts that employ visual references and those that do not. Within both, however, Fern uses the enthymeme to achieve what Burnyeat states is the goal of the rhetorical form: to move audiences to "[reflect] on an issue where conclusive argument is not to be had" (93). As a result of such reflection, Fern's audiences may have been moved to accept social possibilities they would otherwise have rejected.

Clappe and Visual Enthymemes

In 1851, Louise Amelia Knapp Smith Clappe (1819–1906) and her physician husband journeyed to isolated gold-mining camps in the Feather River region of Northern California. During her fifteen months there, Clappe captured her

experience in twenty-three letters. Penned under the narrative persona of Dame
Shirley, Clappe's letters vividly detail her life among the miners. Clappe's letters
are written to her sister in Massachusetts, but, as scholars have argued, they
were clearly intended for a broader audience (Smith-Baranzini xx, xxvii). California historians have spoken highly of Clappe's *The Shirley Letters*, originally published serially in 1854 and 1855 in *The Pioneer; or California Monthly Magazine*,
California's earliest literary magazine.

In her letters, Clappe often combines visual enthymemes with juxtaposition
to highlight incongruities, which typically are indirect critiques. One notable
juxtaposition occurs in her first letter, dated 13 September 1851. Here, Clappe
explains that her husband, Fayette, was advised to go to the mountains after
"suffering for an entire year, with fever and ague, bilious, remittent, and inter-
mittent fevers—this delightful list, varied by an occasional attack of jaundice . . ."
(2). The juxtaposition of Clappe's description of the various forms of fever her
husband has suffered with the words "delightful list" and "an occasional attack
of jaundice" bring levity to what otherwise would be considered a serious health
condition. Clappe follows this statement by noting that a friend, who had just
returned from the locale, encouraged her husband to go to Rich Bar, which, at
the time, had only one doctor and a thousand miners: "and as [Fayette's] strength
increased, he might find in that vicinity a favorable opening for the practice of
his profession, which, as the health of his purse was almost as feeble as that of
his body, was not a bad idea" (2). Here the juxtaposition of "health of his purse"
with the feebleness of his body brings about another humorous opposition, or
zeugma, with the audience taking pleasure in making this unlikely connection.
Furthermore, the comment about her husband's "purse" is slipped in at the end
of a series of suggestions apparently from the friend, providing the appearance
of a logical conclusion rather than a direct critique by Clappe.

Clappe's narratives frequently draw on enthymemes to underscore incongruities in the mining camps, including gender-norm violations relating to her
husband's and the miners' use and decoration of domestic space. For instance,
Clappe draws on a visual enthymeme when describing the decor of her log cabin,
her "beautiful log palace" in Indian Bar, built by her husband and presumably a
few miner friends (52). The ceiling of the tiny cabin is lined "with white cotton
cloth, the breadths of which being sewed together only in spots, stretch grace-
fully apart in many places, giving one a bird's eye view of the shingles above"
(47). The sides are lined with "a gaudy chintz, which I consider a perfect marvel
of calico printing" (47). According to Clappe, the calico is decorated by a male
"artist" who "seems to have exhausted himself on *roses*; from the largest cabbage,
down to the tiniest Burgundy, he has arranged them in every possible variety of
wreath, garland, bouquet, and single flower" (47). The fireplace "built of stones

and mud" is constructed inside rather than outside the cabin, and the mantle-piece "is formed of a beam of wood covered with strips of tin procured from cans, upon which still remain in black hieroglyphics, the names of the different eatables which they formerly contained" (48).

The image created by Clappe's narrative suggests a visual enthymeme, which draws on her audience's nineteenth-century assumptions related to the separation of spheres during this period, with domestic space and decor being the appropriate realm of women (Welter). The image humorously depicts what happens when men, such as those at Indian Bar, attempt to inhabit and decorate domestic space. Clappe, herself, does not need to directly state this gender-sphere violation. Instead, she simply implies the violation through the detailed images and odd aesthetics that emerge, she suggests, when individuals fail to operate within their appropriate spheres.

Clappe not only uses visual enthymemes to note gender-sphere violations, she also draws on the enthymemes to illustrate other category violations, evident in her description of her "coronation dinner" that occurred soon after her arrival at Indian Bar. For instance, Clappe describes the excitement of her cook, Ned, upon finding out he will cook for Clappe: "You see, sir" said Ned, "when the queen (with Ned as with the rest of the world, 'a substitute shines brightly as a queen, until a queen be by,' and I am the only petticoated astonishment on this Bar) arrives, *she* will appreciate my culinary efforts" (52).

Here, Clappe draws attention to Ned's and others' lack of discernment concerning class and rank. In her mining community context, simply the fact the she is the only female on the Bar is enough to elevate her status. Similar to the descriptions of her cabin, Clappe's narrative uses visual enthymemes to underscore the incongruity of her coronation dinner. For instance, the cloth for the dinner table is a remnant of that lining the ceiling. In addition, Ned "had invested an unknown quantity of gold-dust in a yard of diaper," an inexpensive cotton fabric, which he divided to form their napkins. Clappe notes that Ned had apparently "ransacked the whole Bar to get viands," to supply the four-course dinner he prepared (53). The dishes include everything from oyster soup to salmon caught from the river, to mince pie and pudding (made without eggs or milk), to claret and champagne. In her letter to her sister Molly, Clappe writes that the dinner "was one of those scenes just touched with that fine and almost imperceptible *perfume* of the ludicrous . . ." (54). Although her critique is more direct in this instance, through her details and her ability to successfully draw on her audience's assumption about typical coronation dinners involving "queens," Clappe underscores the absurdity of the situation. She typically uses visual enthymemes to encourage her audience "to consider," as Burnyeat says, the incongruities and ultimately see the situation from Clappe's perspective.

Ambiguities Force Enthymemes

In contrast to work on Clappe, scholarship of the late twentieth century has not considered Fern as a woman hesitant to advocate for causes. For example, Joyce Warren argues that Fern "wrote fearlessly" on feminism (2). While other twentieth-century scholars echo Warren's observations (e.g., Adams; Schlesinger), many twenty-first-century scholars have been more measured in their assessments. For example, Fern's work has been described as "porous," allowing for various interpretations (Pettengill 67), as continually deferring to social mores (Cohen), as more transcendentalist than feminist (Moses), and as simultaneously satirical and Christian (Van Nyhuis).

Whatever their opinions, scholars agree Fern was enormously popular in the mid–nineteenth century. Born Sara Willis, Fern developed her pseudonym as she wrote for several Boston periodicals after the death of her first husband. When, in 1854, her autobiographical novel, *Ruth Hall*, and her collection of newspaper columns, *Fern Leaves from Fanny's Portfolio*, were published, Fern had achieved success—so much so that entrepreneur and publisher Robert Bonner hired her at the unheard-of rate of one hundred dollars per column for his reenvisioned newspaper, the *New York Ledger* (Warren 145).

Bonner's newspaper was unusual in two important ways. First, the paper had a circulation of four hundred thousand, which far exceeded its contemporary periodicals (Derby 200–07; Mott 359). Second, Bonner was apolitical within his choice of content. For example, during the Civil War, Bonner remained outside the debate regarding slavery and states' rights; consequently, his newspaper remained popular among Southerners who could access it and among Northerners who were unsupportive of the war. Similarly, when he published a piece arguing for one social or political position, Bonner frequently juxtaposed the article with another presenting an opposing view. These two unique characteristics meant Fern's *Ledger* articles had a huge heterogeneous audience.

Fern frequently authored columns concerning women's rights, but just as frequently she wrote about motherhood, education, poverty, fashion, travel, religion, and other issues. She was loved and hated for her often caustic tone and constant sarcasm and irony; however, she was appreciated because of what readers interpreted as her honesty. Fern herself addressed the issue of honesty, for, example, in her 11 May 1861 *Ledger* "Where Are They?," stating that she "flattered" herself as "approaching" perfect honesty. However, readers accustomed to Fern's satirical nature would not necessarily take Fern at her word that she saw herself as nearly perfect; after all, she continues in the column to mention that she hates politeness and she too can "smile and be a villain"; she longs to "drop this snake-skin of custom and astonish somebody with my long pent-up disgust," telling idiots they are idiots and asking ministers, doctors, teachers, officers of the law, shopkeepers, and others about their hypocrisies.

Fern's contradiction-filled discussion regarding her own honesty illustrates her use of enthymemes. A reader of this passage might find no definitive conclusion from the statements within her discussion. Fern is approaching perfection in the area of honesty, yet she also tells "steep fibs"—or Fern's confession of her dishonesty may be a paradoxical revelation of her honesty. Thus, this column illustrates an example of "an issue where conclusive argument is not to be had" (Burnyeat 93).

One reason conclusive arguments are so difficult to "be had" throughout Fern's texts is that she continually confuses her identity, not only via her pseudonym but also via her use of intertextuality (Gunn). Constantly, Fern reconstructs her own and others' previous discourses to construct new meanings. Thus, according to Claire C. Pettengill, Fern's intentions can be particularly difficult to discern in the twenty-first century—as also probably they were for Fern's contemporaries. For example, in her discussion regarding her honesty, Fern somewhat pretentiously quotes Hamlet's Act I monologue referencing Claudius's corruptness; however, many of her readers might not have recognized the allusion in "smile and be a villain" that aligns Fern with one of Shakespeare's villains. Thus, those who can provide the premise that Fern is like Claudius would come to different conclusions than would people who could not provide that premise. Additionally, for readers who recognize the phrase, the citation could add to the unstated premise that Fern is holding up a "snake-skin" of humbleness while she is really affected; to those who do not recognize the quotation, she appears to be merely damning the bombastic. With her mixed audience and her use of enthymemes, Fern's layers of meaning go deep with multiple interpretations constructed by the individual reader's generalizations of Fern, generalizations shaped by the different cultural norms to which the readers subscribe. With such an unstable identity and with contradictory meanings, Fern's nineteenth-century discourse seems almost postmodern. Fern can easily be quoted to prove that she perceives herself as honest or that she considers herself dishonest—or that she is a feminist or not.

Like Clappe, Fern also uses language to shape visual enthymemes. Many of Fern's columns, including some with titles reflecting their use of the visual (e.g., "A Peep of," "A View of"), are full of descriptive language characterizing scenes. Like the photograph or visual discourse described by modern scholars of visual rhetoric, these columns create images that both seem real and allow the readers to "fill in the blanks" of the argument the column is making (Finnegan 143). Fern's September 1863 "Our City Camps" is one such column, beginning with depictions of Union troops stationed throughout Manhattan. Observing the troops as "pleasant," Fern recounts seeing "a soldier stooping over his allotted bit of candle, writing in pencil a letter home. One can 'guess' what that letter is, from the honest, frank face bent over it."

Unlike an etching or photograph of the camp, this visual rhetoric allows readers to see what they want. Fern's readers knew of the horrors of war, especially since the column was published soon after the Battle of Gettysburg. Yet what readers fill in as images of the "honest, frank face" of the writing soldier vary: the soldier may be wounded, he may be rugged, he may be distraught or determined. Similarly, when Fern states that one sees "something of what 'war' means," readers can supply images of amputees, shocked country boys, or fifteen-year-olds clinging to life—or they can supply images of vigorous soldiers ready for another battle or heartless men eager for killing. Fern's dependence on readers' use of enthymemes is illustrated by her statement that one can "guess" what the soldier's letter contains: she hints, but relies on readers to make their own assumptions.

What makes Fern's use of enthymemes so powerful is her chameleon-like character, and her audience's heterogeneous interpretations of her social and political context. As the May 1861 column illustrates, Fern often contradicts herself, especially within descriptions of herself ("Where Are They"). Therefore, the heterogeneous audience is able to provide conflicting premises, allowing her to make arguments regarding subjects most other columnists would be damned for making, such as support of the women's movement.

Such possibility for conflicting enthymemes is provided to a larger degree later in the same column. After a long paragraph describing the camps mentioned above, Fern says she wishes she could ask the soldiers about the war, and from this wish, Fern launches into a discussion of limitations on women:

> Had I been a man, I should have walked straight up to them, and spoken of all these things . . . ; but being a woman, I could only use my eyes, and hold up my tormenting skirts from the damp grass and "lean confidently" on the arm of my companion. . . . I want a freer range. In plain Saxon, I want to "loaf" about, and see something besides ribbons and laces. I want to be able to go out evenings alone. . . . I know you are ready to ask, "Wouldn't I like to be drafted?" Yes, sir.   ("Our City Camps")

But Fern then switches course, confiding, "Between you and me, . . . I want to be taken care of, and petted as a woman, and yet have the independence and freedom of a man." Thus, this column, moving from a paragraph considering "a pretty camp" to one explicitly stating that she wants "freer range" than she has as a woman, forces Fern's readers to consider a feminist perspective. However, labeling Fern a feminist may be premature since she is also explicit that she wants "to be taken care of, and petted." She creates two diametrically opposed images: a woman without skirts, ribbons, or lace who is willing to be drafted, and a woman leaning on a man's arm, petted and cared for. The two images contradict each other and require the audience to provide enthymemes to resolve the incongruity regarding Fern's identity. Readers sympathetic to the women's suffrage movement construct the enthymeme that Fern supports a change in the status of women. On the other hand, other readers can conclude that Fern is merely a woman who likes to joke. Within Fern's texts exists what Valerie Smith describes of the visual enthymeme: various probable meanings accommodating different audiences.

Unlike many frequently cited nineteenth-century feminists, neither Clappe nor Fern led social movements or called women to action to fight for various women's causes. However, as we illustrate, initially publishing their work in periodicals, they asked their audiences to consider perspectives the audiences might otherwise have never considered. Clappe used words to create visual enthymemes that connected with common assumptions but that typically reflected her perspective, and Fern forced her readers to "fill in the blanks" within her texts (Finnegan 143). In so doing, these women's indirect rhetoric used enthymemes to disrupt the status quo in two ways outlined by Foss: by juxtaposing incongruities and cultivating ambiguity.

As we have seen, Clappe eschews direct claims and instead juxtaposes incongruities as a form of humor and critique, particularly concerning gender-norm violations. Although her juxtapositions might seem lighthearted, Clappe subtly develops in her readers the habit of recognizing these incongruities and gender assumptions, ultimately cultivating "new ways of thinking, acting, and being" (Foss 147). Fern fosters ambiguity by "deliberately construct[ing] messages that are unclear, inexact, equivocal, and open to more than one interpretation." In so doing, she "violates conventional rules of rhetoric to construct messages that are clear and transparent (and thus reductive in meaning)" (Foss 148). Fern rejects reductive notions of clarity and instead favors ambiguous communication that highlights multiple interpretations and complexity. In this way, these women challenged the hegemony while seeming to adhere to convention since their enthymemes forced readers to consider both conventional and unconventional conclusions.

In analyzing the indirect strategies of Clappe and Fern, we suggest the significant connection between enthymemes and marginalized rhetors. Given that these women, similar to many marginalized rhetors of the period, were constrained in what they could say directly or clearly, they needed to use common assumptions to help make their points, or at least to bring their points into consideration. Though we examine only the writing of Clappe and Fern, other women and marginalized rhetors may have used similar strategies as a way to have their ideas considered, ideas that often involved critique and complexity. Recent scholarship on indirection suggests this to be the case (e.g., Barrett-Fox, "Posthuman Feminism" and "Rhetorics"; Bordelon; Kates). We encourage scholars to analyze such indirect methods in the writing of other women and marginalized rhetors, which will demonstrate the prevalence and significance of such rhetorical practices.

Works Cited

Adams, Florence Bannard. *Fanny Fern; or, A Pair of Flaming Shoes*. Hermitage, 1966.

Aden, Roger C. "The Enthymeme as Postmodern Argument Form: Condensed, Mediated Argument Then and Now." *Argumentation and Advocacy*, vol. 31, no. 2, 1994, pp. 54–63.

Aristotle. *On Rhetoric: A Theory of Civic Discourse*. Translated by George A. Kennedy, 2nd ed., Oxford UP, 2007.

Barrett-Fox, Jason. "Posthuman Feminism and the Rhetoric of Silent Cinema: Distributed Agency, Ontic Media, and the Possibility of a Networked Historiography." *Quarterly Journal of Speech*, vol. 102, no. 3, 2016, pp. 245–63.

———. "Rhetorics of Indirection, Indiscretion, Insurrection: The 'Feminine Style' of Anita Loos, 1912–1925." *JAC*, vol. 32, nos. 1–2, 2012, pp. 221–49.

Beetham, Margaret. "Towards a Theory of the Periodical as a Publishing Genre." *Investigating Victorian Journalism*, edited by Laurel Brake et al., St. Martin's, 1990, pp. 19–32.

Birdsell, David S., and Leo Groarke. "Outlines of a Theory of Visual Argument." *Argumentation and Advocacy*, vol. 43, nos. 3–4, 2007, pp. 103–13.

Blair, J. Anthony. "The Possibility and Actuality of Visual Arguments." *Argumentation and Advocacy*, vol. 33, no. 1, 1996, pp. 23–39.

Bordelon, Suzanne. "Louise Clappe and *The Shirley Letters*: Indirect Feminist Rhetoric and the Contradictions of Domestic Space." *College English*, vol. 80, no. 5, 2018, pp. 449–70.

Burke, Kenneth. *Attitudes toward History*. 3rd ed., U of California P, 1984.

Burnyeat, M. F. "Enthymeme: Aristotle on the Rationality of Rhetoric." *Essays on Aristotle's* Rhetoric, edited by A. Oksenberg Rorty, U California P, 1996, pp. 88–115.

Campbell, Karlyn Kohrs. *Man Cannot Speak for Her: A Critical Study of Early Feminist Rhetoric*. Praeger/Greenwood, 1989. 2 vols.

Clappe, Louise Amelia Knapp Smith. *The Shirley Letters: From the California Mines, 1851–1852*. Edited by Marlene Smith-Baranzini, Heyday Books, 1998.

Cohen, Daniel A. "Winnie Woodfern Comes Out in Print: Story-Paper Authorship and Protolesbian Self-representation in Antebellum America." *Journal of the History of Sexuality*, vol. 21, no. 3, Sept. 2012, pp. 367–408, doi:10.7560/JHS21301.

Derby, James Cephas. *Fifty Years among Authors, Books and Publishers*. 1884. Forgotten Books, 2017.

Enoch, Jessica. *Refiguring Rhetorical Education: Women Teaching African American, Native American, and Chicano/a Students, 1865–1911*. Southern Illinois UP, 2008.

Fern, Fanny. "Our City Camps." *New York Ledger*, vol. 29, no. 30, 1863, p. 8.

———. "Where Are They?" *New York Ledger*, vol. 17, no. 10, 1861, p. 8.

Finnegan, Cara A. "The Naturalistic Enthymeme and Visual Argument: Photographic Representation in the 'Skull Controversy.'" *Argumentation and Advocacy*, vol. 37, no. 3, 2001, pp. 133–49.

Foss, Sonja K. *Rhetorical Criticism: Exploration and Practice*. 5th ed, Waveland Press, 2018.

Fredal, James. "The Enthymizing of Lysias." *Advances in the History of Rhetoric*, vol. 20, no. 1, 2017, pp. 1–27.

Gage, John. "An Adequate Epistemology for Composition: Classical and Modern Perspectives." *Essays on Classical Rhetoric and Modern Discourse*, edited by Robert Connors et al., Southern Illinois UP, 1984, pp. 152–69.

Grimaldi, William M. A., SJ. *Aristotle, Rhetoric I: A Commentary*. Fordham UP, 1980.

———. *Studies in the Philosophy of Aristotle's Rhetoric*. Franz Steiner Verlag, 1972.

Gunn, Robert. "'How I Look': Fanny Fern and the Strategy of Pseudonymity." *Legacy*, vol. 27, no. 1, 2010, pp. 23–42. *Project Muse*, muse.jhu.edu/article/381343.

Harper, Nancy. "An Analytical Description of Aristotle's Enthymeme." *Central States Speech Journal*, vol. 24, no. 4, 1973, pp. 304–09.

Johnson, Nan. *Gender and Rhetorical Space in American Life, 1866–1910*. Southern Illinois UP, 2002.

Kates, Susan. "Subversive Feminism: The Politics of Correctness in Mary Augusta Jordan's *Correct Writing and Speaking* (1904)." *College Composition and Communication*, vol. 48, no. 4, Dec. 1997, pp. 501–17. *JSTOR*, www.jstor.org/stable/358455.

Madden, Edward H. "The Enthymeme: Crossroads of Logic, Rhetoric, and Metaphysics." *Philosophical Review*, vol. 61, no. 3, July 1952, pp. 368–76.

Mattingly, Carol, editor. *Water Drops from Women Writers: A Temperance Reader*. Southern Illinois UP, 2001.

———. *Well-Tempered Women: Nineteenth-Century Temperance Rhetoric*. Southern Illinois UP, 1998.

McBurney, James H. "The Place of the Enthymeme in Rhetorical Theory." *Speech Monographs*, vol. 3, no. 1, 1936, pp. 49–74.

Moses, Carole. "The Domestic Transcendentalism of Fanny Fern." *Texas Studies in Literature and Language*, vol. 50, no. 1, Spring 2008, pp. 90–119. *JSTOR*, www.jstor.org/stable/40755501.

Mott, Frank Luther. *A History of American Magazines*. Vol. 2, Harvard UP, 1938.

Mountford, Roxanne. *The Gendered Pulpit: Preaching in American Protestant Spaces*. Southern Illinois UP, 2003.

Pettengill, Claire C. "Against Novels: Fanny Fern's Newspaper Fictions and the Reform of Print Culture." *American Periodicals*, vol. 6, 1996, pp. 61–91. *JSTOR*, www.jstor .org/stable/20771086.

Poster, Carol. "A Historicist Recontextualization of the Enthymeme." *Rhetoric Society Quarterly*, vol. 22, no. 2, Spring 1992, pp. 1–24. *JSTOR*, www.jstor.org/stable/ 3885383.

Schlesinger, Elizabeth Bancroft. "Fanny Fern: Our Grandmother's Mentor." *New-York Historical Society Quarterly*, vol. 38, no. 4, 1954, pp. 501–19. *New York Heritage Digital Collections*, cdm16694.contentdm.oclc.org/digital/collection/NYHSR01/ id/9859/rec/12.

Scott, Anne Firor. "The Ever Widening Circle: The Diffusion of Feminist Values from the Troy Female Seminary, 1822–1872." *History of Education Quarterly*, vol. 19, no. 1, Spring 1979, pp. 3–25.

Smith, Susan Belasco. "Serialization and the Nature of *Uncle Tom's Cabin*." *Periodical Literature in Nineteenth-Century America*, edited by Kenneth M. Price and Smith, UP of Virginia, 1995, pp. 69–89.

Smith, Valerie J. "Aristotle's Classical Enthymeme and the Visual Argumentation of the Twenty-First Century." *Argumentation and Advocacy*, vol. 43, nos. 3–4, 2007, pp. 114–23.

Smith-Baranzini, M. "Introduction." Clappe, pp. ix–xxxv.

Van Nyhuis, Alison. "The American Dream and American Greed in Fanny Fern's *Ruth Hall*: Sentimental and Satirical Christian Discourse in the Popular Domestic Tale." *Analyses/Rereadings/Theories Journal*, vol. 3, no. 2, 2015, pp. 59–69.

Walker, Jeffrey. *Rhetoric and Poetics in Antiquity*. Oxford UP, 2000.

Warren, Joyce W. *Fanny Fern: An Independent Woman*. Rutgers UP, 1994.

Welter, Barbara. "The Cult of True Womanhood: 1820–1860." *American Quarterly*, vol. 18, no. 2, part 1, Summer 1966, pp. 151–74.

Young, Stephanie L. "Running like a Man, Sitting like a Girl: Visual Enthymeme and the Case of Caster Semenya." *Women's Studies in Communication*, vol. 38, no. 3, 2015, pp. 331–50, doi:10.1080/07491409.2015.1046623.

Listening for Contemporary Echoes

"Who Says What Is ... Always Tells a Story": White Supremacist Rhetoric, Then and Now

Patricia Roberts-Miller

When I was in graduate school, there were vehement arguments about periodization in both history and literary studies—how precise we should be in our categories, how we should define and date existing categories, and whether we should abandon the terms entirely. While the argument continues, for the most part the consensus seems to be that history is one damn thing after another, but that, for purposes of a coherent scholarly narrative, course arrangement, and textbook organization, we have to have stories that start at some historical moment and stop at another. Historical periods are admittedly social constructs, generated by consensus, but they can be useful ones.

There are certain events that seem to be such moments of rupture that there is no need to defend beginning or ending with them, such as the American Civil War. American history and American literature survey courses (and textbooks) often use the Civil War as the end point (in both the sense of telos and the sense of stopping point) of one course. Triumphalist narratives of American history make the war a moment that ended slavery and transformed the United States. But muddled arguments as to why we should keep memorials and statues to the Confederacy (it wasn't about slavery; it was about slavery but slavery wasn't really so bad; by removing physical encomia to traitors we are denying our history; the Confederates weren't traitors but should be honored and respected for their stance; and so on) show that we are still, as a nation, clear that the war was some kind of break, but we aren't clear on what broke. We are still fighting about that war; I want to suggest that the way we fight about that war is the way we are still fighting it, and the fight has to do with two kinds of rhetoric: our cultural evasion of antebellum rhetoric, and especially how antebellum rhetoric is represented in popular discussions of that rhetoric (such as in textbooks).

I have experienced many disturbing aspects of working on proslavery rhetoric, and one story epitomizes them. In January 1840, *The Liberator* published the "Narrative of James Curry, a Fugitive Slave." Curry says:

One time, a slave, about forty years old, had bought some wheat of some of the neighbor's boys, which he had stolen from his master. My master's son-in-law, Lewis Morgan, had told this slave, that, if he would buy all the wheat he could of the neighbor's slaves, he would take it of him and give him a profit. One overseer detected him with it on the way to Lewis Morgan's and he confessed how he came by it. The overseer then took him to the master, and they went with him to the plantation where the wheat belonged, and as they passed through the field where we were at work, they took me and another slave along with them.

Curry then describes a horrific beating that went on for hours, during which the master would require the poor slave to confess the truth, and then to deny it, and then back again, and so on, beating the slave from truth to lie, and from a lie to the truth, over and over again. This is violence used to terrorize a person into a demonstration of submission to a narrative that both parties know to be a lie. The point wasn't the truth—the point was the slaver's demonstration that he could, through violence, control discourse. That the confession was a lie was the point.

We are, as we have been for two hundred years, arguing about the place of racism in American history and identity. And that argument is still one of a terrorist beating the oppressed into acknowledging the power of the terrorist to insist on a narrative both of them know to be false. We still have people who will drive cars into protestors, doxx critics, plant bombs, shoot up churches or synagogues. Racists have to worry that they might be criticized at work, perhaps even fired, but critics of Nazis and KKK members have to worry about being bombed.

In four ways, the incident Curry describes epitomizes the difficulties in writing about proslavery rhetoric and ideology, and all them are still ways that entangle us in the traps set in antebellum discourses about race and slavery: proslavery strategic misnaming; violence as a method for determining the limits of the political imaginary; the political force of the irrational rhetor; and consensus as cultural agreement to a lie.

Proslavery Violence and Terms

In the United States, justifications of oppression and extermination are always Daniel-in-the-lions'-den stories, or sometimes David-against-Goliath, in which the oppressing group is justified because it is the real victim here, the plucky individual (or small group) against whom huge animalistic entities are arrayed. These justifications are narratives of in-group victimization, with archetypal characters (the Slave, the Slaveholder, the Slaver, the Abolitionist, the Liberal, the Intellectual, the Feminist) who have as much depth as characters in a mediocre melodrama.

Despite their shallowness, in the antebellum era these stereotypes did important political work. It was striking to me while I was working on the proslavery rhetoric how much that rhetoric relied on claims which the people making the claims knew to be false—that slaveholders kept families together, people of African descent were not troubled by malaria, whipping was rare. And the people making the claims knew that their audience knew the claims were false. And they knew their audience knew they knew. I was tremendously puzzled by the function of these bizarre performances. For instance, the economy of slavery was a brutally pragmatic one, with so much focus on profit that people were willing to engage in extraordinary cruelty, such as selling children as young as three days. The profit in slavery was in the buying and selling of people—it was not, as was admitted at the time, the most cost-effective way to get efficient labor—and people who called themselves planters, slaveholders, masters, or slaveowners engaged in the maximization of profit through treating fellow humans as cattle (see especially Berry; Fogel and Engermann).

At the same time, though, much of proslavery rhetoric (and even literature) insisted on an absolute distinction between the benevolent, paternalistic master who did his best to encourage marriage and protect families, and the slaver who made a living buying and selling people. That (entirely false) distinction was maintained linguistically, with the term *master* (or *slaveholder* or *slaveowner*) used for people whose financial situation came largely (but not entirely) from their buying and selling of people, and those who were explicitly and openly merchants of people—a distinction without a difference, except politically. Distinguishing between *slaveholders* (a term that implies they held on to people) and *slavers* did important political work, especially as the names were reinforced in identities: a character in a novel or a play might be a slaver (evil), a benevolent master (good), "white trash" who rented slaves (bad), but never more than one of these characters. And if a master was not benevolent (as in *Uncle Tom's Cabin*), then the book was political, and abolitionist. But books with seemingly good masters (such as *The Yemassee*, by W. G. Simms; *Nick of the Woods*, by Robert Montgomery Bird; or, more recently, *Gone with the Wind*, by Margaret Mitchell) were not characterized as political and proslavery. The proslavery language, by becoming normalized, could seem apolitical simply because it seemed foundational to discourse. The language in which we talk about slavery—slaves (rather than enslaved people; slaveholders versus slavers)—still does that simultaneous depoliticizing and proslavery rhetorical work.

The terms on which proslavery rhetors insisted, and on which many people still insist, promote the violence inherent to slavery. The terms are violent, and defenders of slavery threaten coercion and violence to insist those are still the terms we use.

Violence as a Method for Determining the Limits of the Political Imaginary

In the antebellum era, calling a slaver paternalistic was strategic misnaming. And the use of that proslavery vocabulary was enforced through violence or the threat of violence. Kenneth Greenberg's analysis of the incident Curry describes emphasizes the terroristic violence as the agent and object of persuasion:

> The master was not at all interested in a thorough investigation. Here we do not see torture used as a mode of interrogation intended to produce true statements. The slave understood this perfectly. No part of his confession ever mentioned that the real instigator of the theft was Lewis Morgan, the brother-in-law of his master. . . . The conversation between master and slave was not about the cause of the theft but about who controlled the truth. By whipping the slave from truth to lie and lie to truth, the master was telling both the slave and himself that truth was a matter of assertion and force—and the master had it in his control.   (41)

This was violence as rhetoric—one of the available means of persuasion—that, paradoxically, relied on believing something was true and knowing it wasn't. This isn't persuasion in support of a claim about theft, but in support of a claim about power.

That's the claim made by the late-1950s (post–*Brown v. Board of Education*) monuments, memorials, and changes to state flags. Putting up statues of George Washington, Jefferson Davis, or Nathan Bedford Forrest wasn't about honoring what did happen in the antebellum era—such monuments weren't any more an attempt to be accurate about the Civil War than was Curry's master trying to get to an accurate understanding of the theft. Those statues and memorials weren't even really about the Civil War; they were a demonstration of power—the power to insist on the cultural submission to a lie. We can't argue about things we can't talk about. Thus, limiting what people can talk about limits what policies we can imagine.

Insisting on a South that honored slavers, terrorists, and traitors limited what policies could be imagined in that moment. It still does, and it's intended to. Ultimately, the statues are a kind of doublethink: their existence demonstrates the power of white supremacists to insist on their version of reality, one which they know and deny to be false. The South wasn't, and isn't, univocally proslavery or opposed to civil rights or interested in honoring the Confederacy; the South always had a large population of enslaved and free African Americans, critics of slavery, critics of the war, critics of segregation. The statues and memorials are about insisting on that false narrative, as a false narrative that cannot be disputed—not without a threat of violence.

The Political Force of the Irrational Rhetor

Elsewhere, I've argued that proslavery antebellum rhetoric was deliberately and performatively irrational; rational and pragmatic policy deliberation was eschewed as unmanly (Roberts-Miller, esp. 18–45). That's interesting.

Initially, the rhetoric seemed to me to be another instance of the doublethink process described above: rhetors insisting that South Carolina had been victorious in the nullification crisis (it hadn't—South Carolina had been trounced), that African Americans thrived in the swamps (their death rate was horrifying), that slaves were happy until and unless abolitionists got to them. But this performative irrationality was more complicated than that, and the irrationality had two parts: first, active refusal to discuss the major issues in pragmatic terms (such as the long-term viability of an economy based in slaving); second, active advocacy of impractical solutions to problems.

To take the second first: the antebellum South was mired in a political discourse of honor, in which what Quintilian famously called the good man speaking well was a man speaking with passionate commitment and loyalty to his state, his party, the South, his college, his stance on manure. This puzzled me, and led me down the trail of scholarship on demagoguery. Hyperbole, passionate commitment to an impractical policy, the willingness to stake everything on one throw, all the things that should make a reasonable polity decide not to entrust deliberative responsibilities in a person became the norm for an ideal political figure. That stance is a rejection of plausible estimations of policy outcomes in favor of belief in the in-group—it's about the will.

At the time I was writing about proslavery rhetoric, I thought this stance was because the antebellum South saw every instance of political determination as bargaining. In a bargaining situation being irrational can be an asset. Bargaining is about threats and promises; proslavery rhetors had no carrots to offer, but they could make threats. And they did. They threatened secession; they threatened lynchings, duels, beatings; they threatened abandoning the party if they didn't get their way. If you are bargaining, and the bargaining is public, and you need to get elected by an electorate that wants to see foaming-at-the-mouth performances of in-group loyalty, then, to get reelected, you need to show that you are refusing to compromise, that you will do anything other than compromise.

What you need is an adult in the room who will hold you back. Much of ante-bellum proslavery discourse strikes me as that dude in the bar who screams *Hold me back!* He doesn't want a fight; he wants to look as though he's willing to fight. He wants someone to hold him back. In that kind of culture, people get elected on the basis of who is more willing to engage in pure commitment to the most extreme position. And democratic deliberation starts swirling in the bowl.

Under those circumstances, if you set the standard of in-group loyalty as hanging abolitionists, seceding, banning abortion while not doing anything that would reduce abortion, building a wall to symbolize hatred of immigrants, de-stroying the Affordable Care Act without providing another safety net for the most vulnerable—eventually that standard stops being an extreme position. Commitment to that standard is beyond policy argumentation. That your posi-tion is internally incoherent and irrational is, actually, the reason in-group mem-bers should be committed to your position.

On the first point, when I was writing about proslavery rhetoric, I assumed that taking the posture of the irrational person who refuses to compromise was a cunning decision. The slaver states did have the power, and they never acknowl-edged deliberation as a way to make decisions (even locally)—the slaver states were all about bargaining. Oddly enough, being thoroughly irrational, if you've got violence behind you, is not a bad way to get your way.

Being irrational is disastrous for public deliberation, since coming to good decisions means acknowledging ways your position might be wrong. But if you don't think of public discourse as deliberation and you just see it as a way to get your way, then taking the stance of someone who will burn down the building if he doesn't get his way can be effective—in the short term.

Secession over slavery was an irrational act. Even when the slaver states did secede, doing so was an unwise and unnecessary move; Lincoln had won because the Democrats were split over how rabidly proslavery they should be, and pro-slavery forces could simply have blocked all his legislation and waited Lincoln out. But, having threatened secession for years if a president was elected who didn't support slavery (perhaps as a bluff), the Democrats could hardly back down without making it clear that they had been bluffing. Perhaps the Demo-crats sincerely believed they would win the war—since rational deliberation was prohibited, they certainly hadn't deliberated pragmatically about their chances. Being irrationally committed to impractical policies means, bluff or not, other interlocutors are unwilling to call the bluff. If a culture frames public delibera-tion as a choice among which figures are most irrationally committed to the in-group political agenda, that culture does not make good policy choices.

In an authoritarian culture, and slaver culture was very authoritarian, there is a tendency to put faith in individuals rather than in policies—to believe that a person with sufficient determination, passion for the in-group, and willingness to do anything to succeed is the ideal leader. Individuals can demonstrate they're that kind of person by saying unreasonable (but very loyal) things about the in-group and its chances pf success. Irrationality in a rhetor is likely to win short-term gains in bargaining, and this quality signifies loyalty to the in-group.

Consensus as Unarguable Claims

The problem is that the irrational policies—that might have started purely as performances of in-group loyalty or bluffs intended to get short-term wins— eventually take on a reality of their own. Even if we at some point in time sort of know they aren't real policies we'd want to pursue (secession over the nullification act), the fact that no one can say so out loud means the policies can increasingly seem like ones that are actually on the table. When you have a blo- viating rhetor who lies in favor of making irrational claims and policies, many people might realize that they should take the rhetor seriously but not literally; there might, however, be members of the rhetor's base who take the rhetor both seriously and literally. Certainly, people in the South knew that slavers whipped people, sometimes to death, even as those people worked not to know it. These people knew that the enslaved hated slavery and wanted to escape, even as they claimed that slaves were happy and, paradoxically, slaves were one surly act away from race war.

Earlier, I said that that proslavery rhetors asserted claims they and their audiences knew were untrue—but this topic is a little more complicated. My ar- gument is that most proslavery rhetoric was a performance of loyalty for the in-group. Yet, as we all know, the actual and intended audience are not the same.

These instances of strategic misnaming, doublethink, and rhetorically ef- fective irrationality, I am saying, would have been experienced as rhetorically powerful claims because such instances were recognized, but not acknowledged, as misnaming, doublethink, and irrationality. But those claims were likely not realized as irrational by people with little or no experience of slavery. That is, people in non-slaver states, not especially concerned about slavery, would have no reason to doubt the hyperbolic claims about slaves being happy, slaveholders being kind, and abolitionists being troublemakers. People in non-slaver states would, most likely, have been motivated to believe those claims. Such nonsense would be a welcome conscience bromide for racists who wanted to find a rea- son not to intervene in the slave system. Those rhetorical claims could, then, be known and not known by people in some regions, and comfortably believed by people in other regions.

The historian David Blight remarked that if winners write the history, then the slaver states won the Civil War. By the mid–twentieth century, the Civil War was narrated as a fight between the Cavaliers and the Roundheads, a battle between the dreamy and impractical romantic-era South attached to the elegant but uneconomic plantation system, and the industrial, hard-headed, forward-looking capitalist Yankee North. It was a fight between brothers, a misunderstanding brought on by fanaticism. Slavery was relegated to the side.

And yet it wasn't. If southerners really believed that the Confederacy had nothing to do with slavery, then it wouldn't have made sense for southerners to protest the 1954 *Brown v. Board of Education* ruling by putting up monuments to the Confederacy, integrating the Confederate battle flag into state flags, insisting upon George Washington's enslaved people. Those statues, flags, and monuments only made sense as a protest if viewers understood them to be connecting opposition to the civil rights movement with support for the Confederacy—a connection that depends on both positions being related to a political agenda of protecting white supremacy.

The political and cultural consensus reached about the Civil War was a politically expedient agreement to lie. The lies about the Confederacy are oddly open to exposure. For years, when I've run across someone who says the Civil War was not about slavery, I've recommended they read the declarations of causes for secession. It's interesting to me that many such people refuse to do so (perhaps all of them), yet they don't change their claim. Their refusal to read disconfirming evidence shows they believe their own beliefs to be only precariously believable.

What I saw in working on the rhetoric for slavery is that proslavery rhetors did manage to achieve a cultural consensus. That consensus was, I said, not just about slavery or race—it was about public discourse: "Their goal, and their success, was to keep the realm of public discourse from being a place in which dominant points of view could be criticized. They won that battle, and they proceeded to lose the expensive and unnecessary war that that first victory ensured" (Roberts-Miller 210). I began working on the book from which the preceding quotation is drawn in 2003, as the George W. Bush administration and its loyal propaganda machine began selling the Iraq invasion. The administration worked to silence dissent through explicit and implicit threats of violence (such as calling anyone who disagreed a traitor or terrorist). The administration won that battle.

"Who Says What Is . . . Always Tells a Story"

If history is often one damn thing after another, it is also often the same damn thing over and over, or, perhaps more accurately, just the same damn thing. The nineteenth and twentieth centuries' white supremacy was rationalized as natural and ethical by grounding the notion in biology, and twenty-first-century white supremacy is rationalized as natural and ethical by being grounded in neoliberalism and the just-world hypothesis. There are differences, of course, but what is the same is that this naturalizing of strategies of oppression in the United States depoliticizes American policy discourse.

I found it difficult to describe accurately the role of proslavery rhetoric in persuasion. It was possible to see what might be called genealogies (or perhaps ecologies is a better metaphor) of claims: Thomas Dew seems to have made some new arguments that very clearly spread as far as speeches in Congress and letters to the editor. People did change their claims—one can see the rise of the slavery-as-necessary-evil topos, and then its displacement by the slavery-as-positive-good topos. A lynching of gamblers transmogrified into the exposure of a massive conspiracy, a horror story that lumbered around proslavery public spheres for years; the nonexistent flooding of pamphlets in 1835 was yet another urban legend that, like a vanishing hitchhiker, still turns up in scholarly discussions of the slave debate.

After World War II, when the Allies decided to do the unprecedented and put the instigators of war on trial, many of the accused made that odd appeal to relativism that authoritarians so often make: all that the accused had done wrong was lose the war; had they won the war, many of them said, no one would criticize them. And they lied. They lied about what they'd done, what they knew, when they knew it. Some of the lies were ones repeated to them over and over—about Aryan superiority, the Judeo-Bolshevik threat, the stab in the back. Hannah Arendt, a Jew who escaped but saw many people she had admired (and even once loved) embrace Nazism, saw people lie and be lied to, and wondered about truth—about how you tell history in the face of so much lying.

In her powerful essay "Truth in Politics," Arendt put forward her most elegant description of her conception of thought as representative:

> I form an opinion by considering a given issue from different viewpoints, by making present to my mind the standpoints of those who are absent; that is, I represent them. This process of representation does not blindly adopt the actual views of those who stand somewhere else, and hence look upon the world from a different perspective; this is a question neither of empathy, as though I tried to be or feel like somebody else, nor of counting noses and joining a majority, but of being and thinking in my own identity where actually I am not. The more people's standpoints I have present in my mind while I am pondering a given issue, and the better I can imagine how I would feel and think if I were in their place, the stronger will be my capacity for representative thinking and the more valid my final conclusions, my opinion. (54)

This is political deliberation as an admittedly imperfect act of imagination: we cannot know what others think or feel, but we can try to imagine it. And the more stories we have from others, the more valid our opinions. Thus, the point of silencing dissent is that it is silencing those other stories—monuments to proslavery forces insist on a single story about the history of the United States, on a single perspective about slavery, racism, and identity.

In that same essay, Arendt says, "Who says what is—'legoi ta conte'—always tells a story, and in this story the particular facts lose their contingency and acquire some humanly comprehensible meaning" (84). Rosine Kelz explains this passage:

> The endurance of a human world, and thus a lasting public sphere, depends on a web of stories that describe shared reality. The importance of stories to grasp reality confirms the non-sovereignty of the political actor. It is not the actor herself but the spectator who can see and express her identity by telling a story about her.   (28)

A web of stories that creates a shared reality in which the daily lived experience, the ancestral memories, of people are silenced through violence—that is what Confederate monuments are monuments to.

Proslavery rhetoric was a series of claims that could be asserted but not argued, a political agenda that the advocates of this rhetoric strove to keep out of the realm of policy argumentation. Slavery was naturalized and depoliticized. The most powerful move of antislavery rhetors was repoliticizing discourse about slavery, and they did so through narratives heavy in details of the facts of their lives. Stories politicize politics. But if the stories we tell have clear endings—if we pretend that the Civil War ended the issues that caused the war—then we depoliticize the issues still facing us.

Works Cited

Arendt, Hannah. "Truth and Politics." *The New Yorker*, 25 Feb. 1967, pp. 49–88.

Berry, Dainah. *The Price for Their Pound of Flesh: The Value of the Enslaved from the Womb to the Grave in the Building of a Nation*. Beacon Press, 2017.

Blight, David. *Race and Reunion: The Civil War in American Memory*. Harvard UP, 2001.

Curry, James. "Narrative of James Curry, a Fugitive Slave." *The Liberator*, 10 Jan. 1840. *Documenting the American South*, U of North Carolina, Chapel Hill, 2003, docsouth .unc.edu/neh/curry/curry.html.

Dew, Thomas. *Review of the Debate (on the Abolition of Slavery) in the Virginia Legislature, 1831–32*. Washington, DC, 1833. Extract from *The Political Register*, vol. 2, no. 25, 16 Oct. 1833.

Fogel, Robert William, and Stanley L. Engermann. *Time on the Cross: The Economics of Negro Slavery*. W. W. Norton, 1995.

Greenberg, Kenneth S. *Honor and Slavery: Lies, Duels, Noses, Masks, Dressing as a Woman, Gifts, Strangers, Humanitarianism, Death, Slave Rebellions, the Proslavery Argument, Baseball, Hunting, and Gambling in the Old South.* Princeton UP, 1996.

Kelz, Rosine. *The Non-sovereign Self, Responsibility, and Otherness: Hannah Arendt, Judith Butler, and Stanley Cavell on Moral Philosophy and Political Agency.* Palgrave Macmillan, 2016.

Roberts-Miller, Patricia. *Fanatical Schemes: Proslavery Rhetoric and the Tragedy of Consensus.* U of Alabama P, 2009.

The Rhetorical Legacies of Chinese Exclusion: Appeals, Protests, and Becoming Chinese American

Morris Young

> I appeal not for myself. I plead not for the strong, but I plead for the those of my fellows who are weak and defenceless, that the people of this great nation may be merciful, that they would repent of their sins, that they may be willing to be just, and force the law-makers to do right.
>
> —Wong Chin Foo

When the United States established the Chinese Exclusion Act of 1882, it was the first of several immigration acts to target Chinese (extended in 1884, 1888, 1892, and 1904),[1] and was followed by laws to curb immigration from all Asian countries and prohibit the naturalization of Asian-born immigrants as citizens of the United States (the Immigration Acts of 1917 and 1924). As a result, the United States saw for the first time restrictive immigration legislation on the basis of race, national origin, and social class, legislation that also set the foundation for the racialization of immigration policy in the United States (Lee 24–25). Anti-Asian discourse circulated widely in California and beyond as Chinese made their way to America looking for economic opportunity during the gold rush and the building of the First Transcontinental Railroad. Increasingly seen as a threat to a way of life built on an ideology of Western expansion (Lee 26–27), the Chinese became a trope for Americans to explain declining economic conditions, to serve as evidence of social decay, and to spur an increasing sense of nationalism during a period of global expansion for the United States. Metaphors of exclusion, such as walls, borders, zones, and gates, flowed through the popular American imagination to reinforce beliefs about who belonged and who did not.[2]

In particular, the Geary Act of 1892, sponsored by the United States Representative Thomas J. Geary of California, sparked outrage in the Chinese community in the United States for two primary reasons: the act extended for ten years the original Chinese Exclusion Act of 1882, which restricted the entry of Chinese laborers and denied naturalization to people of Chinese descent; and it added new requirements, including the registration of each Chinese resident and the submission of photo identification and a sworn witness statement by one white American to testify to each Chinese resident's identity. The Geary Act also stipulated a penalty of hard labor and then deportation if a Chinese resident was found to be in the country illegally. These increased restrictions, regulations, and penalties were met by a range of rhetorical activity by the Chinese—including public speeches, essays, and editorials in journals and newspapers—and by community organizing—including the attempted creation of a new political party (Lee 6; Seligman; K. Wong).[3]

Here I focus on the rhetorical activity of the Chinese in America during this period (1882–1900) as they attempted to address restrictive and discriminatory laws and policies, expose exploitation, and respond to racism. I also consider how anti-Chinese discourse from the nineteenth century provides a foundation for rhetorics of exclusion in the twenty-first century, repeating the deployment of metaphors of exclusion such as walls and borders that appeal to nativist, nationalist, and populist audiences by reinforcing constructions of illegal immigrants as alien others. While there are several important Supreme Court cases that took up petitions by Chinese who challenged their status under these laws (e.g., *Yick Wo v. Hopkins*; *United States v. Wong Kim Ark*),[4] I turn to a specific figure, Wong Chin Foo, who was naturalized as a citizen of the United States before the first Exclusion Act, and who took a very public stance not only in arguing against the discriminatory treatment of Chinese in America but also in making an effort to create a dialogue about Chinese culture and its relation to America. Focusing on the *Appeal of the Chinese Equal Rights League to the People of the United States for Equality of Manhood*, I examine how Wong illustrates what LuMing Mao and I theorize as a "rhetoric of becoming" for Asian Americans "that participates in this generative process, yielding an identity that is Asian American and producing a transformative effect that is always occasioned by use" (Mao and Young, "Introduction" 5). In this sense, Wong's participation in a national discourse about the Chinese in America through a variety of essays, speeches, and pamphlets allows him to assert rhetorical inclusion, requiring America to acknowledge his presence and to imagine the Chinese body as part of the national body of the United States. However, I want to also invoke the *temporal turn* as recently theorized in Asian American rhetorical studies (Monberg et al.; Mao), which seeks to disrupt linear historical narratives by placing past and present in dialogue with each other, and to make visible the recursivity of history as a field of rhetorical production. In this sense, the exigency of exclusion and the response by Wong in the nineteenth century exists as a continuous event which flows through our present and back to the past again, marked by a discourse about immigration predicated on fear, presented as an existential threat to America, and amplified by metaphors of exclusion.

Reimagining Nineteenth-Century American Rhetoric

While the impulse in rhetorical historiography has been to historicize to understand the contexts and conditions for rhetorical activity, to recover and recuperate so as to make visible figures and materials that have been hidden in the narrative of history, and to be revisionist as we reinterpret long-standing historical narratives while identifying increasingly complex and complicated actors and forces, scholars have still been inclined to read these histories as linear narratives that provide contexts and texture for understanding our present day (Gold). However, Mao has offered his own method for rereading rhetorical activity in history that attempts to disrupt this linearity and to foreground the recursivity of rhetoric, perhaps especially in engaging in ideologies that continue to structure institutions and practices. In examining an 1885 letter by Saum Song Bo, who wrote to protest the solicitation of contributions from Chinese for the Bartholdi Pedestal Fund to benefit the construction of the Statue of Liberty, Mao argues:

> While we surely can read the present through the lens of the past, what about the other way around? What about looking back from our current vantage point to understand our past and to prepare for what might become our future? Better still, what about bringing both past and present into simultaneous view, into a dialectical tacking that enables us to move between past and present, between different cultural and rhetorical contexts, and to move into a process of becoming over being?

Additionally, as Terese Guinsatao Monberg, K. Hyoejin Yoon, and Jennifer Sano-Franchini suggest, the project of Asian American rhetoric continues "to subvert the notion of linear history as it weaves across temporalities, bringing together memory from separate historical moments" (17). This attention to becoming over being and the role of rhetoric in this process provides an important analytical framework and is foundational to the definition that Mao and I propose:

> We define Asian American rhetoric as the systematic, effective use and development by Asian Americans of symbolic resources, including this new American language, in social, cultural, and political contexts. Because these contexts are regularly imbued with highly asymmetrical relations of power, such rhetoric creates a space for Asian Americans where they can resist social and economic injustice and reassert their discursive agency and authority in the dominant culture.   (Mao and Young, "Introduction" 3)

In investigating the rhetoric of Wong Chin Foo, I turn to the social and political conditions that shape the discursive field in which Chinese attempted to gain entry as they marshalled their rhetorical resources to respond to rhetorics of exclusion. In particular, I focus on the symbolic resources and rhetorical moves that these Chinese developed and drew upon to appeal to the moral compass of a broader American audience while also agitating the moral outrage of their fellow Chinese in America to mobilize for action. What we see in both the exigency and the response is the deployment of Asian American rhetorics that have spanned across space and time.

The Exigency of Exclusion

While Chinese laborers began to enter the United States in more significant numbers beginning in 1849 to seek their fortune in the gold rush and to lay track through the Sierra Nevada mountain range for the Central Pacific Railroad Company, much of this work had been completed or had dried up by the late 1860s (Salyer 7; Kim 47). The Chinese started to move into the cities and other areas of California and began to enter different industries, including manufacturing, agriculture, and fishing, which began to put pressure on the labor market as the Chinese competed with white Americans during an unstable economic period (Salyer 7–9). California began to enact a series of anti-Chinese laws, and eventually congressional representatives from California and other western states were able to sponsor and pass federal legislation that changed the nature of immigration policy in the United States by excluding and regulating people of Chinese descent who were trying to gain entry to the United States or move between the United States and China.

K. Scott Wong argues that two factors, economics and race, were used as the primary arguments as to why the Chinese constituted such a threat. The Chinese were seen as an economic threat by organized labor, politicians, journalists, and even American missionaries because the Chinese often accepted lower wages than needed to sustain an American family (though immigration and anti-miscegenation laws often prevented the Chinese from bringing or having families) and engaged in economic or pay arrangements with employers or mutual aid societies that were seen as indentured or contract labor, "coolieism," or de facto slavery (K. Wong 5). But perhaps even more damning was the belief by many Americans that the Chinese, by their nature and culture, were unassimilable, biologically inferior, and immoral and unclean (K. Wong 5). This combination of perceived economic threat and broader cultural threat contributed to an emerging yellow peril discourse, which John Kuo Wei Tchen and Dylan Yeats argue is built on

> fear as a recurrent pattern, as a tradition, [and] becomes part of the politics of a people. It becomes ideology and faith. And like all of what we live with every day, we take such patterns for granted. Recurrent fear becomes naturalized like the bogeyman, imminent injury, or death. Yellow Peril fears become systemic, a part of the political culture of daily life. (16)

Exclusion, then, becomes an ideological and rhetorical act meant not only to restrict certain types of bodies on the basis of race, national origin, social class, and culture but also to deny the humanity and legibility of these bodies as part of the social world. Erika Lee describes Chinese exclusion "as an institution that produced and reinforced a system of racial hierarchy in immigration law, a process that both immigrants and immigration officials shaped, and a site of unequal power relations and resistance" (7). We can also think of Chinese exclusion as a rhetorical strategy, fitting into the concept of rhetorical exclusion developed by John Sanchez, Mary Stuckey, and Richard Morris and described as "a rhetorical strategy that defines those who seek inclusion in the larger polity on their own terms as inherently destructive of that polity, questioning the motives of those who challenge governmental power, and a presumption that those involved in such challenges are inherently guilty of crimes against the polity" (28).

In the Chinese Exclusion Acts, we see how state power regulates bodies by legislating exclusion, denying the legitimacy of one's status, and creating bureaucratic barriers that literally detain bodies through denying habeas corpus and interrogating identities. But, undergirding these institutionalized enactments of state power, we see a broader cultural discourse of white supremacy that provides justification for acting against subjects simply on the basis of difference. However, in turn, we see responses by Asian Americans who challenge state power in multiple ways, whether in attempting to disrupt legal norms on their own terms, or in creating innovative forms to address specific exigencies and conditions, or in making rhetorical appeals on the basis of moral certainty and belief in the ideals of America.

Responding to Exclusion: Wong Chin Foo and Rhetorical Appeals

While the Page Act of 1875 and the first Chinese Exclusion Act, in 1882, established the first immigration barriers for Chinese attempting to enter the United States, these acts did not necessarily have an immediate effect on Chinese professionals, merchants, students, or elites who were already in the United States or who had the documentation that allowed them to leave and enter the country without much trouble (Lee 41). However, this relative protection did not mean that the Chinese did not respond to the increasingly hostile climate in the United States, especially for those who began to imagine America as home but who were now aliens ineligible for naturalization as citizens, or for those who were naturalized before 1882 or born in the United States, or for those who simply saw hypocrisy and injustice in the laws of a land that purported to welcome all and provide opportunity to anyone willing to earn it.

In response to these policies and laws, Chinese immigrants began to use legal challenges through the federal courts to both clarify and affirm the rights of those classes of Chinese (merchants and their families, returning laborers, and American citizens of Chinese descent and their families) to enter and reenter the country (Lee 123). Additionally, cases were brought to clarify and affirm the citizenship status of Americans of Chinese descent. In perhaps the most famous case, Wong Kim Ark, born in San Francisco in 1873 to two Chinese nationals, was denied reentry because the government argued that he could not be a citizen of the United States if his parents were subjects of the Chinese emperor. Citing the Fourteenth Amendment, the court decided six to two that Wong was indeed a citizen: "all persons born or naturalized in the United States, and subject to the jurisdiction thereof, are citizens of the United States" (Kim 92–93). However, we see in later citizenship cases that hinged on eligibility for naturalization a decidedly different attitude over who could be a citizen on the basis of racial identification (Coulson).

More broadly, however, we also begin to see Chinese enter into the public sphere as they participated in public debates about Chinese exclusion through a range of rhetorical activities, including the publication of short fiction, editorials in newspapers, and essays in the leading literary magazines of the time (Wang; K. Wong 4; E. Wong 18). As K. Scott Wong argues, these writers often developed a specific rhetorical strategy to persuade audiences that they assumed would be open to certain logical appeals, asserting ethical arguments about the value and standing of Chinese culture while also showing a willingness to draw distinctions between different classes of Chinese immigrants, or to draw distinctions between Chinese and other immigrants from other parts of the world who were facing their own forms of discrimination in the immigration policies and social attitudes of the United States (4). These moves illustrate a sense of rhetorical awareness—to tack between arguments, commonplaces, and topics to construct an identity but to also allow for maneuverability in responding to counterarguments.

I turn to the figure of Wong Chin Foo to illustrate how he enacts these moves in appealing to the moral compass of Americans in seeking to remedy the injustice of the 1892 Geary Act. Wong is a particularly exciting case to illustrate nineteenth-century Chinese American rhetoric since he has existed primarily in his public writings, which range from columns and essays about Chinese culture and customs, editorial and opinion pieces that address political and social issues affecting the Chinese in the United States, and news coverage of his various speeches and activities as he crossed the Midwest and East Coast to promote his various interests.[5] Wong has been characterized as an "unheralded civil rights activist and a pioneer of the Chinese Americanization movement" (Zhang 41);

as "one of the most eloquent nineteenth-century Chinese authors to publish in English," including essays in leading magazines such as *The Atlantic Monthly*, *Harper's Monthly*, and *North American Review* (Hsu, "Wong Chin Foo's Periodical Writing" 83); and as a "muckraker, a rabble-rouser, and a consummate smartass" (Hsiao 68). He is credited, too, as the first person to use the term *Chinese American* when he founded his weekly newspaper, the *Chinese American*, in 1883 (Seligman xii; Zhang 49). But as Hsuan Hsu argues, "Wong Chin Foo made a name for himself by creating and manipulating controversy in the periodical press" ("Connecticut Yankee").

Wong was born in Shandong Province, China, in 1847, was educated by American missionaries, and was then baptized and immigrated to the United States in 1867. He attended the Columbian College Preparatory School (Washington, DC) and Lewisburg Academy (Pennsylvania) before returning to China, where he married and engaged in government service. However, Wong was accused of revolutionary activity in China and fled back to America, was naturalized as a citizen of the United States in 1874 under false pretenses,[6] and began his career as a journalist and lecturer. In 1887, Wong published an essay, "Why Am I a Heathen?," in the *North American Review*, which had solicited essays from well-known religious figures for a series of "Why Am I?" pieces to explain and defend their personal belief systems (Seligman 137). Although he was actually a baptized Christian, Wong took the opportunity to ironically reverse the derogatory term *heathen*, or non-Christian barbarian, to not only make a full-throated critique of Christianity but also tie his analysis to larger issues of Western culture and American capitalism that he saw as operating to devalue Chinese civilization. This essay played off of the circulating anti-Chinese discourse of the time that pointed to the "heathen Chinee" as an existential threat to Americans, when in fact, for Wong, *heathen* exemplified the qualities of reason and morality that distinguished the Chinese from whites.[7]

After the Geary Act became law on 5 May 1892, Wong was part of a group of "leading English-speaking Chinese of the Eastern States" who met on 1 September 1892 in New York to "devise means to do what they could in the way of pleading to the people of this great Republic to deliver their fellow countrymen from this outrageous persecution" (*Appeal* 1). At this gathering of more than one hundred "English-speaking Chinese merchants and professional men," Sam Ping Lee, a merchant from Philadelphia, was installed as president of the Chinese Equal Rights League, and Wong was named secretary. At a meeting on 22 September that attracted "over a thousand prominent Americans and nearly two hundred Chinese merchants," a resolution was presented, adopted unanimously, and concluded: "We, the citizens of the United States, in mass meeting assembled, do hereby resolve and declare that the said bill is monstrous, inhuman and unconstitutional; and we hereby pledge ourselves to the support of that protest against the said bill which has been entered by the Chinese Equal Rights League of New York City" (*Appeal* 1–2).

This resolution and an appeal to the American people were included in a pamphlet, *Appeal of the Chinese Equal Rights League to the People of the United States for Equality of Manhood*, published by the league in New York and sold for ten cents. While the authorship is attributed collectively to the Chinese Equal Rights League, Scott Seligman argues that, based on the style of writing, similarity to his other writings, and proficiency in written English, Wong Chin Foo was most certainly the author of the appeal (201).

The appeal does interesting work as a rhetorical document. Organized in four parts, each section has a specific rhetorical function in making the case to the American people to support the cause of protesting the Geary Act. The first section, titled "The New and Monstrous Anti-Chinese Bill: The Geary Registration Act," establishes the exigency for the formation of the Chinese Equal Rights League, describes the league's origin, and introduces the resolution. The second section is the "Appeal of the League to the People of the United States," where the league makes its case for why the Geary Act is objectionable and should be repealed. The third section provides the text of "The Chinese Registration Act" (The Geary Act) and samples of the required registration documentation, with the brief qualifying introduction: "The following obnoxious and outrageous bill was passed the 52d American Congress, May 5, 1892; the same is to be enforced upon the fifth day of May, 1893." Finally, the fourth section concludes with "Speeches of Senator Sherman and Representative Hitt," who spoke out against the bill and in support of the Chinese upon the passage of the act.

I focus on the second section, "Appeal of the League to the People of the United States," to unpack the rhetorical appeals and moves made that both illustrate the rhetorical strategies deployed by the Chinese (K. Wong 4) and lay the foundation for Chinese American "becoming" that also challenges the founding ideas that structure the becoming of the United States. In this second section, which is just a brief two pages, Wong begins by greeting the American people, addressing them as "Friends of Humanity" (2). In the first two paragraphs Wong begins to position the Chinese in America as people "who have adopted this country and customs in the main" and as residents of the United States who "claim a common manhood with all nationalities, and believe we should have that manhood recognized according to the principles of common humanity, and American freedom" (2). Here Wong attempts to close the difference between Chinese and Americans, to disrupt the claims of anti-Chinese sentiments that race and culture create an unassimilability that cannot be overcome. What Wong also does here is to claim a common humanity, to claim that perhaps despite difference in religion—remember the debate between Christianity and heathenism that Wong participated in—the Chinese are indeed as human as the Americans.

As Wong moves from his tactic of identification through liberal individualism (Clark and Halloran), he makes a specific appeal in the next paragraph to the character of the American people and their "humane, liberty-loving sentiment . . . who are lovers of equal rights and even-handed justice, a people from who sprung such illustrious characters as Washington, Jefferson, Clay, Sumner, lastly, Lincoln, the citizen of the world, the friend of humanity, and the champion of freedom" (*Appeal* 2–3). Wong also invokes military leaders—Sherman, Sheridan, Logan, and Grant—whose "deeds of valor in the cause of freedom are to be seen in the grand march of American development" (3). He identifies a "misguided element who have suffered their feelings to control reason, encouraging a prejudice fiendish in its nature and purpose" against the Chinese, whom he characterizes as "industrious, law-abiding, and honest" (3). Wong closes this paragraph by again invoking a claim of belonging and dismissing the idea that the Chinese are a burden on the American people: "We have and are still paying our portion of government taxation, thereby assisting in supporting the Government, and thereby sharing an equal part in support of the Nation" (3).

In the next three paragraphs, Wong begins each with "We": "We love and admire the Government. . ."; "We, therefore, appeal for an equal chance in the race for life in this our adopted home. . . "; and "We feel keenly the disgrace unjustly and maliciously heaped upon us by a cruel Congress" (3). The use of *we* here does two things. First, it continues the strategy of identification that shapes the opening of the formal appeal, as it reinforces a sense of collective we, people who are all residents (even citizens) of America, people who believe in equality and justice, people who all contribute to the support of the nation by following the rule of law and paying taxes. But the *we* here also functions as a plea from someone in a lower position of power (Fahnestock 290), from a people who, while having claimed equal standing across a number of categories, are still subject to the regulation and disciplining that have been created to target a specific class on the basis of race. Wong also attempts to create a sense of moral outrage by describing the Chinese, for whom he has been making the case as fully human and, if not legal citizens, certainly worthy of citizenship, as subject to inhumane treatment: "respectable Chinese residents should be made to wear a badge of disgrace" or "tagged and branded as a whole lot of cattle for slaughter" or as "objects of scorn and public ridicule" (3).

In the final two paragraphs, Wong concludes by making a final appeal on the basis of identification—"Our interest is here, because our homes, our families and our all [sic] are here. America is our home through long residence"—but then he engages in an act of disidentification by drawing a distinction between

"Chinese immigration as well as Irish, Italian, and other immigration" and "law-abiding citizens in the United States" (3). Here we see where social class and distinction among the Chinese play a role in differentiating the good immigrant from the bad immigrant. Wong ends the appeal with this, perhaps surprising, statement: "Treat us as men, and we will do our duty as men, and we will aid you to stop this obnoxious evil that threatens the welfare of this Republic. We do not want any more Chinese here any more than you do. The scarcer the Chinese here the better would be our conditions among you" (3).

When convenient, Wong and the Chinese Equal Rights League are willing to draw on moral outrage, especially on the basis of racial discrimination and unfair and unjust application of the law. And yet they are also willing to make claims of identification that appeal to social class and assimilability—that is, to claim common ground and citizenship on the basis of legibility to white and privileged Americans. This seeming contradiction raises troubling questions about how we might imagine a rhetoric of becoming for Chinese Americans in this period and beyond. Does a rhetoric of becoming for Asian Americans necessarily mean drawing a distinction between what we might understand as one identity in relation to another? That is, does becoming Chinese American for Wong mean assimilation on the basis of social class, culture, and community? Is the remedy to the injury that Wong and his fellow league members seek a remedy that should not extend to those Chinese immigrants who are perhaps most vulnerable?

Rhetorical Legacies

In examining the rhetorical activity of Wong during the Chinese exclusion period, what we see are remarkable similarities in the circulating discourses that structure discussions about immigration then and now. The invocations from lawmakers and Americans more broadly of economic threat, cultural unassimilability, disease and unfitness, and sexual predation in response to a growing presence of Chinese during the latter half of the nineteenth century are not so unlike what we hear in twenty-first-century America, as fears of unchecked borders, terrorist infiltration, and economic decline are used to shape political and cultural discourses that create an increasing climate of hostility, fear, and violence, with little room to unpack these metaphors and the ideologies that inform them.

Mao's strategy of "bringing both past and present into simultaneous view, into a dialectical tacking that enables us to move between past and present" has afforded me with the opportunity to think about what the recovery of Wong provides and how this might inform a broader understanding of Asian American rhetoric across time and space. First, Wong is a remarkable figure for the range of rhetorical activity he produced, from dozens (hundreds?) of articles and essays in a range of genres, to speeches and other public performances, to the creation of newspapers that helped to establish an Asian American print culture (Hsu, "Wong Chin Foo's Periodical Writing" 85). Wong also lived as a public figure, gaining a celebrity that marked him perhaps as the most well-known person of Asian descent in the late nineteenth century (Hsu, "Wong Chin Foo's Periodical Writing" 83). What Wong's public presence demonstrates is that indeed there was an Asian American rhetorical culture present in nineteenth-century America that encompassed the different areas of American culture broadly, from short pieces introducing Chinese culture to a reading public, to speeches and essays arguing for the benefits of heathenism in contrast to Christianity, to entrances into the political sphere to make claims on rights and responsibilities for the Chinese in America. These are areas far beyond the legal cases that have often been seen as documentation for Asian Americans seeking both legal and rhetorical inclusion.

However, this examination of Wong also brings into focus the complexity, even contradictions, of Asian American rhetoric. While conceptualizing Asian American rhetoric as a rhetoric of becoming highlights the flexibility and rhetoricity of identity formation and draws attention to rhetorical activity in the context of exigency, contexts, and practices, we are also faced, in confronting those cases, with rhetorics of becoming that may create uncomfortable and difficult realities. On one hand, Wong's appeal to the American people draws on and extolls a sense of liberal democracy and American ideals, seeking justice and equal protection under the law. On the other, he is willing to draw a distinction between those Chinese who have long-standing residency and commonalities with Americans and those Chinese immigrants who may only reinforce the worst stereotypes assigned to them by anti-Chinese Americans. Here we see echoes of modern-day affirmative action debates that position one group of Asian Americans who seek equal and fair treatment in admissions on the basis of qualifications against others, often other people of color, whom Asian Americans see as having advantage on the basis of identity. But in both cases we see how privilege and power are institutionalized and structured to keep the marginalized on the margins and the centers of power in place. Ultimately, Wong's arguments did not change the attitudes about the Chinese or other Asians, and, in fact, more substantial immigration policies were enacted against Asians, and only repealed in 1943 when China became an ally against Japan during World War II.

What then is the rhetorical legacy of Chinese exclusion? We see that in the exigency of exclusion there were those like Wong and his compatriots in the Chinese Equal Rights League who were willing to take a public stand, to produce and distribute arguments, and to begin to articulate a sense of belonging and becoming—that is, a belonging to America and a becoming Chinese American—that was rhetorical and not simply ontological. And yet what we also see in the legacy of Chinese exclusion and the resulting rhetorical activity is that rhetoric that challenges structures and ideologies of power (and in this case, white supremacy) may still be subject to those ideologies. For Wong and league members to create distance from other Chinese simply reinforces the ideologies of white supremacy, and Wong's appeals to and identification with Americans leaves in place structures that still maintain privilege and power and deny access and remedy to those seeking justice and equality. And sadly, this is a legacy that is even more stark in the present, as we see the further institutionalization of power and privilege being reinstated in the creation, application, and interpretation of our laws in the United States today.

Notes

1. Before the more expansive 1882 act, the Page Act of 1875 restricted immigration of Chinese who were contract laborers (in effect forced or indentured labor), Chinese women who were identified as immoral and suspected to be engaged in prostitution, and others who were undesirable or unfit for entry (Kim 53; Lee 30).

2. For example, see the political cartoons of Thomas Nast, whose work appeared in *Harper's Weekly* and included cartoons with titles such as "Throwing Down the Ladder by Which They Rose" (23 July 1870), "The Chinese Question" (18 February 1871), and "E Pluribus Unum (Except the Chinese)" (1 April 1882). Nast captured the prevailing anti-Chinese sentiment in the United States, critiqued American hypocrisy, and revealed the injustice experienced by the Chinese (Walfred).

3. See Seligman (241) on the establishment of the American Liberty Party.

4. See Kim.

5. In his critical biography, *The First Chinese American: The Remarkable Life of Wong Chin Foo*, Scott D. Seligman provides a comprehensive catalog of Wong's writings along with sociohistorical context for many of the pieces.

6. Wong filed a Declaration of Intention to apply for naturalization in Grand Rapids, Michigan, on 3 April 1874 and was declared a citizen of the United States the same day. However, Wong did not meet the criteria for naturalization. He had filed his petition under the exemption for minors but in doing so gave false information about his date of birth, date of arrival in the United States, and continued residency in the United States. See Seligman (44–45).

7. Brett Harte's satirical poem "The Heathen Chinee" was often misread and misused by anti-Chinese advocates who saw the poem as propaganda for their cause rather than as a critique of anti-Chinese sentiment. See Romeo.

Works Cited

Appeal of the Chinese Equal Rights League to the People of the United States for Equality of Manhood. Chinese Equal Rights League, 1893.

Chan, Sucheng, and K. Scott Wong, editors. *Claiming America: Constructing Chinese American Identities during the Exclusion Era*. Temple UP, 1998.

Clark, Gregory, and S. Michael Halloran. "Introduction: Transformations of Public Discourse in Nineteenth-Century America." *Oratorical Culture in Nineteenth-Century America: Transformations in the Theory and Practice of Rhetoric*, edited by Clark and Halloran, Southern Illinois UP, 1993, pp. 1–26.

Coulson, Doug. *Race, Nation, and Refuge: The Rhetoric of Race in Asian American Citizenship Cases*. State U of New York P, 2017.

Fahnestock, Jeanne. *Rhetorical Style: The Uses of Language in Persuasion*. Oxford UP, 2011.

Gold, David. "Remapping Revisionist Historiography." *College Composition and Communication*, vol. 64, no. 1, Sept. 2012, pp. 15–34.

Hsiao, Andrew. "100 Years of Hell-Raising." *The Village Voice*, 23 June 1998, pp. 67–70.

Hsu, Hsuan. "A Connecticut Yankee in the Court of Wu Chih Tien: Mark Twain and Wong Chin Foo." *Commonplace*, vol. 11, no. 1, Oct. 2010, commonplace.online/article/connecticut-yankee-court-wu-chih-tien/.

———. "Wong Chin Foo's Periodical Writing and Chinese Exclusion." *Genre*, vol. 39, no. 3, Sept. 2006, pp. 83–105.

Kim, Hyung-chan. *A Legal History of Asian Americans, 1790–1990*. Greenwood Press, 1994.

Lee, Erika. *At America's Gates: Chinese Immigration during the Exclusion Era, 1882–1943*. U of North Carolina P, 2003.

Mao, LuMing. "In the Present and Importantly Present: Enacting a Temporal Turn for Asian American Rhetoric." *Enculturation*, vol. 27, Dec. 2018, enculturation.net/in-the-present-and-importantly-present.

Mao, LuMing, and Morris Young. "Introduction: Performing Asian American Rhetoric into the American Imaginary." Mao and Young, pp. 1–22.

———, editors. *Representations: Doing Asian American Rhetoric*. Utah State UP, 2008.

Monberg, Terese Guinsatao, et al. "Introduction: Re/articulations of History, Re/visions of Community." *Building a Community, Having a Home: A History of the Conference on College Composition and Communication Asian/Asian American Caucus*, edited by Jennifer Sano-Franchini et al., Parlor Press, 2017, pp. 1–30.

Romeo, Jacqueline. "Irony Lost: Bret Harte's Heathen Chinee and the Popularization of the Comic Coolie as Trickster in Frontier Melodrama." *Theatre History Studies*, vol. 26, 2006, pp. 108–36.

Salyer, Lucy E. *Laws Harsh as Tigers: Chinese Immigrants and the Shaping of Modern Immigration Law*. U of North Carolina P, 1995.

Sanchez, John, et al. "Rhetorical Exclusion: The Government's Case against American Indian Activists, AIM, and Leonard Peltier." *American Indian Culture and Research Journal*, vol. 23, no. 2, 1999, pp. 27–52.

Seligman, Scott D. *The First Chinese American: The Remarkable Life of Wong Chin Foo.* Hong Kong UP, 2013.

Tchen, John Kuo Wei, and Dylan Yeats, editors. *Yellow Peril! An Archive of Anti-Asian Fear.* Verso, 2014.

Walfred, Michelle. "Overview." *Illustrating Chinese Exclusion*, 2014, thomasnast cartoons.com. Accessed 22 Mar. 2020.

Wang, Bo. "Rereading Sui Sin Far: A Rhetoric of Defiance." Mao and Young, pp. 244–65.

Wong, Edlie L. *Racial Reconstruction: Black Inclusion, Chinese Exclusion, and the Fictions of Citizenship.* New York UP, 2015.

Wong, K. Scott. "Cultural Defenders and Brokers: Chinese Responses to the Anti-Chinese Movement." Chan and Wong, pp. 3–40.

Wong Chin Foo. "Why Am I a Heathen?" *North American Review*, vol. 145, no. 369, Aug. 1887, pp. 169–79.

Zhang, Quingsong. "The Origins of the Chinese Americanization Movement: Wong Chin Foo and the Chinese Equal Rights League." Chan and Wong, pp. 41–63.

Cultivating Civic Interfaith Activism: Rhetorical Education at Andover Settlement House

Michael-John DePalma

> Diverse societies that achieve pluralism have a strong civic fabric—one that can withstand the provocations of extremists and haters—and bridge their social capital in ways that can take on some of the toughest problems. But bridges don't fall from the sky or rise from the ground; people build them.
>
> —Eboo Patel

In "Toward a Field of Interfaith Studies," Eboo Patel defines an interfaith leader as "someone who has the framework, knowledge base, and skill set needed to help individuals and communities who orient around religion differently in civil society and politics build mutual respect, positive relationships, and a commitment to the common good" (40). In using the phrase *civic interfaith rhetorical activism*, I am extending Patel's notion of interfaith leadership by foregrounding forms of rhetorical engagement that seek to forge collaborations among citizens and communities who orient differently around religion to address pressing public concerns. Civic interfaith rhetorical activists aim to strengthen religiously diverse democracies by cultivating rhetorical identifications and mutual respect among citizens—dynamics that enable cooperation in civic activist work. This proactive rhetorical engagement with religious diversity allows citizens and communities to mobilize the wisdom of particular religious traditions to contribute to the making of a more just world. Civic interfaith activists do not set aside religious commitments in political and civic concerns but instead draw together the insights and practices of diverse faith traditions to respond to complex social problems—many of which are connected directly or implicitly to contested (religious) values. Rather than treating religion as primarily a personal moral code, civic interfaith rhetorical activists hold that individual morality and a commitment to just social conditions are inseparable, thus emphasizing the personal and public dimensions of religion for citizens. Given the ever-increasing religious diversity of our present moment, an exigent project for scholars of rhetoric is fostering rhetorical dispositions and skills needed to "engage religious diversity in a way that promotes peace, stability, and cooperation" (Patel 38).

An important site of nineteenth-century rhetorical activism created in response to a version of this pressing concern was Andover Settlement House

(Andover House hereafter) in Boston's South End—one of the first university settlement houses in the United States. Founded by William Jewett Tucker, professor of sacred rhetoric at Andover Theological Seminary, the goal of Andover House was to institutionalize cooperative moral action among citizens of various religious groups and classes to improve social conditions and human relations. Tucker created Andover House to train rhetors to engage with religious diversity in ways that promoted mutual respect, harmonious relationships, and a commitment to the common good. As Tucker witnessed major shifts in the religious landscape, widening economic disparities, rising tensions over labor conditions, and increasing social disintegration, he struggled to come to terms with how to best train citizens who could respond productively to the religious, economic, cultural, and political tumult around them. A vital part of his response was the founding of Andover House.

Rhetorical Education and Civic Activism in Boston's South End

In a letter written on 9 October 1891, Tucker proposed the establishment of Andover House and described the house's aims as follows: "The house is designed to stand for the single idea of resident study and work in the neighborhood where it may be located. . . . The whole aim and motive is religious, but the method is educational rather than evangelistic. A second, though hardly secondary, object . . . will be to create a center, for those within reach, of social study, discussion, and organization" (Woods and Kennedy 125). A few months later, in January 1892, Tucker and Robert A. Woods, one of Tucker's students at Andover Seminary, opened the doors of Boston's first settlement house.

For both Tucker and Woods, the activist work at Andover House was guided in large part by their Christian motives. The initial impetus for establishing Andover House was Tucker and Woods' belief that "the times demanded a larger and closer application of this idea or principle—the simple Christianity of Christ, to the great problems of life as they confront us in our cities" (Bevington 130). Tucker and Woods, in other words, viewed Andover House as a means of enacting Social Christianity in their local context. They understood settlement house work as embodying God's call to love thy neighbor. However, love of neighbor, for Tucker and Woods, did not mean attending only to spiritual needs or cultivating harmonious interpersonal relationships—activities commonly emphasized in orthodox Protestant Christian circles during the nineteenth century. Love of neighbor also meant attending to the full range of concerns—material, economic, political, environmental, emotional, industrial, health, moral, educational—that affected the condition of human lives and relationships. A core message of what Tucker and Woods referred to as Social Christianity was that Christians had not only an obligation to save souls but also to redeem the brokenness and evil in society by promoting radical reforms in politics, business, and culture.

In response to the radical shifts in the religious and cultural landscape of the late nineteenth century, Andover House was created as a site of rhetorical activism in which residents could research, write about, and work to address community concerns in Boston's South End. Studying the living conditions and social tensions in South Boston through immersion was one of the most important parts of the work at Andover House. Residents researched the living environments, working conditions, social dynamics, and religious tensions in the surrounding community and published their studies to promote the philosophy of the settlement house movement and create "a more responsible public attitude toward industrial districts" (Woods and Kennedy 128). In a periodical published five months after the opening of Andover House, the purposes of Andover House are described as follows:

> To this House, as a centre, graduates of colleges, seminaries, ministers of any creed or church, and other fit persons may come to study what has come to be known as the problem of the city, to study it in all its phases—its social, sanitary, economic, industrial, educational, moral, and religious aspects. And not only come to study the problem but by personal service to touch it with helpful and healing hands whenever it is possible.   (Bevington 130)

Along with gaining a deep understanding of and connections to the community through field research and interviews, a central purpose for workers at Andover House was civic advocacy work that aimed to improve the living and working conditions for citizens of Boston's South End. This activism took several forms: crafting policy arguments, partnering with local community organizations, delivering public presentations of research findings, preaching sermons, and publishing research and policy arguments that reached a national audience. The workers at Andover House used their research, community knowledge, and expertise in rhetoric to engage city officials, politicians, neighborhood clubs, district improvement associations, and religious groups to advocate for good in their communities. Andover House residents worked for the enforcement of building codes, to improve neighborhood sanitation services, and to create playground spaces for children and families. Andover House workers also partnered with public schools in South Boston by connecting with teachers, organizing conferences, mentoring neighborhood children, visiting schools, and establishing credentials for industrial education. Another dimension of their work was partnering with trade union leaders to struggle for improved labor conditions and address high rates of unemployment.

In addition to actively addressing injustice locally, the residents at Andover House were committed to promoting the idea of the settlement house nationally. One primary way that Andover House residents worked to persuade educators and community leaders of the need for and value of settlement house work was through written publications (books, journal articles, news stories). For example, shortly following Andover House's founding, Woods produced a pioneering study of the social conditions in Boston entitled *The City Wilderness: A Settlement Study*. In that study, Woods articulates the dimensions of Andover House's mission and work.

Over nearly three decades, Woods and other residents at Andover House continued to publish research conducted in Boston, advocacy reports for addressing local concerns, and essays, edited volumes, and books that made strong cases for reform. Tucker, Woods, and other residents also gave lectures across the nation to promote reform and to stem the tide of social disintegration among classes and religious sects. Andover House thus functioned as a vital site of rhetorical activism, as well as a training ground for cultivating dispositions and expertise that would enable residents to mobilize their religious motives to work toward civic, economic, social, and spiritual good in their neighborhood and across the United States.

Four Guiding Principles of Rhetorical Activism at Andover House

Key to Andover House's vitality as a site of rhetorical activism is that Tucker and Woods recognized that navigating complex and often strained relations among religious communities, social classes, and ethnic groups required fostering particular dispositions in Andover House residents. To cultivate such dispositions, Tucker and Woods established four principles that guided residents' orientations to their work: personal connection, nonpartisan collaboration, consecrated activism and evangelical restraint, and bottom-up activism.

Personal Connection

The first guiding principle is that the work at Andover House was rooted in personal connections between human beings. Tucker and Woods believed that meaningful connections among citizens were essential for addressing social problems. This position is stated in an 1892 *Christian Union* entry entitled "Personality in Social Reform": "The settlements are founded upon the profound conviction that a personal contact of life with life is what is most needed in the solution of modern social problems. And the success of these enterprises is in exact proportion to the degree to which this idea has been faithfully carried out." Andover House was not to operate as a depersonalized institution with regular, preformulated programs in the way that other traditional religious and civic agencies did. Instead, workers aimed to cultivate personal relationships with residents—relationships that enabled workers to learn how best to cooperate with members of the surrounding community to address local needs. As Tucker states, "A thorough and consistent plan has been formulated, but no programme. . . . The one constant quality is personal influence, personal invention, personal sympathy and courage, the individual and united purpose to increase the moral valuation of the neighborhood" (367).

One primary channel through which the principle of personal connection was enacted by Andover House residents was a system of visiting that "sought to create a counter-current to the momentum . . . of institutionalism, by opening up technical and specialized channels that lead directly out into the neighborhood, its homes and its inter-family circles" (Woods, *Neighborhood* 170). In *The Neighborhood in Nation-Building: The Running Comment of Thirty Years at the South End House*, Woods lists twenty-one kinds of visiting that residents carried out, including general friendly visiting; nurses' neighborhood visits for infant feeding, infant care, prenatal care, and hygiene education; visiting to report kindergarten and Montessori school medical examinations and to see to follow-up treatment; visiting young offenders for the juvenile court to offer counseling and mentoring; visiting in 154 tenements; visiting factories to observe labor conditions; home and school visiting, including instruction on running a household, caring for a family, and following a family budget; and sanitary inspection on request before reporting to the Board of Health (170–71).

Nonpartisan Collaboration

A second principle that guided the work at Andover House was collaboration. The residents at Andover House partnered with every possible organization, club, agency, program, and institution that was working to improve conditions in Boston's South End. John A. Bevington articulates this principle in a description of Andover House that appeared in *Far and Near* in May of 1892; he writes: "where it is practicable we endeavor to establish friendly relations with these different movements so we may work together, helping to solve problems, to improve conditions, and give a general uplift and wider outlook to the unfortunate, the oppressed, and the degraded people of our city" (130). Residents of Andover House did not need to share the same political, religious, or philosophical views or values with local philanthropic, religious, or government agencies to partner with them. Residents and partners simply needed to share Andover House's goal of working to improve the living conditions of Boston's residents. Though there were likely many instances in which the ideas, values, and approaches of Andover House residents differed significantly from agencies with which they partnered, the common ground of seeking the betterment of the community was the central priority in the Andover House workers' hierarchy of values. As Woods asserts:

> Settlement work stands for reform by identification and cooperation. Under the settlement scheme, opposition must be reduced to the minimum. In education matters, in the labor problem, in religion, the settlement house worker is always the possibilist. His steps are guided by the desire to come into fellowship with the people who happen to be about him, not by doctrinaire standards or the abstract passion for perfection. (*Neighborhood* 67–68)

The diverse range of collaborations Woods strategically formed over his thirty years at Andover House illustrates well how the principle of nonpartisan collaboration was enacted to improve living conditions of citizens in Boston's South End. Between 1892 and 1922, Woods was a member of the Central Labor Union Relief Committee, a member of the Commission on Municipal Baths and Gymnasiums, a board member for the Massachusetts Civic League, president of the South End Social Union, a member of the Public Franchise League, chairman of the Citizens' Committee to Promote a State System of Industrial Education, chairman of the board for the State Hospital for Inebriates, a member of the licensing board for the City of Boston, chairman of the Boston War Camp Community Service, chairman of the State Committee to Secure Ratification of National Prohibition, a member of the governing board for the Chamber of Commerce, president of the Wells Memorial Institute for Working Men and Women, and a member of the Mayor's Advisory Committee on Zoning. In surveying his wide-ranging partnerships, it is clear that Woods forged alliances far and wide based on one primary criterion: the organization's ability and willingness to address community concerns in Boston's South End.

Consecrated Activism and Evangelical Restraint

Another key principle that guided workers at Andover House was a commitment to activist service, compelled by deeply held religious motives, that resisted proselytizing. Workers at Andover House viewed their activism and service in Boston's South End as consecrated work. They saw themselves as called by God to love their neighbors by attending holistically to the spiritual, material, social, political, and cultural dimensions of residents' lives. This holy call to love their neighbors did not allow for exceptions. Love, whether in the form of meeting material, social, cultural, economic, or spiritual need, was to be extended freely to

all residents. Religious motives were thus mobilized in diverse ways among Andover House workers. Workers sought to enact their consecrated calling among
all those in their proximity and in whatever forms they could influence the community for good. It was this desire for influence that led workers at Andover
House to avoid making proselytizing their primary goal. The desire for social
unity among residents during a period in which religious differences were a major cause of division was another important consideration. Tucker speaks to this
point when he writes:

> The one end and aim of the House is to create a true social unity, to which all
> may contribute who have anything of value to offer. Its chief object is not that
> of churches. The religious motive informs and permeates its methods, but it
> does not seek chiefly religious results. Religion in and of itself, as illustrated in
> the various communions, will never give the social unity, in any community,
> which is now the most essential element in the change of social conditions.
> (367)

In his efforts to cultivate this kind of disposition in citizens and promote a capacious notion of Christianity and citizenship, Woods regularly delivered sermons
and lectures at local churches and seminaries. An example of Woods's efforts on
this front is a 1912 address delivered to faculty and students at Andover Theological Seminary entitled "The Recovery of the Parish." In this lecture, Woods
lays out a vision of consecrated activism for Protestant Christian churches in
particular, stating:

> I do not hesitate to say that a cultivated and developed neighborly acquaintance
> and neighborly fellowship in action, traversing all the distinctions which keep
> any kinds of human beings apart, is fundamental and indispensable to every
> man, woman, and child who would be to-day's kind of patriot and Christian.
> Nor do I hesitate to say that if the contagion of that sort of local human loy-
> alty and cooperation could lay hold of the Church—as a revival of true and
> ancient Christianity—the Church . . . would soon take the lead of the whole
> reconstruction process. . . . A new statesmanship would be developed out of the
> organized synthesis of actual experience, from neighborhood to neighborhood,
> from town to town, from city to city, of the great dominating mass of people
> of good will from all parties, from all classes, from all races and from all sects.
> (*Neighborhood* 135–36)

This principle of consecrated activism and evangelical restraint not only ani-
mated Woods's and Tucker's public lectures, it influenced the work at Andover
House in practice by serving as the central criterion used in hiring residents. In

an appendix to *The Settlement Horizon: A National Estimate* entitled "Interplay of Religious Loyalties," Woods offers settlement house leaders across the nation his take on the disposition required for settlement workers, asserting that "[t]he most resourceful settlements . . . require each new resident to give indubitable assurances that he or she is not about to use the sacred name of friendship as a subtle cloak for what amounts to propaganda. For the final test of unsectarianism lies not even in the intention of its professors, but in the actual results of their words and actions" (436).

Bottom-Up Activism

Bottom-up activism is another vital principle that guided the work at Andover House. Tucker emphasizes the "development of the neighborhood from within rather than from without" (367). Instead of imposing programs from the top down, as was often the case in community development work, Tucker believed that there was a need for cooperative and reciprocal relations among workers and residents if long-term change was to take hold in the neighborhood. Approaching the improvement of community work from the bottom up, Tucker thought, would allow residents of South Boston to be invested in reform efforts. Tucker also viewed a grassroots approach as essential because such an approach would enable Andover House to partner with community residents who had expertise, access, and community influence that workers at Andover House did not. Related to this, Tucker emphasized bottom-up activism because it was the method that best enabled residents in the community to be empowered and lead ongoing reform efforts in South Boston, independent of assistance from outside entities like Andover House. Among the chief reasons that Tucker emphasized a bottom-up approach, though, is that he believed that deep appreciation of a local context was essential for understanding the most fitting response to social problems in a particular community. It was not possible, in Tucker's view, to develop fitting courses of action to problems in a community without having intimate knowledge of the texture of those problems as they emerged in particular environments. The best means of acquiring knowledge of living conditions in particular contexts was to immerse oneself in a community and build relationships with people in that place. Immersion and close proximity to residents, Tucker thought, created opportunities for identification with members of a community and provided access to narratives of the community and its members that would otherwise remain tacit.

The formation of the South End Improvement Society is an example of bottom-up activism at Andover House. In developing relationships with citizens in Boston's South End, Andover House workers became aware of several pressing needs in the community and were motivated to help residents give voice to their concerns. Thus, the South End Improvement Society was formed as a civic organization to give community members and Andover House workers a coordinated means to collectively investigate and act upon local problems. The first public meeting of the society aimed to address sanitation issues, and community members voiced their concerns to the chief of the local sanitation division. In only a few years, the South End Improvement Society grew to several hundred members. As a result of the society's work, Woods reports, "Now there is a great improvement in the sewer system; now a marked reduction of smoke nuisance; now a gain in transit facilities; now an elaborate pace-making clean-up; now a large achievement in the repaving of streets. Best of all is an increasingly settled spirit of mutual respect and confidence among a large and increasing number of citizens" (*Neighborhood* 186).

Fostering Civic Interfaith Rhetorical Activism in the Twenty-First Century

Nearly every major study of the religious landscape indicates that America is now more religiously diverse than ever before. Given this reality, it is important for twenty-first-century citizens to develop the rhetorical capacities required to cultivate identifications across religious difference and harness diverse religious perspectives to address shared civic concerns. In this final section, I consider three ways that citizens might adapt the principles of Andover House to enact dispositions and foster expertise that enable civic interfaith rhetorical activism. Specifically, I discuss the value of cultivating relationships within communities; cultivating diverse, nonpartisan collaborations; and reconceptualizing notions of religious commitment and religious discourse.

Our current historical moment is characterized by division, partisanship, and mistrust. Far too often there is an unwillingness among citizens to listen to divergent perspectives. In cases of religious differences, there is often a heightened sense of suspicion, misunderstanding, and fear—all of which manifest in uncharitable and uninformed rhetorics about (non)religious groups and citizens. These divisions are deepened by the assumption that differences in religious belief negate the possibility of finding common ground, and such schisms are widened as religious ideas are reduced to disembodied talking points and placed in binary opposition to one another. Rather than sharing experiences and stories of how our complex beliefs have taken shape in relation to and apart from religious institutions, we see our commitments stripped down to sound bites, and citizens become caricatures. When our humanity is reduced to a series of disembodied abstractions, detached from our layered identities, motives, and passions, it is easy to treat one another as targets at which to take aim and unload. When our neighbor is construed as an ideological construct, we are quick to dispose of our humility; when qualification is dethroned by absolutism, we pay little mind to the fact that our language has consequences for other human beings. Public rhetorics that take these shapes erase the ways religion is enacted, practiced, and lived by human beings with diverse motives and orientations.

To recover dimensions of religion as it is lived by citizens and discover the ways in which religious pluralism can be a resource for addressing shared civic concerns, we might take cues from Andover House by recognizing the importance of forming substantive relationships with citizens in our communities who orient differently around religion. The work at Andover House reminds us that engaged citizenship is relational work. Engaged citizenship requires more than mass consumption of newsfeeds, debates on social media, and casting of votes during election seasons. These activities certainly matter a great deal, but if engaged citizenship is predominantly (or only) enacted in these ways, citizens persist as disembodied abstractions from opposing camps, and our knowledge remains limited to our grand narratives, redacting all that is particular, nuanced, and, above all, human. Andover House encourages us to recognize that engaged citizenship demands the intentional building of relationships within and beyond local communities. Engaged citizenship requires human beings who orient differently around religion engaging together in shared activity to address common civic concerns; it demands that we work in intimate proximity to other citizens. And it necessitates humility to recognize that knowledge of our neighbors is always partial and that particular forms of understanding are only available when we are in the company of other citizens.

For this kind of relational work to be generative, the partners we choose are vital. The principles at Andover House once again provide guidance on this front. Efforts to seek wide-ranging alliances with unlikely partners could offer a rich counter-orientation to the divisive cultural milieu in which we are situated. When reductive portrayals of (non)religious citizens are commonplace, demonization across (religious) difference is standard practice, and partisan enclaves are ever fortifying their walls, citizens might be intentional about collaborating with unlikely allies to address shared community concerns. Through such projects, citizens would have opportunities to experience firsthand how diverse forms of wisdom and expertise are brought to bear on complex civic problems. In such cases, citizens might be positioned to disassociate their collaborators from reductive, secondhand narratives and rearticulate narratives that are rooted in informed experience and knowledge. The many considerations that are required for such work would demand a whole other essay entirely, but suffice it to say for now that there is much to be gained by engaging the complexities of religion as lived and embodied practices, enacted by citizens and communities with diverse orientations.

In addition to a prioritization on human connection and nonpartisan collaboration in our efforts to engage in generative ways with religious pluralism, another lesson citizens might adapt from Andover House is the value of forwarding a capacious conception of religious commitment and expanded notions of religious discourse. When considering our conceptions of religious commitment, religious rhetoric, and the interplay between religious motives and rhetorical activism, the work at Andover House reminds us that we must take care in articulating the range of meanings these terms have across traditions and contexts. Along with this definitional work, we must be intentional about acknowledging the diversity of practices that are enacted in response to religious motives—a number of which we would conventionally limit to civic or activist. Complicating our commonplace notions of religious commitment and attending to the wide spectrum upon which religiously motivated activism is enacted might allow us, as citizens, to address two interrelated barriers to interfaith rhetorical activism: defining religious commitment solely in terms of an individual's assent to a particular set of beliefs, and conflating all forms of religious discourse with proselytizing.

In our twenty-first-century context, it is not uncommon for citizens to associate religion with a set of privately held, personal beliefs that have no place in civic engagement. It is true that adherence to particular beliefs are an important dimension of demarcating religious affiliation for individuals and communities. The problem, though, is that religious identity is too often defined solely in terms of an individual intellectual assent to particular theological doctrines or creeds. If religious commitment is defined primarily in terms of individuals' adherence to the dogmas of particular religious institutions, attention is deflected away from the practices that are vital to religious citizens' lives and communities. To view religious commitment holistically, we must thus keep in view the diverse ways in which religious beliefs and practices are interanimated, both for individuals and communities. Such a holistic view requires us to acknowledge the diverse ways that beliefs compel action and that creeds shape deeds, and to acknowledge the mutually constitutive relations between beliefs and practices.

In studying Andover House, we see a model of religious commitment that is enacted though activist practices, and we gain insight into diverse and far-reaching ways that religious motives were mobilized for activist purposes. As such, the work at Andover House provides a rich example that complicates notions of religious commitment defined primarily in terms of individual believers' intellectual assent to particular creeds. For Tucker, redeeming social relationships, living environments, and working conditions for the suffering was holy work that was integral to the spiritual redemption of human beings; and ministering holistically to redeem unfair working condition, bitter class relations, and unhealthy living quarters was a vital part of the Christian's calling. In this regard, Andover House provides citizens a rich counter-orientation for understanding the relations between religious commitment and civic interfaith rhetorical activism.

Along with broadening conceptions of religious commitment, the work of Andover House offers an example of how to expand notions of religious discourse to help citizens imagine generative links between religious motives and rhetorical activism. All too often religious motives are viewed narrowly in our public imagination as linked to one form of religious rhetoric: proselytizing. It is rare, however, to see nuanced representations that illustrate the ways religious motives animate a wide spectrum of rhetorical activist work for citizens. Because religious motives are frequently conflated with the activity of proselytizing, it is often assumed that religiously committed individuals will need to bracket their religious motives if they are going to participate productively in our pluralistic democracy. Andover House provides a productive counter-narrative to the metonymic reduction of religious rhetoric to proselytizing and the view that religious motives must be set aside in civic activist work.

The forms of civic engagement enacted at Andover House were thoroughly compelled by religious motives. Tucker, Woods, and the workers at Andover House viewed engagement in their neighborhood as sacred work. In no sense did they see a need to bracket their religious commitments to participate in community activism. What was required, though, was a capacious view of religious rhetorical practice that was not limited to evangelism. As an ordained and prominent minister and teacher of sacred rhetoric, Tucker highly valued the evangelistic dimension of the church, but Tucker's Social Christianity led him to believe that God's call to love thy neighbor and establish the kingdom of heaven on earth should be of primary import to Andover House workers. Rather than arguing for an ideal version of religion that unified, Tucker frankly pointed to the reality that religion divides some citizens even as it unifies others, and he urged Andover House residents to adopt more expansive notions of religious rhetoric. In the context of Andover House, religious rhetoric, for example, meant arguing alongside trade unions for better working conditions, educating politicians about unsafe living conditions, or constructing policies that combated food insecurity among community residents. Tucker, thus, simultaneously expanded the range of ways Christians might rhetorically enact God's call to love thy neighbor and placed evangelism as one among many activities that Christians might engage in beyond the church. In this scheme, evangelical rhetoric no longer overshadowed other forms of Christian rhetorical practice, nor was it cast as the primary way in which Christians rhetorically enacted their faith. Religious motives instead became primary forces that compelled the intellectual work, rhetorical activism, and community engagement of Andover House workers. For present-day citizens in search of productive pathways for engaging in civic interfaith rhetorical activism, Andover House provides a robust model of religious rhetoric.

The work at Andover House prompts us to reflect on the difficulty and importance of engaging in civic interfaith rhetorical activism. In rhetorical studies, scholarship on religious rhetorics has rapidly proliferated over the past two decades. This burgeoning of work on religion and rhetoric is immediately evident in looking through Paul Lynch and Matthew Miller's excellent contribution in *Present Tense*, "Twenty-Five Years of Faith in Writing: Religion and Composition, 1992–2017." While research on religion and rhetoric is growing in the field, many still see this research as niche work that has relevance only to a select few (e.g., scholars who identify with a religious tradition, teachers who work at faith-based colleges). The subfield of religion and rhetoric, in other words, is not perceived as integral to the field as a whole. These perceptions influence the dearth of engagement with religious rhetorics in the context of civic engagement and civic-minded rhetorical education. For example, in teaching writers to engage in forms of public argument, considerations regarding how best to navigate diverse religious orientations are rarely primary concerns, if they are considerations at all. In other cases, writers are taught to bracket their religious motives when engaging in public deliberation.

Rhetorical activism at Andover House serves as a reminder that religious motives cannot be easily set aside in our work as civically engaged rhetors. It may be the case that Americans are becoming increasingly secularized, but religion still remains a major force in citizens' lives in the United States and around the globe. According to a recent Pew Research Center report, more than seventy-five percent of Americans claim affiliation with a religion, and over eighty-four percent of the world's population identifies with a religious tradition ("Global Religious Landscape"). Thus, for millions of citizens, religious beliefs and values have significant implications in terms of political decision-making and civic action. That said, for citizens who aim to cultivate capacities that are essential to thoughtful civic engagement in the twenty-first century, attention to religious rhetorics ought to be a central concern.

Works Cited

Bevington, John A. "Andover Settlement House." *Far and Near*, vol. 19, May 1892, pp. 130–31.

"The Global Religious Landscape." *Pew Forum on Religion and Public Life*, Pew Research Center, 18 Dec. 2012, www.pewforum.org/2012/12/18/global-religious -landscape-exec/.

Lynch, Paul, and Matthew Miller. "Twenty-Five Years of Faith in Writing: Religion and Composition, 1992–2017." *Present Tense*, vol. 6, no. 2, Aug. 2017, www .presenttensejournal.org/volume-6/twenty-five-years-of-faith-in-writing -religion-and-composition-1992-2017/.

Patel, Eboo. "Toward a Field of Interfaith Studies." *Liberal Education*, vol. 99, no. 4, Fall 2013, pp. 38–43.

"Personality in Social Reform." *The Christian Union*, vol. 45, no. 22, 28 May 1892, p. 1041.

Tucker, William Jewett. "The Work of the Andover Settlement House in Boston." *Scribner's Magazine*, vol. 13, 1893, pp. 357–72.

Woods, Robert A., editor. *The City Wilderness: A Settlement Study*. Houghton, Mifflin, 1898.

———. *The Neighborhood in Nation-Building: The Running Comment of Thirty Years at the South End House*. Houghton, Mifflin, 1923.

———. *The Settlement Horizon: A National Estimate*. Russell Sage Foundation, 1922.

Woods, Robert A., and Albert J. Kennedy, editors. *Handbook of Settlements*. Charities Publication Committee, 1911.

The Long Nineteenth Century and the Bend toward Justice

Jacqueline Jones Royster

Let's consider the founding of the United States of America as a keystone kairotic moment. As Abraham Lincoln reflected in 1863 in the Bliss copy[1] of the Gettysburg Address, the founding of the nation was "a new birth of freedom" that set forth a grand experiment in governance—"by the people," "of the people," and "for the people." Arguably, this short speech stands as the most inspirational speech in American public discourse in terms of its success in being an easily accessible and memorable rededication of commitment to the principles on which the nation was founded. The Gettysburg Address conjures a plainly spoken historical vision, pays a dramatic tribute to the fallen, and invokes a heartfelt invitation to the people of the nation to embrace once again the nation's cause as an innovative model by which it can govern itself by the vision and will of *the people*.

To reflect on the nation's origin story with this document as a touchstone, I note that throughout the seventeenth and eighteenth centuries, the people of African origin had gathered or been gathered in North America to create lives for themselves in a new geographical space under New World conditions which were essentially unfamiliar to them and occupied by others. In simplistic terms, however, while nation-building processes proclaimed the desire for a new model, the Europeans who rose in 1776 to become the lead nation-builders functioned still within an Old World paradigm, one that we recognize today as a Westernized vision, voice, agency, and authority. Specifically infused by their European-defined sense of self, power, entitlement, and control, these nation-builders waged the Revolutionary War, the American colonies against the British Empire, and they won.

Twenty-four years later, by the cresting of the nineteenth century, the nation found itself at a pivotal moment of needing to figure out how exactly to carry forth on a *new continent* the promise of a *new nation* as Lincoln's address would later note. What was that promise? As encoded in founding documents, the promise of nation was the unequivocal declaration of the nation's dedication to *freedom, justice, and equality for all* and the setting of terms and processes *by, of, and for the people.* The quintessential task of nation-building became the implementation of these core declarations. *The people* were at the center of things as the pivot point. The construction of a new paradigm for governance necessarily became creating coherence between founding values and the laws, policies, and practices to implement and sustain them—*by, of, and for the people.*

This framework set the pace for the emergence of robust rhetorical action as the material embodiment of the work of nation-building in this experimental space, with many voices rising to the occasion to determine the arc of implementation and sustainability, the arcing away from Old World ways of thinking, being, and doing, toward different ways. The challenge was to capture and enact the spirit of innovative experimentation, not just in the exploration of New World geographies but more pointedly in the exploration of ways to negotiate uncharted conceptual territories—to conceive of what an adherence to *freedom, justice, and equality for all* might look like and how the honoring of citizen-centric governance might function.

Establishing a National Mythos

As researchers and scholars looking back from our twenty-first-century standpoints toward this era, the basic task is to examine through the lenses of specific rhetorical events the materiality of how, as a nation, we have developed and balanced public discourses in the implementation and consecration (as indicated by the Gettysburg Address) of national principles. The priority is to discern and connect core values—our dedication to truth, freedom, justice, and equality for all—to nation-building processes in a crucial test of the evolving clarity of our national dreams and thereby the evolving integrity of our national mythos.

The test can start by drawing attention to four familiar documents, beyond the Gettysburg Address, that encode and symbolize the essence of who we are as a nation: the Declaration of Independence (1776), the United States Constitution (1789), the Pledge of Allegiance (including its various versions from 1887 to 1954), and the Emma Lazarus poem "The New Colossus" (1883), which was immortalized on the base of the Statue of Liberty in 1903.

The Declaration of Independence

In 1776, the United States emerged as an independent nation when fifty-six men of elite status convened in Philadelphia to sign the Declaration of Independence on behalf of those living throughout thirteen colonies and two territories (counting East and West Florida)—that is, for people, presumably, who had a deep desire to live free of domination, oppression, and sociopolitical control. The iconic language states:

> We hold these truths to be self-evident, that all men are created equal, that they are endowed by their Creator with certain unalienable Rights, that among these are Life, Liberty and the pursuit of Happiness.—That to secure these rights, Governments are instituted among Men, deriving their just powers from the consent of the governed. . . . And for the support of this Declaration, with a firm reliance on the protection of divine Providence, we mutually pledge to each other our Lives, our Fortunes and our sacred Honor.

With this very first national document the terms of engagement were set: the equality of all, unalienable rights and freedoms, the security of these rights (or the expectation of justice), a power base derived from the consent of the people, and a pledge of life, fortune, and honor in defense of this call for change.

The United States Constitution

By declaration, the nation's founders severed the United States' colonial relations with Great Britain, ultimately by the waging of war. With a successful outcome for this revolution, the process toward independence and nationhood continued when the United States Constitution was ratified on 21 June 1788, and became effective on 4 March 1789. The Declaration of Independence and the Constitution set in motion in the eighteenth century a grand experiment in sovereignty—an innovative governance. As stated in the Constitution:

> *We the People* of the United States, in Order to form a more perfect Union, establish Justice, insure domestic Tranquility, provide for the common defence, promote the general Welfare, and secure the Blessings of Liberty to ourselves and our Posterity, do ordain and establish this Constitution for the United States of America.

The Constitution, as a governance model, was designed to support the formation of a more *perfect union* in establishing *justice, domestic tranquility, common defense, and general welfare*, and, perhaps most provocatively of all, to create a nation dedicated to *securing liberty* for its *citizens*. These concepts, however, have been in contention and have given rise to robust rhetorical engagement related to the abolition of slavery, the rights of women, the sovereignty of Native peoples, citizenship for immigrants, and more. A dramatic example of the extremities of the contending forces is that, just seven decades beyond the Constitution, the Southern states and the Northern states waged a bloody Civil War (1861–65), anchored by the question of how the nation would move forward: as a free or a slaveholding nation, as divided into two or united in one.

The Pledge of Allegiance

At war's end, the states supporting freedom and justice—presumably for all (including the formerly enslaved)—prevailed, and the second half of the nineteenth century became a definitional moment for fostering identity, patriotism, and national loyalty as our fast-growing nation began establishing itself as an innovative leader in democracy on a global stage. In 1887, the movement toward one nation took a specific turn, especially with regard to the increasing numbers of immigrants who were migrating from Europe and Asia. Immigrants entered with a range of operational values and patterns from their places of origin, and set in motion immigration issues that continue to reverberate into the twenty-first century.

The Civil War veteran Rear Admiral George Balch composed a pledge of allegiance one sentence in length but filled with allusions to ongoing but generally uninterrogated values: "We give our heads and hearts to God and our country; one country, one language, one flag!"[2] In 1892, Francis Bellamy, a Baptist minister and socialist reformer, created another pledge as part of the celebration of the four-hundredth anniversary of Christopher Columbus's arrival in North America: "I pledge allegiance to my Flag and the Republic for which it stands, one nation, indivisible, with liberty and justice for all" ("Pledge"). On two additional occasions (after World Wars I and II) when there was a perceived need to cement identity, loyalty, and allegiance, the Bellamy statement was revised, with the final revision coming ten years after World War II in the context of the perceived threat of communism. On 14 June 1954, the United States Congress officially incorporated the phrase "under God" into the statement, endorsing the revised pledge as an official national text and a definitive element of American life. The current statement reads: "I pledge allegiance to the Flag of the United States of America, and to the Republic for which it stands, one Nation under God, indivisible, with liberty and justice for all" ("Pledge"). Endowed by the pathetic appeals of founding documents, the experiences of four wars (counting the Spanish-American War in 1898), and the advocacy of political, religious, and social elites, the Pledge of Allegiance emerged. The statement provided a ritualistic mantra, a symbolic shortcut for the late nineteenth century and beyond for fostering love of country, for framing the values of *the nation*—liberty and justice for all—without referring to *equality* but with the addition of *unity* or *oneness*. To be noted, none of these terms was fully interrogated, but a touchstone has been, still, the ongoing proclamation of liberty (or freedom) and justice—*for all*.

The Emma Lazarus Poem

By the last decades of the nineteenth century, the sense of national identity and patriotism had hit a strong and powerful stride as national leaders sought to push the nation to a higher regard on the world stage. A rhetorical opportunity to escalate this momentum came in the form of a gift from the people of France to the people of the United States—the Statue of Liberty. This iconic symbol was dedicated on Liberty Island in New York Harbor on 28 October 1886, more than one hundred years after the nation's founding. It quickly came to symbolize the United States in quite material terms as a beacon of light for people around the globe who seek refuge and asylum and whose agency and possibility may be constrained variously within their places and situations of origin.

Encoding this national message is the poem inscribed on the Statue's pedestal, "The New Colossus," written in 1883 by the Jewish writer Emma Lazarus as a contribution to an exhibition of art and literary works to be auctioned to raise funds for the pedestal's construction. The poem was mounted on the pedestal in 1903 and has proclaimed since then a welcoming invitation to all entering New York Harbor and, symbolically, across other borders as well: "Give me your tired, / Your poor, / Your huddled masses yearning to breathe free. . . ," a statement that tears at the very heartstrings of core national values ("Statue").

While these five documents—the Gettysburg Address, the Declaration of Independence, the Constitution, the Pledge of Allegiance, and Lazarus's poem—are certainly not the full story of the development of our national mythos, they do constitute key contributions to our mythos's evolving developmental process, all converging around notions of the sovereignty of citizens, of freedom, justice, and equality, and the pursuit of individual potential and possibility. A point to be emphasized, however, is not the inspiration and promise that are encoded into these types of documents but the openness with which the documents frame the concept of audience and extend an invitation to *the people*, as an unspecified category, to participate in this new model of *nation*. A basic challenge for implementation, then, is that, once this story of nation was written into being, the documents themselves acquired their own reality and momentum, becoming available to the imagination of anyone who might see and read them or hear them or interpret them from their own point of view, and who might call or seek to call the United States home.

Embedding an Ethical Imperative

Over time, the openness of our declared national values has come to be perceived as an ethical commitment, one through which the nation (and thereby its people) has vowed to honor and live up to its explicitly declared promises of *freedom, justice, and equality for all*. One elephant in the room at the time of the founding of the country and the expression of these principles, however, was the indisputable fact that the nation was a seriously slave-holding nation,[3] where the enslaving of human beings had been institutionalized in all of the colonial territories and intricately entwined socially, politically, economically, and ideologically, and encoded in laws, policies, and practices, even as the colonies declared sovereignty, independence, self-rule.

These contrasts were stunning, with proclamations of *freedom, justice, and equality for all* placed in polar opposition with conceptual blindness to slavery and injustice, and socioeconomic, political, and racist domination. Consider, for example, that in 1776, leaders of the nation declared sovereignty based on *freedom, justice, and equality for all*. However, despite the fact that several states had chosen to abolish slavery before the first Constitutional Convention in 1787 (among them Vermont, New Hampshire, Rhode Island, Massachusetts, Connecticut), national leaders still encoded fugitive slave laws (Article 4, Section 2, Clause 3) into the Constitution. In fact, by the 1790s, the momentum for the discontinuities between core national values and slavery were strong and getting even stronger.

By 1850, this situation spiked significantly when Congress chose to add even more strength to the rights of slaveholders and their agents and established yet another Fugitive Slave Law. This law made the slaveholders' search for their human property easier and made punishments for recaptured African American escapees harsher. The law increased danger, as well, for legally free and freeborn African Americans who were being kidnapped and enslaved without cause, and, in light of a growing Underground Railroad movement, the law went even further in sanctioning punishments for those who harbored escapees. Instructively for the focus of this essay, the 1850 Fugitive Slave Law generated new tensions between values and practices and constituted a vibrant kairotic moment for escalating abolitionist rhetoric and indeed the abolitionist movement.

Within this rhetorical environment, Reverend Theodore Parker (1810–60) built a reputation in the Northeast as a rhetor. He was a Unitarian minister, religious reformer, social activist, and a member of the New England Transcendentalists. Parker was prominent among public speakers in the nineteenth century who received broad attention for making a compelling case for the sustainability of the nation and its principles based on a moral commitment to right action. In one of his sermons, "Justice and the Conscience," first published in 1853, Parker states:

> I do not pretend to understand the moral universe; the arc is a long one, my eye reaches but little ways; I cannot calculate the curve and complete the figure by

the experience of sight; I can divine it by conscience. And from what I see I am sure it bends toward justice. The arc of the moral universe is long, but it bends toward justice. Jefferson trembled when he thought of slavery and remembered that God is just. Ere long all America will tremble.

(Parker and Cobbe 48)

The sermon was well received in its own day, but over the decades since it has also been a regular inspiration for others and persistently used in sociopolitical discourses. Among the frequent users most recently was President Barack Obama, who included a passage from the sermon, for example, in his commemorative address in 2013 for the fiftieth anniversary of the speech by Martin Luther King, Jr., at the March on Washington in 1963. This rhetorical tribute to King was echoic in the sense that King frequently quoted the statement himself in his own presentations.

To be noted, Parker's statement actually makes interesting room for counter-interpretive viewpoints of its meaning. One view suggests that no matter what happens, justice prevails. In essence, the sightline is toward a passive view of morality and ethics and a comfort with the idea that goodness ultimately prevails over evil, with the basic notion that *truth, freedom, justice, and equality* just work themselves out naturally whether there is vigilance about intentional action or not. Another perspective, however, is one accepted in this analysis. By the very existence of longstanding documentation of civil and human rights activism, a counter-interpretation is that intentional action is a better, more ethically proactive choice. With King as an exemplary user of the statement, the *bend of the universe toward justice* has been typically recognized as an ethical, honorable, and dynamic (rather than static) process that does not at all relieve the nation from responsibility. Instead, the highlighting of the arc actually obligates us to work persistently and actively to sustain this arc and achieve these ends as the right thing to do for humans as sentient beings with the agency and authority to act. By this reckoning, the vibrant participation of this rhetorical element in our national discourses brings to visibility a quintessential embedding over these decades of a bold and palpable moral element into the nation's commitment to the active pursuit of truth, freedom, justice, and equality—for all.

From this latter viewpoint, the scope of the long nineteenth century (as defined here from the nation's founding through the turn of the twentieth century) is compelling. This viewpoint positions the waging of the Revolutionary War and the creation of a new nation as a conscientious and intentional act of resistance, designed to support the recognizable rightness of the arc of the universe toward *freedom, justice, and equality for all*—the principles of our *new nation*. With this framing, we have an analytical opportunity in rhetorical studies to examine the long nineteenth century as an amazingly critical and consequential moment for actually creating a new governance model and then making the model work. The founding documents of 1776 constitute the touchstone of that model. Subsequent rhetorical occasions offer, in turn, material points of reference from which to track the evolution of the claims to newness and to interrogate the processes of implementation as we negotiate and intentionally uphold the bend toward justice.

Critical Misalignments

The point to be underscored here is poignant and provocative. While we have in the United States an inspirational, iconic base, we simultaneously have lingering critical misalignments that remind us that the pathways bringing national dreams of *freedom, justice, and equality for all* to reality have been far from smooth. As a nation we have documents that proclaim the considerable pride that we take in our value propositions. At the very same time, we have a bold and rather blatant record of violent domination, oppression, discrimination, and white supremacy. It seems imperative, therefore, in the third century of nation-building, to interrogate our terms and our processes of implementing and consecrating them so that we can be conscious and intentional about negotiating governance pathways, establishing laws and policies, and instituting processes capable of moving the nation toward the goal of creating *a more perfect* state.

Critical among the nation-building issues is that there is a substantial gap between the idea of the grand experiment (enhanced by the rhetorical openness of the invitation to known and unknown audiences) and the implementation of this experimental design in policies and practices. Quite persistently lingering questions have been: Who is included within the categorical scope of the audience for the documents—in other words, who are *the people*? Who is represented as belonging within the scope of the United States as a representative democracy? Which people? Who counts? How so? How not? Who has the right, privilege, and authority to be represented, to call the new nation home, to claim presence within the category of *citizen*? How does the nation align its policies and practices within the scope of its innovative, inspirational design and in keeping with its principles, values, and declarations? Such were the questions as time passed. They were the questions in 1776 when the nation was establishing its sovereignty as a slave-holding nation and as an invader of Native territories. They were the questions in 1861 when the Civil War pitted brother against brother—an inadequate phrasing that we understand more clearly today, in light of historical data that has established the level of disregard of participants other than white brothers in the highly racialized, gendered, and sociopolitical space

of that time period. They were the questions in the latter decades of the nineteenth century, when there was a large influx of immigrants from Europe and
Asia. They were the questions in the 1950s and '60s during peak moments of the
modern civil rights movement, for citizens of diverse heritage as peoples of color.
And they are the questions now in the twenty-first century, in the face, for example, of the nation's struggle to support Spanish-speaking immigrants who entered the country illegally to create new lives for themselves, but whose children,
though undocumented, know no other home, or the struggle to offer asylum and
humanitarian kindness to those around the globe who are seeking respite from
violence, danger, and devastations of various kinds in their homelands.

In national discourses, these contentious spaces have constituted a zone of
invisibility and inaudibility in the national mythos. *All* has not in practice meant
every one. The metaphor that comes to mind is the notion articulated by George
Orwell in *Animal Farm* (1945) that "[a]ll animals are equal, but some animals are
more equal than others" (134). With this conundrum, protest and resistance in
rhetorics of the United States have been lively—from the beginning, with these
protests grounded by the very same founding principles of *freedom, justice, and
equality for all* that the protestors typically did not see in evidence for all—only
for some. A longstanding example, in this regard, is the activism of African
Americans generally, and African American women especially.

Nation-Building as an Activist Imperative

As a nation, while we revel in our national mythos, we simultaneously face an
ethical imperative[4] to recognize that researchers, scholars, and others have documented, first, a long history of opacity about the interrelated complexities in
the Americas of conquest, chattel slavery, sociopolitical oppression and domination, and both overt discrimination and implicit operational bias; second, an
equally long history of resistance and protest against all of these circumstances
and material conditions by those made invisible, inaudible, and disempowered
by these sociopolitical constructions; third, the recurring divides and disrup-
tions from the founding of the nation in the late eighteenth century, through
the nineteenth and twentieth centuries, and continuing into the current era related to the persistent absence of *freedom, justice, and equality for all*—still—for
particular segments of the people of the United States; and fourth, the lingering
invisibility and inaudibility in public discourses around these critical misalignments as the nation continues its quest to become *a more perfect nation.* Such
misalignments have created ever-present kairotic occasions from which imperatives for advocacy and action persistently arise, between fact and fiction, myth
and reality, presumption and evidence, constraint and freedom, oppression and

justice, proclamations and implementation. Such is the story of African American women's advocacy and activism.

One example is Elizabeth Freeman, known in her earlier adult years as Mum Bett. Born in 1742, at six months old Freeman was purchased by John Ashley from Sheffield, Massachusetts, and worked as his slave for almost forty years. During this time, she married and had one daughter, Betsy, but Freeman's husband was killed while fighting in the Revolutionary War. After the war, there was a catalytic event. While there is some confusion about who was the target, one day Ashley's wife struck out at either Freeman's daughter or her sister (who had been sold to Ashley at the same time as Freeman) with a hot shovel. Freeman blocked the strike and was wounded. Freeman's response was to take Betsy and leave the Ashley house. She refused to return.

While Freeman was illiterate, she had heard the words of freedom and equality in the Ashley household in the talk about the Bill of Rights and the 1780 Constitution of Massachusetts, and, when Ashley tried to get Freeman back, she sought out the help of Theodore Sedgewick, a lawyer and abolitionist from Stockbridge. Freeman's case was joined with another slave in the Ashley household. *Brom and Bett v. Ashley* went to Common Pleas Court in Great Barrington with favorable results, and Freeman became the first African American woman to be set free under the Massachusetts Constitution. This case was instrumental in the abolition of slavery in Massachusetts.

In freedom, Freeman changed her name from Bett to Elizabeth Freeman; worked the remainder of her life as a servant in the Sedgewick household; and saved her money, bought her own home, and raised her family. One hundred years later, that family included W. E. B. DuBois, who was born in Great Barrington in 1868 and was the first African American to receive the doctoral degree from Harvard University in 1895. DuBois was renowned as a leading scholar, educator, and author; sociologist, historian, and philosopher; civil rights activist and founder of the NAACP. Interestingly, DuBois died in 1963 after leaving the United States and becoming a naturalized citizen of Ghana.

Despite this story of activism, challenges to maximize opportunities for African Americans were fierce. These citizens were caught in thick webs of social, political, and economic oppression, imposed inequalities, and pervasive injustice. Before and after the founding of the nation, African Americans struggled to fully exercise freedom and equal opportunities, and to obtain equal justice under the law. Their efforts did gain traction in national law with the Emancipation Proclamation in 1863, and with the ratification of the Thirteenth, Fourteenth, and Fifteenth Amendments to the Constitution. However, even after laws were in place in the mid–nineteenth century, these citizens were increasingly terrorized by acts of oppression, discrimination, racial domination, and also torture, as lynching came to be common practice. In juxtaposition, African American activism to counter injustice continued with African American women playing prominent roles.

Ida B. Wells, for example, the renowned African American journalist, wrote her first anti-lynching editorial in 1892, launching her national and international prominence as a crusader for justice. Victoria Earle Matthews of New York (also a journalist and community organizer) and Maritcha Lyons of Brooklyn (a leading educator and community organizer) called a meeting in New York's Lyric Hall of leading African American women from New York, Pennsylvania, and Massachusetts so that they could hear Wells tell her story. Josephine St. Pierre Ruffin (a leading clubwoman and community activist) was in attendance from Boston. When she returned home, Ruffin started the *Woman's Era* magazine, the first journal owned, managed, and edited by an African American woman to be dedicated to issues related to the lives and progress of African American women. This journal became the voice and organizing tool of the Black clubwomen, a well-educated national group of elites, as they launched in 1896 a powerful wave of advocacy and activism for human and civil rights. In *A Voice from the South* (1892), Anna Julia Cooper, an educator and clubwoman from Washington, DC, declared, "Only the Black Woman can say 'when and where I enter, in the quiet, undisputed dignity of my womanhood, without violence and without suing or special patronage, then and there the whole Negro race enters with me'" (31). This statement captured for generations to come the commitment of African American women activists to *freedom, justice, and equality for all.*

A well-documented pattern of response and engagement from the work of nineteenth-century women was that they understood: the need to see and seize opportunity; to be inventive in finding ways to speak the truth—persistently, relentlessly, and persuasively; and also the need to work with friends and allies to foment change. This pattern of action was not new. It was a habitual part of African American women's cultural practices (see Royster). What was likely a more distinctive innovation with the rise of literacy, educational opportunity, and the freedom to engage in collective action is African American women's recognition of the ways and means of power, authority, and entitlement, with their habit of taking into account three quite strategic questions: Who has the power and authority to change systems, policies, and prevailing practices? What sorts of strategic frameworks are available to influence those who have such power? What activist design might be usable by an enterprising person or group to engender sentiments capable of convincing people with power to act?

At the end of the nineteenth century and the dawning of the twentieth century, then, the table was set for strategic action going forward to sustain the bend toward justice for the twentieth century.

A Never-Ending Quest

As we approach the third century of the nation's founding, another priority emerges: we can expand the test for credibility and integrity of national values with an eye toward identifying signs of endurance and sustainability, in search of evidence that suggests that the center (the central principles and processes) still holds. From the long nineteenth century forward, the nation has experienced a relentless continuation of acts of violence, injustice, and social, economic, and political domination. The occasions for resistance remain urgent with a relentless stream of new voices emerging to resist, including Black Girls Matter, Black Lives Matter, Me Too, Times Up, and a substantial slate of others. In essence, in the twenty-first century we are bearing witness to an ongoing, twofold tragic flaw in the incredible story of our nation. On one hand, we have an inspired vision of possibility. On the other, we have a persistent inability to enact and fully embody that vision's promise and its invitation. At the intersection, we have an equally persistent imperative for sociopolitical turmoil and vigilant rhetorical action.

The basic question concerns what and where twenty-first-century evidence of the nation's commitment to *truth, freedom, justice, and equality for all* might be, and what the patterns of practice might suggest, not simply about continuities of belief but also continuities of ethical practice. One challenge is to take to heart that our core values are all constantly in contention and negotiation and that it is vigilance, as Parker, King, and others have suggested through the generations, that keeps the bend toward justice. Challenges remain: Are we committed as a nation with our proclaimed principles and values to being a free and just nation? Do we continue to have champions who can lead and light the way? As this third century of our story of nation continues—flaws and all, contestations and all—it seems that our national promises remain open and at stake: *freedom, justice, and equality for all*—or not?

Notes

1. There are five known official copies of the Gettysburg Address written in the hand of Lincoln and presented by him to the people for whom the versions are named. There are the John Nicolay copy and the John Hay copy, both of which are in the Library of Congress. Nicolay and Hay were Lincoln's private secretaries. There is the Edward Everett copy, located in the Illinois State Historical Library. Everett was the main speaker for the Gettysburg event and requested a copy. There is the George Bancroft copy, located in the Carl A. Kroch Library at Cornell University. Bancroft was a historian of American history during this era and former

secretary of the Navy; he requested a copy for publication that ended up not being usable because Lincoln had written on both sides of the paper. The fifth copy is the Alexander Bliss copy, displayed in the Lincoln Bedroom of the White House. Bliss, Bancroft's stepson and a publisher, was presented a copy that Lincoln had titled, signed, and dated. This copy is considered the standard version of the address.

2. In this section and in the following section, I use several nonacademic sources, as indicated in the list of works cited and consulted. I recognize and honor the capacity of public research to enrich the general knowledge base about the documents and stakeholders discussed in these sections. While the sources are credible, the primary audience for such information is typically the general public rather than academic researchers and scholars. In trying to expand interpretive frameworks in academic research and scholarship, therefore, my assertion is that the inclusion of such materials in contextual accounts in academic volumes is useful even when the contextual account itself does not quote directly from a specific text.

3. Because of space limitations, this essay does not bring into the analysis the genocide of untold numbers of Native peoples in the acquisition of territory and the domination of resources in the making of the nation, but obviously this history is also part of the pattern here.

4. See Royster and Kirsch.

Works Cited and Consulted

Constitution of the United States. 1787. *National Archives*, 19 Nov. 2019, www.archives
.gov/founding-docs/constitution-transcript.

Cooper, Anna Julia. *A Voice from the South*. 1892. Oxford UP, 1988.

The Declaration of Independence. 1776. *National Archives*, 19 Nov. 2019, www.archives
.gov/founding-docs/declaration-transcript.

"Elizabeth Freeman." *Elizabeth Freeman Center*, www.elizabethfreemancenter.org/who
-we-are/elizabeth-freeman/.

"Elizabeth Freeman (Mum Bett)." *Africans in America / PBS*, www.pbs.org/wgbh/aia/
part2/2p39.html.

"Emma Lazarus." *Jewish Women's Archive*, jwa.org/people/lazarus-emma.

Foner, Eric. *Give Me Liberty! An American History*. Seagull 5th ed., vol. 1, W. W. Norton,
2017.

Gura, Philip F. *American Transcendentalism: A History*. Hill and Wang, 2007.

Jones, Jeffrey Owen. "The Man Who Wrote the Pledge of Allegiance." *Smithsonian
Magazine*, Nov. 2003, www.smithsonianmag.com/history/the-man-who-wrote
-the-pledge-of-allegiance-93907224/.

King, Martin Luther, Jr. *Where Do We Go from Here: Chaos or Community?* Beacon, 2010.

Lincoln, Abraham. "The Gettysburg Address." 1863. *Abraham Lincoln Online*, www
.abrahamlincolnonline.org/lincoln/speeches/gettysburg.htm.

Melamed, Dennis. "Under God: The Pledge of Allegiance." *American History Magazine*, 15 Nov. 2016, www.historynet.com/god-evolution-pledge-allegiance.htm.

"NAACP History: W.E.B DuBois." *NAACP*, www.naacp.org/naacp-history-w-e-b -dubois/.

Orwell, George. *Animal Farm*. 1946. Signet Classic, 1996.

Parker, Theodore, and Frances Power Cobbe. *The Collected Works of Theodore Parker*. 1879. Leopold Classic Library, 2016.

"The Pledge of Allegiance." *United States Department of Veterans Affairs*, www.va.gov/ opa/publications/celebrate/pledge.pdf.

Royster, Jacqueline Jones. *Traces of a Stream: Literacy and Social Change among African American Women*. U of Pittsburgh P, 2000.

Royster, Jacqueline Jones, and Gesa E. Kirsch. "Ethics and Action: Feminist Perspectives on Facing the Grand Challenges of Our Times." *Rewriting Plato's Legacy: Ethics, Rhetoric and Writing Studies*, edited by Lois Agnew and John Duffy, U of Utah P, 2019, pp. 117–39.

"Statue of Liberty." *National Park Foundation*, www.nationalparks.org/explore-parks/ statue-liberty-national-monument.

Notes on Contributors

Mollie Barnes is assistant professor at the University of South Carolina, Beaufort. She works on nineteenth-century transatlantic literature, focusing on representations of social reform and revolution. She has published on Elizabeth Barrett Browning, Fanny Kemble, and Edith Wharton. Her current projects—including a series of articles on Charlotte Forten and Margaret Fuller—explore transatlantic triangulations, with emphases on the complex recovery histories and reformist imaginaries that emerge in activist networks, especially in newspapers and in private and public letters. Her book project, *Unifying Ambivalence: Transatlantic Italy and the Anglo-American Historical Imagination*, studies problem texts by Anglo-American expatriates.

Patricia Bizzell is distinguished professor of English, emerita, at the College of the Holy Cross, in Worcester, Massachusetts. She won the Conference on College Composition and Communication Exemplar Award in 2008. She is also a Fellow of the Rhetoric Society of America and its past president. Among her publications are *Academic Discourse and Critical Consciousness*, on composition theory (1992), and *The Rhetorical Tradition: Readings from Classical Times to the Present*, a critical anthology coauthored and edited with Bruce Herzberg, and with Robin Reames in the third edition (2020); the first edition won the Conference on College Composition and Communication Outstanding Book Award in 1992.

Suzanne Bordelon is professor and chair of the department of rhetoric and writing studies at San Diego State University. Her teaching and research interests include feminist rhetorics and pedagogies, rhetorical education, literacy studies, archival research, and composition pedagogy and theory. She is the author of *A Feminist Legacy: The Rhetoric and Pedagogy of Gertrude Buck*. In addition, her writing has appeared in *Advances in the History of Rhetoric*; *College Composition and Communication*; *Rhetoric Society Quarterly*; *Rhetoric Review*; *JAC: A Journal of Rhetoric, Culture, and Politics*; and other journals. She is chair of the editorial board of *Peitho* and a member of the advisory board of the Coalition of Feminist Scholars in the History of Rhetoric and Composition.

Meaghan Brewer is assistant professor at Pace University, where she teaches courses in rhetoric, composition, and literacy theory and directs the writing across the curriculum program. Her research interests include teacher education for graduate students, literacy theory, and rhetoric and women's science education in nineteenth-century America. She has published articles in *Peitho, Composition Studies, Applied Linguistics Review, Journal of Adolescent and Adult Literacy,* and *Composition Forum.* Her book, *Conceptions of Literacy: Graduate Instructors and the Teaching of First-Year Composition,* was published in 2020.

Martin Camper is associate professor of writing at Loyola University Maryland. His book, *Arguing over Texts: The Rhetoric of Interpretation* (2018), offers a method for analyzing debates over textual meaning grounded in stasis theory. Research for his second book project, tentatively titled *How the Bible's Meaning Changes: Argument and Controversy in the Christian Church,* has been supported by grants from the National Endowment for the Humanities and the International Society for the History of Rhetoric. His other work has appeared in *College Composition and Communication, Rhetoric Review,* and *Advances in the History of Rhetoric.*

Michael-John DePalma is associate professor of English and coordinator of professional writing and rhetoric at Baylor University. He is immediate past chair of the Rhetoric and Religious Traditions Standing Group of the Conference on College Composition and Communication. His research centers on religious rhetorics, transfer, and rhetorical education. His recent work has appeared in *College English, College Composition and Communication, Composition Studies, Rhetoric Review,* and various edited collections. With Jeffrey M. Ringer, he edited *Mapping Christian Rhetorics: Connecting Conversations, Charting New Territories* (2015). He is the author of *Sacred Rhetorical Education in Nineteenth-Century America: Austin Phelps at Andover Theological Seminary* (2020).

Jessica Enoch is professor of English at the University of Maryland and director of the Academic Writing Program. Her books include *Refiguring Rhetorical Education: Women Teaching African American, Native American, and Chicano/a Students, 1865–1911* (2008) and *Domestic Occupations: Spatial Rhetorics and Women's Work* (2019).

Brian Fehler is associate professor of English and advisor for the doctoral program in rhetoric at Texas Woman's University, where he teaches graduate courses in history of rhetoric and feminist rhetorics and undergraduate courses in writing studies. A lifetime member of the Rhetoric Society of America, his articles have appeared in *Rhetoric Review* and *RSQ: Rhetoric Society Quarterly.* He is coeditor (with M. Elizabeth Weiser and Angela M. Gonzalez) of *Engaging Audience: Writing in an Age of New Literacies* (2009).

Kristie S. Fleckenstein is professor of English at Florida State University, where she teaches graduate and undergraduate courses in rhetoric and composition. Her research interests include feminism and race, especially as both intersect with material and visual rhetorics. She is the recipient of the 2005 Conference on College Composition and Communication Outstanding Book Award for *Embodied Literacies: Imageword and a Poetics of Teaching* (2003), and the 2009 W. Ross Winterowd Award for best book in composition theory for *Vision, Rhetoric, and Social Action in the Composition Classroom* (2009). Her current project explores nineteenth-century photography and debates about racial identities.

Lynée Lewis Gaillet is distinguished university professor and chair of the English department at Georgia State University. She has received a National Endowment for the Humanities Award and an International Society for the History of Rhetoric fellowship. Her publications include *Scottish Rhetoric and Its Influences* (1998); *Stories of Mentoring: Theory and Praxis* (2008); *The Present State of Scholarship in the History of Rhetoric: A Twenty-First Century Guide* (2010); *Primary Research and Writing: People, Places, and Spaces* (2016); and *Remembering Women Differently: Re-figuring Rhetorical Work* (2019). She is past president of the Coalition of Feminist Scholars in the History of Rhetoric and Composition, and past executive director of the South Atlantic Modern Language Association.

Brenda Glascott is director of the honors college and associate professor of humanities at Portland State University. Her research areas includes the history of women's rhetorics and literacy practices, gender and rhetoric, and public sphere theory. She has published in *College English, Reader, Reflections: A Journal of Community-Engaged Writing and Rhetoric*, and several edited collections. She is cofounder and managing editor of the peer-reviewed, open-access journal *Literacy in Composition Studies*. Her current research is a rhetorical history of women's labor activism in early-twentieth-century New York City, particularly in relation to the Triangle Shirtwaist Factory fire.

Sarah Hallenbeck is associate professor of English and composition coordinator at the University of North Carolina, Wilmington. She is author of *Claiming the Bicycle: Women, Rhetoric, and Technology in Nineteenth-Century America* (2016), and her work has appeared in *Rhetoric Society Quarterly, Rhetoric Review*, and *Technical Communication Quarterly*, among others.

Wendy Hayden is associate professor of English and codirector of the first-year writing course at City University of New York, Hunter College. Her book, *Evolutionary Rhetoric: Sex, Science, and Free Love in Nineteenth-Century Feminism*, was published in 2013. Among her publications are articles in *College Composition and Communication, College English, The Journal of Academic Librarianship, The Journal of Interactive Technology and Pedagogy, Rhetoric Review*, and *Rhetoric Society Quarterly*.

Elizabeth Lowry is lecturer at Arizona State University. Her research interests include religious rhetorics, Indigenous rhetorics, and gender studies. She is author of *Invisible Hosts: Performing the Nineteenth-Century Spirit Medium's Autobiography* (2017); *The Seybert Report: Rhetoric, Rationale, and the Problem of Psi Research* (2017); and *Indigenous Rhetoric and Survival in the Nineteenth Century: A Yurok Woman Speaks Out* (2018).

Nancy Myers is associate professor of English, and she was the class of 1952 distinguished professor of English for 2017 to 2019, at the University of North Carolina, Greensboro. She served as the president of the Coalition of Feminist Scholars in the History of Rhetoric and Composition from 2010 to 2012. She is coeditor with Kathleen J. Ryan and Rebecca Jones of *Rethinking Ethos: A Feminist Ecological Approach to Rhetoric* (2016). Her publications include essays in *Women at Work: Rhetorics of Gender and Labor, Remembering Women Differently: Refiguring Rhetorical Work, In the Archives of Composition, Political Women: Language and Leadership*, and *Women's Oratorical Education*.

Julie Prebel is associate professor of American studies and director of the writing program and writing center at Occidental College, Los Angeles. Among her publications in composition and rhetoric are essays in *Composition Forum, enculturation, Pedagogy*, and *WLN: A Journal of Writing Center Scholarship*. She has also contributed chapters in edited volumes on topics in American literature and culture, and on Richard Wright, Toni Morrison, and Charlotte Perkins Gilman.

Angela G. Ray is associate professor in the communication studies department and associate dean for academic affairs in the graduate school at Northwestern University. Her book *The Lyceum and Public Culture in the Nineteenth-Century United States* (2005) won awards from the American Forensic Association, the National Communication Association, and the Rhetoric Society of America. She is coeditor, with Paul Stob, of *Thinking Together: Lecturing, Learning, and Difference in the Long Nineteenth Century* (2018). Her scholarship also appears in book chapters and journals such as *Argumentation and Advocacy, Quarterly Journal of Speech, Rhetoric and Public Affairs*, and *Women's Studies in Communication*.

Patricia Roberts-Miller is professor of rhetoric and writing and director of the University Writing Center at the University of Texas at Austin. She is author of *Rhetoric and Demagoguery* (2019); *Demagoguery and Democracy* (2017); *Fanatical Schemes: Proslavery Rhetoric and the Tragedy of Consensus* (2009); *Deliberate Conflict: Argument, Political Theory, and Composition Classes* (2007); and *Voices in the Wilderness: Public Discourse and the Paradox of Puritan Rhetoric* (1999).

Jessica A. Rose serves as associate director of research and community for the writing studio at Georgia State University. Her research investigates the intersections of feminist rhetorics and pedagogies, multimodal rhetorics, cultural studies, composition studies, and archives. She won Georgia State University's Graduate Writing Award for her essay "American Song" in 2017. Her current works include an article entitled "Critical Imagination through Difficult Collections," cowritten with women, gender, and sexuality archivist Morna Gerrard, and "Misogyny in Higher Education," published in *Misogyny in American Culture: Causes, Trends, and Solutions*, edited by Letizia Guglielmo (2018).

Jacqueline Jones Royster is professor of English in the School of Literature, Media, and Communication at the Georgia Institute of Technology. Her research focuses on the history of rhetoric, feminist studies, and cultural studies with specific interests in human and civil rights. She has received several prestigious awards, including the Mina P. Shaughnessy Prize, the Frances Andrew March Award, the Braddock Award, the Conference on College Composition and Communication Exemplar Award, and the Winifred Bryan Horner Award. She is also a fellow of the Rhetoric Society of America.

Paul Stob is associate professor of communication studies at Vanderbilt University. His research explores the intersection of rhetoric, intellectual culture, and public advocacy in Gilded Age and Progressive Era United States. He is author of *Intellectual Populism: Democracy, Inquiry, and the People* (2020) and *William James and the Art of Popular Statement* (2013). He is also coeditor (with Angela G. Ray) of *Thinking Together: Lecturing, Learning, and Difference in the Long Nineteenth Century* (2018).

Lisa Suter is assistant professor of English at Metropolitan State University of Denver. Her research analyzes the connections between the women's elocutionary movement and rhetorical education in women's colleges in the late nineteenth century, and her publications have focused on recovering the accomplishments of the American Delsartists.

Megan Vallowe is assistant professor of English at Dalton State College, in northwest Georgia. Her recent article in *American Periodicals* reexamines the *Cherokee Phoenix* and the politics of reprinting in nineteenth-century print culture. Her book project, *Indigenous Women's Resistance in Nineteenth-Century Popular Media*, examines the biopolitics of Indigenous women's manipulation of settler-colonial rhetorics in the long nineteenth century.

Shevaun E. Watson is associate professor of English and director of composition at the University of Wisconsin, Milwaukee. Her essay "'Good Will Come of This Evil': Enslaved Teachers and the Transatlantic Politics of Early Black Literacy," won the 2010 Conference on College Composition and Communication Richard Braddock Award. Her other publications have appeared in *Rhetoric Society Quarterly*, *WPA: Writing Program Administration*, *Writing Center Journal*, *Composition Studies*, *Rhetorica*, *Peitho*, *Early American Literature*, and *College and Research Libraries*, as well as in various edited collections. She is currently working on a book about race, tourism, and public memory in Charleston, South Carolina, as well as a coedited collection, *Public Memory, Race, and Heritage Tourism of Early America* (forthcoming from Routledge).

Patty Wilde is assistant professor of English and writing program administrator at Washington State University's Tri-Cities campus. Her current research focuses on feminist history and historiography, particularly as it relates to American Civil

War rhetorics by and about women, archival research, and composition theory and pedagogy. Her work has appeared in *Rhetoric Review*, *Praxis*, *WPA: Writing Program Administration*, and *Peitho*, as well several edited collections.

Elizabethada A. Wright, professor at University of Minnesota, Duluth, teaches in the department of English, linguistics, and writing studies and also serves as coordinator for the women, gender, and sexuality studies program. Additionally, she is a faculty member at the University of Minnesota Twin Cities' Literacy and Rhetorical Studies Program. She has published in *Rhetoric Society Quarterly*, *Rhetoric Review*, *Markers: The Annual Journal for the Association of Gravestone Studies*, and *Studies in the Literary Imagination*, as well as in a number of other journals and books.

Morris Young is professor of English at the University of Wisconsin, Madison. His work focuses on writing and identity, the intersections of literacy and rhetorical studies, and Asian American culture. His current project considers the function of rhetorical space in response to exigencies of exclusion, marginalization, and containment. His book, *Minor Re/visions: Asian American Literacy Narratives as a Rhetoric of Citizenship* (2004) received the 2004 W. Ross Winterowd Award and the 2006 Conference on College Composition and Communication Outstanding Book Award. His coedited collection (with LuMing Mao), *Representations: Doing Asian American Rhetoric* (2008), received honorable mention for the 2009 MLA Mina P. Shaughnessy Award.

Lisa Zimmerelli is associate professor and chair in the writing department and director of the writing center at Loyola University Maryland. She won the *Rhetoric Society Quarterly* Charles Kneupper Award for best essay in 2013. For her work in community engagement, she won the Loyola University Maryland Faculty Award for Excellence in Engaged Scholarship in 2015, and her essay, coauthored with her community partner, was selected for inclusion in *Best of Journals in Rhetoric and Composition 2017*. Among her publications are *The Bedford Guide for Writing Tutors* and essays in *Rhetoric Society Quarterly*, *Rhetoric Review*, *WLN: A Journal of Writing Center Scholarship*, *Writing Center Journal*, as well as in edited collections.